MN

FOOD TRENDS
and the
Changing Consumer

Ben Senauer, Elaine Asp, Jean Kinsey

eagan press
St. Paul, Minnesota, USA

Library of Congress Catalog Card Number: 91-071616
International Standard Book Number: 0-9624407-2-8

Printed in the United States of America.

Eagan Press
3340 Pilot Knob Road
St. Paul, MN 55121, USA

To Sylvia Lane, Professor Emeritus

Preface

What are Americans eating and who is preparing it? Where are they eating and how is it changing? What is a healthy diet and what food is safe? How is the U.S. population changing and what effect are those changes having on food consumption patterns? How do various lifestyles and economic factors—prices, income, information, and the value of time—affect consumer food behavior? What are the unique food needs and problems of the elderly and the poor? How do we know what consumers are purchasing and eating; where do we get the facts?

The answers to these questions are of some interest to everyone, since we are all consumers of food. The answers are critically important to the food industry. Marketing success is based on knowing what the customers want and providing it. Successful food marketers—from fast-food outlets to supermarkets—focus on meeting the needs and desires of consumers. The consumer is setting the agenda for the entire food system. Consumer demands are transmitted from food retailers to wholesalers and processors and ultimately back to the farmers. The industry has become consumer-driven.

Major changes have occurred in the way Americans consume food. Increasingly, they do not want to buy food to cook; they want to buy meals to eat—at home or away from home. Consumers are far more diverse than in the past, leading to more diversity in food preferences. Consumer behavior is also studied more widely than ever before, and more is known about changes in eating habits. Concerns about health and safety have emerged as major issues affecting food choice. All these factors mean that for the food industry knowledge of consumer trends and their marketing implications are more important than ever. These topics are the subject of this book. The first chapter provides an introductory overview.

This book was written for those with either a professional or casual interest in consumer trends, food consumption, nutrition, or the food industry. First, professionals in management, marketing, and technical positions in the food industry should find this book useful. It provides a comprehensive reference on consumer and food trends, sources of data, nutrition guidelines, and an overview of major food safety issues. Farmers and other agricultural producers might also profit from a better understanding of the consumer-oriented markets in which they sell their products.

Second, government policymakers and regulators who monitor food and the food industry should find in this book a useful discussion of food safety and other current food and nutrition policy issues. Third, researchers and educators at colleges and universities and their students in disciplines such as agricultural and applied economics, consumer economics, food science, marketing, nutrition, and public health will find it useful for understanding the major factors that affect food choices and eating patterns. This group would also include nutrition educators and dietitians.

Although not written specifically as a textbook, it could readily serve as such, or a supplemental reading, in several college-level courses in the disciplines mentioned above. More and more programs in a number of specialties related to agriculture, food, or nutrition are finding the need for students to have a broad understanding of the food industry and its markets. And last, but far from least, the general public has an intrinsic interest in the food they eat and in the trends being set by others around them.

About the Authors

Professors Senauer, Asp, and Kinsey are on the faculty of the University of Minnesota. Ben Senauer and Jean Kinsey are in the Department of Agricultural and Applied Economics and Elaine Asp is in the Department of Food Science and Nutrition. Dr. Senauer's Ph.D. is from Stanford University, Dr. Kinsey's is from the University of California at Davis, and Dr. Asp's is from the University of Minnesota. Collectively, they have over 60 years of professional experience related to the topics covered in this book. In addition to academic research, teaching, and service activities, among them they have advised or worked with the California State Department of Agriculture, the Marketing Order Board for California Pears, the Economic Research Service and the Agricultural Research Service of the U.S. Department of Agriculture, the International Food Policy Research Institute, Kraft Foods Company, the National Center for Food and Agricultural Policy at Resources for the Future, and the Nutrition Coordinating Center of the University of Minnesota.

Their research has been supported primarily by the Agricultural Experiment Station at the University of Minnesota, but various research projects have been funded by several other sources, including the Graduate School at the University of Minnesota, the Greater Minnesota Corporation, the National Cancer Institute, and the U.S. Department of Agriculture. Dr. Asp and Dr. Senauer have jointly taught an upper division/graduate course in Food Marketing Economics for the last nine years. Dr. Kinsey and Dr. Senauer have collaborated on a number of research projects over the years. Dr. Kinsey and Dr. Asp have collaborated on research grants.

They have also participated in various regional research committees, which bring together experts from many universities. Dr. Senauer has for many years been a member of a Regional Research Committee on Changing Patterns of Food Demand and Consumption Behavior. Dr. Kinsey worked for several years with a Regional Research Committee on Food and Agricultural Policy and Dr. Asp is a member of a Regional Research Committee on the Market Value of Wheat for Domestic and International Foods. In addition, they have worked as consultants for the Minnesota Department of Health, the U.S. Department of Agriculture, the U.S. Agency for International Development, and the University Consortium. Dr. Kinsey serves as a director of the Federal Reserve Bank of Minneapolis.

Dr. Senauer wrote the first drafts of Chapters 1, 5, 6, 9, and 10. Dr. Asp wrote the first drafts of Chapters 4, 7, and sections of 2, while Chapters 3, 8, and sections of 2 were initially written by Dr. Kinsey. All of the authors wrote parts of Chapter 11 and all reviewed and edited each other's chapters. Early drafts of several chapters were circulated as staff papers and/or presented at seminars in order to receive comments and feedback from colleagues.

The authors discovered that writing this book was both more work and more rewarding than they anticipated. Having been involved professionally for many years with the topics covered in this book, they each had much they wanted to say. They trust that readers will find it interesting as well as useful.

Acknowledgments

The authors are grateful to many persons who helped them throughout the writing process, especially their spouses, colleagues, and graduate students. A special acknowledgment is due Evert Van der Sluis, who produced most of the figures for Chapter 2. Susan Bifulk, a member of the civil service staff of the University of Minnesota, handled the complex word processing requirements of this book. She is without a doubt a Wordperfect virtuoso. The following people are thanked for reviewing or providing comments on one or more chapters of the book: Frank Busta, Oral Capps, David Eastwood, Geraldine Gage, Joan Gordon, Bonnie Morrison, William Schaefer, John Seltzer, and Burt Sundquist. In addition, we appreciate the assistance and guidance we received from the staff at Eagan Press.

A very special expression of gratitude goes to Sylvia Lane, Professor Emeritus at the University of California, Berkeley, who reviewed the entire book, chapter by chapter as it was written. Moreover, Dr. Lane has been a mentor to Drs. Kinsey and Senauer over many years, as well as to many of our colleagues. This book is dedicated to her.

Ben Senauer
Elaine Asp
Jean Kinsey

Contents

FOOD
TRENDS
and the
Changing Consumer

Introduction:

Major Trends
in a Consumer-Driven
Food System

CHAPTER 1

The major eating patterns of American consumers have changed dramatically. Our breakfast eating habits provide an excellent example of these changes. In the 1950s the typical American family, most mornings, sat down together to a hot meal such as bacon and eggs, prepared by the wife and mother, who was usually a full-time homemaker. That is how breakfast was portrayed on such popular television shows of the time as "Leave It to Beaver" or "Father Knows Best." Today the average family may eat breakfast together on weekends, if at all. During the week, all but the very youngest family members typically fend for themselves, and one of the most widely consumed breakfasts is a bowl of ready-to-eat cereal. In the need for haste, breakfast for many oftentimes consists of only a muffin and, perhaps, a glass of orange juice consumed on the run. Others may stop by a fast-food outlet on the way to work or skip breakfast altogether.

Such consumer trends have important implications for the food system in the United States. The food system links farmers and consumers; produces, moves, stores, and transforms basic commodities into food products and services; and is the source of nourishment for the American people. By any measure, the U.S. food system is a huge industry. In 1988, the total food and fiber system accounted for about 15% of the value added in the U.S. economy and about one of every six jobs.[1] The

---

This chapter appeared in earlier versions in *Choices* (4[4]:18-21, 1989), published by the American Agricultural Economics Association, and in the *Journal of Agricultural Economics* (41:422-430, 1990), published by the British Agricultural Economics Society, and is used here with permission. However, it was originally written with the specific intention of serving as the first chapter of this book, which is indicated in both publications.

farm value of food products sold in 1988 was $97 billion, and the final sales of the food marketing system to consumers reached about $638 billion.[2]

This enormous industry is increasingly driven by consumers rather than by producers. The emphasis is shifting more and more from production to marketing.[3] The basis of successful marketing is understanding the ultimate customer, in this case the American food consumer. In this environment, the consumer is setting the agenda for the food industry and the most successful firms have acquired a consumer-focused marketing orientation. Companies that succeed focus on satisfying the needs and wants of food consumers. They try to find out just what consumers want and then market products with attributes that will meet those wants. The major attributes that consumers look for in food products are quality, taste, convenience, nutrition, wholesomeness, and value.[4]

The poultry industry is an excellent example of an industry that has enjoyed great success, in part, by catering to consumers. Poultry consumption in the United States rose by 65.2% from 1976 through 1989. During that period, beef consumption declined 26.7%.[5] Poultry has benefited from a lower real price than beef and from health-related concerns about beef. In addition, the poultry industry, and particularly the large chicken processors, have provided scores of new brand-name, value-added products processed for consumers' convenience.

A knowledge of major consumer trends and an understanding of their marketing implications has become crucial in the food industry. This chapter outlines major consumer trends and their implications for the U.S. food system.

DEMOGRAPHIC FACTORS, LIFESTYLES, AND MARKET SEGMENTATION

The demographic characteristics of the U.S. population are undergoing major changes, and these changes have important implications for the food industry. Perhaps the basic factor with the most obvious significance for food demand is the declining rate of population growth. The Census Bureau is now projecting that, under the most likely scenario, the population of the United States will actually start to decline within the next 50 years.[6]

In addition, the population is growing older, living longer, residing in smaller households, and moving south and west. Also, the ethnic mix is changing. The median age of the population will increase from 32 in 1990 to 36 by the year 2000.[7] The baby boom generation, born between 1946 and 1964, is becoming middle-aged. The population between 30 and 50 years old expanded by 20 million between 1980 and 1990.[8] In just one example of the impact of these trends, we see adults and families being targeted by more fast-food industry advertising as the teenaged proportion of the population declines.

The number of people 65 years of age and older is projected to more than double in the next 50 years, going from 30 million now to 68 million in 2040.[9] Most, although certainly not all, of these seniors will be healthy, active, and financially secure. An aging America will be more concerned about nutrition and health implications of food and will want products that meet their special needs, such as low-sodium and low-fat items. Already much of the advertising of ready-to-eat breakfast cereals is targeted at the older consumer and stresses nutrition and possible health benefits. These targeted advertisements are particularly obvious during the evening national network news programs, which large numbers of older Americans watch.

The average household size was down to 2.62 members in 1989 from 3.33 in 1960.[10] Singles living alone, composed primarily of two distinctly different groups—the young and the old—account for about a quarter of U.S. households.[11] Over half of all households are composed of only one or two persons. Not surprisingly, there is an increasing demand for food products in smaller packaging units. Singles and small families also typically consume more of their food away from home.

Projections are that 6 out of 10 Americans will live in the Sunbelt by the turn of the century.[12] About half the population growth between now and the year 2000 will occur in just three states: California, Texas, and Florida.[13] Typically, when people move, they shed some of their old food habits and acquire some of the tastes of their new region. The increased consumption of Mexican and Southern-style food may be partly explained by regional migration.[14]

Due to differential birth rates and immigration, the ethnic mix of the U.S. population is changing. The fastest growing ethnic groups are Hispanics and Asians. There are now 19 million Hispanics in the United States, and the projection for the year 2000 is 30 million.[15] The largest group, about 12 million, is of Mexican origin, which is obviously also a major factor in the increased demand for Mexican food products.[16]

Increasingly, food companies need to target products at particular market segments. Back in the 1950s, the great middle class defined the American mass market.[17] Consumer products were marketed to the predominant, largely homogeneous middle class.[18] The stereotypical U.S. family consisted of a working father, a mother who was a full-time homemaker, and at least two children. That stereotypical family represented only 7% of all households by 1987.[19] Consumers have become heterogeneous, with distinctly different food consumption habits. The market is breaking up along regional and demographic lines.

Companies are learning how to target consumers in ever smaller market niches. With access to computerized supermarket sales data they can learn much more about the market for their products and how it varies geographically. In the future, more of the marketing budget will be spent on local promotions, including trade discounts and coupons, than on national advertising.[20]

Many food companies now categorize consumers into groups by lifestyle and market their products accordingly. The Pillsbury Company has divided food consumers into five such categories: the Chase and Grabbits, 26% of consumers; the Functional Feeders, 18%; the Down Home Stokers, 21%; the Careful Cooks, 20%; and the Happy Cookers, 15%.[21] The Chase and Grabbits are yuppies, young urban singles and married couples without children. They are willing to try new and different foods, and they want convenience but not necessarily convenience foods. They are a rapidly growing group. Functional Feeders are typically older; the husband works in a blue-collar, union job. They are interested in preparing traditional meals in more convenient ways.

Down Home Stokers eat traditional regional and ethnic foods. Their incomes are lower, and when the wives work, it is from economic necessity. Careful Cooks are better educated, older, frequently retired, and have higher incomes. They try to eat a healthful, nutritious diet but still want to enjoy their food. Happy Cookers are households where one of the members enjoys cooking and baking. They buy basic ingredients and nutritious products such as fresh fruits and vegetables. The Chase and Grabbits and Careful Cooks are growing market segments, whereas the other three are declining.

Different lifestyle profiles have been developed by various food market researchers. Many of these categories overlap, even though the specific titles differ. One developed by the Community Nutrition Institute, for example, categorized consumers into Meat Eater, People on the Go, In-a-Dither, Conscientious, and Healthy Eater households.[22] Almost all seem to have catchy names for their categories.

WORKING WOMEN AND CONVENIENCE

One of the major social and economic trends of the last quarter century is the increased participation of women in the labor force. The overall labor force participation rate for women went from 34.8% in 1960 to 56.6% in 1988.[23] For married women 35-44 years old, the rate went from 36.2 to 72.7%. Even for married women whose youngest child is less than six years old, the rate has reached 57.4%.[24]

Not surprisingly, convenience is now one of the most important attributes of food products. There is an increasing willingness to pay more to buy convenience and service. People want to do less cooking. One survey found that half of all women do not like to cook every day, and three-quarters of them want to get the cooking over as quickly as possible.[25] Women still do over 90% of the cooking in American families.[26]

The time crunch has spawned an enormous and growing convenience-oriented industry. Time-pressured consumers do not want to buy ingredients for preparing meals; they want to buy meals. Much of the time, they do not even want to take the time to eat in a sit-down restaurant. There is a growing demand for meals that go from the freezer to the microwave to the table and into the trash in the same container, with virtually no cooking or cleanup.[27] There is now a microwave oven in 75–80% of households in the United States.[28] In addition, over 60% of those employed have access to a microwave at their place of work.[29] Supermarkets are being flooded with products designed for the microwave.

An economic model of household behavior helps us more fully understand the implications of these trends. The model first developed by Gary Becker of the University of Chicago states that households face not only a budget constraint but also a time constraint.[30] In addition, work activity is viewed as occurring within the household as well as in the labor force. As incomes rise and pressure on the available time increases, many consumers feel increasingly dollar rich and time poor. The pace of life seems to keep speeding up.

Women in the labor force face the greatest time pressures because not only do they work outside the home, but they also continue to do most of the work within the home. The time men spend on household work has increased measurably, however, especially for men who have preschool children, as discussed in detail in Chapter 3. Despite the faster pace of life, leisure time for some people is rising, because they are marrying later, having fewer children, and retiring earlier. Labor force participation among men over age 55 fell from 89% in 1955 to 71% in 1987.[31]

CHANGING EATING PATTERNS

Our fundamental eating patterns are changing dramatically. For many Americans, a typical breakfast is a bowl of cereal, which they quickly eat while standing. Lunch is a cheeseburger and fries picked up in the drive-through lane at the fast-food outlet and eaten while driving. Dinner may be a home-delivered pizza or some things picked up at the deli counter in the supermarket on the way home from work. Then, as a reward for making it through a tough day, some have a big bowl of premium ice cream while watching television at night. This behavior reflects

Pillsbury's Chase and Grabbit group, the most rapidly growing category.

Fewer and fewer consumers are sitting down to eat the traditional three square meals a day.[32] In a nationwide survey, only 50% of adults said they ate three regular meals a day.[33] The term "grazing" was coined to describe the continuous snacking or frequent, light eating behavior of a growing portion of the population.[34] Fast-food chains aim for products that are finger foods that can be eaten with one hand on the steering wheel. Family sit-down meals are becoming rare in many households under the pressure of busy schedules.[35]

Increasingly, different members of the same family eat quite different things. In the past, one could think of a gatekeeper, typically the wife and mother, who made the crucial decisions about food and diet for the entire family. Now more and more individuals make the key decisions about their own diets, even as children. More convenience foods are being designed with the individual eater in mind. The increased prevalence of single-serving size containers is a reflection not just of single-person households, but of individual-choice eating as well.[36]

The microwave is not treated as Mom's appliance the way the range and conventional oven were.[37] Typically, everybody in the family cooks in it, and it is frequently used to prepare foods that will be eaten by only one person. Even young children use the microwave, although this raises some safety concerns.

Human behavior is frequently contradictory, and many individuals' eating patterns are no exception. Many consumers seem to be almost schizophrenic in their eating habits.[38] They carefully monitor the calorie and fat content of their main dishes, eating salads and lean entrees, and then splurge with a super rich dessert. The sales of both "lite," low-calorie products and calorie-rich, high-fat desserts and snack products are doing very well.[39] The explanation for these patterns is provided by the many roles food plays beyond simply filling nutritional needs. Food can also be a pleasure, a cultural and social medium, a comfort, and a reward.[40]

FOOD SAFETY, NUTRITION, AND HEALTH

Food safety issues have become a major concern for consumers. In a 1989 survey of food shoppers conducted for the Food Marketing Institute, 82% rated pesticide and herbicide residues as a serious health hazard. Sixty-one percent, when asked, said they felt antibiotics and hormones in poultry and livestock feed were a serious hazard. The percentage rating irradiated food a serious hazard was 42%, nitrates in food 44%, additives and preservatives 30%, and artificial coloring 28%.[41]

These concerns seem to be largely latent; they are revealed when consumers are specifically questioned about such possible hazards, but most consumers have not altered their food purchases as a result of these concerns. In a survey by a food produce trade group, only 18% of those consumers concerned about pesticide residues indicated that they had actually changed their food buying behavior.[42] In the Food Marketing Institute's 1989 survey of consumers, 81% said they were completely or mostly confident that the food in their supermarkets was safe.[43]

Under the glare of intense media attention, specific consumer food safety concerns can erupt into widespread alarm. A recent example occurred when use of the chemical daminozide (sold under the brand name Alar) on apples was questioned. Although there was no clear scientific consensus on the health risk posed by Alar, the public reacted strongly. The concern focused particularly on children, who are heavy consumers of apple products. Some school systems stopped selling apples in their school cafeterias.[44] The federal government and the food industry both need to take food safety concerns seriously and play an active role in maintaining consumer confidence in the food system.

The major nutritional concerns in the United States have largely shifted from a focus on diseases related to nutrient deficiencies to the linkage between diet and the major chronic diseases. Widespread nutritional problems today are related to overconsumption, rather than to shortages of certain nutrients. In general, the typical American's diet contains too much fat, particularly saturated fat and cholesterol, too much sodium, and, frequently, too many calories for the level of physical activity. The average diet contains too few fruits and vegetables and too few of the complex carbohydrates found in cereal grains and their products.[45]

About two-thirds of the two million deaths in the United States each year are due to heart disease, cancer, and stroke.[46] Medical evidence is increasingly strong that these three major causes of death are affected by diet and other lifestyle factors. Initially, the public had reason to be somewhat confused because there was scientific disagreement over the exact link between diet and these chronic diseases. However, the message to the public from scientific report after report has become increasingly clear and consistent.

The strongest message is that the typical U.S. diet contains too much fat, particularly saturated fat.[47] The message seems to be getting through to consumers. In the 1989 Food Marketing Institute survey, 94% of the respondents indicated they were very or somewhat concerned about the nutritional content of their food. The proportion who indicated that fats in food pose a serious health hazard increased from 42 to 58% between 1985 and 1989. For cholesterol, the increase was from 44 to 61%.[48] In another survey, 75% of the respondents were aware of the link between diet and chronic diseases and the awareness for some diseases was as high as 90%.[49]

The average American consumes 36% of his or her calories in the form of fat, which is down from 41% in 1977-1978.[50] The average per capita consumption of some products high in saturated fats—such as red meat, animal fat shortening, butter, whole milk, and eggs—is down. However, we still have a long way to go to meet the dietary recommendation to reduce fat to 30% of total calories, and an even lower fat diet may yield further health benefits.[51] For many Americans, there is a dichotomy between their awareness of what constitutes a nutritious, healthy diet and what they actually eat.

This resistance to changing unhealthy food habits suggests there is great market potential for food products that have altered nutritional characteristics but retain the quality and sensory attributes, such as flavor, of the traditional product. Many people would like to eat a healthier diet without fundamentally changing their consumption pattern. For this reason, the consumer demand for animal product options, such as leaner beef, should be substantial.[52] The great appeal of noncaloric sweeteners, such as NutraSweet (aspartame), is that individuals can reduce their caloric intake without cutting back on their consumption of sweetened products, such as soft drinks.

FOOD RETAILING CHANGES

The food retailing industry has responded to these consumer trends by changing quite dramatically. There is a trend towards fewer and bigger supermarkets. With fewer but larger supermarkets, the number of smaller convenience stores continues to increase. The conventional supermarket is being replaced by the warehouse store, the gourmet market, and even the hypermarket, which places a warehouse supermarket and general discount store under one roof.[53] The two fastest growing market segments are at the upscale and discount ends of the grocery business.[54] Consumers either want to buy the best or want the best buy. Many times, the same people will shop at both types of stores, stopping for some items at the upscale supermarket and for others at the warehouse outlet.

Within stores, supermarkets are generally stocking more convenience and take-out foods and are giving more space and attention to the fresh produce section. Many stores are moving towards one-stop shopping, with an in-store bakery, deli, florist, dry cleaner, and even a post office. Grocers are going after a larger share of the food service business. To an increasing extent, grocers are becoming meal retailers. Deli and take-out food sections have been greatly expanded and are particularly attractive because of their higher profit margin. With the proliferation of new products, the competition for shelf space in supermarkets is becoming hotter. In addition, computerized scanner technology is giving grocers a much better idea of product movement and sales performance of specific items.

Americans spent $210 billion at food service establishments in 1988.[55] The most distinctively American part of that industry is fast food. Some 128,000 fast-food outlets dot the United States, and they serve about one-fifth of the American public on a typical day.[56] McDonald's alone has 10,000 outlets (8,500 in the United States) and serves 23 million people per day worldwide.[57] The rate of sales growth for the fast-food industry has fallen from the double-digit rate enjoyed previously.[58] As the market has become saturated, the level of competition has intensified. One of the major challenges facing the industry is the declining number of teenagers in the population. They have traditionally been not only the best customers but also the largest source of employees for jobs behind the counters of fast-food outlets.

Perhaps the most dynamic area of food retailing is in take-out-to-eat (TOTE) food and home meal delivery. This fast-growing segment encompasses food purchased for off-premise consumption, frequently at home, and includes supermarket deli counter sales, pizza home delivery and take-out, fast-food drive-through, and restaurant carry-out meals. By 1989, take-out and delivery sales were $51 billion.[59] A Food Marketing Institute survey found that 81% of all households buy take-out food over a one month period.[60] Between take-out food and dining out, some households have virtually given up cooking except for special occasions. Take-out or delivered food is especially appealing to households where all the adults are employed in the labor force, even though its price is two to three times that of comparable homemade dishes.[61] These people are tired and hungry at the end of the day and do not want to cook, but they want the comfort and ease of eating at home. The term "cocooning" has been coined to describe the movement of more activities back into the home.[62]

ATTRIBUTES, PACKAGING, ADVERTISING, AND BRANDS

In 1985, some 5,600 new food products were introduced, and this number reached 9,200 in 1989.[63] Such runaway product proliferation creates intense competition for supermarket shelf space, and only a small percentage of the new products introduced will succeed.

An economic model developed by Kelvin Lancaster suggests that consumers view products as bundles of attributes or characteristics; this model can provide important insights when applied to consumer food demand.[64] In this model, consumers want products with desired combinations of attributes. The increasing importance of convenience as an attribute in many products has already been discussed. There are many examples of product line extensions in which the new products differ by only a few characteristics or even a single one, such as low-sodium or low-calorie versions of a product. Food scientists are increasingly being asked to develop products with certain combinations of characteristics. The considerable power of food technology to create products is certainly evident in items like surimi, in which inexpensive fish is transformed into high-value seafood facsimiles such as crab legs and lobster tails.

Our concept of a food product should be expanded to include characteristics attributable to the product's packaging and advertising. Some eight cents of every dollar spent for food and beverages is for packaging.[65] The food products purchased in 1988 contained $32 billion worth of packaging.[66] A package's appearance may be as important as its content or its price in the consumer's decision. If shoppers do not find the package appealing, they may never buy the product. Increasingly, packaging may affect product characteristics other than appearance. New packages for fresh produce with membranes custom designed for the respiration rate of each type of produce may yield fresher fruits and vegetables.[67] Now, with the microwave, the package may actually be the cooking utensil.

The downside of all this packaging for appearance, convenience, and quality is that the average American discards over 1,250 pounds of waste a year.[68] About two-fifths of the waste is packaging, much of it from food products.[69] One-third of the states are running out of landfill capacity to dispose of this waste. In response to these problems, there are growing pressures to reduce packaging or to make the material recyclable or degradable.

The expenditures on advertising and promotion by the food industry are enormous. Total food-related advertising reached $11.5 billion in 1988.[70] McDonald's spent $362 million on advertising in 1987 and Kellogg's spent $309 million.[71] Through advertising, companies try to create a certain impression or perception of their product among consumers. More specifically, the goal is to differentiate their product from competing ones. The basic idea is to convince the consumer that the attributes of a particular product are different from and better than those of competitors' products. The goal is to foster brand loyalty to a product. Successful advertising may create product differentiation when there are, in fact, no substantive differences in attributes between products.

The impact of advertising has strengthened the importance of brands in the food industry. Brand names may be intangible factors, but in many cases their value rivals, or may even outweigh, that of the physical product itself. The importance of a brand is the perception of product value and worth that is engendered in consumers.[72] Much of the take-over activity in the food industry in the last few years has been largely motivated by a desire to acquire market-leading brand names.

AGRICULTURAL PRODUCTION

Consumers are at one end of the food chain and farmers are at the other. However, consumer-driven changes work their way through the food system from the retailer to the wholesaler to the food processor and back to the farmer. Agricultural producers need to help processors, distributors, and retailers meet the demands of consumers for fresh, safe, nutritious, convenient, and high-quality food products. Farmers and ranchers supply the raw materials to the food industry. Consumers are increasingly asking that the industry convert those commodities not just into food products but into actual meals. Processors will increasingly want uniform materials for their production processes.[73] To meet the needs of consumers, distributors and processors will do more buying of animals and crop products raised to meet certain specifications. More production will also be done under contract.[74]

McDonald's, the fast-food chain, is an example. They require that their lettuce suppliers harvest a week earlier than normal to prevent the core from becoming too crunchy. The potatoes need to meet strict size and moisture standards, or incentive payments are reduced.[75] Major poultry processors subcontract the rearing of their chickens. They supply the chicks and feed, supervise the rearing, and the farmer receives payment, almost like a salary.[76] Farmers in the future will probably give up more of their independence in exchange for greater security. In particular, with such arrangements they will increasingly have more secure markets for their products.

Obviously, those who raise products that move directly to retail sale will profit from responding to consumer preferences. However, even those engaged in the production of basic commodities, such as grain or beef, cannot afford to ignore the market-driven requirements of agribusiness. Farmers need to shift their approach from raising what grows best or is under a government program to producing what sells best. When the consumption of products made with oats and oat bran rose rapidly a few years ago, food manufacturers had to turn to imports because U.S. production was insufficient.[77]

Furthermore, farmers and the organizations that represent them must become accustomed to the desire of consumers and their organizations to have an increasing impact on food and agricultural policy. Consumers have a right to have a say in the determination of policies that influence the food they eat. Producers and consumer groups need not be adversaries. Farmers and consumers have a mutual interest in having a safe, nutritious, high-quality food supply.

A GLANCE AT THE OTHER CHAPTERS

This chapter has set the stage for the remainder of this book by introducing the major trends. Chapter 2 takes a detailed look at changes in the American diet, both major long-run trends in food consumption and current trends in eating patterns, dietary recommendations, and attitudes. The major demographic trends are analyzed in Chapter 3 and major lifestyle classification systems that segment the market in Chapter 4. Chapter 5 analyzes the effects of two key economic factors, income and prices, on consumer food demand. In Chapter 6, important extensions to the basic economic model of the consumer are described and applied to understanding food consumption behavior. In Chapter 7, the various sources of basic data, both government and private, on food expenditures and consumption are discussed. Chapters 8 and 9 look at two unique groups of food consumers with special preferences and problems: older Americans and poor Americans. Chapter 10 provides an overview of major food safety concerns and examines the issue of safety from a conceptual perspective. Chapter 11 briefly describes each of the various sectors of the total food industry, from farming to retailing, and then focuses on the implications of the consumer trends discussed earlier in the book.

Trends and Traditions in the American Diet

CHAPTER 2

"We are what we eat." We are thin or fat, healthy or ill, chic or dowdy. "Some live to eat, others eat to live." Food is a basic necessity and, for most, a source of pleasure. Food is defined by cultural tradition and taboo. Consumption patterns are affected by social and economic forces. In the modern world, food not only nourishes the body, it "serves as a high-touch counterpart to a high-tech society."[1]

The production, processing, packaging, distribution, preparation, presentation, form, and style of food continually respond to changing technologies and consumer preferences. In recent years, rapid changes have occurred in the way food is prepared, in who cooks it, and in the places it is consumed. Our traditional thinking about what is food, and what food is, has been challenged by new technologies, new information, and new values.

This chapter first explores the long-run trends in per capita consumption of basic foodstuffs in the United States, highlighting recent departures from those trends and the implications for a healthier population. Concerns about health and diet, and dietary recommendations consistent with new scientific information and lifestyles, are then discussed in some detail. Trends in consumers' tastes and marketing techniques point the way for future food consumption patterns. As we enter the 1990s, price, taste, and variety remain important to food shoppers, but the dominant themes are quality, nutrition, safety, and convenience.[2]

LONG-RUN TRENDS

A universally observed, long-run correlation between rising per capita income and increased per capita consumption of food from animal sources has played itself out in the United States. Animal sources of food are desired for their taste and nutrition, but it costs more to produce food from animals than from plants. Therefore, higher per capita incomes are necessary to afford food supplied by animals. Figure 2.1 shows that during the last century, the per capita consumption of animal products in the United States increased in relation to crop products, but not dramatically. A noticeable increase after 1935 has been followed by a gradual decline since the 1950s. By 1987, animal products made up about 40% of total food consumed (by pounds per capita), compared with 38% in 1910 and 42% in 1945, the peak year for animal products.[3]

A saturation level, not only of animal products, but of total food, has been reached in affluent societies like the United States; this is shown in Figure 2.1. When income allows the purchase of more food than the human body needs, the rate of growth in food consumption must decline and the quantity consumed stabilize. The top line shows that total per capita food consumption has actually declined in the United States since 1945, with the largest share taken out of crop products. Other evidence of food saturation is shown by looking at the stability of the energy content in the food supply in terms of Calories (1 Calorie = 1 kilocalorie in the metric system). In 1987, 3,500 Calories per day were available in the food supply, compared with 3,400 available in 1910, and a low of 3,100 in 1957.[4]

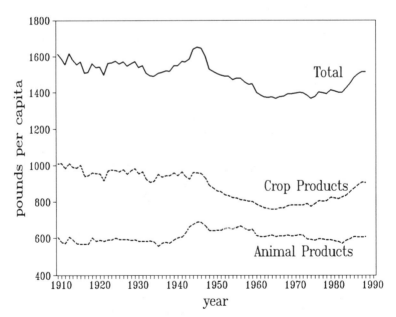

Figure 2.1. Per capita consumption of total food, crop products, and animal products from 1909 to 1988. (Data from Hiemstra, 1968; Putnam, 1989a, 1990a. An explanation of how food consumption graphs were generated appears in the Appendix to Chapter 2.)

Animal Products

Changes in the consumption of common animal products are illustrated in Figure 2.2. These lines illustrate an index of the quantities (in pounds per capita) consumed each year relative to 1909 consumption levels (see Appendix, Chapter 2). All consumption data on the graphs in this chapter represent quantities of food that "disappeared" into the consumer food market.[5] As discussed in Chapter 7, these data overstate the amount actually eaten because they include food wasted, trimmed off, or discarded. They do, however, provide a good picture of the long-run trends in food consumption. The indexed data in Figure 2.2 illustrate that a spectacular increase in the consumption of meat, poultry, and fish was matched by an equally spectacular rise and fall in egg consumption. The consumption of dairy products, measured in milk equivalents, also fell, with a marked rise in the 1980s due mostly to increased cheese consumption.

Meat, poultry, and fish components are depicted in Figure 2.3. The rise in consumption of poultry (80% of which is chicken), the rise and fall of beef, and the long-run stability of pork can be readily observed. By 1989, poultry consumption per person surpassed beef by 16 pounds and pork by 22 pounds. Measures are in retail weight for red meat and ready-to-cook weight for poultry. For meat, this is the weight of the

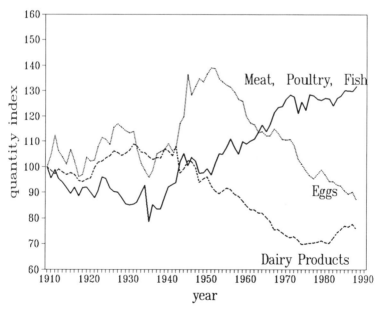

Figure 2.2. Per capita consumption index for meat, poultry, and fish; eggs; and dairy products from 1909 to 1988. (Data from Hiemstra, 1968; Putnam, 1989a, 1990a.)

product as sold in retail stores; it includes some bones and fat. Poultry weights include bones, fat, skin, neck, and organs. Fish is weighed without bones and skin, so quantities of fish are not strictly comparable to meat and poultry amounts in Figure 2.3.

More and more, meat is purchased closely trimmed and without bones, and poultry is purchased as parts and without bone. In order to compare amounts of "edible" meat and poultry on the same basis—without bone, fat, or skin—the data on meat and poultry weights were revised in 1986 by the U.S. Department of Agriculture (USDA). The effect of the revision was to decrease the measure of poultry consumed relative to that of red meats. For instance, the difference between the old retail weight and the new boneless, trimmed weight for beef decreased consumption figures by only 3.7 pounds per capita, whereas the difference between the old ready-to-cook weight for poultry with bones and the new boneless weight was a decrease of 14.7 pounds per capita in 1989. On a boneless, trimmed-weight basis, the 1989 per capita consumption of poultry was 4.5 pounds less than beef and 18 pounds more than pork. On this basis, according to USDA projections, poultry consumption was expected to surpass that of beef after 1990.

However it is measured, poultry consumption is expected to continue upwards at the expense of red meats; poultry accounted for 19% of total

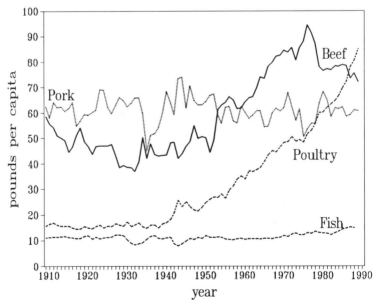

Figure 2.3. Per capita consumption of pork, beef, poultry, and fish from 1909 to 1988. (Data from Hiemstra, 1968; Putnam, 1989a, 1990a.)

meat, poultry, and fish consumption in 1966 and 32% in 1989.[6] Part
of its popularity is due to a large market in fast-food chains, where 40–45%
of all chicken is sold.[7] The percentage of red meat entrees in restaurants
fell from 35% in 1982 to 22% in 1988. During that time, the percentage
of restaurant patrons who ordered steaks or prime rib fell from 19 to
12%.[8]

Figure 2.4 illustrates how a change in technology changes the form
in which food is consumed. Refrigeration and freezers allowed fresh and
frozen fish to replace cured fish, much the same as frozen fruits and
vegetables replaced many fresh and canned ones. Thirty-seven percent
more fish was consumed in 1989 than in 1971, but as a proportion of
total meat, poultry, and fish, it increased from 6.3 to only 8.3%.[9]

Relative prices of various animal products have a strong influence
on the relative amounts consumed and, as discussed in Chapter 5, rising
incomes and falling relative prices have increased the consumption of
individual animal products. But, with affluence, consumers respond less
to retail food prices, and the demand for the various forms of animal
protein becomes more sensitive to demographic factors, health concerns,
long-term trends, and short-term fads. Although more than 95% of the
annual observed variation in beef, pork, and poultry consumption can
be explained by year-to-year changes in their relative prices and household

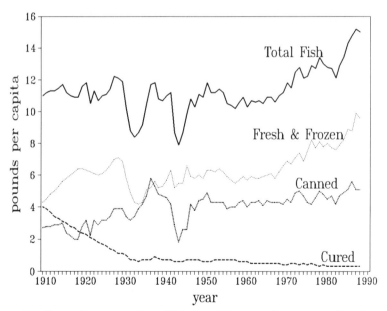

Figure 2.4. Per capita consumption of fish—total, fresh and frozen, canned, and cured—
from 1909 to 1988. (Data from Hiemstra, 1968; 1989a, 1990a.)

income, long-run demographic and lifestyle trends are pulling the consumption of animal products in different directions.[10]

For example, fish has fewer calories than red meat, and it has been suggested that certain fish oils help reduce blood serum cholesterol. Between 1967 and 1988 the consumption of fish increased 42%, although its price increased 418%, more than twice as much as red meat and almost three times as much as poultry. However, during that time, red meat consumption dropped 11% and poultry rose 89%.[11] This indicates a shift in consumers' preferences. Likewise, egg consumption declined in the face of almost flat egg prices. In the early 1980s, dairy prices fell, and so did consumption. "All other factors affecting demand—such as changes in the prices of substitutes, demographics, lifestyles and health concerns—apparently outweighed the positive effects of declining prices and rising incomes to push total consumption (of dairy products) down."[12]

Dairy Products

Changes in the mix of dairy products consumed since 1909 are illustrated by a quantity index in Figure 2.5. Whole fluid milk levels fell while low-fat milks (including low-fat, skim, buttermilk, and low-fat yogurt) rose. Between 1950 and 1987, total fluid milk consumption

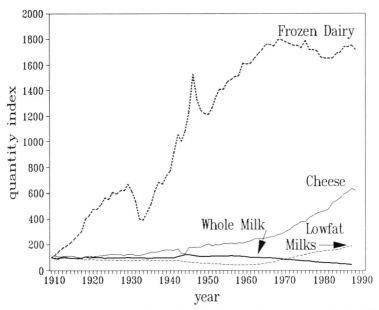

Figure 2.5. Per capita consumption index for frozen dairy, cheese, whole milk, and low-fat milks from 1909 to 1988. (Data from Hiemstra, 1968; Putnam, 1989a, 1990a.)

fell by more than 100 pounds per person. By 1987, low-fat milk accounted for 115 pounds per capita compared with 110 pounds of whole milk.[13] About 22% of fluid milk was used on breakfast cereals, a 36.6% increase since 1967. Increased consumption of cereal and the milk used with it offset more than 20% of the decline in fluid milk consumption that otherwise would have occurred during the past 20 years.[14] Changes in the demand for fluid milk may be partially attributed to consumers' concern for the high fat and calorie content of whole milk and also to the decreased number of children in the population, discussed in Chapter 3. Children consume more fluid milk than adults.

In both a 1987 nationwide survey concerning milk consumption and in the 1989 Prevention Index, half of the respondents said they were "somewhat" or "very" concerned about the cholesterol and fat in milk and other foods and tried "a lot" to avoid eating too many high-cholesterol foods.[15] A significant correlation was found between concerns about fat and cholesterol and decreased consumption of milk, beef, pork, and eggs.[16] On the other hand, the increased consumption of cheese indicates that consumer response to (or information about) high-fat products has been limited, since most cheese is high in fat. Increased cheese consumption accounted for 73% of the increase in dairy products between 1981 and 1986. Much of that increase was due to the consumption of pizza. Only 38% of cheese is purchased, as such, for consumption at home; 39% is eaten away from home, and 23% is sold as an ingredient in various processed foods, which may be eaten at or away from home.[17] Cheese accounted for 17% of all dairy product consumption (not counting fluid milks) in 1960 and 31% by 1987; however, when measured in retail pounds per capita, it makes up only about 4% of all dairy products including fluid milks.[18]

Ice cream accounts for two-thirds of frozen dairy products, which make up about 6% of all dairy consumption by retail weight.[19] Ice cream consumption has been flat since 1965.[20] Very recently, ice cream sales have declined by about 11% while frozen yogurt sales have increased 170%, indicating that the increases in frozen dairy product consumption are also from newer and lower fat products.[21] Even so, nearly 98% of all American households eat some ice cream, and 33% eat at least a half gallon per week. The biggest eaters are in the Northeast and Upper Midwest and between ages 2 and 17, or over 45. Although gourmet ice creams and exotic flavors are growing in popularity, basic vanilla and chocolate make up more than one-third of sales. Ice cream consumption increases with income and education; households without children buy the upscale brands.[22] Perhaps we will see the substitution of low-fat frozen milk products for ice cream in the future on a scale comparable to the substitution of low-fat milks for whole milk in the past. The introduction of fat substitutes for use in frozen desserts promises to further diminish the use of butterfat and the consumption of traditional ice creams.

Fats and Oils

Figure 2.6 shows that Americans have steadily increased their overall consumption of fat while substituting vegetable for animal fat. With some annual fluctuation, the consumption of animal fats has declined, especially since 1940, and the consumption of vegetable oils has increased steadily since 1909. In 1952, vegetable oils overtook animal fats and have climbed at a rate of 3.5% per year since, pushing up total fat consumption by 1.2% per year. For every 1-pound decline in animal fat consumption since 1950, there has been an increase of 2.8 pounds in consumption of vegetable oils.

Total fat consumption was overstated by at least 10% in recent years (Figure 2.6), because it included an increased use of fat and oil for frying by restaurants. Much of this fat is not consumed but is reprocessed by renderers for animal feed, pet food, or other nonfood uses. Only 36% of fats and oils is sold at retail for home consumption; the rest is sold to processors and the food service industry.[23] Butter consumption declined from 6.5 pounds per capita in 1965 to 4.5 pounds

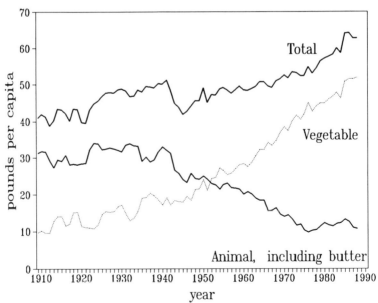

Figure 2.6. Per capita consumption of fats and oils—total, vegetable, and animal— from 1909 to 1988. (Data from Hiemstra, 1968; Putnam, 1989a, 1990a.)

in 1989.[24] Only about 30% of butter, like cheese, is consumed at home. The rest is consumed as an ingredient in processed foods and in foods served away from home.[25]

Figure 2.7 shows sources of fat and cholesterol in the American food supply in 1985. Since about one-fourth of this fat is not actually consumed, the distribution of fat in the diet is somewhat different from that pictured in Figure 2.7.[26] For example, fats and oils provide 47% of the fat in the food supply but only about 44% of the fat in the American diet, with 18% available by way of salad dressings. Most of the remaining fat in the food supply and the diet comes from meat, poultry, and fish (31%). This has changed very little since 1940. Dairy products provide about 15% of the fat in the diet, down from 22% in 1940.[27] Eggs supply a small

FAT

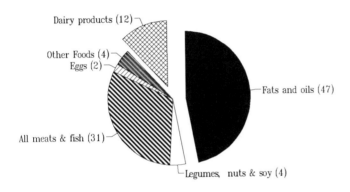

CHOLESTEROL

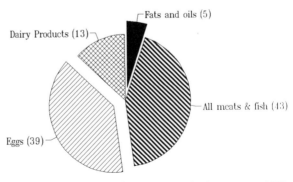

Figure 2.7. Sources of fat and cholesterol in the U.S. food supply, by percent, 1985. (Data from U.S. Department of Health and Human Services, Public Health Service, 1989.)

percentage of the total fat but a large part of total cholesterol, as can be seen in Figure 2.7. More than 80% of dietary cholesterol comes from eggs, meat, poultry, and fish.

Soybean oil has the largest share of the vegetable oil market at 70%, with corn oil next at 7.7%.[28] These two oils are used largely in salad and cooking oils. Only 3% of fats and oils used in edible products were imported tropical (coconut and palm) oils in 1989. This is down from 4.9% in 1983.[29] Tropical oils represented less than 4% of total fat intake and about 8% of saturated fat intake by American consumers in 1985.[30] Tropical oils are the only vegetable oils that are mostly saturated fat. Public concern about saturated fat has led several major food companies to eliminate tropical oils from foods that could be readily processed with other oils. Palm and coconut oils have properties that make them especially good for coffee whiteners, whipped toppings, and some crackers, but the USDA has estimated that the amount of tropical oils in foods could be reduced by half without noticeable changes.[31]

Figure 2.8 shows the percentage of saturated fatty acids in 12 common fats and oils. All animal fats have saturated fatty acids. Continued concern about a link between saturated fat and heart disease probably foretells further declines in animal fat consumption. The trend toward increased consumption of total fats and oils is out of step with current dietary

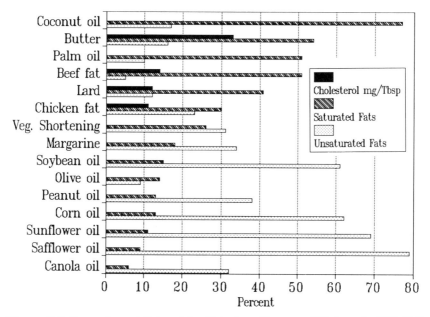

Figure 2.8. Comparison of dietary fats. (Data from Reeves and Weihrauch, 1979; U.S. Department of Agriculture, Agricultural Research Service, 1963.)

recommendations and concerns. Underlying this trend and consistent with particular health concerns about saturated fats is the fact that the largest increases have been in mono- and polyunsaturated fats. Consumption of the latter has more than doubled since 1909. Consumption of omega-3 fatty acids, found in fish, has also increased, as has the consumption of linolenic acid, a polyunsaturated fatty acid found in plants, especially soybeans.

Consumption of saturated fats has changed very little since 1940.[32] Older people eat less fat overall but more saturated fat, probably a holdover from old eating habits. People who are more highly educated eat more fat, but less saturated fat, reflecting their improved knowledge about the negative effects of saturated fat.[33] Since 1971, average cholesterol consumption declined from 509 to about 443 milligrams (mg) per day for men and from 318 to 300 mg per day for women. This is still above the currently recommended 300 mg per day.[34] Despite a general moderation in the consumption of foods that contain animal fats since the mid-1980s, there was a slight upturn in the consumption of high-fat, mixed-grain dishes such as macaroni and cheese and high-fat desserts.[35]

Flour and Cereal Products

The noticeable drop in crop product consumption since the 1940s is due mostly to a decline in flour and cereal products (from 300 pounds per capita in 1909 to 172 pounds per capita in 1988) and in fresh fruits (from 123 pounds per capita in 1909 to 94 pounds in 1988).[36] Between 1967 and 1987, consumption of breakfast cereals increased 44% to 14.1 pounds per capita, accounting for a substantial part of recent increases in consumption of cereals and grains.[37] Between 1987 and 1989, cereal sales rose 22%, with cereals containing oat bran rising 70% in 1989 alone.[38] This is attributed to the quest for increased fiber in the diet, to aggressive advertising and health claims by food processors, and to the convenience of these foods for breakfast.

Figure 2.9 illustrates a downward trend in flour and cereal consumption and an erratic pattern of consumption for beans, peas, and nuts. Legumes are recommended for healthful diets, adding fiber and protein without excess fat, whereas nuts are high in fat. Legumes made up less than 1% of per capita consumption of food crops in 1984. Most of the increased consumption of legumes and nuts shown in Figure 2.9 is due to a 181% increase in nut consumption since 1909.

Fruit

Marketing research shows that more consumers reported eating more fresh produce in the late 1980s. Total fresh produce consumption increased 21% between 1977 and 1987, most growth occurring after 1983. Even though fruit consumption has increased since 1970, Americans ate much more fresh fruit before 1950 than they have since. This is surprising in light of the recent popularity of fresh produce. It can be explained partly by the demise of homegrown and home-processed fruit during the first half of the century. Both growing and processing fruit are too time-consuming for urban dwellers working outside the home. After the 1940s, home-produced fruits were replaced by commercial crops and new processing technologies, especially freezing.

Explanations of a recent upward trend in fresh fruit consumption were reported in a 1988 survey of 2,000 consumers.[39] Of the reasons given for eating more fresh fruit, 73% were related to concern about a well-balanced diet and 61% to concerns about nutrition; 79% of respondents were eating more fruit as snacks, and 36% were consuming more in salads. In the same survey, consumers chose apples, bananas, and seedless grapes as their three favorite fresh fruit snacks, followed by oranges and peaches.[40]

Figures 2.10 and 2.11 illustrate changes in the forms of fruit consumed. Even with a large increase in frozen fruit products (especially juice), there was a sharp decline in total fruit consumption between 1947 and 1963, with a modest increase since then (Figure 2.11). Fruit juices, of which 79% was orange juice, accounted for 42% of all fruit consumption

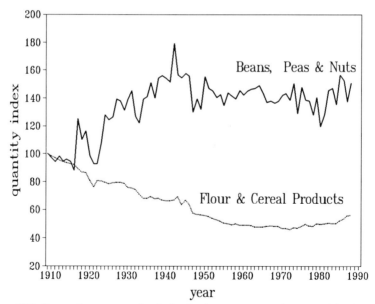

Figure 2.9. Per capita consumption index for beans, peas, and nuts and for flour and cereal products from 1909 to 1988. (Data from Hiemstra, 1968; Putnam, 1989a, 1990a.)

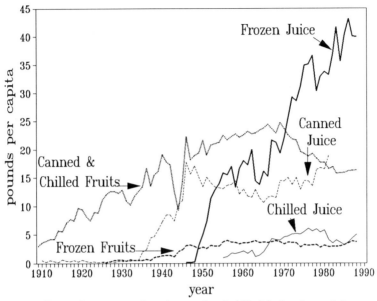

Figure 2.10. Per capita consumption of canned and chilled fruits, frozen juice, canned juice, chilled juice, and frozen fruits from 1909 to 1988. (Data from Hiemstra, 1968; Putnam, 1989a, 1990a.)

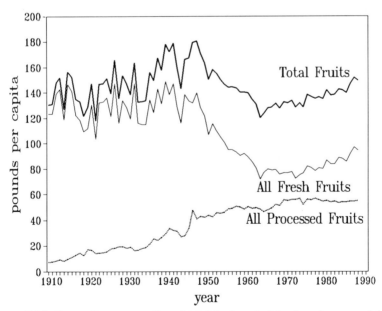

Figure 2.11. Per capita consumption of total fruit and of fresh and processed fruits (including juices) from 1909 to 1988. (Data from Hiemstra, 1968; Putnam, 1989a, 1990a.)

(by weight) in 1981, an increase from 12% in 1950. In terms of fresh fruit consumption, apples, bananas, and oranges predominated. When figures on consumption of fresh and processed fruits and fruit juices were added together, oranges still had the largest share.

Figure 2.12 shows the dominance of the ABCs (apples, bananas, and citrus) in fresh fruit consumption over time. Citrus is represented by oranges, which make up about 60% of all fresh citrus fruits. Apples declined while bananas increased. An increase in noncitrus fresh fruits like grapes, strawberries, avocados, and pineapples has diminished the importance of the ABCs in the fresh fruit market and probably also contributed to the decline of other old favorites. For example, watermelon consumption has declined 41% since 1960,[41] kiwi fruit has risen 87% since 1983,[42] and fresh grapes have increased 135% since 1976.[43]

Vegetables

Vegetables available in the market have been increasing during the entire century. Since 1970, total fresh vegetable consumption has increased 42%, with broccoli consumption up 400% to 3.5 pounds per capita, carrots up 57% to 9.9 pounds per capita, cauliflower up 257% to 2.5 pounds per capita, and onions and tomatoes up 44 and 36%,

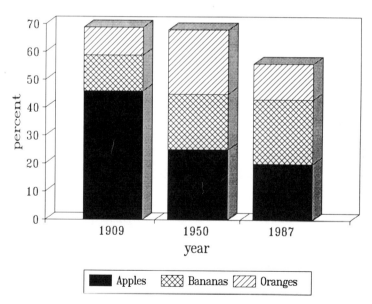

Figure 2.12. The A B C's of fresh fruit consumption: apples, bananas, and citrus, as a percent of fresh fruit consumed in 1909, 1950, and 1987. (Data from Hiemstra, 1968; Putnam, 1989a, 1990a.)

respectively, to about 15 pounds per capita each.[44] As with fruit, the most common reasons given for increasing fresh vegetable consumption are concerns about health and nutrition.[45]

Most of the 100 new items added to produce sections of grocery stores since the 1970s are specialty vegetables and herbs. Production increases are also in evidence. For example, Arizona tripled the acreage devoted to specialty salad greens between 1981 and 1986.[46] The western United States not only grows most of the specialty items, but its inhabitants consume more than the rest of the country as well. The large Asian and Hispanic populations in the West account for much of the consumption of more exotic vegetables.

In 1986, about 18% of fresh produce was imported, with vegetable imports increasing 80% since 1977. In 1986, 32% of the imported fresh produce came from South America, 27% from Mexico, and 16% from Europe.[47]

Restaurant customers have been ordering more main dish salads, up 10% between 1982 and 1986. During that time, potato orders increased almost 4% and hot vegetable orders increased 5.5%. Of the hot vegetables ordered in 1987 in restaurants, the four favorites were corn, green beans, cauliflower, and mixed vegetables.[48]

Although overall vegetable consumption increased, over the long run there was a large decline in potato consumption (73% of all vegetables

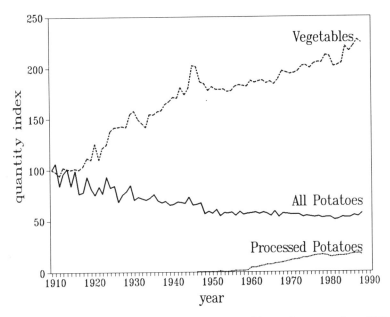

Figure 2.13. Per capita consumption index for vegetables and potatoes from 1909 to 1988. (Data from Hiemstra, 1968; Putnam, 1989a, 1990a.)

in 1909 and only 30% in 1987). French fries and other processed potatoes have rescued the potato from further decline in the American diet. Figure 2.13 shows how quantities of vegetables increased and potatoes decreased relative to 1909 consumption levels. Since 1946, the first year in which data were collected separately on fresh and some processed potatoes, one can see the increase in processed potatoes (see Appendix, Chapter 2). This reinforces observations of a trend towards more highly processed, value-added foods—foods that take less time to be prepared by busy household members. In 1987, 60% of all potatoes were purchased fresh, compared with 76% in 1970.

Fifty-two percent of other vegetables consumed were purchased fresh in 1966 compared with 42% in 1987. Besides potatoes, the big three fresh vegetables are lettuce, onions, and tomatoes, which make up more than 64% of all fresh vegetable consumption (excluding potatoes).[49] Recent increases in fresh fruit and vegetable consumption may seem to defy the trend towards convenience foods, but, to the extent that fresh produce can be eaten raw, with minimal preparation, or cooked quickly, it is a naturally convenient food. Grocers have added to convenience by cleaning and precutting fresh vegetables commonly used in salads, dips, or stir-fry dishes. Pineapples are peeled and melons cut. Even in the fresh produce section, value-added products are popular.

Sweets

Americans like their sweets. The increase in all types of sweeteners is phenomenal, up 25% between 1966 and 1987 to 152 pounds per capita per year. The composition of this increase is important. Figure 2.14 shows that refined cane and beet sugar consumption has declined since 1972, whereas corn sweeteners and noncaloric sweetener consumption increased. In 1987, 42% of all sugars and sweeteners were from refined sugar, 45% from corn sweetener, and 13% from a noncaloric source. This compares with 81% from refined sugar in 1966, 13% from corn sweetener, and 5% from a noncaloric source. This switch resulted from a combination of factors including government policy, which raised the price of sugar, and the development of economical processes for making corn sweetener. Other factors were consumers' concerns about excess calories and dental health, which led them to select noncaloric sweeteners. The rise in total sweeteners is connected to the rise in the consumption of soft drinks, almost all of which are now sweetened with either corn sweetener or a noncaloric sweetener.

Beverages

The shift in beverage consumption is an interesting trend. Coffee consumption peaked in 1946 at 20 pounds per capita, falling back to its

1914 level of a little more than 9 pounds in 1977, and then rising and holding steady at about 10-11 pounds per capita.[50] The average American coffee drinker downed 1.67 cups a day, or 38 gallons per year, in 1988, compared with 3.12 cups per day, or 71 gallons per year, in 1962, while the percentage of coffee drinkers fell from 74.7 to 52.5%. Much of the recent upswing in coffee, tea, and cocoa consumption is due to decaffeinated coffees and to an increase in specialty gourmet coffees. The latter went from about 4% of the coffee market in 1983 to about 11% in 1990.[51]

There are some parallels here with the switch to new fruit and vegetable varieties; people have discovered (and can afford) good flavor. Seeking to compete in price, large coffee companies in America used the cheaper robusta bean rather than the high-grade arabica bean, creating a coffee with a mediocre taste.[52] Though many coffee drinkers are accustomed to the mild taste, those who have discovered the gourmet blends exhibit a distinct preference for them. Coffee is still the beverage of choice in the morning for 47% of consumers, followed by juice (21%), and milk (17%).[53]

Figure 2.15 shows the trends in beverage consumption since 1966 in gallons per capita. The overall decline in fluid milk consumption can be seen here; overall milk consumption ends up being almost equal to

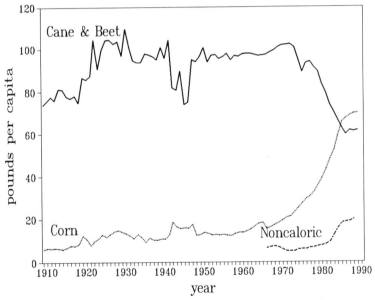

Figure 2.14. Per capita consumption of sweeteners—cane and beet, corn, and noncaloric—from 1909 to 1988. (Data from Hiemstra, 1968; Putnam, 1989a, 1990a.)

that of coffee. Tea consumption is unchanged and juice consumption has increased slightly. Soft drink consumption increased notably, from less than 20 to above 30 gallons per capita. The reasons soft drinks are being substituted for milk and coffee are thought to be related to concerns about overweight as well as to their snappy taste, their convenience, and advertising. Diet soft drinks made up one-third of all soft drinks consumed by younger women and half of those consumed by older women in the 1986 Continuing Survey of Food Intake by Individuals.[54] Thirty percent of the soft drinks sold in grocery stores are diet drinks.[55]

Although consumption of alcoholic beverages rose in tandem with soft drinks between 1966 and 1982, it has declined since. Hard liquor consumption fell to an 18-year low in 1988, 2.5% below 1970.[56] Sales of wine and beer were also down. In 1989, Americans drank 2.11 gallons of wine per capita, down 5.8% from 1988, which was down 5% from 1987. Americans over age 18 drank an average of 33.7 gallons of beer and 2.16 gallons of distilled spirits in 1989.[57]

Industry specialists speculate that growing health consciousness, greater enforcement of drunk driving laws, and an aging population are forces converging to suppress alcohol sales. However, alcohol consumption

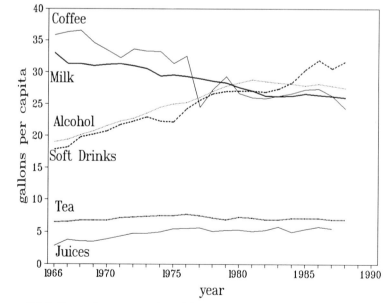

Figure 2.15. Per capita consumption of beverages—coffee, milk, alcohol, soft drinks, tea, and juices—from 1966 to 1987. (Data from Hiemstra, 1968; Putnam, 1989a, 1990a.)

has fallen fastest among young people under age 24. One can only conclude that these young people are better informed and more responsive to information about the consequences of alcohol than former generations. Indeed, among 15–19 year olds, automobile deaths related to alcohol fell from 6,281 in 1982 to 2,170 by 1988, a whopping 65% decrease.[58] The challenge to the producing industries is to differentiate in advertising between use and abuse of alcohol. In the alcoholic beverage industry, as in the coffee industry, the sales of higher quality "good wines," white liquors, and scotch with snob appeal increased in an otherwise declining market.[59] A shift in demand for higher quality products is indicated once again.

Major Shifts

The long-run picture for food consumption in the United States shows that we have decreased total food consumption, which is consistent with our aging population, our increased knowledge about health risks from overeating, and a reduction in food needs accompanying increasingly sedentary lives. Few, if any, foods that we ate in 1909 have disappeared from our diets, but they appear in different forms—more processed, more packaged, more labeled, more convenient, and sometimes, more mysterious. In an earlier time when nearly all food was produced and prepared at home, and when just obtaining enough food for life and health was a major concern, food was believed to be good for you by definition. Now, when a variety of foods is available and affordable, and overeating is a major health problem, some food characteristics have taken on negative qualities, and food is selected with more care and discrimination. There are several examples of long-term substitutions of one food for another by American consumers: poultry for red meat, vegetable oils for animal fats, processed fruit juices for fresh fruits, processed for fresh potatoes, noncaloric for caloric sweeteners, low-fat for high-fat milk, and soft drinks for most other beverages.

The possibility that consumers might gain some control over chronic diseases and morbidity through careful food selection drives and reinforces trends in food consumption. Other forces operating are changing attitudes and aspirations of consumers as well as new life-styles and time demands. Almost half of produce wholesalers attributed recent changes in their industry to changing consumer attitudes; another one-fifth attributed the changes to new technology.[60] Technological change has made it possible for many new forms of food and food service to be available. Changes in food shopping and the places people eat also influence the types of food eaten.

A study of women's food consumption between 1977–1978 and 1986 showed that their calorie consumption at restaurants increased by 60%, at fast-food restaurants by 160%, and at cafeterias by 38%.[61] This indicates the pace and extent of the trend toward eating more food away from home during the 1980s. Eating at fast-food outlets appears to be declining, however, especially among the heaviest users, the 18–34-year-old crowd. Forty percent of consumers reported decreasing their visits in June of 1990, mostly because of publicity about the fat and cholesterol content of the foods. Patronage also decreased by age; 18–34 year olds ate at a fast-food chain 3.01 times per month, compared with 1.86 times for 35–44 year olds, and 1.06 for those over age 55.[62] The aging of the population alone dictates that patronage at traditional fast-food outlets will decline.

Figure 2.16 shows how the percentage of food expenditure on food away from home has risen since 1966. The grocery business will have to compete increasingly hard for the consumer's food dollar. Figure 2.17 shows that the bulk of expenditures on food away from home was in eating and drinking places, followed by retail sales and direct selling in clubs, or cafeterias, vending machines, and other outlets. Food expenditures at schools and colleges were greater than at motels and recreational facilities.[63] As take-out-to-eat (TOTE) food increases in importance, the distinction between at-home and away-from-home food

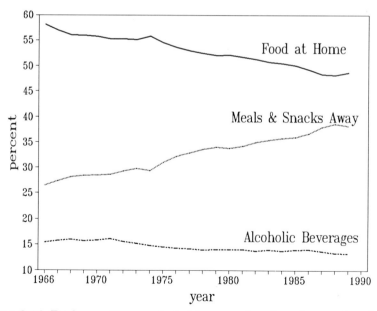

Figure 2.16. Total expenditures on food at home, meals and snacks away from home, and alcoholic beverages, as a percentage of total food and beverage expenditures, from 1966 to 1989. (Data from Hiemstra, 1968; Putnam, 1989a, 1990a.)

expenditures becomes more blurred and less significant, since food for "off-premise use" (usually at home) may be fully cooked away from home, and it may be purchased in a restaurant or a grocery store. Trends in the food industry are discussed in some detail in Chapter 11. Trends in information and attitudes about diet and health are explored next.

DIET AND HEALTH

A major shift in the way we think about food is related to its role in promoting health and longevity. By definition, food nourishes the body and promotes growth and strength. Traditional dietary recommendations were concerned with eating enough calories, protein, vitamins, and minerals. Now, some foods (or food components) traditionally thought to be "good for you" (in moderation) are thought to be "bad for you" (in excess). For example, fats provide calories for energy, but they also promote obesity, and some are suspected of promoting heart disease and possibly cancer. We are now more concerned with negative components of food that may need to be decreased or avoided than we are with obtaining positive nutrition.

A national campaign to lower the blood cholesterol levels of Americans is under way. The National Cholesterol Education Program, launched

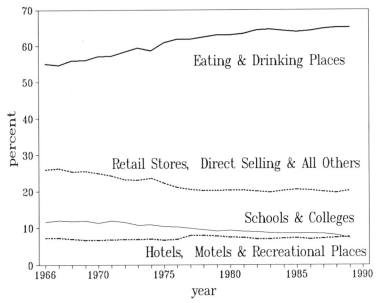

Figure 2.17. Expenditures on food away from home by place, as a percentage of total expenditures on food away from home, from 1966 to 1989. (Data from Hiemstra, 1968; Putnam, 1989a, 1990a.)

in 1985 by the National Heart, Lung and Blood Institute (a major division of the National Institutes of Health) promised to inform Americans about the dangers of high levels of blood cholesterol, and especially high levels of low-density lipoprotein, the cholesterol-containing component that is thought to contribute to clogged arteries.[64] On February 27, 1990, an expert government panel on Population Strategies for Blood Cholesterol Reduction called for expanded and standardized nutrition labeling of food, no matter where it is sold. They further challenged the food industry to provide consumers with "good tasting, safe foods."[65]

There is still, however, considerable controversy about the link between the amount of cholesterol eaten and the level of blood serum cholesterol in human beings and even some questions about whether lowering blood serum cholesterol will lengthen lives.[66] Early in 1989, the National Research Council reported that a 10% reduction in blood serum cholesterol levels could reduce the risk of heart disease 20%.[67] About one-third of the adult population is believed to have a high risk of heart disease and, therefore, might benefit from reduced blood serum cholesterol.[68] However, in a widely read article, Moore argued that the possibility of lowering blood serum cholesterol through diet change is limited in most people to about a 10% reduction, and only about 14% of people respond well to such diets.[69]

Despite the controversy about the role of dietary cholesterol, there is a consensus that excessive saturated fat in the diet is one factor that leads to clogged arteries, heart disease, and heart attacks.[70] In 1990, it was also shown that hydrogenated, unsaturated fatty acids, specifically *trans*-monounsaturated fatty acids, also raise blood serum cholesterol.[71] There is a noted correlation between a decrease in deaths from heart disease since 1960 and a decline in the consumption of animal (saturated) fats in the American diet. For example, the death rate from heart disease for American men declined from 439.5 to 342.8 per 100,000 between 1960 and 1985. This 22% decline was accompanied by a 1.2% increase for American women.[72] However, heart disease is still the leading cause of death in the United States, with about 765,000 deaths per year, followed by cancer, with 469,000 deaths per year. Both are far ahead of strokes, the next largest killer at 150,000 deaths per year. All may be attributed at least partially to overconsumption of dietary fat.[73]

Proving a direct relationship between fat intake and heart disease or cancer has been difficult, partly because of numerous intervening factors including genetics, smoking, and other health problems like high blood pressure. "A hundred years from now, people will look back on this century and realize there was an epidemic of heart disease in the Western world that was unique in history."[74] The reason: widespread prosperity allowed ordinary people to indulge in rich food and sedentary lifestyles.[75]

Dietary Recommendations

In the past 20 years, a veritable flood of research and a massive number of reports have documented connections between diet and health and longevity. New dietary recommendations reflect a shift from concern about preventing diseases associated with nutritional deficiencies to emphasis on the contributions of nutrition to further improve health and possibly decrease risks of chronic diseases.[76] These reports were stimulated by the 1977 U.S. Senate Select Committee on Nutrition and Human Needs, which defined a set of *Dietary Goals for the United States,* shown in Tables 2.1 and 2.2 (items 1 and 2). These goals addressed health problems linked to the overconsumption of fats, sugar, and sodium, and served to publicize diet and health linkages that scientists and nutritionists had been studying for some time.[77]

The committee's *Dietary Goals* were very controversial and were not initially publicized by the Senate or by the USDA. They served, however, as the basis for dietary recommendations subsequently publicized by a large number of influential government, health, and scientific organizations. These dietary recommendations for body weight, fat, and cholesterol appear in Table 2.1. Recommendations for carbohydrates, sodium, alcohol, and other components appear in Table 2.2. Virtually all of the organizations recommend that consumers eat a wide variety of foods. They also emphasize the importance of diet in the prevention and control of a variety of major chronic diseases, as well as the harmful effects of overconsumption rather than underconsumption of specific nutrients.[78]

Overall, the recommendations of different groups are remarkably similar. Differences concern intended audience, that is, whether the recommendations are for the general public or professionals—whether they address the risk of a particular chronic disease, or whether they are made for everyone in order to improve health and decrease risk of a "whole spectrum of chronic diseases."[79] Some recommendations are tailored for specific age-sex groups. In 1986, the American Dietetic Association put out special dietary recommendations for women.[80] The American Academy of Pediatrics proposed dietary recommendations for children, and the National Cholesterol Education Program targeted people with heart disease.[81] Some are quantitative, providing numeric recommendations for specific nutrients and food components, others are qualitative, providing descriptive recommendations, and some are a combination of the two.[82]

The trend to develop new dietary recommendations and revise existing ones is continuing into the 1990s. In mid-1990, new quantitative reference values for food labeling were proposed by the U.S. Food and Drug Administration to replace the U.S. Recommended Dietary Allowances

Table 2.1. Recommendations for Weight, Dietary Fats, and Cholesterol[a]

Source[b]	Body Weight	Fat — Total	Fat — Saturated	Fat — Polyunsaturated	Cholesterol
Government Agencies					
1. U.S. Senate, *Dietary Goals for the United States*, 1st ed., 1977	...[c]	30% of energy intake	10% of total energy	20% unsaturated (10% mono, 10% poly)	300 mg/day
2. U.S. Senate, *Dietary Goals for the United States*, 2nd ed., 1977	To avoid overweight, consume only as many calories as expended	Reduce to 30% of total energy	Reduce to 10% of total energy	Intake should be 20% of total energy (10% mono, 10% poly)	Reduce to 300 mg/day
3. DHEW, *Healthy People: Surgeon General's Report on Health Promotion and Disease Prevention*, 1979	Exercise and balance calories to maintain weight	Reduce excess intake	Consume less	...	Consume less
4. DHHS, *The Surgeon General's Report on Nutrition and Health*, 1988	Achieve and maintain a desirable body weight	Reduce consumption	Reduce consumption	...	Reduce consumption
5. DHHS-FDA, *Daily Reference Values (DRV) for Nutrition Labeling*, 1990	...	30% of reference calorie intake	10% of reference calorie intake	20% of reference calorie intake from unsaturated fatty acids	300 mg
6. USDA and DHHS, *Nutrition and Your Health: Dietary Guidelines for Americans*, 3rd ed., 1990	Maintain healthy weight	Choose a diet low in fat, saturated fat, and cholesterol 30% or less of calories	Less than 10% of calories		Choose a diet low in fat, saturated fat, and cholesterol

Health Organizations					
7. American Medical Association, *Concepts of Nutrition and Health*, 1979	Maintain a desirable weight through dietary control and exercise	Moderation in intake	Proportion of saturated and unsaturated fat not of universal importance		Level in the diet not of universal importance
8. *Nutrition and Cancer: American Cancer Society Guidelines, Programs and Initiatives*, 1990	Avoid obesity	Reduce to 30% or less of total caloric intake	...	...	...
9. National Cancer Institute, *NCI Dietary Guidelines: Rationale*, 1988	Avoid obesity	Reduce to 30% or less of calories	...	...	...
10. American Heart Association, *Dietary Guidelines for Healthy American Adults*, 1988	Maintain recommended body weight	Less than 30% of calories	Less than 10% of calories	Not to exceed 10% of calories	Not to exceed 300 mg/day
11. American Heart Association, *The Healthy American Diet*, 1990	Achieve and maintain a reasonable body weight	Reduce consumption	Reduce consumption	...	Reduce consumption
National Academy of Sciences					
12. *Toward Healthful Diets*, 1980	Adjust calorie intake to maintain appropriate weight for height	Reduce intake if overweight or if energy needs are low	Recommendations not warranted for the public		Recommendations not warranted for the public

(*continued on next page*)

Table 2.1 (*continued*)

Source[b]	Body Weight	Fat				Cholesterol
		Total	Saturated	Polyunsaturated		
13. *Diet, Nutrition, and Cancer*, 1982	...	Reduce intake to 30% of total caloric intake	Reduce intake	Reduce intake		...
14. *Diet and Health*, 1989	Balance food intake and physical activity to maintain appropriate body weight	Reduce to 30% or less of calories	Reduce to 10% or less of calories			Less than 300 mg/day
15. *Recommended Dietary Allowances*, 10th ed., 1989	Balance calorie intake with output to maintain desirable weight	Reduce to not more than 30% of caloric intake	Limit intake to less than 10% of calories			Less than 300 mg/day

[a] Adapted from Cronin and Shaw, 1988.
[b] The full names of organizations and reference to the master bibliography listing (where it differs) follow:
  1. U.S. Senate Select Committee on Nutrition and Human Needs, 1977a, p. 12.
  2. U.S. Senate Select Committee on Nutrition and Human Needs, 1977b, p. 4.
  3. U.S. Department of Health, Education, and Welfare, 1979.
  4. U.S. Department of Health and Human Services, Public Health Service, 1988.
  5. U.S. Department of Health and Human Services, Food and Drug Administration (Federal Register, 1990d).
  6. U.S. Department of Agriculture and U.S. Department of Health and Human Services, 1990.
  7. Council on Scientific Affairs, American Medical Association (American Medical Association, 1979).
  8. American Cancer Society (Nixon, 1990).
  9. National Cancer Institute, National Institutes of Health, U.S. Department of Health and Human Services (Butrum et al, 1988).
  10. American Heart Association, 1988.
  11. American Heart Association (Food Chemical News 1990b).

12. Food and Nutrition Board, National Research Council, National Academy of Sciences (National Research Council, 1980).
13. Committee on Diet, Nutrition, and Cancer, National Research Council, National Academy of Sciences (National Academy of Sciences, 1982).
14. National Research Council, 1989a.
15. Subcommittee on the Tenth Edition of the RDAs, Food and Nutrition Board, National Research Council, National Academy of Sciences (National Research Council, 1989b).

[c]Indicates that no specific dietary advice is stated in the published report. If a group specifically states that recommendations are inappropriate or unwarranted, this is noted.

Table 2.2. Recommendations on Carbohydrates, Sodium, and Alcohol[a]

| Source[b] | Carbohydrate | | | Sodium | Alcohol | Additional Recommendations |
	Starch	Fiber	Refined Sugars			
Government Agencies						
1. U.S. Senate, *Dietary Goals for the United States*, 1st ed., 1977	Carbodyrate consumption at 55–60% of total energy intake	...[c]	15% of total energy intake	3 g salt/day	...	...
2. U.S. Senate, *Dietary Goals for the United States*, 2nd ed., 1977	Increase complex carbohydrates and naturally occurring sugar to 48% of total energy	...	Reduce to 10% of total energy	Decrease salt intake to 5 g salt/day	...	...
3. DHEW, *Healthy People: Surgeon General's Report on Health Promotion and Disease Prevention*, 1979	Consume more complex carbohydrates		Consume less	Consume less salt	...	Dietary supplements, fluoride
4. DHHS, *The Surgeon General's Report on Nutrition and Health*, 1988	Increase consumption	Increase consumption	...	Reduce intake	Take alcohol only in moderation if at all	Fluoride, sugars, calcium, iron, dietary supplements
5. DHHS-FDA, *Daily Reference Values (DRV) For Nutrition Labeling*, 1990	Carbohydrate should constitute 55% of calories			2,400 mg (6 g salt)	...	Protein: 14 g, infant; 16 g, child < 4 yr; 50 g, age 4 to adult; 60 g, pregnant; 65 g, lactating

6. USDA and DHHS, *Nutrition and Your Health: Dietary Guidelines for Americans*, 3rd ed., 1990	Choose a diet with plenty of vegetables, fruits and grain products	Use sugars in moderation	Use salt and sodium in moderation	If you drink, do so in moderation	Dietary supplements, fluoride
Health Organizations					
7. American Medical Association, *Concepts of Nutrition and Health*, 1979	...	...	Moderate intake of salt to less than 12 g/day (4,800 mg of sodium/day)	Moderation in intake	Dietary supplements
8. *Nutrition and Cancer: American Cancer Society Guidelines, Programs and Initiatives*, 1990	Eat more high-fiber foods	...		Limit consumption of alcoholic beverages, if you drink at all	Include a variety of vegetables and fruit in the daily diet. Limit consumption of smoked, cured, and nitrate-cured foods
9. National Cancer Institute, *NCI Dietary Guidelines: Rationale*, 1988	Increase fiber intake to 20-30 g/day with an upper limit of 35 g	...	...	If you drink, do so in moderation	Limit foods preserved by salt curing
10. American Heart Association, *Dietary Guidelines for Healthy American Adults*, 1988	Carbohydrate intake should constitute 50% or more of calories, with emphasis on complex carbohydrates		Limit to 3,000 mg/day	Not to exceed 1-2 oz. ethanol/day	Protein (15% of total calories)

(*continued on next page*)

Table 2.2 (continued)

Source[b]	Carbohydrate			Sodium	Alcohol	Additional Recommendations
	Starch	Fiber	Refined Sugars			
11. American Heart Association, *The Healthy American Diet*, 1990	Increase consumption	Increase consumption	...	Reduce intake	Consume alcohol in moderation, if at all	Reduce risk for dental caries, osteoporosis, and iron deficiency anemia in specific groups
National Academy of Sciences						
12. *Toward Healthful Diets*, 1980	...	...	Reduce intake if energy requirement is low	Use salt in moderation: 3–8 g/day (1,200–3,200 mg of sodium/day)	Reduce intake if energy requirement is exceeded	Fluoride
13. *Diet, Nutrition, and Cancer*, 1982	...	...	...	...	If consumed, do so in moderation	Vitamins A and C, limit foods preserved by salt curing and smoking
14. *Diet and Health*, 1989	Increase to more than 55% of total calories	Eat fruits and vegetables, do not use fiber supplements	Do not increase intake	Limit to 6 g of salt/day	Intake of alcohol not recommended. For those who drink, limit to 1 oz. pure alcohol daily	Protein: <1.6 g/kg body weight for adults, <15% of total calories; calcium; dietary supplements; fluoride
15. *Recommended Dietary Allowances*, 10th ed., 1989	Increase consumption of complex	Achieve desired fiber intake from	Do not increase intake	Safe minimum intake 500	...	Dietary supplements; protein (g/kg) per day: 2.2

carbohydrates. More than half the energy requirement from carbohydrates	mg/day. Limit daily intake to 6 g of salt (2.4 g sodium) or less per day	age 0-6 mo., 1.6 age 6 mo.-1 yr, 1.2 age 1-3, 1.1 age 4-6, 1.0 age 7-14, 0.9 boys 15-18, 0.8 adult
vegetables, fruits, legumes, whole grain cereals, not fiber concentrates		

a Adapted from Cronin and Shaw, 1988.

b The full names of organizations and reference to the master bibliography listing (where it differs) follow:

1. U.S. Senate Select Committee on Nutrition and Human Needs, 1977a, p. 12.
2. U.S. Senate Select Committee on Nutrition and Human Needs, 1977b, p. 4.
3. U.S. Department of Health, Education, and Welfare, 1979.
4. U.S. Department of Health and Human Services, Public Health Service, 1988.
5. U.S. Department of Health and Human Services, Food and Drug Administration (Federal Register, 1990d).
6. U.S. Department of Agriculture and U.S. Department of Health and Human Services, 1990.
7. Council on Scientific Affairs, American Medical Association (American Medical Association, 1979).
8. American Cancer Society (Nixon, 1990).
9. National Cancer Institute, National Institutes of Health, U.S. Department of Health and Human Services (Butrum et al, 1988).
10. American Heart Association, 1988.
11. American Heart Association (Food Chemical News 1990b).
12. Food and Nutrition Board, National Research Council, National Academy of Sciences (National Research Council, 1980).
13. Committee on Diet, Nutrition, and Cancer, National Research Council, National Academy of Sciences (National Academy of Sciences, 1982).
14. National Research Council, 1989a.
15. Subcommittee on the Tenth Edition of the RDAs, Food and Nutrition Board, National Research Council, National Academy of Sciences (National Research Council, 1989b).

c Indicates that no specific dietary advice is stated in the published report. If a group specifically states that recommendations are inappropriate or unwarranted, this is noted.

(U.S. RDAs).[83] The new values are called the Reference Daily Intakes (RDIs) and the Daily Reference Values (DRVs). The DRVs can be found in Tables 2.1 and 2.2 (item 5) and in more detail in Table 2.3. The Nutrition Labeling and Education Act of 1990 adds more requirements for nutrition labeling. Additional qualitative recommendations were published in an American Heart Association report for the general public, which appeared as "The Healthy American Diet" in 1990 (Tables 2.1 and 2.2, item 11).[84]

In 1990, a third revision of the USDA and the U.S. Department of Health and Human Services' (DHHS) recommendations was published as *Nutrition and Your Health: Dietary Guidelines for Americans* (Tables 2.1 and 2.2, item 6).[85] The 10th edition of *The Recommended Dietary Allowances* was published late in 1989. It is a referenced report for professional use presenting quantitative and qualitative recommendations for nutrients and other food components (Tables 2.1 and 2.2, item 15).[86] And last, but not least, the two most comprehensive of the recent referenced reports for professionals that relate diet to chronic disease are *The Surgeon General's Report on Nutrition and Health*, which made qualitative dietary recommendations in 1988,[87] and the National Research Council's report, *Diet and Health*, which made qualitative and quantitative recommendations in 1989 (Tables 2.1 and 2.2, items 4 and 14).[88]

The main purpose of the Food and Drug Administration's proposed RDIs and DRVs is to establish a standard basis for the percentages calculated for the Daily Values to appear on food labels for consumers' information. A food label would list the percentage of Daily Values of nutrients available in a serving of food, discussed further in Chapter 6. The Daily Values for protein and 26 vitamins and minerals are based on the RDIs; these would replace the old U.S. RDAs. The RDIs, in Table 2.4, are general reference values, not dietary allowances for

Table 2.3. Daily Reference Values for Nutrition Labeling[a]

Nutrient or Food Component	Amount	Percent of Calories[b]
Fat	75 g	30
Fatty acids		
Saturated	25 g	10
Unsaturated	50 g	20
Cholesterol	300 mg	...
Carbohydrate	325 g	55
Fiber	25 g	...
Sodium	2,400 mg (6 g salt)	...
Potassium	3,500 mg	...

[a]Federal Register, 1990d.
[b]Reference calorie intake established is 2,350 Calories.

individuals. They are population-adjusted means of nutrients for five population groups based on the 10th edition of the RDAs. The Daily Values for eight additional food components (Table 2.3) are based on the DRVs. The DRVs include some food components for which dietary recommendations suggest a limited intake and some that are based on a reference caloric intake established at 2,350 Calories. These standards are used to calculate the percentage of calories available from a particular food component, such as fat or carbohydrate.

Table 2.4. Reference Daily Intakes for Nutrition Labeling[a]

Nutrient	Unit of Measurement	Adults and Children 4 Years or Older	Children Less than 4 Years[b]	Infants[c]	Pregnant Women	Lactating Women
Biotin	Milligrams	60	20	13	···	···
Calcium	Milligrams	900	800	500	1,200	1,200
Chloride	Milligrams	3,150	1,000	650	3,400	3,400
Chromium	Milligrams	120	50	33	···	···
Copper	Micrograms	2.0	0.9	0.6	···	···
Fluoride	Micrograms	2.5	1.0	0.5	···	···
Folate	Micrograms	180	50	30	400	280
Iodine	Micrograms	150	70	45	175	200
Iron	Milligrams	12	10	8.0	30	15
Magnesium	Milligrams	300	80	50	320	355
Manganese	Micrograms	3.5	1.3	0.6	···	···
Molybdenum	Milligrams	150	38	26	···	···
Niacin	Niacin equivalents[d]	16	9.0	5.5	17	20
Pantothenic acid	Milligrams	5.0	3.0	2.5	···	···
Phosphorus	Milligrams	900	800	400	1,200	1,200
Protein	Grams	50	16	14	60	65
Riboflavin	Milligrams	1.4	0.8	0.5	1.6	1.6
Selenium	Micrograms	55	20	13	65	75
Thiamin	Milligrams	1.2	0.7	0.4	1.5	1.6
Vitamin A	Retinol equivalents[d]	875	400	375	800	1,300
Vitamin B-6	Milligrams	1.5	1.0	0.5	2.2	2.1
Vitamin B-12	Micrograms	2.0	0.7	0.4	2.2	2.6
Vitamin C	Milligrams	60	40	33	70	95
Vitamin D	Micrograms[e]	6.5	10	9.0	10	10
Vitamin E	Alpha-tocopherol equivalents[d]	9.0	6.0	3.5	10	12
Vitamin K	Micrograms	65	15	7.5	65	65
Zinc	Milligrams	13	10	5.0	15	19

[a] Source: Federal Register, 1990d.
[b] "Children less than 4 years" includes persons 13 and through 47 months of age.
[c] "Infants" means persons not more than 12 months of age.
[d] 1 Retinol equivalent = 1 microgram (μg) of retinol or 6 μg of beta-carotene; 1 alpha-tocopherol equivalent = 1 milligram (mg) of d-alpha-tocopherol (RRR-alpha-tocopherol); 1 niacin equivalent = 1 mg of niacin or 60 mg of dietary tryptophan.
[e] As cholecalciferol.

Two additional labeling proposals were made in 1990. First, a report from the National Academy of Sciences Institute of Medicine, called "Nutrition Labeling—Issues and Directions for the 1990s," was commissioned by the U.S. Public Health Service and the USDA. It recommended that nutrition labeling be required for packaged foods, meat, seafood, fresh produce, and many restaurant foods. Second was the Nutrition Labeling and Education Act of 1990, which requires national uniformity in nutrition labeling and makes nutrition labeling mandatory for most packaged foods. It requires definitions of terms such as "free," "low," "lite," and "reduced" and development of a consumer education program on food labeling. It further directs the Food and Drug Administration to issue final regulations within two years.[89]

The newly proposed RDAs (10th ed., 1989, shown in Tables 2.5–2.9) give amounts of 30 nutrients and dietary components to be consumed daily; the recommendations are differentiated for 15 groups categorized by age and sex and for pregnant and lactating women.[90] RDAs "provide a nutrient standard for planning adequate diets for groups of people."[91] The RDAs are intended to be adequate for the needs of almost all healthy people, on average and over time.[92] It is important to remember that the RDA for each nutrient except calories (energy) contains a safety factor and, therefore, is higher than the requirement for most people. The RDA stated for energy (calories) is considered a requirement without a built-in safety factor (Table 2.9). The RDAs were first established in 1941 and first published in 1943. They have been revised approximately every five years except between 1980 and 1989.[93] Each edition incorporates new knowledge and provides more information than the previous one.

The Surgeon General's reports on *Healthy People,* in 1979, and on *Nutrition and Health,* in 1988 (Tables 2.1 and 2.2, items 3 and 4),[94] and the National Research Council's reports in 1982 on *Diet, Nutrition and Cancer* and, in 1989, on *Diet and Health* (Tables 2.1 and 2.2, items 13 and 14)[95] addressed the diet-related risks for several chronic diseases, including coronary heart disease, cancer, stroke, hypertension, diabetes, obesity, osteoporosis, dental disease, and diseases of the liver, kidney, and gastrointestinal tract. The Surgeon General's 1988 report concluded that overconsumption of certain dietary components is a problem for Americans, the worst being the high amounts of fat. Dietary recommendations in these reports include qualitative and quantitative recommendations that focus on avoiding overeating, maintaining a balance of nutrients in a healthy diet, and reducing the risk of chronic disease.[96]

The American Heart Association has been a particularly active and

Table 2.5. Recommended Dietary Allowances for Protein and Vitamins, Revised 1989[a,b]

Category	Age (years)	Weight[c] (kg)	Weight[c] (lb)	Height[c] (cm)	Height[c] (in.)	Protein (g)	Fat-Soluble Vitamins Vitamin A (μg RE)[d]	Vitamin D (μg)[e]	Vitamin E (mg α-TE)[f]	Vitamin K (μg)	Water-Soluble Vitamins Vitamin C (mg)	Thiamin (mg)	Riboflavin (mg)	Niacin (mg NE)[g]	Vitamin B-6 (mg)	Folate (μg)	Vitamin B-12 (μg)
Infants	0.0–0.5	6	13	60	24	13	375	7.5	3	5	30	0.3	0.4	5	0.3	25	0.3
	0.5–1.0	9	20	71	28	14	375	10	4	10	35	0.4	0.5	6	0.6	35	0.5
Children	1–3	13	29	90	35	16	400	10	6	15	40	0.7	0.8	9	1.0	50	0.7
	4–6	20	44	112	44	24	500	10	7	20	45	0.9	1.1	12	1.1	75	1.0
	7–10	28	62	132	52	28	700	10	7	30	45	1.0	1.2	13	1.4	100	1.4
Males	11–14	45	99	157	62	45	1,000	10	10	45	50	1.3	1.5	17	1.7	150	2.0
	15–18	66	145	176	69	59	1,000	10	10	65	60	1.5	1.8	20	2.0	200	2.0
	19–24	72	160	177	70	58	1,000	10	10	70	60	1.5	1.7	19	2.0	200	2.0
	25–50	79	174	176	70	63	1,000	5	10	80	60	1.5	1.7	19	2.0	200	2.0
	51+	77	170	173	68	63	1,000	5	10	80	60	1.2	1.4	15	2.0	200	2.0
Females	11–14	46	101	157	62	46	800	10	8	45	50	1.1	1.3	15	1.4	150	2.0
	15–18	55	120	163	64	44	800	10	8	55	60	1.1	1.3	15	1.5	180	2.0
	19–24	58	128	164	65	46	800	10	8	60	60	1.1	1.3	15	1.6	180	2.0
	25–50	63	138	163	64	50	800	5	8	65	60	1.1	1.3	15	1.6	180	2.0
	51+	65	143	160	63	50	800	5	8	65	60	1.0	1.2	13	1.6	180	2.0
Pregnant						60	800	10	10	65	70	1.5	1.6	17	2.2	400	2.2
Lactating First six months						65	1,300	10	12	65	95	1.6	1.8	20	2.1	280	2.6
Second six months						62	1,200	10	11	65	90	1.6	1.7	20	2.1	260	2.6

[a] Source: National Research Council, 1989b, last page. Reprinted, by permission, from *Recommended Dietary Allowances*, ©1989 by the National Academy of Sciences, National Academy Press, Washington, DC.

[b] Designed for the maintenance of good nutrition of practically all healthy people in the United States. The allowances, expressed as average daily intakes over time, are intended to provide for individual variations among most normal persons as they live in the United States under usual environmental stresses. Diets should be based on a variety of common foods in order to provide other nutrients for which human requirements have been less well defined. See text for detailed discussion of allowances and of nutrients not tabulated.

[c] Weights and heights of reference adults are actual medians for the U.S. population of the designated age, as reported by NHANES II. The median weights and heights of those under 19 years of age were taken from Hamill et al, 1979, pp. 16–17. The use of these figures does not imply that the height-to-weight ratios are ideal.

[d] Retinol equivalents; 1 retinol equivalent = 1 μg of retinol or 6 μg of beta-carotene.

[e] As cholecalciferol; 10 μg cholecalciferol = 400 IU of vitamin D.

[f] Alpha-tocopherol equivalents; 1 mg d-α-tocopherol = 1 α-TE.

[g] 1 NE (niacin equivalent) is equal to 1 mg of niacin or 60 mg of dietary tryptophan.

Table 2.6. Recommended Dietary Allowances for Minerals, Revised 1989[a]

Category	Age[b] (years)	Calcium (mg)	Phosphorus (mg)	Magnesium (mg)	Iron (mg)	Zinc (mg)	Iodine (μg)	Selenium (μg)
Infants	0.0–0.5	400	300	40	6	5	40	10
	0.5–1.0	600	500	60	10	5	50	15
Children	1–3	800	800	80	10	10	70	20
	4–6	800	800	120	10	10	90	20
	7–10	800	800	170	10	10	120	30
Males	11–14	1,200	1,200	270	12	15	150	40
	15–18	1,200	1,200	400	12	15	150	50
	19–24	1,200	1,200	350	10	15	150	70
	25–50	800	800	350	10	15	150	70
	51+	800	800	350	10	15	150	70
Females	11–14	1,200	1,200	280	15	12	150	45
	15–18	1,200	1,200	300	15	12	150	50
	19–24	1,200	1,200	280	15	12	150	55
	25–50	800	800	280	15	12	150	55
	51+	800	800	280	10	12	150	55
Pregnant		1,200	1,200	320	30	15	175	65
Lactating								
First six months		1,200	1,200	355	15	19	200	75
Second six months		1,200	1,200	340	15	16	200	75

[a]Source: National Research Council, 1989b, last page. Reprinted, by permission, from *Recommended Dietary Allowances,* ©1989 by the National Academy of Sciences, National Academy Press, Washington, DC.
[b]Reference weights and heights for age and sex categories are given in Table 2.5.

Table 2.7. Estimated Safe and Adequate Daily Dietary Intakes of Selected Vitamins and Minerals, Revised 1989[a,b]

		Vitamins		Trace Elements[c]				
Category	Age (years)	Biotin (mg)	Pantothenic Acid (mg)	Copper (mg)	Manganese (mg)	Fluoride (mg)	Chromium (μg)	Molybdenum (μg)
Infants	0–0.5	10	2	0.4–0.6	0.3–0.6	0.1–0.5	10–40	15–30
	0.5–1	15	3	0.6–0.7	0.6–1.0	0.2–1.0	20–60	20–40
Children and	1–3	20	3	0.7–1.0	1.0–1.5	0.5–1.5	20–80	25–50
adolescents	4–6	25	3–4	1.0–1.5	1.5–2.0	1.0–2.5	30–120	30–75
	7–10	30	4–5	1.0–2.0	2.0–3.0	1.5–2.5	50–200	50–150
	11+	30–100	4–7	1.5–2.5	2.0–5.0	1.5–2.5	50–200	75–250
Adults		30–100	4–7	1.5–3.0	2.0–5.0	1.5–4.0	50–200	75–250

[a]Source: National Research Council, 1989b, p. 284. Reprinted, by permission from *Recommended Dietary Allowances,* ©1989 by the National Academy of Sciences, National Academy Press, Washington, DC.
[b]Because there is less information on which to base allowances, these figures are not given in the main tables of Recommended Dietary Allowances (2.5 and 2.6) and are provided here in the form of ranges of recommended intakes.
[c]Since the toxic levels for many trace elements may be only several times usual intakes, the upper levels for the trace elements given in this table should not be exceeded habitually.

vocal group in promoting diets to prevent heart disease. Their 1988 *Dietary Guidelines for Healthy American Adults* (Tables 2.1 and 2.2, item 10), which were widely publicized, reiterated the quantitative goals set forth in the 1977 U.S. Senate Select Committee's *Dietary Goals.* In 1990, the association put forth a qualitative set of recommendations, the "Healthy American Diet," that addressed total nutritional needs and control of risk factors for cancer, diabetes, cardiovascular disease, and stroke (Tables 2.1 and 2.2, item 11).[97] This qualitative version of their recommendations is also significant in that it represents agreement and endorsement of five private health organizations. Although governmental agencies do not endorse such reports, four of them, according to Myron Weisfeldt, president of the American Heart Association, "have discussed the concepts at length and applaud the intent of the document."[98]

The third edition of *Nutrition and Your Health: Dietary Guidelines for Americans,* promulgated by the USDA and the DHHS, presents qualitative and quantitative recommendations designed to help healthy consumers make daily food choices.[99] The qualitative guidelines were first developed as a joint effort between the USDA and DHHS and issued in 1980 to interpret quantitative recommendations of the 1977 *Dietary Goals for the United States,* second edition,[100] and findings of the 1979 *Surgeon General's Report* (Tables 2.1 and 2.2, items 1 and 3).[101]

The USDA was under considerable pressure from farm producer groups not to publicize the quantitative 1977 *Dietary Goals for the United*

Table 2.8. Estimated Sodium, Chloride, and Potassium Minimum Requirements of Healthy Persons, Revised 1989[a]

Age	Weight[b] (kg)	Sodium[b,c] (mg)	Chloride[b,c] (mg)	Potassium[d] (mg)
Months				
0–5	4.5	120	180	500
6–11	8.9	200	300	700
Years				
1	11.0	225	350	1,000
2–5	16.0	300	500	1,400
6–9	25.0	400	600	1,600
10–18	50.0	500	750	2,000
>18[e]	70.0	500	750	2,000

[a] Source: National Research Council, 1989b, p. 253. Reprinted, by permission, from *Recommended Dietary Allowances,* ©1989 by the National Academy of Sciences, National Academy Press, Washington, DC.
[b] No allowance has been included for large, prolonged losses from the skin through sweat.
[c] There is no evidence that higher intakes confer any health benefit.
[d] Desired intakes of potassium may considerably exceed these values (~3,000 mg for adults).
[e] No allowance included for growth. Values for those below 18 years assume a growth rate at the 50th percentile reported by the national Center for Health Statistics (Hamill et al, 1979) and averaged for males and females.

Table 2.9. Median Heights and Weights and Recommended Energy Intake, Revised 1989[a]

Category	Age (years)	Weight (kg)	Weight (lb)	Height (cm)	Height (in.)	REE[b] (Cal/day)	Multiples of REE	Average Energy Allowance (Cal)[c,d] Per kg	Per Day
Infants	0.0-0.5	6	13	60	24	320	...	108	650
	0.5-1.0	9	20	71	28	500	...	98	850
Children	1-3	13	29	90	35	740	...	102	1,300
	4-6	20	44	112	44	950	...	90	1,800
	7-10	28	62	132	52	1,130	...	70	2,000
Males	11-14	45	99	157	62	1,440	1.70	55	2,500
	15-18	66	145	176	69	1,760	1.67	45	3,000
	19-24	72	160	177	70	1,780	1.67	40	2,900
	25-50	79	174	176	70	1,800	1.60	37	2,900
	51+	77	170	173	68	1,530	1.50	30	2,300
Females[e]	11-14	46	101	157	62	1,310	1.67	47	2,200
	15-18	55	120	163	64	1,370	1.60	40	2,200
	19-24	58	128	164	65	1,350	1.60	38	2,200
	25-50	63	138	163	64	1,380	1.55	36	2,200
	51+	65	143	160	63	1,280	1.50	30	1,900

[a] Source: National Research Council, 1989b, p. 33. Reprinted, by permission from *Recommended Dietary Allowances*, ©1989 by the National Academy of Sciences, National Academy Press, Washington, DC.
[b] Calculation of resting energy expenditure (REE) based on Food and Agriculture Organization equations, then rounded. (1 Calorie = 1 kilocalorie or kcal).
[c] In the range of light to moderate activity, the coefficient of variation is ±20%.
[d] Figure is rounded.
[e] The allowance for pregnant women is increased by 300 calories per day in the second and third trimesters, and for lactating women by 500 calories per day.

States and chose to issue qualitative guidelines to educate the public.[102] Criteria used to develop all editions of the guidelines include "faithfulness to the science base, utility to the general public, and consistency with Federal agencies' policy."[103] The 1980 guidelines were reviewed by the first Dietary Guidelines Advisory Committee in 1983, revised, reissued in 1985, and widely distributed through health professionals, educators, and the media.[104] The wording of the new 1990 guidelines and associated explanations make them more health-oriented, more positive, and in some cases more specific than those in the previous editions.

The remaining sets of dietary recommendations listed in Tables 2.1 and 2.2 include two early reports, one by the National Research Council in 1980 (item 12), and one by the American Medical Association in 1979 (item 7). Both downplayed the importance of fat consumption or any need to recommend changes in the American diet. The American Cancer Society's 1984 report recommended a decrease in fat and an increase in fiber.[105] In 1988, the National Cancer Institute articulated quantitative guidelines for fat and fiber (Tables 2.1 and 2.2, item 9). The American Heart Association issued its pathbreaking guidelines in the same year (Tables 2.1 and 2.2, item 10). In 1990, the American Cancer Society issued a recommendation that fat intake be 30% or less of calories (Table 2.1 and 2.2, item 8). The history of these various recommendations shows that it took about a decade between the time the 1977 U.S. Senate committee first put forth its quantitative *Dietary Goals* and the development of widespread public education concerning these goals. On November 5, 1990, the USDA and the DHHS finally endorsed an upper limit on dietary fat intake as part of their *Dietary Guidelines,* third edition. They, like other organizations, recommend no more than 30% of calories come from fat and no more than 10% from saturated fat. These guidelines apply to children over two years old and adults.[106]

Food Guidance and Education

To implement dietary change by the general public, dietary recommendations must be translated into educational tools that help people select healthy foods. Cooperation from government agencies, the food industry, health professionals, educational institutions, and the mass media is needed to do this.[107] The mass media have become a primary educator about food risks, and governmental agencies, primarily the USDA and DHHS, have long taken a leading role in developing educational tools that help Americans select nutritious diets within limited budgets. To help simplify consumers' decisions, food guides have existed as a guidance tool since 1917.[108] Food guides group foods with similar compositions and nutrient contents and prescribe the number of servings of a designated size from each group that should be eaten in a day.

One of the earliest food guides, issued in 1933, included 12 food groups and four cost plans. It was based on "new" knowledge that became available during the 1920s about nutrients and food sources of vitamins and minerals. It also incorporated information from the USDA's first official government food guide published in 1917 called "Food for Young Children." Food groups designated in this guide were flesh foods, starchy foods, fat foods, watery fruits and vegetables, and sweets.[109]

One of the first food guides to be widely used, published in 1943 and 1946, listed the Basic Seven (Table 2.10).[110] This was the first guide that used the RDAs to evaluate the nutritional adequacy of diets.

For at least two decades, the Basic Four food guide promulgated in 1958 was a standard for nutrition educators and consumers regarding food choice (Table 2.10). It was a condensation of the earlier Basic Seven.[111] In 1979, the Basic Five or, the "Hassle-free Guide to a Better Diet," added a group for fats, sweets, and alcohol to the Basic Four. In 1989, a list of six food groups issued by the USDA split up fruits

Table 2.10. Food Guides

Food Guide	Food Groups Recommended
Basic Seven[a] (1943, 1946)	Leafy green and yellow vegetables Citrus fruit, tomatoes, raw cabbage Potatoes and other fruits and vegetables Milk, cheese, ice cream Meat, poultry, fish, eggs, dried peas, beans Bread, flour, cereals Butter and fortified margarine
Basic Four, from *Food for Fitness, a Daily Food Guide*[b] (1958)	Milk Meat Vegetable, fruit Bread, cereal
Basic Five—Hassle-free guide to a better diet[c] (1979)	Vegetable-fruit Bread-cereal Milk-cheese Meat, poultry, fish, and beans Fats, sweets, alcohol
A pattern of daily food choices[d] (1989)	Breads, cereals, and other grain products Fruits Vegetables Meat, poultry, fish, and alternates Milk, cheese, and yogurt Fats, sweets, and alcoholic beverages

[a]From Haughton et al, 1987.
[b]U.S. Department of Agriculture, Agricultural Research Service, 1958.
[c]U.S. Department of Agriculture, Science and Education Administration, 1979b.
[d]U.S. Department of Agriculture, Human Nutrition Information Service, 1989.

and vegetables and added new foods to old groups (Table 2.10). The most recent guide represents current trends in food consumption and new nutritional knowledge.

Since 1933, food guides have been remarkably similar in purpose and emphasis. Foods are grouped to provide variety and adequate nutrition. It has been assumed that nutritionally adequate diets would be affordable and that entire food groups should not be removed from the diet in order to decrease costs. The assumption was also made that food habits and preferences could be a guide, though probably not always the best one, for the selection of nutritionally adequate foods. The evolution of the food groups reflects these fundamental criteria and a conservative response to new tastes, technology, and information.

The Human Nutrition Information Service of the USDA developed Food Plans in the mid-1930s that have been standards for family food use and food costs for more than 50 years.[112] Food Plans are lists of quantities and types of foods that provide nutritionally adequate diets for people in 11 age-sex groups at four cost levels—Thrifty, Low-Cost, Moderate-Cost, and Liberal.[113] The current plans are developed using a computerized mathematical programming model that selects the optimum amount of each type of food listed, subject to cost constraints, food consumption patterns derived from Nationwide Food Consumption Survey data (described in Chapter 7), and nutritional guidelines based on the RDAs and the dietary guidelines outlined in Tables 2.1 and 2.2. Costs of the plans are updated quarterly using the Consumer Price Index and are published in the *Family Economics Review*. As discussed in Chapter 9, the Thrifty Plan is used to determine food stamp allotments, and all the Food Plans are used by professionals to advise consumers on planning nutritionally adequate food intakes within their food budgets.[114]

Consumer Response

American consumers are becoming cognizant of the new dietary recommendations. Many of the trends in food consumption move in the direction pointed to by the recommendations. The nutritional status of the U.S. population is monitored by the USDA and the DHHS using data collected on food consumption from individuals and households.[115] In 1989, a report of expert panelists concluded that Americans are choosing lower fat meat and dairy products and are increasing their consumption of grains.

A 1986 survey conducted by the Food and Drug Administration found that 61% of people reported eating differently because of health concerns.[116] A 1987 survey found that almost half of adults try very hard to decrease the high-fat foods and cholesterol they eat; another 29% try moderately hard. Less than one-quarter do not worry about it.[117] A 1988 poll found 54% avoided eating too much fat, 42% limited cholesterol, and 35% exercised strenuously three times a week.[118] In a 1990 Louis Harris poll, half of adults reported "trying a lot" to avoid high-cholesterol foods and 58% avoided eating too much fat.[119] In 1990, 46% of shoppers surveyed said fat was their worst nutritional problem, an increase from 29% one year earlier; 44% said cholesterol was a worry, and 30% worried about too much salt.[120] Another 1990 survey found more than half of shoppers said a new product should be allowed on supermarket shelves only if it had little cholesterol, little fat, and few calories.[121] These consumers are clearly selecting foods by avoiding undesirable characteristics rather than seeking positive nutrition.

New food labeling will help provide even more information to consumers and will make it easier for them to select foods having preferred characteristics. The number of consumers that reported using labels to avoid or limit their intake of sodium increased from 14% in 1978 to 44% in 1986. For fats and cholesterol, the percentage increased from 7 to 15%. In 1986, 43% reported being on a low-sodium diet, 24% on a blood serum cholesterol lowering diet, and 19% on a weight reduction diet.[122]

Changes in the average amounts of various foods eaten in 1977 and 1985 by adult men and women are recorded in Table 2.11.[123] The trends revealed are similar to those in Figures 2.1–2.6 and 2.9–2.15. One should note that meat mixtures seem to be replacing "just meat" in the American diet, so that declines in poultry, pork, and beef are overstated in Table 2.11. Some portions of the meats listed reappear in a variety of meat mixtures. Declines in egg and whole milk consumption are evident. Increases in fish, low-fat milk, grain, and soft drink consumption are also obvious.

Even though there is evidence that consumers are slowly adopting eating patterns consistent with new dietary recommendations, a major nutrition concern about overeating remains. More than one-fourth of American adults are overweight, with higher percentages among women in ethnic minorities, especially blacks and Hispanics. Table 2.12 shows the percentage of people in various ethnic groups deemed to be overweight or severely overweight in a national health survey in the late 1970s and early 1980s.[124]

A 1990 Louis Harris poll found that 61% of adults were overweight; they weighed more than 10% above the recommended weight range for their height and build.[125] Since the risk of heart attack increases directly with excess weight, this is a significant health problem for American consumers.[126] Education concerning and attention to obesity prevention needs to be targeted at very young people, especially women, and at the poor. As discussed in Chapter 9, poverty in America often leads to obesity in the face of malnutrition.

Individual nutrients most likely to be underconsumed by Americans, especially women, are iron, calcium, vitamin B-6, and folacin. Nutrient intakes of small children also are low in iron, and those of poor, young, Hispanic children appear to be low in vitamin A.[127]

Nine percent of adults reported drinking an average of one or more ounces of alcohol (ethanol) per day, which is considered sufficient to be a problem.[128] This corresponds closely to results from a Louis Harris poll in 1990 that found 91% of adults drank only moderately or not at all.[129] Although consumption of alcohol has been considered unhealthy

Table 2.11. Percentage of Persons (ages 19–50) Using Selected Foods, Mean Intakes in One Day in 1985, and Percent Changes in Mean Intakes from 1977[a,b]

	Men			Women		
	No. Using (%)	Mean Intakes[c]		No. Using (%)	Mean Intakes[c]	
		1985 (g)	Change from 1977 to 1985 (%)		1985 (g)	Change from 1977 to 1985 (%)
Food Group or Subgroup						
Total meat, poultry, and fish	93	268	−9	88	181	−3
Meat mixtures	40	110	+5	37	88	+35
Beef[d]	28	52	−35	23	27	−45
Pork[d]	25	26	−7	20	14	−22
Poultry[d]	16	25	−22	19	22	−8
Fish and shellfish[d]	11	21	+50	12	13	+18
Total fluid milk	48	205	−5	51	141	−5
Whole milk	27	117	−25	26	64	−35
Lowfat or skim milk	21	87	+53	26	77	+60
Cheese	33	17	+6	34	18	+6
Eggs	28	26	−26	24	18	−28
Total vegetables	85	272	+3	83	173	−8
Total grain products	94	278	+8	94	209	+29
Grain mixtures	25	94	+31	26	74	+72
Total carbonated soft drinks	61	433	+74	54	287	+53
Regular soft drinks	48	332	+43	36	179	+28
Low-calorie soft drinks	16	101	+494	20	105	+123

[a] Source: U.S. Department of Health and Human Services, Public Health Service, 1989, p. 37.
[b] Data for men were collected on a day in the summer; data for women were collected on a day in the spring. Comparisons of 1985 data with data collected in 1977 should be made cautiously. Changes in data collection procedures and probing techniques may affect conclusions about increases or decreases in the intake of certain foods.
[c] Mean values represent intakes of all persons.
[d] Reported separately.

by most people, and immoral by some, for centuries, it persists. There is even limited evidence that in moderation, alcohol may have health benefits. Apparently, it can raise the count of high-density lipoprotein, the blood serum cholesterol-containing fraction that is linked to a reduced incidence of heart disease.[130]

Total fat consumption is still too high. In 1980, it was linked to high serum blood cholesterol (greater than 200 mg/deciliter) in over 55% of the population aged 20-74.[131] High sodium intake has been linked to hypertension, which affects up to 44% of the adult population. Blacks have a higher rate of hypertension, and white women who smoke eat higher amounts of fat, both of which are believed to contribute to heart disease.[132]

As discussed previously, the calories available in the food supply have varied little during the past century; there were 3,500 available per capita per day in 1985.[133] Calorie intake averaged about 1,517 per day for adult women (aged 19-50), 2,558 for adult men, and 1,440 for children under age 5 in 1985.[134] This represents a change from 1,604 for women, 2,433 for men, and 1,551 for children in 1977-1978.[135] Average calorie consumption appears to be falling for women and children according to recent food consumption surveys.

In 1985, 20% of calories in the food supply were available from fats and oils; 20% from grains; 19% from meat, fish, and poultry; and 18% from sweeteners.[136] Table 2.13 shows the percentages of calories consumed from fat, protein, and complex carbohydrates for men and women between ages 20 and 50 in 1977-1978 and again in 1985-1986. One can readily see that the calories obtained from fat declined and those from carbohydrates increased by about five percentage points for both men and women, even though 1985-1986 intakes ranged from 106.3 grams of fat per day for men to 67 grams per day for women. Comparisons

Table 2.12. Age-Adjusted Percentage of Overweight Persons Aged 20-74 Years[a,b]

	Percent Overweight		Percent Severely Overweight	
Ethnic Group or Race	Male	Female	Male	Female
Mexican American	30.9	41.6	10.8	16.9
Cuban	27.6	31.6	10.7	6.6
Puerto Rican	25.6	40.2	8.0	15.7
Nonhispanic white	24.2	23.9	7.7	9.4
Nonhispanic black	26.0	44.4	10.0	19.8

[a]Source: U.S. Department of Health and Human Services, Public Health Service, 1989, p. 49.

[b]By sex and ethnic group or race: Hispanic Health and Nutrition Examination Survey, 1982-1984, and second National Health and Nutrition Examination Survey, 1976-1980. Overweight and severely overweight are statistical measures defined as being in the 85th and 95th percentile of body mass measures (weight/height) among the relevant populations. It is not a measure based on an individual's healthy weight.

of the types of fatty acids in Table 2.13 should be done with caution because the data come from two different survey methods. Still, the percentage of total grams of fat from saturated fat changed very little, actually increasing somewhat for women. Men increased their intake of monounsaturated fat and both men and women increased the percentage of polyunsaturated fat. Men ate considerably more cholesterol-laden foods than women during both periods but decreased their intake over time.

In Pursuit of Health. Diet and exercise habits of Americans are changing. Between one-fourth and one-third of Americans consciously behave in a "healthy" way. About 24% reported practicing 19 out of 24 preventative health measures in a 1989 poll by Louis Harris and Associates.[137] In a 1987 survey, 30% reported watching the amount of calories they ate,[138] and 15–20% were on weight reduction diets at any one time.[139] In 1989, 36% of adults in the United States took nonprescription vitamin and mineral supplements—41% of women and 31% of men.[140] Half reported making changes in their diets in the past few years.[141]

Although 40% of U.S. adults exercised or played active sports regularly in 1988, only 28% were considered "physically active" (by a standard of burning up 3 or more Calories for every pound of body weight during exercise each day).[142] In 1990, 35% reported exercising strenuously at least three time a week, 42% of men and 29% of women. Women were more likely to watch their diet closely and men were more likely to exercise.[143]

Table 2.13. Percentage of Diet from Fat, Protein, Carbohydrates, and Fatty Acids for Men and Women (ages 20–50) in 1977–1978 and 1985–1986[a]

Sample	Percent of Total Calories				Percent of Total Grams of Fat from Fatty Acids		
	Fat	Protein	Carbo-hydrates	Cholesterol (mg/day)	Saturated	Mono-unsaturated	Poly-unsaturated
Men							
1977–1978	41.6	16.3	40.0	449[b]	36.5[c]	37.4[c]	13.8[c]
1985–1986	36.6	16.0	45.3	435	36.0	38.2	18.0
Women							
1977–1978	41.0	17.0	41.0	228	35.5[c]	36.6[c]	15.0[c]
1985–1986	36.7	16.6	46.3	301	36.3	36.7	19.0

[a]Data from U.S. Department of Health and Human Services, Public Health Service, 1989, pp. II-40, 46, 53, 59, 65, 69, 81. The 1977–1978 data are from the National Food Consumption Survey (Hama and Riddick, 1988). The 1985–1986 data are from the CSFII Surveys (U.S. Department of Agriculture, Human Nutrition Information Service, 1986b, 1987a).
[b]Data from the HANES II survey (Woteki et al, 1988a).
[c]Data from the HANES II survey (Woteki et al, 1988a) for years from 1976 to 1980.

Middle-aged, college-educated women were found most likely to lead healthy lifestyles, and white men with blue collar positions had the worst health habits.[144] Those who are most likely to be among the healthy one-third are women and older people.[145] Older Americans were most likely to be found among "healthy eaters" as they shifted to foods that would help prevent cancer and heart disease as early as 1980.[146] The aging of the population implies that more people are likely to become healthy eaters in the future.

Foods that are healthful and taste good—especially foods people remember from their childhood—are still the most popular. A survey of 2,000 consumers found that, although over half had reduced their consumption of red meat, eggs, cholesterol, sodium, sugars and sweets, and fried foods, they also indulged in ice cream and chocolate when they felt depressed (21 and 13%, respectively). About 15% would gladly go back to their old eating habits if research showed it would be healthy.[147]

Consumers send conflicting messages concerning food and health concerns. They indulge in gourmet ice cream and give up eggs. They cut out whole milk and eat Brie. They eat oatmeal for breakfast, a hamburger and french fries for lunch, and work out at the gym before dinner. The young (aged 18–29) are the most contradictory, endorsing healthy food and often exercising vigorously but eating more snack food and exercising less often than older people on average.[148]

Some interpret this contradiction as a workout-pigout mentality, looking for quick fixes to overindulgence.[149] Alternatively, it may be interpreted as a conscious balancing act—an attempt to balance the calories, nutrients, and taste of food. It is a personal short-run–long-run, benefit-cost analysis where the benefits of food that tastes good are balanced with the benefits of bodies that look and feel good. It is also an attempt to balance the various roles that food plays. Besides nourishing the body, food is sometimes a psychological salve, sometimes a display of good taste or good manners, and much, much more. It should, perhaps, be considered a sign of a well-informed and disciplined consumer if adequate compensation is made elsewhere for the occasional culinary indulgence. To the extent that what appears as inconsistent or irrational behavior is a balancing of nutrients over time, it may represent an informed, nutritional sophistication. However, the proportion of the population that is overweight suggests that uncontrolled indulgence may still be a serious problem for many.

TRENDS THAT AFFECT EATING BEHAVIOR

A trend indicates a general movement or direction of change in attitudes or behavior that has the strength and endurance to change the course of overall consumption patterns. It has been called a "grown-up fad"—a fad that has been tried, liked, and adapted by a significant number of people.[150] In 1987, 10 trends in consumer attitudes and behavior were identified for the Food Marketing Institute by futurist Faith Popcorn.[151] These trends are consistent with the observations of many others and show promise of continuing for some time to come.

Neotraditionalism. A desire for premium quality products and a willingness to pay more to obtain them is reflected in the increased demand for gourmet foods, produce guaranteed to be pesticide-free, and foods with especially good flavor. The latter explains a rise in demand for items like gourmet coffees, specialty cheeses, and newer varieties of crisp, sweet apples. As one Washington apple grower said, "Taste has finally come to the fore."[152]

Called "neotraditionalism," this trend embodies values that demand fewer but higher quality and more durable goods. Quality includes minimizing the environmental impacts of consumption. Most consumers will consider themselves to be some shade of "green" as they seek out "environment-friendly" goods.[153]

This trend is consistent with and reinforces the demand for safe and wholesome food and for food packaging and processing that help protect the environment. McDonald's switch from polystyrene to paper packaging was a direct response to consumers' sensitivities about environmentally safe products.[154] An important aspect of high-quality food is that it protects the long-run health and well-being of consumers. In addition to tasting good, consumers want food that is in good taste; that is, it adds noticeable value to their lives.

Adventure. A trend towards adventure expresses itself in a desire for variety, for new tastes and new foods, for adventure that involves little real risk. Consumers increasingly want more variety and diversity in their diets, as individuals and as a society. It is known that as incomes increase, consumers increase the number and variety of goods they purchase, including foods. One study found that household composition was, however, more important in predicting the demand for food variety than increased income. Small households and those with more adult women were the most likely to display diversity in food purchases.[155] Another factor that predicts an increase in the demand for diversity is an increasingly diverse population. Also, as discussed in Chapter 3, a population that is wealthier and better traveled is often searching for satisfying alternatives to old food habits. This search is closely tied to increasing boredom with old products or availability of new ones. For example, big hits in the early 1990s were predicted to be organic coffee and gourmet ice.[156]

Indulgence. A trend towards indulgence is consistent with the trend toward quality, adventure, and individualism. It arises from an attitude that says, "I deserve it and I want gratification now." Surely this is fostered by the large number of working adults who have very little leisure time and who feel they have earned the right to indulge. In their precious free time they seek out mini-adventures, which often involve new food experiences. Quite apart from truly addictive consumer behavior, many people indulge in occasional treats that enhance their pleasure or their status. With more income, these treats will be more frequent and more conspicuous, but food treats are relatively affordable to all Americans. In a world where consumers increasingly try to control their diets, controlled indulgences can be expected to continue.

Individualism. An individualistic lifestyle allows consumers to make statements about who they are and what they believe through their choices of food and other products. Increasingly, individuals in a household are choosing the food they want to eat, independent of the homemaker. "The microwave oven is also the embodiment of the '80s style individualism, turning each family member into a private chef. Gone is the sanctity of the family meal. Irretrievably altered is the role of mom, the nurturer."[157] At least two-thirds of children prepared at least one meal a week without supervision in 1990, and even preschoolers used microwave ovens to prepare food for themselves.[158]

Although we increasingly express our individuality through food choices, the practice of eating evening meals with family members is certainly not dead yet. In a 1988 nationwide survey, 80% of household heads reported cooking dinner at home several times a week. Household members ate dinner together three or more times per week in 70% of the households.[159] Among that 70%, dinner was eaten together by all members nearly six times per week on average, a durable habit indeed. In 86% of these households, the female household head was the main dinnertime cook.[160] This is corroborated by another survey that found nearly half the people who lived with others ate together almost every night of the week; less than 15% ate together fewer than three to five nights a week.[161]

Households of people over 55 years old and with women who do not work outside the home ate dinner together at home the most often, whereas those with working women without children ate dinner at home least often. Eating dinner together at home and cooking regularly decreased as income increased. Eating together was very or somewhat important for nearly all respondents, and most of them anticipated eating dinner together in the future as frequently as they did at the time of the 1989 survey.[162] This is consistent with the next trend, which calls for spending even more nonworking time in the home.

Cocooning. A trend towards staying home, termed "cocooning," reflects people's desires to protect themselves from the hassles of public appearances and uncertainties of social interactions. It may also reflect fear about the safety of some urban environments and the need for a change of pace after long days of interacting with people on the job. With almost 70% of all adults in the labor force, the desire to "go out" for social or mental stimulation diminishes. It may also be seen as a time management tool whereby some tasks, such as eating, can be accomplished faster at home. Other tasks can be accomplished while eating. Two-thirds of people surveyed in a Gallup poll in 1989 reported watching television, reading, working, or doing something else while they ate besides conversing with fellow diners.[163]

The working population is likely to continue cocooning, but forces that will limit it are a growing number of elderly and single-person households and their needs for social interaction. Predictions indicate, however, that people will be spending more time at home, working and playing there. Home entertainment and electronic gadgets for the home will be the single strongest growth market of the nineties according to some trend watchers.[164] Using computers, televisions, and telephones, consumers will shop from home, ordering food for customer pickup or home delivery.[165] Some fast-food places are reportedly even taking orders from fax machines to shorten the waiting time at pick-up.[166] Cocooning means a higher demand for TOTE food, for frozen foods, for home-delivered foods, and for technology that enables self-sufficiency. It may foretell a decrease in food *eaten* away from home but not in food *prepared* away from home.

Grazing. At home or away, people will graze more and eat fewer full, sit-down meals. This is consistent with the need for adventure and for food variety. It is consistent with individualism and with time management needs for convenient, ready-to-eat foods. Consumers eat on the run, eat little amounts more often, select the foods themselves, and, at least during the day, eat independently of other family members. To the extent that people who work spend more time away from home, this trend is likely to continue. Take-out food, finger food, food on a stick, buffet service, vending machines, and microwave ovens all facilitate this trend, which is limited only by the nutrition, quality, and taste of the food available for grazing.

Wellness. In the 1970s and 1980s, physical fitness was quite the craze. This has matured into a trend towards wellness, a more holistic concept that includes physical fitness and the effect of diet and other personal habits on long-term health. This is consistent with an aging and better informed population. For many, living to a ripe old age is not desirable unless it is accompanied by good health and independence. To the extent that dietary habits can influence this, they are likely to be pursued. Pursuing good health is a tradition. What has changed is how individuals attempt to achieve wellness through diet and exercise that might prevent chronic illness in addition to reliance on the medical profession for cures.

Controlling Time. "Time will be the currency of the nineties."[167] An increased need to manage one's time has and will continue to lead to great demand for convenience in foods and other goods and services. Time demands often conflict directly with the desire to eat healthfully, and balancing these two needs is a constant challenge for consumers and food sellers alike. "People haven't learned how to cook healthy quickly."[168]

Again, given the amount of time all adults spend in the labor force, the need for convenient foods and shopping services will continue. A survey of consumers showed that the most prized recent inventions were those that gave them convenience and control, such as the microwave oven, the television remote control, and the automatic coffee maker.[169] Consumers are tired of overly complex products that are difficult to operate and require time-consuming maintenance.

Shopping is an inconvenient and undesirable activity for many busy Americans. Consumers' pet peeves include standing in checkout lines and waiting for home deliveries.[170] Furthermore, they have shopping fatigue. They would rather order from a catalog or be able to buy everything at one store. "Shopping around" is not what busy people want to do.[171] About 30% of consumers do like to shop; the rest find little pleasure in it. Between 1982 and 1989, the average number of stores visited at a shopping mall dropped from 3.6 to 3, and the average length of the stay dropped from 90 to 68 minutes. Six out of 10 shoppers reported abandoning a store for poor service, especially shoppers with high incomes.[172] Those who like to shop are most likely to be under age 30, female, hold a white collar job, and live in California.[173]

Selectivity. Consistent with a quest for quality and convenience, consumers are increasingly intolerant of unsafe, poorly constructed, and overpriced products. In a market where consumers can evaluate how much satisfaction they get from a product, they have three choices: exit, voice, or loyalty.[174] In order to allow consumers to voice their complaints, businesses have installed a plethora of toll-free 800 numbers. It may be more convenient to call than to travel, but the satisfactory handling of consumer complaints via 800 numbers is very uneven. Consumers who are dissatisfied can exit. They can switch to another brand, product, or store. At least half of consumers switch brands of food products readily, especially if the product does not have a unique characteristic such as a flavor or status niche. People most likely to be loyal to brands are elderly, male, have blue-collar jobs, and live in the Midwest.[175] A study of brand-name foods in Canada found that those with the biggest rise in sales between 1984 and 1988 emphasized healthiness, indulgence, single-serving sizes, and product innovation. The fastest growing were brand-name beverages and frozen entrees.[176]

Ethics. The 1990s will see a return of the ethics and culture of the 1930s to 1950s. Declining narcissism and a search for moral stability will lead consumers to seek value in those things that will endure.[177] The environmental concern over fast-food packaging is an attack on a "throw-away, fast-food lifestyle" as much as a concern with solid waste buildup.[178] This represents, in part, the natural cycle of conservative and liberal attitudes that are observable through history. In the 1990s and beyond, the need to be socially responsible for environmental degradation, to become tolerant of diversity in society and to get along with one's neighbors, and the need to improve education and health care will dictate an increase in community spirit. Greater concern about extremes in poverty and hunger, especially about the homeless, and more generous food assistance for the poor might be on the horizon.

GLOBAL FOOD TRENDS

Although this book is primarily about the American food industry and the consumer trends that drive it, it would be a mistake to think that these operate independently of the rest of the world. For one thing, we import a significant share of our food. For example, in 1988 we imported 8.5% of the red meat consumed, 32% of the fresh fruits, 40% of the broccoli, 31% of the cauliflower, 91% of the spices, and 100% of the coffee, tea, and cocoa. Except for the last four items, the proportion of these foods that is imported has increased substantially since 1970.[179] In 1989 the United States imported $21.5 billion worth of food and agricultural products and exported $39.7 billion worth. The United States had 14% of the world share of all agricultural exports and 7% of the world's agricultural imports in 1989.[180] Food is a global business, and eating patterns around the world seem to be moving in directions that will make them increasingly similar in the future.

As incomes rise during economic development, typically the proportion of calories coming from cereals and starchy foods declines and the proportion from vegetable oils, fats, sugar, meat, and other animal products rises. An increase in the consumption of animal products has been particularly marked in Eastern Europe and the USSR over the last 30 years; still, consumption remains low by Western standards.[181] Although rice is still the major staple of the Japanese diet, per capita rice consumption is declining and meat consumption is increasing.[182]

Rising incomes also mean that a smaller percentage of total household expenditures is needed for food. This trend can be observed around the world. For example, between 1970 and 1986, the portion of personal consumption expenditures for food in Hong Kong fell from 31 to 16%, in the USSR from 35 to 28%, and in Japan from 26 to 19%.[183] These fundamental trends are bringing overall food consumption patterns closer together around the world.

In societies with high incomes, particularly the United States and Western Europe, the proportion of food from animal sources is leveling out and may even be declining as concerns about overeating and fat consumption replace concerns about having enough food. For example, the trend in the United States towards declining beef and increasing poultry consumption has also been observed in England.[184] More generally, over the past 20 years, the consumption of dairy products, sugar, potatoes, and grains has declined across Europe, while meat held steady and vegetable consumption increased.[185]

The globalization of food consumption patterns is occurring along two tracks. First, basic food commodities available and eaten in rich and poor countries are becoming more alike. Concerns regarding food safety and quality and environmental integrity are also spreading around the entire world, though more rapidly in advanced, well-fed nations. Simultaneously, more diverse food preferences are developing within countries, and a greater variety of foods are being purchased by individuals. International trade, telecommunications, travel, and an increasingly international media are fostering the homogenization of food consumption patterns and concerns across countries and the diversification of food preferences within countries. These food trends are occurring in the context of the more general globalization of world economies and mass culture.[186]

The globalization of eating habits does not imply a narrowing of consumer tastes, but a broadening of the range of preferences and an increased diversity in consumption patterns within individual countries. As Peter Timmer, a professor at Harvard University, said, "There will be Coke and McDonald's everywhere, but also Sichuan, Indian curries, paella, and tortillas."[187] Dietary variety is a luxury good as measured by economists. That means that the demand for variety rises as incomes increase, and they are increasing in most of the world.

Furthermore, many of the underlying demographic trends and economic forces in the United States that will be discussed in the next several chapters of this book are occurring elsewhere and pushing consumption patterns in similar directions. Rising incomes, shifting relative prices, aging populations, and women entering the labor force are widespread phenomena. For example, one explanation for the rising consumption of wheat in developing countries, particularly in the form of commercial bread, and the decline of traditional foods like millet and sorghum that require long hours of preparation, is the rising value of women's time.[188]

GENERAL IMPLICATIONS

In terms of basic food commodities, there is a gradual trend for the consumption of meats to level out if not decline. The substitution of crop-based foods for animal-based foods will be driven by concerns about health and nutrition, especially the overconsumption of fat and, perhaps to a limited extent, by concern for animal welfare. Unsaturated fat and fat substitutes will replace much of the saturated and animal fat in foods of the future. Concerns about heart disease and a virtual war on fat dictate this trend. Given the desire for weight control, the use of noncaloric sweeteners is almost certain to continue to increase. These trends are all indicative of the fact that Americans in general eat more food than their bodies can use and, for many, enough extra to be harmful. Overall, average calorie consumption has been falling since at least 1970, consistent with more sedentary lives and the availability of lower calorie foods. Liking to eat and being able to afford to eat whatever they like, Americans increasingly seek "good tasting" food that does not add to their weight or health problems. They will purchase foods that serve both their penchant to indulge today and to feel good tomorrow.

As discussed in Chapter 11, concerns for the environment and their own health are leading consumers to prefer food that has been subjected to a minimum of chemical treatment, preharvest and postharvest. This concern extends to preferences for degradable or recyclable packaging and safe processing. Social conscience will have an increased influence on food preferences in the future, but its total effect is likely to be small compared to the desire for quality and convenience.

The desire for convenient food will continue to drive the demand for processed food, already cooked food, or ready-to-eat fresh food. TOTE food is already purchased by 8 out of 10 households in any given month. About 15% of food expenditures go for TOTE food, and 19% is spent on restaurant food.[189] "Today, women are 'assembling' meals rather than preparing them. With a scarcity of time, more and more contend that quality time for their families or themselves is too important to waste in the kitchen. Their needs are changing the entire food retailing and service industries."[190] Food today must be fast and fresh. In fact, several "F" words describe current trends in food consumption: fast, fresh, fit, fancy, fun, finished, fad, fiber, foreign, famous, friendly, fat(non), and fractional (small servings).[191]

The individualistic nature of Americans, as well as their increased diversity, desire for variety, and economic ability to express themselves through food choices, indicate that nontraditional food marketing will be needed. The mass, middle-of-the-road, universal marketing of food is losing its effectiveness. To appeal to consumers' sense of uniqueness and adventure and provide food choices that satisfy consumers' diverse and changing preferences, market segmentation and targeting of market niches will be necessary.

The next chapter explores population and demographic trends in the United States. Labor force participation, income growth, and changes in income distribution are also examined for their ability to foretell future food consumption patterns.

APPENDIX

The food trend graphs (Figures 2.1–2.6 and 2.9–2.15) are based on data that have been compiled and published by the United States Department of Agriculture (USDA) since 1909. They can be found in a series of publications titled *Food Consumption, Prices and Expenditures*. The 1968 edition by Hiemstra and the 1989 and 1990 editions by Putnam were used for these figures. In addition, much of the data from 1965 forward are available on personal computer diskettes from the Economic Research Service of the USDA.

Data from the 1968 edition were added to the data available on diskette to complete the data series back to 1909, or to the earliest date for which data were available. Some of the most recently published data reflect a change in the way data are currently collected and tabulated. When these new series data created a disjointed trend line for recent years, the new and old series were merged in order to draw a continuous line. This was done by shifting the new trend line up (or down) to the old line on the first date at which there was a difference and then mapping the new series.

The data are reported in pounds per capita and are presented this way in many of the graphs. Some of the graphs are quantity indexes that can more readily illustrate the changes in per capita consumption since 1909 and relative to other food products. The quantity indexes were created by simply dividing the per capita consumption in every subsequent year by the per capita consumption in 1909 and multiplying by 100. These are different from the expenditure-weighted indexes by the USDA reported in Chapter 7. The indexes in this chapter show changes in quantity unadjusted for price changes.

Data for aggregate food groups were created by simply adding together data from the published series. For example, beans, peas, and nuts were added together for the top line in Figure 2.9. Various categories of fruits and degrees of fruit processing were aggregated in Figures 2.10 and 2.11 to illustrate changes in the form of fruit we eat. Vegetable data illustrated in Figure 2.13 are summed from commercially sold fresh, frozen, and canned vegetables. They do not include fresh vegetables produced at home, which until 1945 exceeded fresh vegetables sold in retail stores by a considerable amount. For example in 1909, 126 pounds per capita of fresh vegetables were produced at home and 63 pounds per capita were sold commercially. By 1945, the 113.5 pounds sold commercially exceeded home production, and after 1966 home-produced vegetable data were no longer published. The processed potato data are summed from data on canned, frozen, chipped, and dehydrated potatoes, which first appeared in 1946. The processed potato index was created by dividing the quantity of processed potatoes by the total quantity of potatoes in 1909 to make it comparable to the index for total potatoes of which it is a subset. In cases where the new data series were dramatically different and shorter, as with fruit juices in Figure 2.15, the older data series was graphed because it provided a longer trend line.

Demographic Trends
Foretell Food Trends

CHAPTER 3

Demographic, cultural, and economic diversity are increasing in the United States. There are more people with different ethnic backgrounds, lifestyles, and tastes than ever before. One of the ways people from different cultural origins and demographic groups express their differences is through the foods they eat. According to Tim Hammonds and Judith Kozacik of the Food Marketing Institute, "Tastes and preferences for food products are rooted in the fundamental forces of demographics and lifestyles. They move slowly and powerfully."[1]

Demographics grow more important for determining how much and what types of food are consumed as the size of the overall population grows more slowly, changes composition, and becomes more affluent. The demographic composition of the past and current population is well known and can be projected ahead 10 or 20 years with reasonable accuracy.[2] Beyond that, statements about population change are largely speculative, based on the assumption that past trends will continue. However, compared to other exogenous forces affecting the demand and supply of food (weather, wars, pests, government policies, inflation), the influence of demographics is relatively predictable. One can debate which changes are most important and more enduring, but smaller households and larger numbers of the elderly, nonwhites, educated workers, and employed women are typically credited with leading the biggest changes in the way we live and eat.

Demography is the scientific study of population size and composition and its changes, how these determine population trends, and the influence of those trends on social, political, and economic activities.[3] Demographic trends in the United States and their influence on food consumption are explored in this chapter. Trends covered are population growth and composition, ethnic diversity, household composition of families and nonfamilies, aging, income by region and education level, and changes in labor force participation. The projected impact of combined demographic and income trends on food expenditures is presented first. Then each of the demographic trends is discussed in some detail, including its expected effect on food consumption. The evidence suggests that markets, as well as people, will grow increasingly diverse. A growing mass market for homogeneous food commodities may be a thing of the past.

PROJECTED CHANGES IN FOOD EXPENDITURES

Foretelling future changes in food consumption and expenditures may be as much an art as a science. Demographic changes serve as indicators of changing tastes and preferences in most economic models designed to study food expenditures. Projections of the combined effects of demographic changes and real income growth on changes in national food expenditures between 1980 and 2010 are shown in Table 3.1. This is a summary of the projected effects of changes in the regional, racial, and age distribution of the population based on a middle level estimate of population growth and a 1% growth rate in real income.[4]

The projected increases in per capita expenditures are greatest for food bought away from home (16.5%), alcoholic beverages (14.7%), fish (18.4%), fruits (13%), and vegetables (14.2%). At the national level, expenditures are projected to increase more than 30% for food away from home, pork, fish, fresh fruits, fresh and processed vegetables, and alcoholic beverages. Rising incomes tend to dominate these results by pushing all expenditures up, and some potentially important factors were left out, such as changes in relative prices and preferences. This helps to account for the projected increase in beef and pork exceeding that of poultry. The results are, however, a good indication of expenditures for one type of food relative to another. For example, expenditures on dairy products are projected to increase less than for most other foods except cheese, and expenditures on fresh produce will outstrip those on processed fruits and vegetables.[5]

These projections also show that the most important demographic changes are a decline in the rate of population growth and an aging population. An increase in the number of elderly increases expenditures on all types of food except food away from home and alcoholic beverages. The impacts of regional shifts in population are minor, but some of the effects of regional differences that have been noted are increased expenditures on fresh fruits and vegetables, fats, and oils, and miscellaneous foods, and decreasing expenditures on meats, cereals, and butter. Increased ethnic diversity tends to decrease overall food expenditures. Effects of rising income were projected to increase expenditures on all foodstuffs except eggs. The largest expenditure increases due to income changes were for fish, cheese, and alcoholic beverages.

POPULATION GROWTH

Population growth is slowing down. In 1990, the U.S. population of 250 million people was growing at half the rate it had been in the middle of the 20th century. An average growth rate of 1.3% per year led to a total population increase of 80% during the 30 years before 1980. The population is expected to increase by only 15% in the 30 years after 1980, and the growth rate is expected to be less than 0.2% per year.[6] European growth rates are already down to 0.3% per year, and global growth rates are 1.7%, with the highest rates in Africa (3%), Latin America (2%), and South Asia (1.9%).[7]

Table 3.1. Projected Percent Increase in Real Food Expenditures Due to Combined Demographic and Income Changes Between 1980 and 2010[a,b]

Category	Percent Increase	
	Per Capita	Nationwide
Total Food	13.7	32.1
Food away from home	16.5	35.0
Food at home	10.8	28.9
Meat, poultry, fish, and eggs	12.5	31.1
Beef	11.2	29.2
Pork	12.3	31.3
Other meat	6.9	24.3
Poultry	10.7	29.1
Fish	18.4	37.4
Eggs	5.3	22.4
Cereals and bakery products	7.5	24.7
Dairy products	6.0	22.9
Milk and cream	1.5	17.2
Cheese	11.0	29.2
Other dairy products	9.6	26.8
Fruits	13.0	31.2
Fresh	13.8	32.2
Processed	11.7	29.4
Vegetables	14.2	33.1
Fresh	15.1	34.5
Processed	12.0	30.2
Sugars and sweeteners	7.2	23.8
Nonalcoholic beverages	7.4	25.3
Fats and oils	10.4	28.4
Butter	11.6	28.9
Margarine	9.4	27.4
Other	8.9	26.6
Miscellaneous	8.7	25.6
Alcoholic beverages	14.7	33.2

[a]Source: Blaylock and Smallwood, 1986, pp. 36 and 41.
[b]The "middle-series" poulation projection of the Census Bureau, which projects a U.S. population of 283 million by 2010, was used. An average annual growth rate of 1% was assumed for real income growth. In addition to population and income growth, the projections reflect the effect of changes in the age, regional, and racial distribution of the population.

Growth rates in the United States are quite uneven among ethnic groups. Nonhispanic whites increased at a rate of 0.5% in 1990. Hispanics and other races except blacks grew at a rate of 2.7%, blacks at a rate of 1.5%. By 2010, these rates are estimated to be 0.15% for whites, 1.8% for Hispanics, and 1.1% for blacks.[8] (The currently preferred term, African-American, is not used in this book to keep the names of ethnic groups consistent with those used in the census data.)

Figure 3.1 illustrates the slowing of overall population growth and the change in the mix of ethnic groups using the middle level population projections of the Census Bureau.[9] The nonwhite proportion of the total continues to increase throughout the period illustrated. For all ethnic groups, population growth is projected to taper off by about 2030 and to grow at a negative rate (−0.2%) for whites. This leads to the question of how economic sectors and industries such as the food industry, designed to thrive on growing markets, will adjust.

The slowing of domestic population growth and population growth in other "developed" countries means that growth in the quantity of food demanded in the developed world will also slow down. Most

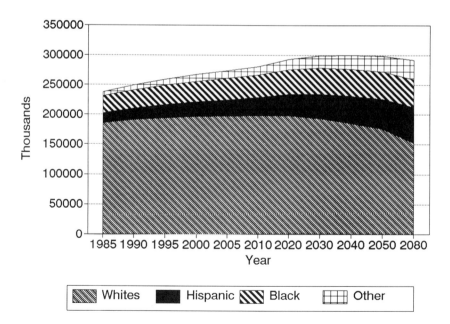

Figure 3.1. Total U.S. population by ethnic group from 1985 to 2080. (Data from U.S. Department of Commerce, Bureau of the Census, 1965, 1984a, 1989b; Spencer, 1986.)

Americans are already eating as much food as they can and many eat more than they should. More than one-fourth of adults are considered obese and 56% reported dieting to lose weight in 1986.[10] Food vendors face increased competition for a share of each consumer's stomach, while the number of stomachs is increasing at a slower pace.[11]

Population growth has traditionally depended upon fertility rates, but future population growth in the United States will depend mainly on declining mortality, continued immigration, and the fertility of nonwhite women. The demand for specific foods will depend less on population growth and more on the diversity of consumers' preferences. "As American consumers grow more educated and diverse, and demand increasingly customized service, the future will belong to those who target local differences cost-effectively."[12]

ETHNIC DIVERSITY

The faces and places of immigration have changed dramatically over the past century. During the 1800s, 95% of immigrants were from northern and western European countries. During the first two decades of the 20th century, this group dropped to 41% of the immigrants, with southern Europeans making up another 44%. The Europeans settled mostly in the American Northeast and Midwest. The 1965 Immigration Act abolished national origin quotas, opening up U.S. borders to unprecedented numbers of Asians and Hispanics. By 1986, less than 15% of immigrants were Europeans; 41% were Asian and 37% were Latin American. These new immigrants moved primarily into the South, the West, and the Middle Atlantic states.[13]

Immigration accounted for 28% of the population growth in the late 1980s and by 2030 will account for all the growth if birth rates do not change.[14] Immigration continues relatively unchecked in the United States, where 5% of the world's population takes in 50% of the international migrants each year, not counting refugees and illegal immigrants.[15] In the past two decades, more than three-fourths of the legal immigrants have come from Third World countries, principally from Mexico, the West Indies, Cuba, Korea, and the Philippines. About one-fourth of the increase in Hispanics since 1980 is attributed to illegal immigration.[16] Estimates of the total number of illegal immigrants in the United States are not very precise, ranging from 1 to 12 million.[17]

Hispanics

In 1989, Hispanics were more than 8% of the population, a 39% increase in nine years. Half of the increase was due to immigration.[18] Between now and 2010, half of the total population growth will be due to increasing numbers of Hispanics.[19] In the Southwest, Hispanics outnumber blacks. Hispanics make up at least one-fourth of the population in Texas and more than one-third in California; they are the majority in New Mexico. Hispanics are relatively young with about one-third under the age of 15. Almost two-thirds have Mexican roots. Mexican Hispanics are not only the largest group of immigrants, they have the highest fertility rate of all ethnic groups (2.8 births per adult woman's lifetime).[20]

If integration of an immigrant group into our society normally takes about three generations, many Hispanics will not be integrated for another one or two generations. They are largely Spanish speaking, many are Catholic, males tend to be dominant in households, and there are relatively few interracial marriages.[21] Though most are still relatively poor (21.3% in poverty)[22] and undereducated (49% have not completed high school),[23] the rate of college education among Cuban Americans is ahead of that for the nation as a whole (25% vs. 20%).[24] The 1987 median income of Cuban Americans was $1,304 more than the national median household income, and 1.4 times as much as the median Hispanic income of $19,305.[25] There is obviously considerable diversity among the Hispanic population. Figure 3.2 shows the distribution of Hispanics in the United States and their median incomes in 1987.

Ethnic Groups and Food Consumption

Immigrants from Third World countries, typically lacking skills and financial resources, swell the ranks of low-income households and boost the need for low-priced consumer goods, especially food and housing. These immigrants also provide a low-wage labor pool that U.S. consumers and businesses (though not laborers) have historically welcomed. This has been particularly true for farm labor and the food service industry. In countries like the United States where indigenous population growth has virtually stopped, immigrants provide a means of continuing economic growth by filling jobs and decreasing the dependency ratio caused by an aging population. Some observers argue that immigrants work harder, save more, and are more innovative than other Americans, and that their numbers ought to be increased to help foster economic innovation and growth.[26] Others argue that, although a large supply of low-wage labor may increase the global competitiveness of U.S. businesses in the short run, it ultimately reduces their incentive to adopt new, more efficient technology.[27]

Over the next half century, ethnic diversity will increase the diversity of types of consumer goods that will be demanded. The nonwhite population is relatively young. In 1988, the median age of blacks was 27.5 years, compared with 25.8 for Hispanics and 33.3 for whites.[28] Twenty years from now, almost 40% of children in grades one through eight will be nonwhite compared with 31% today.[29]

The mix of races in American schools, workplaces, supermarkets, and restaurants is changing fast. The challenge to food marketers is to anticipate increasingly diverse needs and changing preferences. Studies of food consumption found that, relative to whites, nonwhites eat fewer fruits and vegetables but more dark green vegetables. They are more likely to consume rice, legumes, pork, fish, poultry, eggs, and sweet beverages. They are less likely to drink milk or eat milk products, butter, margarine, beef, or desserts.[30] This pattern is quite consistent with general trends in per capita food consumption discussed in Chapter 2.

In the late 1980s, blacks spent an average of $1,000 per year less on food than whites, and a smaller portion of their food budget was spent eating away from home (21% compared with 33% for other groups combined).[31] This largely reflects a lower average income. In the early 1980s, however, blacks were found to spend 10% more than the average on meat and eggs and 30% more on fish and poultry, even though they spent less on food overall.[32]

Ethnic diversity creates market niches. For example, some Hispanics prefer high-fat milk. While the rest of the nation was moving to lower fat milk products, a specialty market for milk with 3.8% rather than 3.5% butter fat (whole milk) developed in some Hispanic sections of New York City.[33] Other market niches are created by strong cultural and

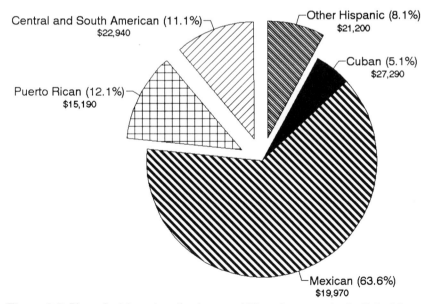

Figure 3.2. Place of origin and median income of Hispanic persons in the United States in 1987. (Data from U.S. Department of Commerce, Bureau of the Census, 1987f, 1988h.)

religious beliefs about food. In some local markets, Jewish needs for kosher food or Indian taboos on beef, for example, influence food consumption.

Various ethnic groups not only increase the diversity of foods demanded but introduce new foods into the American diet by selling them to the larger population. Asian Americans, the fastest-growing ethnic group in the country, are more likely than other minority groups to own their own business. Chinese and Japanese Americans owned 40% of the 225,642 U.S. firms owned by Asians in 1986. Most of these were in a retail trade, with one-quarter of the total receipts ($18 billion per year) coming from food stores or eating and drinking places.[34]

Consumers from all ethnic backgrounds are becoming more cosmopolitan eaters. At the same time ethnic groups are adopting more traditional American foods like hamburgers and french fries, Americans are adopting ethnic foods like pizza and tacos as their own. Between 1982 and 1986, the traffic in Asian restaurants increased 54%. It increased 43% in Mexican restaurants and 26% in Italian restaurants, compared with a 10% overall increase in restaurant patronage.[35]

REGIONAL DIFFERENCES

Regional differences revolve around demographics, ethnic cultures, population growth, and income trends. The population continues to shift to the South and West. The South gained 13% and the West gained 22% between 1980 and 1990; they are expected to grow by another 11 and 13%, respectively, by 2000. The Northeast grew 3.4%, and the Midwest only 1.4%. By 2000, it is projected that growth in the Northeast will be down to 2.4% and in the Midwest down to 0.3%.[36] States that gained the most population between 1980 and 1990 were Alaska (37%), Arizona (35%), Nevada (50%), Florida (33%), California (26%), and New Hampshire (20%). States that lost population during that time were Iowa (−5%), West Virginia (−8%), North Dakota (−2%), Wyoming (−3.6%), and the District of Columbia (−5%). Many of the North Central states are expected to lose population by 2000.[37] However, there is evidence that some may be holding their own or starting to grow.[38]

Americans are rather mobile, but they do not move very far. About 18% of the population, or 43.7 million people, move each year but most relocate within the same county. Three percent, or 7.5 million people, move across a state line. Thirty-five percent of people in their early twenties move each year.[39] They leave home to go to college or to find jobs, mostly in nearby suburban neighborhoods.

Migration from rural to urban centers continues. Almost half of the people in the United States live in metropolitan areas of 1 million or more, and in 1988 three-fourths lived in areas designated as metropolitan.[40] Those living on farms constituted only 2% of the population.[41] Rural, nonfarm people made up the other 23% of the population. Mobility helps to introduce a variety of food preferences across the country, but differences in food tastes and consumption patterns persist between regions. Urbanization increases the number of meals eaten away from home, estimated to be at least 50% of all meals in urban centers in the 1980s.[42]

More than half of Hispanics live in the Southwest. In 1989, 34% lived in California, 21% in Texas, and 10% in New York. Florida and New Mexico each had 8% of the Hispanic population, and the rest were scattered throughout the United States[43] American Indians, who numbered about 1.4 million, were heavily concentrated in New Mexico, Arizona, South Dakota, and Oklahoma. About two-thirds did not live on Indian reservation land.[44] Census data show Indians and Hispanics to be relatively poor and undereducated. Their food needs are reflected in the demand for low-cost, basic foods consistent with their preferences.

In the 1980s, one-fifth of Asian Americans lived in California, Hawaii, or New York. Other states with large numbers of Asian Americans were New Jersey, Texas (Vietnamese), Illinois (Laotian), Washington (Cambodian), and Minnesota (Hmong and Laotian). Although Asian Americans were only 1.6% of the total population during the 1980s, they accounted for 5% of the population in the West. At least 25 different Asian and Pacific Island groups make up the 3.5 million Asian-American population, 90% of which is (in order of decreasing numbers) Chinese, Filipino, Japanese, Asian Indian, Korean, Vietnamese, Laotian, and Thai.[45]

Since 1980, the proportion of blacks living in the South grew from 52 to 56%, while the proportion in the Northeast declined. This reversal of a long-standing trend for blacks to leave the South is expected to continue.[46]

Age distribution varies by region. Those counties with the highest percentages of people under age 5 in 1988 were located mostly in the Western Mountain states (Utah, Wyoming, Idaho, New Mexico) and Texas. Counties with the highest percentage of people over 65 were mostly in Florida, with some in Texas and Arizona.[47]

Other regional differences may also affect food consumption. For example, the counties with the highest unemployment rates were in the South, but those with the lowest per capita income were mostly in the Plains states (Nebraska, North Dakota, South Dakota, and Montana). Both lead to poorer households and demand for lower cost foods. In contrast, 15 out of the 25 counties with the highest per capita incomes were in a corridor from Washington, D.C. to Boston.[48]

The Boston–Washington, D.C. corridor also had one-sixth of the total

U.S. population and one-fourth of the metropolitan population.[49] Except for San Francisco, it also had the six most densely populated metropolitan areas and was the largest continuous urban area in the country.[50] This density largely explains the fact that, as recently as the early 1980s, half of the U.S. population lived in the Eastern time zone; only 15% of the population lived in the Pacific time zone.[51] The population distribution continues to shift westward, however. The East Coast area is very urban, cosmopolitan, and relatively wealthy. Food choices here reflect a wide variety of preferences consistent with high incomes and fast-paced lives. This area sets many of the food trends for high-income households across the country. It contains pockets of wealthy households, the type that produced the famous yuppie markets of the 1980s.

Regionality and ethnicity contribute not only to homogeneous and persistent consumption patterns among people within an area but to diversity between areas.[52] In the Southwest, demand has been relatively high for fruits, vegetables, and fish, but low for butter and cheese. Southerners reported eating less fruit and fewer dairy products but more dried beans and peas, quick breads, meat, fish, poultry, and eggs than the rest of the nation.[53] Those in the North Central region or Northeast were more likely to eat desserts; snack food was more prevalent in the North Central region.[54] People in the West and the Northeast spent more on fruits and vegetables, cereals, and bakery and dairy products as well as on food away from home. In the Northeast more was spent on poultry, meat, fish, and eggs. In the West, more was spent on prepared foods.[55] This is consistent with the relatively urban, dense populations and high incomes in the Northeast and California and the concomitant demand for convenience.

HOUSEHOLD COMPOSITION

Household composition is the foundation of demographic trends. Its most important components are household size, age distribution, and marital status. The general trend in American households has been towards smaller, older households with fewer married couples and fewer children. Fewer children are a result of declining fertility rates, rates that vary considerably by ethnic group.

Fertility

As early as the 1920s, the fertility rate began to drop among European and American women. By the 1960s, the idea of zero population growth became a popular cause among those concerned with preserving an ecological balance and preventing the Malthusian (mass starvation) hypothesis from coming true. Among the Northern European countries and the white population of the United States, zero population growth has been a reality since at least 1972.[56] That is, the total fertility rate in these populations has been less than 2.1 children per adult woman during her lifetime. The French and other European nations have tried various ways to curtail the fall in their birthrates in order to stimulate economic growth.[57] In the United States, fertility has been falling in all age groups since the end of the baby boom in 1964. Figure 3.3 shows the average fertility patterns of American women since 1940 and projected to 2010. The only recent upward trend has been in the late 1980s among women ages 30–40. This has been called a baby "echo" and is expected to level off.

Since the Hispanic population is growing faster than the black population and both are growing faster than the white population, by the year 2005, the black and Hispanic populations will be roughly equal and together make up more than one-fourth of the total population. Fertility rates among blacks, at 83.8 births per 1,000 women age 15-44 in 1987, were 35% higher than for whites.[58] Hispanic fertility rates were 50% higher than for white Americans and 9% higher than for black Americans. Fertility among foreign-born women was 99 per 1,000 women in 1986, compared with 68 per 1,000 for American-born women,

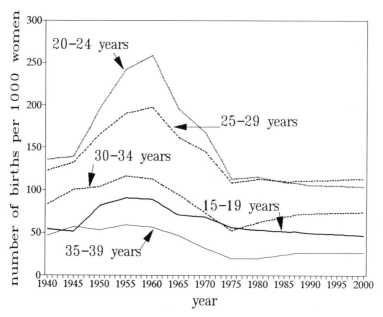

Figure 3.3. Fertility rates by age group of mother from 1940 to 2000. (Data from U.S. Department of Commerce, Bureau of the Census, 1988a, 1989b, 1990a.)

and 54 per 1,000 for European women.[59] Even so, in 1987 the absolute number of white births in the United States (2,992,000) was more than seven times the number of Hispanic births, 4.6 times the number of black births, and 23 times the number of births among other ethnic groups.[60]

Households and Families

The average number of people per *household* was down to 2.6 by 1988 due to a growing number of singles and a decline in fertility. The average number of people per *family* was down to 3.2 because there were fewer children and an increase in single-parent families. Families and households both averaged 4.8 persons in 1900 and 3.8 persons in 1940. After that, their average sizes diverged. All families are households but not all households are families. By definition, families are those households where members living together are related by blood, marriage, or adoption. Households can be thought of as "living units," 72% of which are families; the rest are nonfamilies made up of unrelated individuals who share a dwelling or live alone. Figure 3.4 outlines the composition of families.

Married couples declined as a percentage of families from 87% in 1970 to 80% by 1987. Families of married couples with children declined from 50 to 38%; of these families, one-fourth had at least one stepchild present.[61] The decreased percentage of married couple households is partly due to later marriages. The median age of marriage was at a record high of 23.6 years for women in 1987 and at a near record high of 25.9 years for men.[62] The percentage of persons aged 25–29 who had never been married doubled since 1970, from 19 to 42% of men, and from 11 to 19% of women.[63] This has created a growing market for goods and services for young single adults.

Single-parent families accounted for almost one-half of the increase in the number of families during the 1980s. Four out of five single-parent families were headed by women who were divorced or widowed or who had children outside of marriage. During the past 20 years, two-thirds of families headed by females had children present, making up about 10% of all families. Among Hispanics, 19% of families were headed by women.[64] In the first half of the 1980s, the birthrate among unmarried women rose 12% (mostly among whites), while it dropped 3% among married women. In 1987, 30% of all infants were born to unmarried women, 16% of white infants and 62% of black infants.[65] This phenomenon increased the number of single-parent households and the number of poor households in the economy headed by women.

The number of families headed by men without spouses also grew rapidly in the eighties, making up 3% of all families in 1987.[66] Families

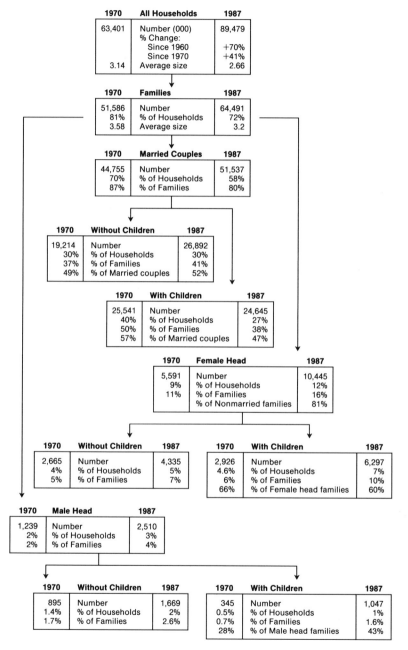

Figure 3.4. Change in composition of family households between 1970 and 1987. (Data from U.S. Department of Commerce, Bureau of the Census, 1985a, 1985b, 1987c, 1987d; Waldrop, 1989a.)

headed by unmarried men were almost twice as likely to have children present in 1987 than in 1970. Two-thirds of families headed by unmarried men and 40% of families headed by unmarried women had no children under age 18 present. Together, they made up 7% of all households.

Increases in families headed by unmarried men and women can also be attributed to divorce. Divorce rates increased 173% between 1970 and 1980, peaking in 1981. They leveled off, remaining at about 5 per 1,000 in the population for the rest of the 1980s. Almost half of all marriages were likely to end in divorce, and about 2% of all married couples divorced in any given year.[67] Divorce creates a larger number of small households that has been sustained by a decline in the rate of remarriage (123 per 1,000 divorced women in 1970, compared with 82 per 1,000 in 1985).[68] The proportion of divorced women who ultimately remarry is expected to be about 70% in the future.[69] This means that the number of nontraditional families will continue to be large.

Children

There were seven million fewer children in the population in 1985 than in 1970, the result of a large decline in the birth rate. Figure 3.5 shows that the proportion of households with children under age 18

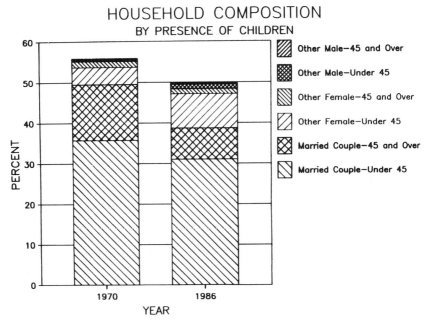

Figure 3.5. Composition of households with children present. (Data from U.S. Department of Commerce, Bureau of the Census, 1987d.)

declined between 1970 and 1986, especially for married couples over age 45. This decline was matched, however, by an almost equal increase in the percentage of households with children that were headed by women.

There are still a few large families. In 1987, among families with children present, 20% had three or more children, 37% had two children, and 43% had only one child.[70] Families with three or more children had a lower median income but spent a higher proportion (20%) on food. Accounting for 10% of all expenditures on food, they are important for the continued marketing of large-volume packages and basic ingredients. They were much more likely than other families to report baking as a leisure activity. These families accounted for 58% of the children living in poverty, although 20% of children in large families lived in homes with annual incomes in excess of $50,000 per year.[71]

Nonfamily Households

During the 1980s, the number of households grew faster than the population (14% vs. 8.5%)[72]. Nonfamily households and families headed by unmarried men or women, of which 81% were headed by single mothers, were the fastest growing household types. Figure 3.6 outlines the composition of nonfamily households. Among nonfamily households with two or more members, 62% were headed by men, 20% had some children present, one-fourth had members who were divorced, 60% had members who had never been married, and the median age was 32. This includes unmarried couples as well as other adults who share a housing unit through various rental arrangements.

Unmarried couples made up about 4% of all couples (married and unmarried)—a fairly stable proportion throughout the second half of this century. About 20% of the unmarried couples were under the age of 25, and over 80% were under the age of 45.[73] Forty percent of unmarried couple households had children present, compared with 48% of married couples.[74] In terms of their food consumption patterns, unmarried couples behave very much like married couple households.

Nonfamily households accounted for 43% of new households in the eighties. This trend can be seen in Figure 3.7. The growth in single-person households increased the top part of the bar, and the increase in single-parent families pushed down the bottom section representing married couples, who accounted for only 21% of new households during the 1980s. This helps to illustrate that households are becoming smaller and more diversified in their needs and preferences. A market geared to married couple families with children, now only about one quarter of all households, will be missing a very large proportion of consumers. Another one quarter of all households contained only one person, and 53% of households had no children. The households resembling the traditional stereotype—married couple with two or more children under age 18, wife not in the labor force—dropped from 23% of all households in 1955 to 7% by 1987.[75]

Living Alone

A growing number of single-person households is partially a sign of affluence. Individuals can afford to establish and maintain separate

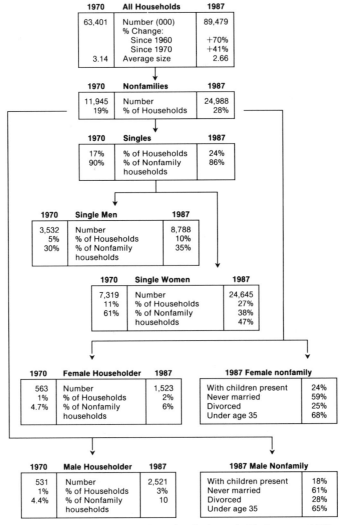

Figure 3.6. Change in composition of nonfamily households between 1970 and 1987. (Data from U.S. Department of Commerce, Bureau of the Census, 1985a, 1985b, 1987c, 1987d; Waldrop, 1989a.)

housing units. Households of only one person increased from 10% in 1940 to 24% by 1987.[76] In 1988, 6.88 million men and 6.33 million women under the age of 65 were single and living in their own households.

Young singles, under the age of 34, made up about one-fourth of all single-person households in 1985, up from to 13% in 1970. In both years, one-third of single-person households were women over age 65, but the proportion composed of elderly single men declined from 11 to 8%. The median age of women living alone was 65; for men it was only 41.[77] Half of the women who lived alone were widowed, and one-fourth were over the age of 75. With the number of elderly people expected to double in the next 50 years, the importance of households of single, elderly people (80% women) will increase dramatically.[78]

Single-person households are diversified by both age and gender. This implies that no one marketing strategy will successfully reach all of them. Single women spent a larger proportion of their budgets on food at home and only half as much as single men on restaurant food ($500 per year vs. $1,000 in 1987).[79] This reflects, in part, the fact that single women's median income was only 64% as high as men's and that more women know how to cook.

In spite of a long-term trend towards Americans living alone, the trend for young people to do so actually turned downward during the eighties.

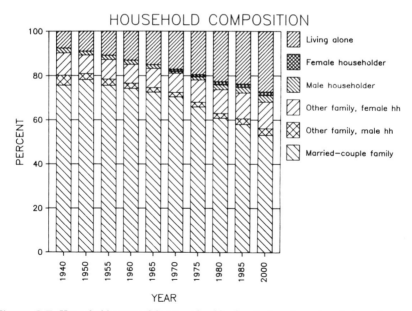

Figure 3.7. Household composition trends. (Nonfamily female and male householders were assumed to be the same percent in 2000 as in 1985.) (Data from U.S. Department of Commerce, Bureau of the Census, 1986a, 1987d.)

For example, among men between the ages of 18 and 25, 54% lived with one or more parents in 1970, whereas 60% did so in 1985. Women were less likely to stay at home with their parents, but the numbers of those who did rose from 41% in 1970 to 48% in 1985.[80] Adult children who lived in their parents' homes were more likely to have incomes under $10,000, indicating that economic necessity drives some to this choice. On the other end of the income scale, one-third of men and women in their twenties who lived "at home," lived in homes where the family income was over $50,000 per year.[81] They may prefer to continue living in a style to which they have become accustomed rather than establish a household of their own at a much lower level of consumption. It takes young people who have grown up in affluent families longer to find employment that will support their consumption habits. For many college students, their parents' home remains their official residence even though they live away from home most of the year.

Smaller Households

More than half of all U.S. households had only one or two members in 1990. Smaller household size tends to increase per capita food expenditure, since economies of scale cannot be realized in food purchasing and preparation. Economies of scale in household food consumption are illustrated by the cost of the USDA food plans discussed in Chapter 2. In 1989, a moderate-cost food plan for food eaten at home was estimated to cost $509.60 per month for a family of four with one teenager. The increased cost for an additional fifth or sixth person was 5% less than the cost of adding the fourth person. Marginal food costs for more than six persons actually declined by 10% for each additional person.[82]

The Continuing Consumer Expenditure Survey data from 1985 show that actual food expenditures increased by 66% between one and two person households, by 27% for the third person, by 14% for the fourth person, and by 7.5% for the fifth person. Households with six persons or more actually spent 2% less for food than those with five.[83] In these data, the annual *per capita* food expenditures for household units of various sizes were $1,935 for one person, $1,603 for two, $1,355 for three, $1,160 for four, $999 for five and $816 for six persons or more. An earlier study found that the average per capita value of food consumcd fcll by $7.40 per month for each extra person in a household (converted to 1990 dollars).[84] The greatest economies of household size have been in the consumption of fruits and vegetables, followed by bakery products, cheeses, soups, and sauces.[85]

Small households increase the demand for food away from home, take-out-to-eat food, conveniently prepared food, and food that can be purchased in small portions. Single persons spend up to 50% of their food budget on food away from home.[86] For single men, rising income was found to increase food expenditures more than for single women.[87] Singles were found to consume relatively large amounts of poultry, fruit and vegetables (not potatoes), and dairy products. They consumed less pork, beef, eggs, processed vegetables, sugar, and sweets than those in larger households.[88]

Signals for food markets are somewhat mixed. Smaller households spend more per capita on food, but on average they have lower incomes. The overall impact of a larger number of small households has been shown to increase aggregate expenditures on food away from home, dairy products, poultry, and processed and fresh fruits. It decreased total expenditures on beef, milk, and processed vegetables between 1972 and 1981.[89] As household size continues to decline, these food expenditure trends can be expected to continue.

The growing number of households headed by unmarried men is a phenomenon that is largely unexplored in terms of food marketing. Most of these men shop and cook for themselves. They are less likely than women to use shopping lists or coupons.[90] They tend to be conservative about trying new products, and their cooking skills are often minimal.[91] They eat away from home more often than other people. They have higher incomes than female household heads and can afford to purchase high-quality food with built-in services.

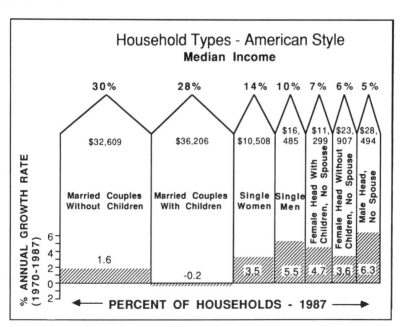

Figure 3.8. Percentage of household types, their annual growth rate, and median income in 1987. (Data from U.S. Department of Commerce, Bureau of the Census, 1988a, 1989a.)

Figure 3.8 summarizes the proportion of households made up of various combinations of men, women, and children in 1987, and how rapidly each type of household grew between 1970 and 1987. It is easy to see that households headed by unmarried men grew the most rapidly (5.5% per year for singles and 6.3% for others) and that the number of married couples with children declined. The median income for each household type clearly shows that male household heads have higher incomes.

Group Quarters

Not counted among the households in Figures 3.4–3.7 are those who live in group quarters. In 1980, about 2.5% of the population, or 5.7 million people, lived in group quarters such as college dormitories (1.1%) or institutions (0.9%), including homes for the aged or mentally ill and prisons. Places where more than 40 persons per 1,000 lived in group quarters were Hawaii (largely military), Washington D.C., and North Dakota and Vermont (mostly students). The average U.S. group-quarters population was 25 people per 1,000.[92]

The type of group quarters can make a difference for food marketing. A large number of students in college dormitories with dining halls and no cooking facilities may create a high demand for inexpensive restaurants and take-out food. If large numbers eat in institutions, wholesale food business will increase. Local market niches can be determined to a large extent by the type of group quarters present. The trend is towards fewer institutional homes for the elderly and the ill and more for college students and prisoners.

AN AGING POPULATION

The baby boom lasted from 1946 to 1964, with the birthrate peaking in 1957 at 25.3 births per 1,000 population.[93] Baby boomers were ages 26 through 44 in 1990; they will swell the ranks of older middle-aged households (ages 46 through 63) until 2010, when they will begin to swell the ranks of the retired population. The nation's median age was 30 in 1980, 32 in 1990, and will be over 40 by 2030.[94]

The aging of the population is illustrated in Figure 3.9. It shows that, for all races in the United States, the ratio of old to young will increase dramatically by 2030. Unless there is an unpredictable change in fertility, the percentage of young people will decrease and the distribution of ages will look much more like the shaded column than a pyramid. The top-heavy shaded column for whites and the bottom-heavy shaded columns for nonwhites illustrate that the ethnic minority populations will remain younger than whites. This is largely due to differential fertility rates.

By far the most common household type in every age group (except those over age 74) is a married couple household. Figure 3.10 shows the percentage of households in each age group in 1988 that were married couples, married couples with children, or single-parent families with

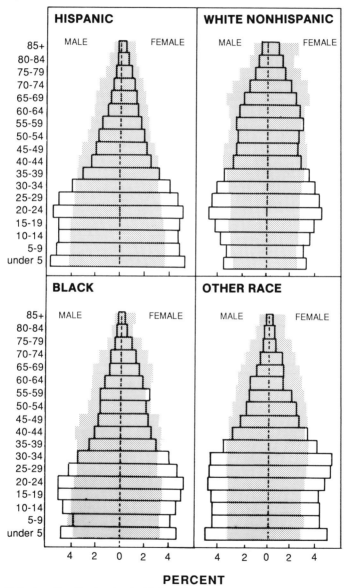

PERCENT

Figure 3.9. Age distribution in the United States by gender and race: percent of men and women in each age group. The shaded areas show projected percentages for 2030. (Reprinted from the U.S. Department of Commerce, Bureau of the Census, 1984c; Spencer, 1986.)

children. Figure 3.11 shows households in each age group headed by single men or women. One can readily see that the married couple bar is the tallest in each age group, except for those over age 74, where female single-person households dominate. More than half of single women heading households were over age 64 (6.55 million); of these more than half were over age 74. Only 22% of single men heading households were over age 64. In the future, there should be more married couple households among those over age 64 as the life expectancy of men increases.

People aged 15-24 headed 6% of all households in 1987, and those from 25 to 34 headed 23%. The number of people in these age groups will decline by the end of the century. Twenty-one percent of household heads were 35-44 years old, and 15% were from 45 to 54. By the year 2000, people in these age groups will increase dramatically. Householders aged 55-64 made up 14% of the total, and those aged 65-74, 13%. Their numbers will also increase by 2000, but more dramatically by 2010. Households headed by a person over age 74 made up only 9% of the total but will grow 26% by 2000 and more thereafter.[95]

Mortality has declined dramatically for the elderly, with life expectancies increasing one and one-half times during the 20th century. This is illustrated in detail in Chapter 8. The greatest increases

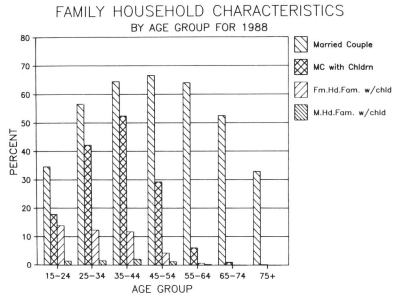

Figure 3.10. Percent of family types in each age group in 1988. (Data from Waldrop, 1989a.)

throughout the century have been in the doubling of life expectancies of nonwhites. Increased life expectancies over the century have created a growing population of elderly people. For example, less than 12% survived to age 80 in 1900, whereas 50% are expected to do so by 2000.[96]

Aging and Food Consumption

Age affects food consumption because caloric and nutritional needs change as people age. Preferences and choices also change with income changes and experience. Children consume more milk products, eggs, soups, snack foods, sugar-based beverages, and desserts but fewer fruits, vegetables, table spreads, and meat than older people.[97] With fewer children in the population, the demand for these foods should adjust accordingly. Those aged 35–44 in 1990 spent about 2.5% less per capita on food than the average consumer.[98] Total food expenditures were up for this age group only because there were so many of them. As they move into the elderly group, they will affect the food demand of the elderly after 2010. Food needs for elderly, single-person households are different from the food needs and preferences of younger singles who eat more, eat out more often, and are more inclined to follow food fads. Households headed by persons aged 55–64 spent about 10% more on food than the average household, while those over age 65 spent about 12% less. On a per capita basis though, elderly households

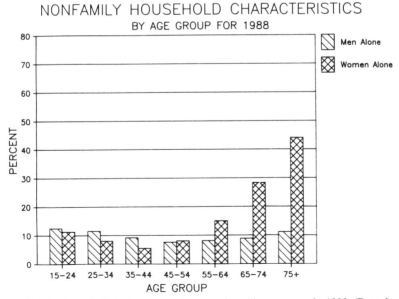

Figure 3.11. Percent of single men and women in each age group in 1988. (Data from Waldrop 1989a.)

under age 75 spend 14% more, mostly due to the small household size that requires larger food outlays per person.[99]

The aging of the population is considered one of the most important trends in the socioeconomic environment of the United States. Some argue that it is the single most important story on the demographic scene.[100] This trend can be identified with considerable certainty and it foretells changes in preferences and food demand. Thus, Chapter 8 is devoted to an extended discussion about the impacts of a growing elderly population on future food consumption.

EDUCATION

The major trends in education are an increasing number of people over age 25 with a high school and college education and a persistent disparity in educational achievement between whites and nonwhites. Overall, completion of at least four years of high school increased from 24% of the population in 1940 to 76% in 1986. Among whites and Asians, that percentage was about 77%; among blacks, 51%; and among Hispanics, 44%. One-fifth of adults had completed college in 1988, compared with 5% in 1940. The rate for whites was 21%, compared with 33% for Asians, 11% for blacks, and 10% for Hispanics. Twenty-three percent of men and 17% of women held college degrees, but among younger people ages 25–29, differences narrowed to 23% for men and 21% for women.[101]

Among teenagers aged 16–17 in 1980, the highest levels of school enrollment were among Americans of Japanese and Chinese descent (96%), the lowest was among Hispanics (80%), with 89% for all whites. Among those 20–24 years old, Chinese Americans had the highest proportion enrolled in school (60%); all whites had 24%, blacks had 21%, and Hispanics had 18%.[102] The increase in the number and percent of people with higher education foretells higher incomes for a larger proportion of the population. It also helps to explain the disparity in income between the educated and others. Table 3.2 shows the direct relationship between education and earnings in 1984. Four-year college graduates earned an average of 76% more than high school graduates at that time. In 1987, their average earnings were 86% greater than the average earnings of someone with only a high school degree.[103]

Since 1980, more young women have been enrolling in college than men. The percentage of women aged 18–21 enrolled in college increased from 32% in 1975 to 42% in 1988, while it increased from 35 to 38% for men age 18–21.[104] As a group, ethnic minority men appear to be leaving the educational process. For black men aged 18–21, 55% had a high school degree in 1975; in 1988 it was 65%. The number of black men aged 18–21 enrolled in college, however, fell from 24% in 1975 to 21% in 1988. The number of black males enrolled in college declined from a high of 590,000 in 1984 to 494,000 in 1988.[105] For Hispanic males aged 18–21, the numbers enrolled in college increased between 1975 and 1988, but the proportion enrolled fell from 25 to 20%. The numbers of white males enrolled in college declined during that time, but these numbers represented an increase from 37 to 40% of white males aged 18–21.

A continuing disparity in education and concomitant incomes means that a persistent group of food consumers will be poor. They will be mostly nonwhite households or single mothers and, at the extreme, the homeless. These consumers are very sensitive to price and will be purchasing lower cost food and fewer services. The regions of the country where education levels were the lowest in 1985 were the South (69% high school graduates and 18% college graduates) and nonmetropolitan areas in general (69% with high school diplomas). The West, where 80% were high school graduates and 24% college graduates, and metropolitan areas, where 78% were high school graduates, will be areas with higher average incomes and a demand for food that meets upscale preferences for more convenience, more variety, and more food prepared away from home.[106]

A higher number of college educated women implies that more will be in the labor force, earning more money, having fewer children, and making food choices that reflect a need for convenience and a desire for healthy diets. Education has been found to be the most important determinant of knowledge about nutrition.[107] College graduates were 67% more likely to report dieting to lose weight.[108] They will be a large part of the market for low-calorie foods. Those with more education tend to be more adventuresome in their food selections and will adopt new

Table 3.2. Income and Education[a] (All U.S. Persons over Age 18, 1984)

Persons by Education	Mean Monthly Income ($)	Percent of Persons
Doctorate	3,265	0.5
Professional	3,871	1.0
Master's	2,288	3.4
Bachelor's	1,841	10.6
Associate	1,346	3.6
Vocational	1,219	1.8
Some college, no degree	1,169	17.8
High school graduate only	1,045	35.5
Not high school graduate	693	26.0
All persons	1,155	100.0

[a]Source: U.S. Department of Commerce, Bureau of the Census, 1987b, p. 7–8.

food varieties more quickly. They eat out more often. Educated people are also better informed about food safety issues and will demand higher quality food and food service. Price will be less of a deciding factor for them than food quality and diet compatibility.

INCOME TRENDS

There is a popular perception that average household incomes in the United States are declining and that the rich are getting richer and the

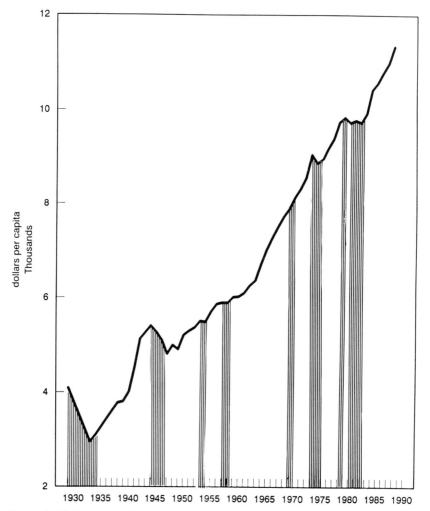

Figure 3.12. Per capita disposable income from 1929 to 1988 (in constant 1982 dollars). (Data from Council of Economic Advisors, 1987.)

poor are getting poorer—that the large middle-class, mass market is diminishing, and that an underclass of permanently unemployable persons has developed. Considerable evidence supports this perception. Aggregate income statistics such as per capita personal disposal income,

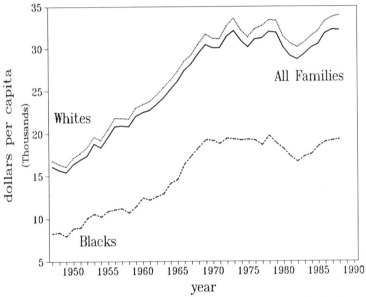

Figure 3.13. Median family income from 1947 to 1988 (in constant 1988 dollars). (Data from U.S. Department of Commerce, Bureau of the Census, 1988a, 1989a, 1990a.)

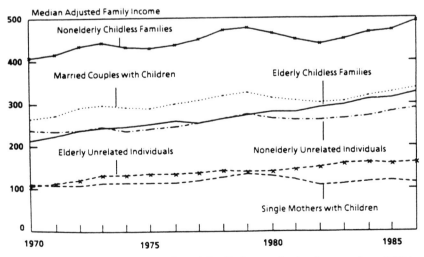

Figure 3.14. Trends in median adjusted family income by family type, from 1970 to 1986. (Reprinted from Congressional Budget Office, 1988a.)

median family income, and individual wage earnings reveal much the same picture—incomes rising until about 1973 and stagnating thereafter. This reversal in income growth has been called "the major economic story of the postwar period."[109]

Per capita personal disposable (after tax) income (PDI) in the United States was $14,107 in 1988. Its growth slowed less in recent years than median family income because it is calculated by dividing total income from all sources evenly across all persons. In recent years, PDI increased despite low productivity because there have been more workers (earners) and fewer children (nonearners) among which to divide total income.[110] As long as the economy grows, that is, gross national product grows faster than inflation, PDI tends to increase. Figure 3.12 shows the trend in real PDI (in 1982 dollars). One can clearly see that its growth slows during periods of recession, represented by the shaded areas. Although widely used as a measure of economic well-being, like most aggregate measures, PDI hides as much as it reveals. To learn about the spending power of households and their relative well-being, one has to look at how income is distributed among households with different characteristics.

Real (adjusted for inflation) median family incomes increased steadily

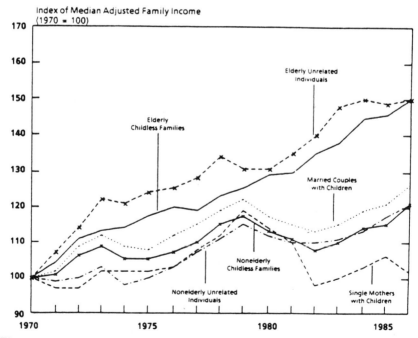

Figure 3.15. Trends in median adjusted family income relative to 1970, for selected family types, from 1970 to 1986. (Reprinted from Congressional Budget Office, 1988a.)

in the post-World War II period, doubling between 1947 and 1973. In the 1973-1975 recession, this income fell by $1,700 in real terms. It more than recovered by 1979, only to fall again between 1980 and 1982. In 1984, it was $46 less (adjusted for inflation) than it was in 1975. By 1989, it was $28,910, which was above the level in 1979, a prior peak year.[111] Figure 3.13 illustrates the trends in median income for all families and for whites and blacks. The trend for Hispanics was similar to that for blacks, only the level was about $2,000 higher. It is easy to see that the rate of increase began to level out in the early 1970s. Real median income for unrelated individuals rose less rapidly over the long run but continued to rise while family incomes fell.[112]

Real median income does not account for the relative status of different types of households. Adjusted family income (median income as a percentage of the poverty level) as plotted in Figure 3.14 shows that since 1970, nonelderly childless families had incomes more than four times as great as single mothers, whose adjusted family incomes have stayed around the poverty level since 1970.[113] Indexing adjusted family incomes so that 1970 equals 100, and plotting income trends for various family types, shows that by 1986, cash incomes rose to 163% of the poverty level for the elderly, while they stayed around the poverty level for single mothers. The relative well-being of families clearly depends on family structure and age, as shown in Figure 3.15.

Income Distribution

How income is distributed among households is measured by plotting the percent of aggregate household income received against the percent of households. This produces a "Lorenz curve." The size of the area between the Lorenz curve and the "line of equality," that is, the 45 degree line on which the percent of income received and the percent of households is equal, provides a measure of how evenly income is distributed. This is illustrated in Figure 3.16 for the United States in 1984 by the darkened area. Two times the size of that area is called the Gini coefficient. The closer the line of equality is to the Lorenz curve, the smaller the darkened area, the smaller the Gini coefficient, and the more equally distributed is income. Figure 3.16 shows that in the United States, the 20% of households with the lowest incomes received about 5% of all household income. If income were evenly distributed, the lowest and highest 20% of households would each receive 20% of aggregate income, the Lorenz curve would lie on top of the straight line of equality, and the Gini coefficient would be zero.

The Gini coefficient has changed very little since the 1940s, although it fell slightly between 1947 and 1969 and then rose again. This illustrates, in a modest way, how incomes tend to become more evenly distributed when general incomes are rising. The Gini coefficient rose between 1979 and 1984, indicating that incomes were becoming less equally distributed. Table 3.3 shows that the poorest 20% of households received 5.6% of all household income in 1969, a year in which the richest 20% received 40.6%. By 1989, the richest 20% of households received 46.8% of aggregate household income.[114]

Using money income to measure consumer well-being and income distribution, though common, has its faults. It includes government transfer payments in cash but not in kind. Those who receive food stamps, health care, housing, tax breaks, or production subsidies have consumption power above that of their cash income. Those with large families have less spending power per person for any given level of cash income. Money income does not account for accumulated wealth, which, if added to money income, produces even larger Gini coefficients. For example, in 1984 the top 20% of households, by money income standards, held 75% of the assets owned by households; the top 2% held 26% of the assets.[115]

Table 3.4 summarizes the distribution of income among households of various types in 1987. Despite many changes in the relative sizes of age groups and their relative incomes, it shows that middle-aged

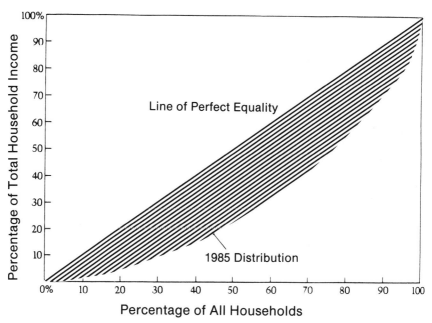

Figure 3.16. Lorenz curve of income distribution for the United States in 1985. (Data from U.S. Department of Commerce, Bureau of the Census, 1988a.)

householders (ages 35–54) still had the highest median incomes and the greatest proportion who made more than $50,000 per year. The income profile for those under age 24 and those over age 64 looks very similar. The big difference is in their ownership of assets and net worth (assets minus debts). American households had a median net worth of $44,000 in 1986 and an average of $145,000.[116] Median net worth rises steadily until age 65, when it is drawn down slightly. Although only 12% of householders under the age of 35 had a net worth of more than $50,000, 56% over age 65 had a net worth of $50,000 or more.[117]

The distribution of earnings, as opposed to income, has been much less evenly distributed historically and is growing even more uneven. The Gini coefficient for earnings across all families rose from 0.415 in 1949 to 0.460 in 1984.[118] This increase is largely due to an increase in the number of families with no earners at all, up from 5.4% in 1949 to 15.1% in 1984. The number of "no earner" families increases as retirement age declines and more families of all ages are headed by women.

Unearned income (government transfers, pensions, interest, and dividends) has replaced part of earnings as a source of spending power for many American households. The proportion of total personal income from wages and salaries fell from 66 to 59% between 1970 and 1986, while transfer payments rose from 10 to 15%, and interest and dividends

Table 3.3. Distribution of Family Money Income[a] (United States, 1947–1984)

| | | | | | | Top Income in Each Quintile, 1984[b] | |
Category	1947 (%)	1959 (%)	1969 (%)	1979 (%)	1984 (%)	Families ($)	Unrelated Individuals ($)
Percentage of all family income going to							
First quintile (poorest)	5.0	4.9	5.6	5.2	4.7	14,849	5,826
Second quintile	11.9	12.3	12.4	11.6	11.0	25,812	10,107
Third quintile	17.0	17.9	17.7	17.5	17.0	37,453	16,659
Fourth quintile	23.1	23.8	23.7	24.1	24.4	53,862	26,236
Fifth quintile (richest)	43.0	41.1	40.6	41.7	42.9	87,070[c]	46,334[c]
Richest 5%[d]	17.5	15.9	15.6	15.8	16.0	...	...
Gini coefficient							
Of family income inequality		0.376	0.361	0.349	0.365	0.385	
Of unrelated individuals income inequality		0.552	0.522	0.481	0.435	0.448	

[a] Source: Levy, 1987, pp. 14–16, 20–21.
[b] In 1989 dollars.
[c] Beginning of top 5%.
[d] Included in top quintile.

rose from 11% to 16%.[119]

On balance, aggregate income figures do not reveal many dramatic changes regarding income distribution. They even seem to defy common observations and attitudes about the demise of the middle class. However, shifts in income and earnings among different household types—by age, size, gender, and ethnic group—lend credence to popular perceptions. For example, Table 3.5 shows that the proportion of households in the second and third quintiles that were elderly increased considerably between 1949 and 1984, while their representation among the poor in the first quintile declined. Husband-wife families ages 35–64 grew as a proportion of the upper two quintiles at the expense of younger families. Families headed by females under age 64 made up more than twice the proportion of poor families in 1984 than they did in 1949. Related to these movements among household types is labor force participation. Notice that in the lowest quintile, 44% of families had no earners in 1984. No-earner families have more than doubled since

Table 3.4. Median Household Income and Net Worth by Age, Race, and Household Size[a] (United States, 1987)

Household Category	Median Income ($)	Percent of Group with Median Income		Percent Below Poverty	Median Net Worth ($)
		Below $10,000	Above $50,000		
Age					
of householder					
15–24	16,204	30.4	4.5	15.9	...
25–34	26,923	13.5	13.9	10.7[b]	5,764[c]
35–44	34,929	10.4	26.4		35,581
45–54	37,250	10.5	33.1	9.1[d]	56,791
55–64	27,538	17.4	22.0		73,664
>64	14,334	34.4	6.4	12.2	60,266
All	25,986	18.4	18.5	13.5	32,667
Race					
of householder					
White	27,427	16.1	19.7	10.5	39,135
Black	15,475	35.6	7.2	33.1	3,397
Hispanic	19,305	25.9	7.9	28.2	4,913
Persons					
per household					
1	12,544	40.8	3.7	...	
2	26,481	13.2	17.4	8.7	
3	32,348	10.9	24.6	10.5	
4	36,805	8.0	30.2	10.3	
5	35,825	9.5	28.6	14.8	
6	33,871	12.5	26.6	22.0	
>6	30,800	13.4	26.4	29.5	

[a] Source: U.S. Department of Commerce, Bureau of the Census, 1988a.
[b] Ages 25–44.
[c] Ages 15–34.
[d] Ages 45–64.

1949 in all quintiles, even as wives were entering the labor force in unprecedented numbers.

A Declining Middle Class

A picture of offsetting income trends has developed. More families are entering the low- and high-income brackets, that is, below $10,000 and above $50,000 per year.[120] Interpretation of this change is twofold. One view is optimistic. Since a smaller share of households has middle level income, and the percent with $20,000 or less has been a constant 31%, more families must be moving up into higher income brackets, leaving fewer in the middle income ranges. This view suggests that families are growing better off.

The pessimistic view stems from a decline in spending power of middle level incomes since 1973. The rate of increase in real income for people in the middle rose very slowly compared with their expectations. They could not increase their levels of consumption as rapidly as their parents had in the past. Young people and those with low and middle incomes had to spend a larger portion of their income on necessities like food, shelter, and energy. During the 1970s, the price of necessities rose 15% faster than the overall Consumer Price Index, resulting in a greater decline in real incomes among middle and low income households.[121] Adjustments in their spending patterns show that they had to increase expenditures for necessities by about $1,000

Table 3.5. Income Distribution (Percent) by Type of Family and Number of Workers, 1949 and 1984[a]

Family Type	First Quintile (poorest)		Second Quintile		Third Quintile		Fourth Quintile		Fifth Quintile (richest)	
	1949	1984	1949	1984	1949	1984	1949	1984	1949	1984
Head aged 65 or over (male or female)	25	24	11	23	7	11	6	7	8	7
Husband-wife family aged 35–64	42	25	48	36	61	47	58	60	71	74
Husband-wife family aged 34 or under	18	16	33	25	28	32	32	30	17	15
Female head aged 64 or under	15	35	8	16	4	10	4	3	4	4
Total	100	100	100	100	100	100	100	100	100	100
Proportion of all families in quintile with working wife	11	15	15	30	16	49	26	57	26	67
Proportion of all families with no working member	25	44	8	16	2	8	1	4	1	3

[a] Source: Levy, 1987, pp. 200–201.

per year (in 1984 dollars) between 1973 and 1981. Consumer expenditures that decreased in order to accommodate these necessities were for furniture, clothes, personal care, and charitable contributions. A large number of young households buoyed the restaurant business and gave the impression that money for food away from home was plentiful, but average annual household expenditures on food away from home went up only $47 (in constant 1984 dollars) between 1973 and 1981.[122]

Besides a fall in real income growth, the loss of many middle income (blue-collar) and agricultural jobs, the type held by many men with little education, led to thousands of displaced workers whose family incomes declined. There was also a recent rash of displaced white-collar workers from middle management positions. In 1986, there were more than 5.1 million displaced workers; half came from manufacturing industries that closed their plants. Layoffs in the wholesale-retail trades and financial services (mostly white-collar jobs) accounted for another 27% of the displaced workers, only two-thirds of whom were reemployed. The latter group may find it easier to relocate or retrain, but the opportunities at the top are shrinking relative to the supply of qualified labor. Fifteen percent of displaced workers dropped out of the labor market altogether.[123]

The despair felt by displaced workers and the fear that threatened layoffs instill in all workers come as much from a decline in opportunity for advancement as from a decline in relative income. The change in income growth relative to expectations is dramatically illustrated in Figure 3.17, which shows the average gain in men's income between the ages of 40 and 50 for roughly the past three decades. Income growth over a lifetime has slowed considerably for men.

The composition of families with the lowest 20% of income has also changed dramatically. This has widespread implications for government policy, national productivity, and consumer demand of all sorts including the demand for food. Families with incomes below $20,000 headed by women increased from 23 to 31% between 1973 and 1986.[124] The result is that more than one-third of all the nation's children live in homes where income is under $20,000. Twenty-one percent of children live in families with incomes over $50,000. Levy argues that the popular picture of a declining middle class is not especially applicable for all families taken together, but it is appropriate for families with children.[125] This implies that there will be a continued and perhaps increasing need for investment in education and child nutrition programs.

Dual-Earner Households

The separate distribution of earnings of men and women reinforces the impression that, at least for men, middle level incomes are declining.

The percentage of men earning under $20,000 or over $50,000 per year increased between 1973 and 1986. The share of women earning low incomes declined, but more than two-thirds of women continued to earn less than $20,000 per year. The relative change in women's and men's earnings reflects major changes in the labor force and facilitates major changes in family structure and in how family members make purchase decisions. Sociologists and psychologists say that it changes the balance of power in household decisions. This earnings shift also changes the relative value of family members' time and how time is allocated to household tasks such as food shopping and cooking.

The net impact of more wives entering the labor force has been to tilt the income distribution towards the rich. In 1979, in the top-income quintile, a larger share of wives worked (72.2%) than in the middle quintiles (67.4%) or the low-income quintile (45.8%). In 1988, the percentage of wives in the labor force had increased the most in top-income quintiles (9.2%) and the least in the low-income quintile (2.7%).[126] As more and more wives from high-income households entered the

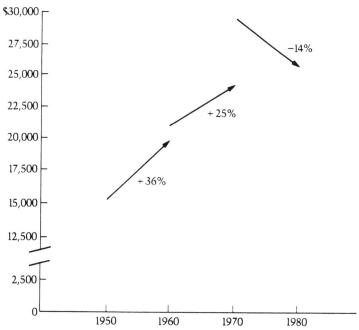

Figure 3.17. Average income gain for men passing from age 40 to age 50 in the United States since 1950 (in 1984 dollars). (Reprinted, by permission of the Russell Sage Foundation, from *Dollars and Dreams: The Changing American Income Distribution*, by Frank Levy. ©1987, The Russell Sage Foundation.)

labor force, they pushed up the income of those households even further.

Meanwhile, wives from poor households prevented incomes in the lowest quintile from slipping further behind than they otherwise would have. In 1984 earnings of wives whose husbands had low incomes (less than $15,000) raised their family incomes relatively more (by 40%) than the earnings of wives whose husbands earned more than $35,000 (by 15%).[127] In 1989, wives who worked full-time year-round earned 68% as much on average as men working full-time.[128] In 1983, one-fifth of working wives earned more than their husbands. Of those who did, 51% had no children under age 18, 24% had four or more years of college, and 31% had executive or professional jobs. Seventy-two percent worked full-time year-round compared with 43% of all employed wives.[129]

Dual-earner families at all levels of income have improved their spending power relative to single-earner families. For example, the real median family income in 1969 (in 1985 dollars) for married couples with both spouses employed was $25,062 and $20,051 where only the husband worked. By 1987, that income increased 58% to $39,516 (constant 1985 dollars) if the wife was employed, and by 47% to $29,393 if she was not. Between 1981 and 1987, wives' earnings grew 23% compared with 12% for husbands'. The proportion of wives working full-time increased from 44 to 50%. By 1987, the annual income of a family with two full-time working spouses was $49,030, which was 59% higher than the income of $31,010 where only the husband worked.[130]

Table 3.6 compares the number of men and women workers, their incomes by age and education in 1986, and the changes since 1973. Since this includes all men and women who worked at all in those years, the ratio of women's to men's earnings, even for young people with four years of college, was only 0.65. For college educated women and men who worked year-round, full-time, the ratio was 0.73. This table does not include people with more than four years of college education, so highly paid professional jobs are not represented. With those caveats, one can still see that the percent changes in wages, earnings, and hours are all negative for men except the youngest men with four years of college. The changes are all positive for women. These changes are closely correlated with changes in the number of hours worked by men and women.

As women make up a larger and larger part of the labor force, their average wages and earnings will grow more slowly. When most employable women have entered the labor force and many work full time, the chance for households to increase their future real incomes by increasing total hours of labor will slow. Therefore, future growth in household incomes will depend more on growth in productivity and wages than on the ability of individuals to pool incomes. Increased education and training for higher paying jobs will be the only way "up" for individuals and households in the future. A report titled "The Forgotten Half," issued in 1988 by the W.T. Grant Foundation, concluded that "during his or her lifetime, a college graduate can expect to earn double the money of a high school graduate and more than triple that of a high school drop-out."[131] The gap in annual incomes between high school and college educated males increased $6,439 per year, in real dollar terms, between 1979 and 1987; it increased $2,326 per year for college educated women.[132]

Income by Region

How income is distributed by region affects markets for food and other goods, but former large disparities in household income between regions have largely disappeared. The South has typically had the lowest incomes. In 1989, its median household income was still the lowest ($25,870); the highest was in the Northeast ($32,640). The percent of total aggregate personal income attributed to each region was, however, highest in the South (30.9%) and lowest in the West (21.5%).[133]

The larger disparities are now between rural and urban regions and

Table 3.6. Employed Men and Women: Numbers, Earnings, and Hours by Age and Education[a] (Percent Change from 1973 to 1986)

Age and Education[b]	1986 Workers (Millions)	Change in Group Size (%)	1986 Mean Annual Earnings[c]	Percent Change Annual Earnings[d]	Wages	Annual Hours Worked
Men, 25–34						
High school	8.4	58	19,387	−21	−16	−6
College	3.3	83	28,792	1	−1	2
Men, 35–44						
High school	5.4	38	24,992	−12	−7	−5
College	2.5	127	37,728	−11	−7	−4
Men, 45–55						
High school	4.4	2	27,027	−8	−2	−6
College	1.4	27	42,696	−4	...	−4
Women, 25–34						
High school	6.5	85	11,182	16	3	13
College	2.9	164	18,924	30	12	16
Women, 35–44						
High school	5.5	96	12,570	18	11	6
College	1.7	240	20,050	30	12	23
Women, 45–55						
High school	4.2	40	13,199	10	7	3
College	0.8	100	19,503	6	11	5

[a] Source: Levy, 1988, pp. 125–151.
[b] Education categories based on four years of attendance at high school or college.
[c] In 1987 dollars.
[d] Annual earnings for those who worked year-round, full-time.

between cities and suburbs. The size of the gap between city and suburban family incomes was 11% in favor of those in the suburbs in 1959, growing to 24% by 1983.[134] This was mainly due to the different types of families who live in cities and in suburbs. One-quarter of central city families were headed by women whose incomes were relatively low. To what extent gentrification of the central cities will decrease the urban-suburban income gap is not known, but the implications for food marketing are fairly clear. Lower cost food and fewer services will be in demand where incomes are relatively low, particularly in rural areas and central cities. The market niches for high variety, high quality, and high service will be in the suburbs and in pockets of cities with well-paid households.

The primary effects of income on food consumption and the role it plays in estimating the demand for various types of food are discussed in detail in Chapter 5. However, in an affluent society, the effects of rising incomes on food consumption patterns are intimately tied to the effect of labor force participation on the value of time.

LABOR FORCE PARTICIPATION

The greatest changes in the labor force over the past two decades have been an increase in the percentage of married women and a decrease in the percentage of men working outside the home. Future changes in the labor force will center around the decreasing share of white male workers. In 1947, two-thirds of the labor force was composed of white males.[135] Figure 3.18 shows that in 1988, 47% of the labor force was white males and 37% was white females. By 2000, only 43% of the labor force will be white males and 20% will be nonwhites of both genders.[136]

Between 1940 and 1988, women in the labor force doubled—from 27.4 to 56.6%. For men, the percentage fell from 79 to 76.2%. The share of married women in the labor force increased more than three times, while that of single, widowed, and divorced women increased by a factor of 1.4.[137] Table 3.7 illustrates changes in labor force participation by sex, age, and marital status since 1960. There was a steady drop in the percentage of married men in the labor force in all age groups, especially for those over age 45.

For married women the story was reversed. There was a steady climb in numbers of women in the labor force except for singles over age 44 and widowed or divorced women over age 65 (Table 3.7). The latter may be partially explained by rising incomes among the elderly through indexed Social Security payments, pensions, and other financial investments that allow older people to retire earlier.

The labor force participation rates of men and women are converging. Those of single men and women are very close at all ages under 65. Almost 70% of married women in prime childbearing years (ages 20–44) were in the labor force in 1988.[138] Despite their maternal roles, more than half of mothers with children under age 6 and more than 70% of those with children between the ages of 6 and 17 were in the labor force in 1988. This development is illustrated in Table 3.8. Participation in the labor force by women with children under age 6 has increased more than fivefold since 1950. Half of married mothers with infants return to work within the first year after birth.[139]

Only part of the picture on the extent of labor force participation can be obtained by looking at the data on full- and part-time workers. Over the last decade, the percentage of all full-time workers who were women increased from 35 to 39%, with a concomitant decrease in the percentage of men. Three-fourths of women who worked, worked full time.[140] In 1985, mothers most likely to work full time were those who were divorced followed by those who were married. About 80% of the married mothers who worked full time also worked a full year.

Overall, 62% of working women worked 50–52 weeks, 18% worked 27–49 weeks, and 20% worked less than half a year.[141] Single mothers who had never been married were the least likely to work full-time (29%), mostly because they lacked the education and skills or child care support to do so.[142] Even though all employed women are not in the work place full time year-round, their increased participation in the labor force has dramatically altered the lifestyle, income,

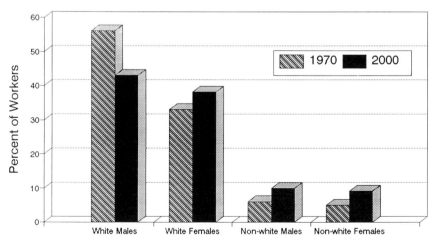

Figure 3.18. The workplace diversifies: U.S. workforce, 1970 and 2000. (Data from U.S. Department of Commerce, Bureau of the Census, 1987a; Solomon, 1989.)

consumption needs, spending habits, and use of time in the American household.

In addition to their primary job away from home, 5.8% of employed men and 4.6% of employed women report holding another job, spending an average of 13 hours a week on a second job in 1985. Those most likely to hold a second job were between the ages of 25 and 44; they worked more than 53 hours a week outside the home.[143] In a small sample of 335 U.S. couples in 1976, employed husbands worked an average of 9.5 hours a day and employed wives worked an average of 6.5 hours per day in the labor force, for a ratio of women's to men's hours of 0.68. The ratio of women's to men's earnings was about 0.60

Table 3.7. Labor Force Participation Rate (Percent) by Age Group, Gender, and Marital Status, 1960-1988[a]

| Year | Age | | | | |
Marital Status	16–19	20–24	25–44	45–64	Over 65
Men					
1960					
Married	96.0	97.5	98.5	93.0	37.1
Single	34.4	76.6	85.3	74.4	24.3
Widowed or divorced	⋯	88.6	83.0	78.1	18.2
1970					
Married	95.5	95.0	98.2	91.6	30.2
Single	49.0	69.0	84.2	66.6	21.0
Widowed or divorced	⋯	73.2	77.6	75.9	16.5
1980					
Married	97.3	96.8	97.3	84.8	20.4
Single	56.8	79.6	83.6	65.2	20.0
Widowed or divorced	⋯	92.9	92.4	69.9	13.0
1988					
Married	95.3	95.7	96.8	82.8	17.5
Single	49.7	80.1	86.9	65.7	20.7
Widowed or divorced	⋯	93.2	90.3	71.2	11.6
Women					
1960					
Married	25.3	30.0	40.0	34.2	5.9
Single	25.3	73.4	79.8	75.1	21.6
Widowed or divorced	37.3	54.6	61.5	58.3	11.6
1970					
Married	36.0	47.4	43.3	44.1	7.9
Single	39.5	71.1	77.0	67.8	17.6
Widowed or divorced	46.5	59.7	66.4	60.7	9.9
1980					
Married	47.7	60.5	60.9	46.9	7.2
Single	49.0	72.2	81.4	62.8	12.0
Widowed or divorced	51.0	68.5	76.8	59.5	8.6
1988					
Married	46.8	65.9	70.7	52.7	7.4
Single	48.7	74.8	81.6	65.2	10.9
Widowed or divorced	64.5	67.7	78.9	62.6	8.2

[a]U.S. Department of Commerce, Bureau of the Census, 1988a, 1989b.

Table 3.8. Labor Force Participation Rates (Percent) of Married Women (Husband Present) by Presence and Age of Children, 1950–1988[a,b]

Year	Total	With No Children Under 18	With Children Under 18		
			Total	6–17	Under 6
1950	24.8	30.3	18.4	28.3	11.9
1955	29.4	32.7	24.0	34.7	16.2
1960	31.5	34.7	27.6	39.0	18.6
1965	35.7	38.3	32.2	42.7	23.3
1970	41.4	42.2	39.7	49.2	30.3
1975	45.1	44.0	44.9	52.2	36.8
1980	50.7	46.0	54.3	61.7	45.3
1988	56.7	49.1	65.2	72.6	57.4

[a]Source: U.S. Department of Commerce, Bureau of the Census, 1988a, 1990a.
[b]Children are defined as never-married sons and daughters, stepchildren, and adopted children. Excluded are other related children such as grandchildren, nieces, nephews, and cousins, and unrelated children.

in 1976, but by 1989 it was 0.68.[144] This suggests that part of the earnings differential between men and women can be explained by the number of hours they work.

The Second Shift

Meanwhile, over the past three decades, average time spent in household tasks declined for women (from 27 to 19.5 hours per week) and increased for men (from 4.6 to 9.8 hours per week). The ratio of women's to men's time in household tasks has declined from 6:1 in 1965 to 2:1 in 1985, according to a 1988 nationwide survey.[145] Long-run, aggregate data suggest that women's household time fell less (from 32 to 28 hours per week between 1959 and 1983), and men's household time increased less (from 11.5 to 12 hours per week), than recent surveys have suggested, but the direction of change is consistent.[146] Women are spending less time on household tasks and men are spending more.

Adding household time to labor force time, married, employed men worked between 57 and 64 hours per week and married, employed women worked between 49.5 and 61 hours per week on average. The ratio of women's to men's total work time was between 0.85 and 0.95. Clearly, there is wide variation around these average numbers, with parents, and particularly mothers, of small children working considerably more hours than those without children.

This gives rise to conflicting stories about whether Americans are gaining or losing leisure time and whether or not they are better off or more stressed than ever. The fact is, a large number of families headed by those between the ages of 25 and 50 have more working members than ever. Families with two working spouses and small children have time demands greater than those ever known when women stayed at home or extended families were available to take care of children and help with other household tasks, such as running errands. By 1988, both spouses were employed in 60% of married couple households, and two-thirds of them had children at home. As the baby boom generation moves through ages 25 to 50, many will experience decreased leisure time.

While 17.8 million married couple families with children and working mothers (27% of all families and 19% of all households) cope with extraordinary time demands, others are gaining leisure time.[147] Factors that lead to an aggregate increase in leisure time are a decrease in the number of children in households, longer portions of lives spent unmarried, and earlier retirements. Between 1965 and 1975, young men and elderly men and women gained significant hours of leisure, as did middle-aged women.[148] Leisure, as defined here, is time spent after taking care of all work tasks and personal grooming and sleeping. It includes time spent in school; participating in clubs and organizations, sports, recreational activities, and hobbies; watching television, reading, and visiting with friends and relatives.

On average, women have gained 5.5 hours of leisure per week since 1965, leaving them with 39 hours per week by 1985. Men had 40 hours per week in both periods. Men and women aged 36–50 had the least leisure time, about 34.5 hours per week. On average, married men and women each had 37 hours, decreasing to 31 if there was a child under age five in the home. Single men and women had the most leisure time, 48 and 43 hours each. Men without children had 12 more leisure hours per week than those with preschoolers; women without children had 7 hours more.[149] The greatest gains in leisure since 1965 were for the elderly, who averaged 22% or 8–9 hours more per week and, in general, for women, who averaged 15% more hours per week.[150] Earlier retirement has led to more leisure for the elderly, and women have gained leisure hours by having fewer children, shifting some child care to fathers, remaining single longer, and finding more efficient ways to conduct household tasks.

Since 1982, the proportion of women aged 18–44 without children has remained at 38%.[151] Childfree 25–29-year-old women increased from 31% in 1976 to 41% in 1988, and those aged 30–34 increased from 16 to 25%. Women most likely to be childfree were white, college educated, and in professional occupations.[152] Among married couples where both spouses had a college education, 70% were dual-earner households. Thirty-six percent of these highly educated, dual earners had no children in 1987. In comparison, of all married couples, 58% were dual-earner couples and 20% had no children.[153] Among women aged 30–39 who earned more than $25,000 a year in 1983, half had no children in their homes.[154]

Increased education, labor force participation, and income have increased the value of women's time and resulted in fewer children and new ways to substitute capital for labor in housework. Only by decreasing their hours in the household have women been able to keep their total work time within the constraints of a 24 hour day and meet normal sleep and personal care requirements. Although some household tasks have shifted from wives to husbands, looking for ways to be more efficient and cut down on household time has become a quest for men and women alike. A conceptual framework that incorporates the value of time will be presented in Chapter 6.

Time, Money, and Food Consumption

One of the primary ways of cutting household time has been to spend less time in the kitchen.[155] Microwave ovens have helped, as have convenience foods, take-out food, fast food, and home-delivered food. Since 86% of employed women still do most of the cooking and 91% do most of the shopping, they are looking for ways to feed themselves and their families quickly. Most spend less than a half hour preparing an evening meal; 20% spend less than 15 minutes.[156]

Increased labor force participation on the part of women has instigated massive changes in the way consumers shop, eat, and cook. Even though they demand healthy and nutritious food, convenience is a powerful lure. One study showed that, among married couples under age 55 with two earners, almost 40% of food expenditures were for food away from home, while among married couples where the wife was not in the labor force, only 24 to 30% of food expenditures were for food away from home.[157] Since total food expenditures of the two groups were quite similar, the higher incomes and scarcer time of the dual earners led them to select more food prepared outside the home.

Earlier research showed, however, that a greater proportion of increased earnings went for food away from home when the wife worked part time than if she worked full time.[158] This indicates that the time constraints on full-time working wives lead them to either purchase less expensive food away from home, such as fast food, or to eat out less often.

If leisure continues to increase, however, the demand for restaurant meals could increase. In 1989, eating out was reportedly the number one choice of leisure time activities.[159] Another recent survey found that those who spent the most time eating meals away from home were older people, college graduates, unmarried people, and those with incomes between $25,000 and $35,000.[160] These are also the categories of people who have the most leisure time. The elderly with more leisure time are seeking activities with a slower pace rather than ways to be more efficient. Eating in restaurants is one such activity. Those whose incomes are not particularly high have less valued time and can eat more frequently and leisurely in restaurants. College graduates, on average, marry later and have fewer children. They need less time, overall, for household tasks. They can eat out more often because they have both more time and more money than others.

Labor force participation affects the productivity of individual households, businesses, government services, and the nation. It also determines household income and its distribution. As we become more affluent, food commands a smaller and smaller portion of household income. As discussed in Chapter 5, the average U.S. household spent only 7.3% of its after tax income for food eaten at home in 1989 and only 11.7% for all food.[161] As the proportion of income needed for food falls, consumers become less concerned with food prices and more concerned with taste, convenience, variety, status, and healthfulness. As markets grow more competitive, projecting retail sales on the basis of prices and income, though important, is not enough. Projections based on cost alone ignore critical changes in age, household structure, and lifestyle that affect consumer behavior.[162]

In contrast to the growing affluence of some groups were the 2.5 million families with cash incomes of less than $5,000 in 1988. Their average family size was three persons, half were black or Hispanic, and two-thirds were headed by a woman.[163] This group needs inexpensive, nutritious food sources and increasingly relies on government programs for income and food. The poor and their food needs are discussed in detail in Chapter 9.

Diversity is and will continue to be the key to food marketing. Although everyone needs food to eat, ideas about what type of food is good, healthy, or affordable vary significantly. New tastes are discovered as people travel and have new experiences. New technology allows new forms of food to be delivered. New information turns good food into bad food (and vice versa). Varied lifestyles call for an increasing potpourri of food presentation and delivery.

GENERAL IMPLICATIONS

"A very significant portion—perhaps the overwhelming majority—of all waking hours of all mankind throughout all of history have been associated with getting enough food. All individuals of a group shared this need, and . . . the strategy for getting enough food . . . affected every other aspect of the group's culture."[164]

Compared to the historical quest for adequate food, contemporary Americans treat food acquisition rather casually—but perhaps we have changed less than we think. Americans purchase virtually all of their food with money that they obtain through employment. Maintaining the spending power of the household so that food consumption can continue to be treated as a matter of fact, rather than a matter of quest, has required more intensive labor force participation by household members and increased investment in food and agricultural technology.

Demographic trends will have an increasingly important impact on food markets. Most of them can be predicted accurately for 10 to 20 years hence, but in demographics, as well as economics, it is difficult to separate irreversible trends from cyclical and episodic events. Among the phenomena discussed in this chapter are some of each. Which are truly trends? With some trepidation, three are identified here as trends likely to last for the next 20 years: 1) continued slow rates of population growth, 2) increasing ethnic diversity, and 3) increasing average levels of education.

Current trends such as the increasing percentage of women in the labor market, a population shift to the Southwest, declining mortality, increased immigration, increased divorce rates, and a decline in the number of children among whites and college educated people will likely stabilize at different levels than in the past, but their rates of change must slow. When saturation levels are reached, all trends must either level out or reverse. This does not mean that permanent changes in food markets are not taking place. Rather, it means that changes will continue to take place, and that catching the episodes and identifying the trends will continue to be critical for successful food marketing.

Disparate Lifestyles

CHAPTER 4

Marketing strategies are changing in today's more consumer-oriented food marketplace. Marketing to the masses is gradually being replaced by micromarketing, which uses a variety of marketing strategies designed to reach small groups or specific segments of consumers that differ greatly in background, tastes, and needs.[1] According to Joel D. Weiner of Kraft USA, "The mythological homogeneous America is gone. We are a mosaic of minorities. All companies will have to do more stratified or tailored or niche marketing."[2]

Originally, markets were segmented largely along geographic lines by region or area and by demographic factors such as age, gender, and income.[3] Now, a multitude of lifestyle classification systems is being used to help describe and predict consumer behavior. During the last 10 years, market research and advertising companies have evolved into what is being called the consumer information industry.[4] Many companies in this industry began by analyzing U.S. census data on the demographic characteristics of consumers in different geographic areas.

During the 1980s, consumer information companies integrated demographics with psychographics (attitudes and values) to develop consumer lifestyle classification systems. These systems, along with information about consumer media preferences from television meters and purchasing behavior from customer records, survey data, and supermarket scanner data, have been combined into comprehensive, sophisticated, microcomputer-based consumer information systems.[5] These systems, when used with operations data from businesses, describe who and where the customers are, what they want, what they buy, and how they can be reached.

For food retailers, consumer lifestyle classification systems are one component of marketing strategies that help determine the product mix offered and the advertising needed to attract consumers to the store.[6] Other techniques used by retailers to identify the preferences of consumers in their market area include focus groups, in-store intercept surveys, telephone surveys, and tracking origins of license plates in the parking lot and redemption rates of coupons mailed to specific consumer groups.

Understanding how consumer lifestyles may affect buyer behavior can be important to food product development as well as to the entire food manufacturing and distribution system. When the needs and desires of consumers are met, new, appropriately formulated food products tend to be more readily accepted and move more quickly from retailers' shelves. This success is then evident at each step of the food distribution system.

Techniques used to develop lifestyle classification systems differ in their approaches to identifying people with different lifestyles. Demographic techniques, one of the first approaches, used U.S. census data to analyze consumer behavior. This provided valuable but limited information to marketers.[7] Geo-demographic techniques, which combine geographic and demographic information, are now being used to describe the population, housing, income, expenditure, age, and other characteristics of consumers in specific geographic areas.[8] These characteristics are then used to develop lifestyle descriptions that help to provide information about purchasing, consumption, media usage, and financial behavior of consumers in a defined geographic area. Psychographic techniques, which combine concepts from psychology and demography, are based on the inclusion of sociopsychological, political, theological, and economic factors in the background and environment of an individual.[9] Psychographics help describe, explain, and classify changes and interrelationships in the values and lifestyles of individuals.

Consumer lifestyle classification systems are generalizations; they cannot be expected to be exact descriptions of individual consumers. They may either be general systems applying to all consumers or specific systems classifying the food-related behaviors of certain groups of consumers, i.e., food shoppers. As examples, three general systems, six specific ones, and one international system will be discussed in this chapter. Most of these, as well as others that have been developed, are proprietary, and are available only to those who subscribe to the services of market research firms, advertising agencies, or other consumer information companies.

GENERAL CLASSIFICATION SYSTEMS

Values and Lifestyle Systems—VALS 1 and VALS 2

One of the earliest general systems that attempted to relate the lifestyles of consumers to their purchasing behavior was the original Values and Lifestyle System (VALS), now called VALS 1 (Table 4.1). The concept of VALS 1 originated in 1960 at Stanford Research Institute International.[10] It was further developed during the 1960s and 1970s, and its use expanded rapidly during the late 1970s and early 1980s.

In 1980, the VALS 1 classifications were enhanced with data from a mail survey of over 800 questions answered by 1,635 respondents selected from a national probability sample of Americans 18 years and older in the 48 contiguous states.[11]

VALS 2, which updated and extended VALS 1, was introduced in 1988 (Table 4.1).[12] VALS 2 is based on data from two surveys. Data from the first survey of 2,292 respondents representative of the U.S. population were used to refine components of the population segments and establish the eight lifestyle classifications for VALS 2. The second survey of 2,591 respondents investigated relationships between the new classifications and selected aspects of consumer behavior.[13]

VALS 1 recognized that people's values change as they achieve their goals and mature, that values and lifestyles change more often and to a greater extent for some people than for others during their lifetime, and that values seem to affect behavior.[14] Values include "the entire constellation of a person's attitudes, beliefs, opinions, hopes, fears, prejudices, needs, desires, and aspirations, that, taken together, govern how one behaves."[15] Lifestyles are affected by these values.

The conceptual structure of VALS 1 systematized both values and lifestyles into a double hierarchy (Table 4.1 and Figure 4.1) in an attempt to explain "why people believe and act as they do."[16] The survey data were used to try to identify attitudinal and demographic factors that seem to affect a person's quality of life, and then to predict how a person might be expected to behave under a variety of other circumstances. According to this framework, as people change psychologically from immaturity to full psychological maturity, they move up the levels of the hierarchy incrementally from one lifestyle category to another. They

Table 4.1. Values and Lifestyle Systems[a]

VALS 1	Percent of Population		VALS 2	Percent of Population	
Outer- and Inner-Directed		2	Actualizers		8
Integrated	2		Principle-Oriented		27
Inner-Directed		20	Fulfilleds	11	
Societally Conscious	8		Believers	16	
Experiential	7		Status-Oriented		26
I-Am-Me	5		Achievers	13	
Outer-Directed		67	Strivers	13	
Achievers	22		Action-Oriented		25
Emulators	10		Experiencers	12	
Belongers	35		Makers	13	
Need-Driven		11	Strugglers		14
Sustainers	7				
Survivors	4				

[a]Data from Mitchell, 1983; SRI International, 1989.

replace some old values and attitudes with new ones and change others very little or not at all.[17]

People in the *Integrated* lifestyle group at the top of the VALS 1 hierarchy (Table 4.1 and Figure 4.1) tend to be at full psychological maturity. Most people at this level are very well educated, have higher than average incomes, and are in their middle to upper years. They have a mature and balanced viewpoint, can be leaders or followers depending on the situation, and are self-confident, mission oriented, and adaptable. Movement upward to the Integrated level can be through either the Outer- or Inner-Directed pathways.[18]

The *Inner-Directed* path includes the *Societally Conscious, Experiential,* and *I-Am-Me* lifestyle groups. As a group, Inner-Directed people have excellent educations and incomes, hold professional or technical jobs, and are independent, self-aware, concerned about inner growth, holistic health, and societal issues that affect quality of life. Inner needs tend to be more important to them than money and material goods.[19]

The *Outer-Directed* path includes the *Achievers, Emulators*, and *Belongers* lifestyle groups. These people are diverse, large in number,

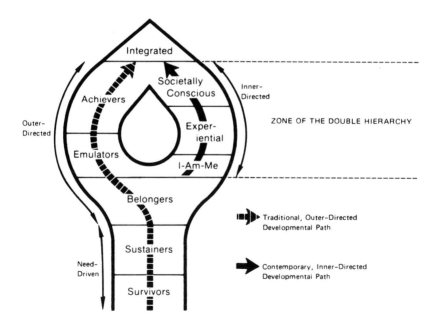

Figure 4.1. Double hierarchy of VALS 1. (Reprinted with permission of Macmillan Publishing Company from *The Nine American Lifestyles* by Arnold Mitchell. Copyright ©1983 by Arnold Mitchell.)

make up the mainstream of middle America, and dominate the economy. They tend to have a concern for people and are greatly influenced by what others think; therefore visible material goods are important to them. They also seem to be conservative and value conventional behavior, honesty, family, belonging to many groups, and being in control of their lives.[20]

The *Need-Driven* lifestyle group at the bottom of the hierarchy includes the *Sustainers* and *Survivors*. These people live in poverty, have very limited resources and high unemployment; a high proportion are women and minorities. They appear to deny their values and needs rather than to express their preferences, mistrust authority, and feel hopeless and alienated. They are at the lowest level of maturity psychologically, seem to be inflexible, prefer the traditional, tend to be unaware of current events, and live outside the cultural mainstream.[21]

Implications of VALS 1 for Food Marketing

To apply VALS 1 to food marketing, food behaviors of people in four of the lifestyle levels were predicted and characterized.[22] These included Inner-Directed (20%), Achievers and Emulators (32%), Belongers (35%), and Need-Driven (11%) (Table 4.1).

All the Inner-Directed lifestyle groups and the Achievers and Emulators of the Outer-Directed path have money to spend for food, therefore food marketers target products to them. Inner-Directed consumers tend to be interested in fresh foods and exotic types of food. They consider appearance, flavor, and the health and nutritional aspects of food very important. Achievers will try anything new. They prefer the highest quality items, value convenience, eat away from home frequently, and shop in gourmet and specialty stores. The demands of these groups for foods that are nutritious and healthful as well as quick and convenient are met by processed foods with little salt or sugar and by frozen or refrigerated entrees and meals.[23]

Belongers have brand preferences and tend to avoid new foods and new cooking methods. Their main meal of the day is the traditional meat, potatoes, and a vegetable. Canned foods fit Belongers' purchasing patterns because they are convenient yet inexpensive relative to fresh or frozen foods. Need-Driven consumers tend to be very price conscious, prefer private-labeled foods, shop for loss leaders, use coupons, and may pay for food with food stamps or checks from welfare or Social Security.[24]

Retail food stores seem to be changing their marketing strategies in order to supply the products and services that better meet the demands of different consumer lifestyle groups.[25] They have added new food and nonfood departments and designed entire stores for certain consumer segments, such as warehouse stores for the price-conscious, and superstores with variety and service for those who often value time and one-stop shopping more than money (see Chapter 11 for details about food stores).

VALS 2

According to the Stanford Research Institute, VALS 2 tends to emphasize the psychological and demographic dimensions of consumer behavior more than VALS 1.[26] It is based on three self-orientation groups and eight consumer segments of similar size arranged in a network (Table 4.1 and Figure 4.2). The three groups, as explained by Stanford Research Institute, are principle-, status-, or action-oriented according to how people appear to make decisions about which products, services,

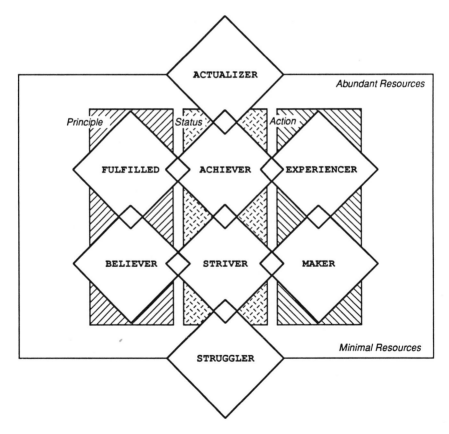

Figure 4.2. Organization of VALS 2. (Reprinted, by permission, from SRI International, 1989.)

and experiences will satisfy them. Resources for each self-orientation group, according to VALS 2, may be psychological, physical, or demographic and either abundant or limited. Resources include income, health, self-confidence, eagerness to buy, intelligence, and energy level. They tend to change with stages of the life cycle, illness, and economic conditions.

People in the *Actualizers* group at the top of the VALS 2 system tend to be guided by any or all of the orientations, depending on the situation. They have abundant resources and are leaders in business and government. They are active, independent, sophisticated, successful, like to find new challenges, have many interests, value the finer things in life, and live rich, diverse lives.

The *Principle-Oriented* group includes the Fulfilleds and Believers segments. As a group, the purchasing behavior of these people appears to be consistent with their belief in how the world is or should be. *Fulfilled* consumers are well-educated professionals with abundant money resources, yet they tend to be conservative, practical, responsible, family-centered people who look for functionality, value, and durability in their purchases. *Believers* are moderately educated people with moderate incomes who tend to be conservative, traditional, predictable, and favor American products and name brands.

The *Status-Oriented* group includes Achievers and Strivers who have or desire to have approval by those of higher social status. *Achievers* are conservative, career-, work-, and family-oriented consumers who find material possessions, image, success, recognition, and reward from their work important; thus, they tend to favor established, prestigious products and services. *Strivers* lack self-confidence, money, and social and psychological resources, are impulsive, and seek approval from others; they want to be stylish in order to emulate people with impressive possessions.

The *Action-Oriented* group, according to VALS 2, includes Experiencers and Makers, who consider activity, variety, and risk when making purchases. *Experiencers* are young, enthusiastic, impulsive, risk-takers who enjoy excitement, sports, exercise and social activities. As consumers, they tend to spend money on clothes, fast food, music, movies, and videos. *Makers* value self-sufficiency and traditional family life, have skills to do complicated projects, and are suspicious of new ideas. As consumers, they tend to prefer material goods that are practical and functional.

The *Strugglers*, at the bottom of the VALS 2 system, are not grouped by self-orientation. They tend to be elderly, poor, ill, or psychologically immature, with few skills or social contacts. As consumers, they live from day to day, are cautious and concerned about safety and security, show brand loyalty, and constitute only a small part of the market for goods and services.[27]

Vision System

Consumer information firms now are combining demographic data from the census with consumer buying data in specific geographic areas to produce complex consumer classification systems with large numbers of lifestyle types. An example of such a system is the Vision system, developed by National Decision Systems, with 12 market segment groups and 48 lifestyle types. Two other similar systems are PRIZM (Potential Rating Index by Zip Market), with 12 market segment groups and 40 lifestyle types, developed by Claritas Corporation, and ACORN (A Classification of Residential Neighborhoods), with 13 market segment groups and 44 lifestyle types, developed by CACI, Inc.[28] Only the Vision system will be discussed in detail here to illustrate how these systems classify consumers.

The Vision system is based on data from market research firms and from government sources such as the Bureau of the Census, Bureau of Economic Analysis, and Bureau of Labor Statistics.[29] It was developed using data from 117 demographic, socioeconomic, and housing characteristics of consumers living in 260,000 neighborhood block groups in the United States.

The goal of the Vision system is to identify homogeneous groups or segments of consumers who respond in similar ways to marketing strategies and to products and services offered in the marketplace.[30] First, 12 general market groups of consumers were identified based on geographic location and listed in order, based on affluence (Table 4.2). Next, 48 specific market segments were identified within these general market groups based on consumer characteristics such as age, stage in life cycle, household size, ethnic group, education, occupation, income, housing, and degree of urbanization (Table 4.2). Then each segment was described in detail, given a one-line summary description and a catchy name. After that, one of the 48 specific market segments was assigned to each of the 260,000 neighborhood block groups.

When applied to food retailing, the Vision system can classify consumers in the trading area of a supermarket according to the foods they might purchase, based on the neighborhood block groups included in the area. In addition, scanner data for existing products can be used to profile product categories and brands actually purchased in the trading area to discover market potential for products and to learn whether or not consumers buy what retailers think they buy. When applied to new product development, a food manufacturer can define a target market or niche and identify viable test markets for a product using Vision segments. Vision enables both retailers and manufacturers to experiment with targeted marketing in ways that have not been possible before.

Table 4.2. Vision Lifestyle Classification System[a]

Market Group	Percent of U.S. Households	Market Group	Percent of U.S. Households
Very High Socio-economic Status		**Low Socioeconomic Status**	
Suburban Wealthy	3.0	Rural Middle Class	5.3
Suburban Gentry		Mobile Homeville	
Nouveau Riche		Ranches	
Tuition and Braces		and Farmlands	
		Country Pleasure	
Urban Affluence	2.7		
Urban Gentry		Suburban Lower Income	8.7
Young Urban		Young Beginners	
Professionals		Young Hispanics	
Condos and Palms		Just Making It	
High Socioeconomic Status		Urban Lower Income	8.2
		Single Starters	
Suburban Affluence	10.3	Metro Hispanic Mix	
Suburban Up		Urban Melting Pot	
and Comers		Black Urban Fringe	
High Tech Frontiers		Fixed Income Blues	
The Good Life		Teeming Tenements	
Comfortable			
Suburbanites		Town Lower Income	4.7
Leave It to Beaver		Sun City	
A Good Start		Appalachian Trail	
		Collegetown USA	
Suburban Middle Class	23.1		
Little League		Rural Lower Income	7.8
and Barbecues		Tractors and Pickups	
Baby Boom Again		Golden Years	
Industrial Upper Deck		Prairie People	
Porch Swings and		Tough Times	
Apple Pie			
Carports and Kids		**No Socioeconomic Status Designated**	
Declining Suburbia			
Ethnic Industrial		Special Population	1.8
		Books and Beer	
Urban Middle Class	6.8	G.I. Joe	
Brownstones		Institutions	
and White Steps		and Unclassified	
Black Middle Class			
High-Rise Blacks			
Town Middle Class	18.8		
Mainstreet USA			
Town and Country			
Hamlet and Hardhat			
Tom Sawyerville			

[a]Source: National Decision Systems, 1987.

SPECIFIC CLASSIFICATION SYSTEMS

Dual-Earner Couples

A demographic-based classification system for dual-earner couples developed by *American Demographics* classified them into seven lifestyle groups (Table 4.3).[31] The system clearly shows that these couples, often considered a homogeneous group by marketers, tend to be quite diverse in terms of lifestyles and stages of the life cycle. Dual-earner couples, who are the majority of all couples, are important to marketers because they possess nearly half of all discretionary income in the United States, that is, income not needed for essentials.

Data used in this classification system were derived from Census Bureau data in the 1986 Current Population Survey and were limited to two-earner couples with one member younger than age 65. Even with this limitation, more than 90% of all two-earner couples were included in the analysis. Life-cycle stage was the basis for designating the segments, as shown in Table 4.3. The segments are divided into two categories, couples with children at home (about two-thirds) and couples with no children at home (about one-third).

According to this system, of the couples with children at home, *Full Nesters* with children aged 6–17 are the largest segment. As a group, they have intermediate incomes. They tend to be careful consumers, practical, spend time at home with the family when not at work, and enjoy material goods and family travel. Teenagers in these households make many purchase decisions as the family shopper and also for themselves, since many of them work part-time and have their own spending money.

Crowded Nesters, the next largest group, have children aged 18–24 at home and may also have younger children. These couples have the highest

Table 4.3. *American Demographics* **Dual-Earner Couples System**[a]

Segment	Percent of Dual-Earner Couples
Children at Home	
Full Nesters	24
Crowded Nesters	18
New Parents	15
Young Families	10
No Children at Home	
Empty Nesters	13
Honeymooners	13
Just-a-Couple	7

[a] Source: Townsend and Riche, 1987.

incomes but may not have the highest spending power because they support children attending college. Little is known about how grown children living at home spend their money; they may represent a different lifestyle in the same household.

New Parents with preschool children under age 6 at home are the next largest segment. These couples have incomes that are at an intermediate level and money seems to be a problem for most of them. Many of the women in these families are college educated and delayed having children until they were established in their profession. For these households, as incomes increase, convenience and quality become more important attributes of goods and services than price.

Young Families, the smallest segment, have one or more children under age 6 as well as one or more in the 6–17 age range, and their incomes are at an intermediate level. For these couples, it is generally the wife's income that raises the family into the middle class. Their purchases include bigger homes, two cars, VCRs, and exercise equipment for family leisure activities. They also save money for college educations for the children.

Of the two-earner couples with no children at home, the Empty Nesters and the Honeymooners are the two largest segments. The *Empty Nesters*, aged 50–64, have raised their families. Some couples in this group are affluent and some have intermediate incomes. Those who are affluent purchase investments, own second homes, and expect to travel when they retire. Other couples strive to save for retirement while helping their children with college, house, or business expenses and their aged parents with medical bills. As a group, these two-earner couples save money, yet are willing to pay for goods and services that meet their needs in retirement.

Honeymooners, the next largest segment, are in their 20s to 30s and have intermediate incomes. Two incomes are essential for these couples to finance a house and to satisfy other desires. They lack discretionary income, and many of them struggle to maintain economic stability. They want whatever good things in life they can afford before having children, such as eating in expensive restaurants, attending concerts, and traveling. They also tend to establish brand loyalties.

Just-a-Couples, older baby boomers aged 35–49, are the smallest segment. They are affluent, self-indulgent, set trends, and live for themselves. Some of them may have children in the future. Quality is important to them in all aspects of their activities and purchases.[32]

Nutrition Profile Classifications

Dietary practices of American households are divided into five segments in the nutrition profile system developed by the Community Nutrition

Institute and the Marketing Science Institute (Table 4.4).[33] The data analyzed were collected by interview in a national survey of 700 households in 1978 and 1979. Data on 185 different food items were first selected as indicators of food purchasing behavior, and then segments of consumers with common nutritional patterns were identified. The percentage of the sample in each category shown in Table 4.4 may have changed considerably since 1978–1979.

Meat Eaters, the largest segment, eat meat three times a day and find the cost of food a problem because meat is expensive. They eat all kinds of meat, more than average amounts of sugar and sweets, and less than average amounts of fruits, vegetables, and whole grains. French fries are their favorite vegetable and they dislike skim milk. They like to cook but do not like to try new foods. Cholesterol and sodium are high in their diets. They want to know more about protein but not in order to lower their consumption of meat. This group is probably smaller now than in 1978–1979, whereas the remaining four groups may be larger.

Healthy Eaters, the next largest segment, habitually eat well. They eat less meat, fat, sugar, and sweets and more vegetables, fruits, and whole grains than average, and they spend more than average per person on food. Their households are the smallest in this classification system, and they are older and tend to live alone. They prefer lean meat, poultry, and fish; they eat cauliflower, cucumbers, mixed vegetables, beets, and celery and consume less cholesterol than any other segment. Their dislikes include convenience foods, frozen entrees, sugared cereals, Kool-Aid, and pizza. They enjoy cooking, trying new recipes, and entertaining and prefer plain cooking. Their knowledge of nutrition is average, but they rate it high.

In-a-Dither households, the third largest segment, prefer convenience foods, dislike cooking of any kind, eat out more often, own more microwave ovens than those in any other segment, and spend the least on food at home. Their consumption of sugar and sodium is high because they eat more than average amounts of commercial food mixes, sweetened cereals, doughnuts, cookies, sugar, puddings, and sweets; less than average amounts of fruits and vegetables; prefer TV dinners, canned

Table 4.4. Nutrition Profile System, Community Nutrition Institute[a]

Segment	Percent of Sample
Meat Eaters	30
Healthy Eaters	25
In-a-Dither	16
Conscientious	15
People on the Go	14

[a]Source: Leonard, 1982.

stews, frozen pot pies, sausages, onion rings, and frozen vegetables in sauces; and they do not like to try new foods. They are more concerned about food safety than nutrition.

Conscientious households, the next largest segment, prefer nuts, legumes, whole grains (especially popcorn), and vegetables, and they dislike convenience foods except for frozen entrees. They spend less money on food than the other segments, consume less meat and fat than the average, and have lower than average intakes of cholesterol and sodium. They like to cook and try new foods. Their nutrition knowledge is the best of any segment.

People on the Go, the smallest segment, eat away from home most often and spend the most money on food of all the segments. They prefer dairy products, milk, yogurt, cheese, butter, whole grain bread, and raw vegetables; eat less than average amounts of meat, sugar, sweets, fruits, and vegetables; and dislike convenience foods. They use the microwave oven for cooking from scratch. They like to cook, especially for entertaining, are not concerned about cholesterol, are not confident about their nutrition knowledge, and would prefer not to bother with good nutrition. This group particularly is expected to have grown since 1978-1979.[34]

What's Cookin' Classifications

As discussed in Chapter 1, eating behaviors of Americans are divided into five segments according to the "What's Cookin'" system developed by The Pillsbury Company (Table 4.5).[35] The segments in this system were derived from eating pattern data from menu census food diaries collected from more than 3,000 individuals for 15 years (from 1971-1972 to 1985-1986) by the Market Research Corporation of America. The analysis included factors such as what, when, with whom, how often, and where people ate; the form of the food; and how food was prepared.

The *Chase and Grabbits*, the largest segment, increased 136% in the last 15 years. These consumers tend to be young, urban, educated, affluent, single or dual-earner couples without children who like to spend money. Although interested in nutrition, their nutrition information is

Table 4.5. What's Cookin' Classifications, Pillsbury[a]

Segment	Percent of Sample
Chase and Grabbits	26
Down Home Stokers	21
Careful Cooks	20
Functional Feeders	18
Happy Cookers	15

[a]Source: Pillsbury Company, 1988.

limited. Foods these people eat at home include fast-food hamburgers and sandwiches, frozen dinners, and carry-out or frozen pizzas. They do not appear to be concerned about food. Food is not especially important to them, although they like trying new foods. They eat only because they have to, and when more interesting things are going on, anything can become a meal at any time.

The *Down Home Stokers*, the next largest segment, has decreased by 34% in the last 15 years. This segment is regional, primarily found in the South, Midwest, and New England. It is composed of blue-collar workers with moderate incomes and some education. Many women in this segment work because of economic necessity, and convenience foods have replaced home cooking from scratch in these families. Their interest in nutrition is peripheral; they know about trends but do not follow them. These people like traditional, regional foods and do not like trying new foods or foods from other cultures.

Careful Cooks, the next largest segment, increased 122% in the last 15 years. People in this group are older, tend to be retired, are well educated, affluent, interested in understanding food as well as eating it, and follow the nutritional recommendations they know. The concept of convenience foods interests them but not the ingredient content. They enjoy food, explore new foods and cuisines, and eat to stay healthy. Foods typically eaten by this segment include wheat bread, skim milk, yogurt, fresh fruits and vegetables, fish and chicken (no skin), and salads.

The *Functional Feeders* segment decreased by 28% in the last 15 years. These consumers tend to be middle-aged people with above-average incomes and larger families living primarily in the Middle Atlantic or East North Central states. Many women work, but for reasons other than necessity. Food is not a high-priority item in their budgets. They value convenience and shortcuts in food preparation more than trying new foods and tend to use convenience foods as ingredients to make traditional cooked-from-scratch meals or as side dishes. Foods typical for this segment include canned soups, frozen macaroni and cheese, pancakes and waffles, store-bought cookies, and instant potatoes.

Happy Cookers, the smallest group, decreased by 35% in the last 15 years. These are either young mothers or mature women who operate a traditional, well-equipped and well-stocked kitchen and take pride in making much of the food from scratch. Rather than experiment with new cuisines, they tend to substitute ingredients in recipes. Younger members of this segment know about the nutritional needs of their family but do not always follow recommendations. Foods typical for this segment include homemade pies, cakes, cookies, fruit crisps, meat dishes, casseroles, fresh fish, and raw and cooked fresh vegetables.

Predictions of segment sizes based on two scenarios of economic conditions in the year 2000 were included in the analysis. Scenario A predicts slow economic growth, decreased per capita income, increased unemployment, and high interest rates. In this scenario, smaller families will eat inexpensive foods and eat at home more often. Innovation in the food industry will be decreased and low-priced foods will be most successful. In this scenario, the Functional Feeders, Down Home Stokers, and Happy Cookers segments are expected to increase in size; the Chase and Grabbits are expected to decrease and the Careful Cooks to remain the same. Scenario B predicts high economic growth, increased per capita income, high employment including more working women, low interest rates, and increased international trade. In this scenario, food technology will advance rapidly and nutritious, international foods will be introduced. In this scenario, the Chase and Grabbits, Functional Feeders, and Careful Cooks segments are expected to increase in size, and the Down Home Stokers and Happy Cookers to decrease in size.[36]

Classifications of Food Shoppers

Three different classification systems for food shoppers have recently been proposed by the Food Marketing Institute (FMI), Condé Nast Publications, and the Coca-Cola Retailing Research Council as shown in Table 4.6. Classifications in the FMI system are based on consumer behavior, attitudes, and demographics of 1,007 food shoppers surveyed in January 1987.[37] Those of the Condé Nast system are based on shopping

Table 4.6. Classifications of Food Shoppers[a]

System and Segments[b]	Composition of Segment (%)
Food Marketing Institute system	Percent of Sample
Quiet Majority	29
Committed Shoppers	22
Impatient Shoppers	18
Uninvolved Shoppers	18
Leisurely Shoppers	13
Condé Nast classification of female shoppers	Percent of Sample
Committed Careerist	33
Traditional Homemaker	30
Displaced Homemaker	26
Free Spirit	11
Coca Cola Research Council system	Percent of U.S. Households
Avid Shoppers	26
Kitchen Strangers	20
Constrained Shoppers	18
Hurried Shoppers	17
Unfettered Shoppers	13
Kitchen Birds	6

[a]Data from Food Marketing Institute, 1987; Sansolo, 1989; Prepared Foods, 1989; Schubring, 1989.

attitudes of 1,799 female shoppers surveyed for a report "Women and Food II: A Study for Food Marketers in the '90s" by National Family Opinion.[38] The Coca-Cola Retailing Research Council system categories are based on eating, cooking, and shopping habits of consumers derived from U.S. census data by the consulting firm Booz, Allen, and Hamilton.[39]

FMI System. Women and men shoppers were segmented by the FMI classification system into five groups according to how they view and select a supermarket.[40] The *Quiet Majority* segment is "middle of the road" in terms of features in a supermarket that are important to them, features such as food quality and variety, convenience, available brands, bakery, and deli. It is the midpoint of the segments in average income and age (41.9 years) and the next to highest in average weekly grocery bills. The *Committed Shoppers* segment chooses supermarkets for specific reasons, such as quality and variety of food, convenience, availability of nutrition information, stocking of national and generic brands, and availability of specialty sections. It is the lowest in average income, oldest in average age (49.2 years), and has the lowest average weekly grocery bill.

The *Impatient Shoppers* segment values time and will pay for services offered by supermarkets. Only a few of these shoppers shop for bargains, read food advertisements, or read labels. Shoppers in this segment have the highest average income, are the next to youngest (40.4 years), and have the highest average weekly grocery bills. The *Uninvolved Shoppers* segment places little value on supermarket services and has little interest in particular features when selecting a supermarket. It is second highest of the segments in average income, youngest (39.3 years), and has the third highest weekly grocery bills. The *Leisurely Shoppers* segment has a casual view of shopping, likes to browse and shop for bargains, and does not value fast checkout. It is the next to lowest segment in average income, next to oldest in average age (46.1 years), and has the lowest average weekly grocery bills.

Condé Nast System. Women shoppers were classified into four groups in the Condé Nast system, based on how their values affect their attitudes toward food shopping.[41] *Committed Careerists* work because they want to, dislike cooking, are not concerned about the price of food, and will pay for convenience. They use microwave foods frequently, prefer frozen dinners to fast food, and shop less frequently than those in the other segments. *Traditional Homemakers* generally do not work outside the home, cook for their families, and are concerned about food prices. They are less likely than the other segments to own a microwave oven; therefore, they are less likely to buy microwave foods. Of all segments, they shop the most carefully and frequently and have the lowest income. The size of this segment is rapidly decreasing.

Displaced Homemakers work because they have to, share the attitudes of Traditional Homemakers who cook for their families, prefer fast food to frozen dinners at home, use the microwave oven primarily to reheat foods, and buy fewer foods at the supermarket but pay more per item than the other segments. *Free Spirit* shoppers do not fit in with the other groups. They dislike cooking but will accept doing it, are concerned about price, and prefer frozen dinners at home to fast food.

Coca-Cola System. Shoppers were segmented into six groups by the Coca-Cola Retailing Research Council System (Table 4.6). This system, based on 1985 census data, also projected changes in the sizes of the segments by the year 2000.[42] *Avid Shoppers*, the largest segment, generally do not work outside the home, like to cook, shop for bargains, are considered "core" customers by supermarkets, are a variety of ages, and come from all income levels. By 2000, this group will decrease in size. *Kitchen Strangers,* the next largest group, eat at restaurants more often than they shop at supermarkets, are sophisticated, childless singles or married adults younger than age 64. By 2000, the size of this group will increase.

Constrained Shoppers have limited educations and incomes and are not very sophisticated. By 2000 the size of this group will increase. *Hurried Shoppers* are women who work outside the home, are busy, and look for ways to cut down on shopping and cooking. They may be from low-, moderate-, or high-income homes. By 2000, the size of this group will decrease. *Unfettered Shoppers* have little need to shop for bargains, are older, and are relatively affluent. By 2000, this group will increase in size. *Kitchen Birds*, the smallest segment, are very careful shoppers, eat very little, and are over age 75. By 2000, this group will increase slightly in size.

International Lifestyle Classifications

A survey called GlobalScan reported in 1990 was conducted in several countries to seek an understanding of consumers' attitudes toward factors thought to affect their purchasing behavior.[43] Countries surveyed included Western Europe, Canada, Hong Kong, Japan, Mexico, Venezuela, and the United States. Consumers were grouped into five segments according to how they thought and felt about materialism, families, the environment, and roles of working women.

In all the countries, the *Strivers* segment was the largest. Consumers in this group tend to be materialistic, do things that make them look good, and are achievement-oriented, pressured, lonely, and looking for a different and better life. *Achievers* tend to be similar in economic status but more sophisticated than Strivers. They buy high-quality items and support equal status for women.

Pressured People are women and other consumers from a variety of social classes who seem to feel lonely despite living in families and are unable to keep up with their lives. When the food they select contradicts what they know they should eat, they tend to feel guilty and anxious. *Traditionals* tend to be conservative, inflexible about roles and values, and concerned about health and finances. *Adapters* tend to be happiest with their lives. This segment seems to show the most concern about nutrition.

GENERAL IMPLICATIONS

Consumer lifestyle classification systems will likely become more and more important to food product developers, food manufacturers, and food retailers as they concentrate on developing skills in segmented marketing. Success in marketing has always depended on knowing the needs and desires of the customers. However, consumers are an increasingly heterogeneous group; all do not want the same product or service.

Successful micromarketing, that is, marketing targeted to small, diverse groups of consumers, requires being able to differentiate among consumers and divide them into subgroups by differences in who they are and what they want. The ability to divide consumers into functional subgroups is fundamental to micromarketing. In addition to providing customized products aimed at specific market niches, micromarketing has brought a shift away from mass advertising techniques to targeted promotions. Some companies aiming at micromarkets are sponsoring sports events and festivals, advertising on cable television and in specialized magazines, and doing more in-store advertising.[44]

Food Economics:
Insightful and Not So Arcane

CHAPTER 5

Many people think economics deals with only those things that have to do with money. Actually, economics is best thought of as providing a structured way of viewing the world and human behavior. It offers much to enrich our understanding of food consumption patterns. Consumers are assumed to seek to maximize their own utility or satisfaction through a series of choices that are constrained by their limited income. This theoretical model suggests that economic factors, such as income and prices, should have a major impact on the types and amounts of food products and other goods purchased by consumers.

For any skeptics who need to be convinced of the importance of economic factors, such as prices, the following account should be eye-opening. The Coca-Cola and Pepsi bottlers in the Phoenix area, as well as in many other parts of the country, were engaged in a price war for market share in the fall of 1988. At one Phoenix grocery store that featured six-packs of Coke for 59 cents, "shoppers were thick as ants." There were traffic jams in the store's parking lot. The store sold 2,900 cases of Coca-Cola a day.[1]

As the following anecdote suggests, economists view human behavior through abstract models. Two economists were walking down a sidewalk, when one said, "Look, there's a dollar bill on the sidewalk." His companion replied, "No, it isn't." When the first insisted, "Yes, it is," the other replied, "No—If it were a dollar bill, somebody would have picked it up already."[2] Some people find the abstractions of economics appealing and insightful; others find them out of touch with reality. Economists would like to think those in the second group simply do not understand their discipline sufficiently to appreciate its value.

Models of economic theory are a group of abstractions that represent simplifications of a very complex reality. The benefits of such theoretical models are that they allow one to focus on the essential factors or interactions in a relationship, provide a method of structuring the analysis, and hence, yield insights into real events and human behavior

133

one would not have been able to see without theory as an aid. The usefulness or "goodness" of a theoretical model can be judged by a very practical standard, its ability to explain and predict real events and behavior.[3] Our particular interest is in the ability of economics to explain food consumption patterns and the behavior of food consumers.

The traditional economic model views the consumer as purchasing the bundle of goods and services that yields the highest level of utility or satisfaction, given his or her own particular tastes and preferences. Consumers are rational in that they can decide whether one bundle of goods is preferable to another or whether they are indifferent to differences between the two bundles. Each consumer is constrained by having only a limited amount of money to spend and faces a set of prices for consumer goods that is outside his or her control. Demand relationships, which reflect the optimum amount of each good to purchase, depend on the consumer's income, the set of prices, and the consumer's preferences. Demand functions can be obtained by maximizing the consumer's utility (satisfaction) subject to the budget constraint.

Economists typically do not attempt to study or measure utility directly. The empirical work of economists concentrates on the resulting demand functions and uses the underlying utility theory to enrich their understanding of that relationship. Demand functions indicate that prices, income, and sociodemographic factors such as those discussed in Chapter 3 should have a major impact on the types and amounts of food a consumer buys. Income and prices, two key economic factors that affect the demand for food and other goods, will be examined in detail in this chapter.

ENGEL'S INSIGHTS: INCOME AND FOOD CONSUMPTION

In 1857, Ernst Engel, originally a Prussian mining engineer who became interested in social statistics, published a study that examined the expenditure patterns of families at different income levels.[4] He observed that "the poorer a family is, the greater the proportion of total expenditures (income) which it must use to procure food."[5] The effect of income on the level and pattern of expenditures has been one of the most extensively studied empirical relationships in economics. Engel's observation concerning food is one of the few patterns that has been observed with sufficient persistence to be called a law in economics. Engel's law in its modern version says that as "consumer incomes increase, the proportion of income spent for food decreases," assuming other influencing factors remain unchanged.[6]

The relationship between consumption and income is referred to as the Engel function or Engel relation. This relationship may be studied either with simple comparisons and graphs or sophisticated statistical techniques, which are referred to as econometrics. The Engel relationship may be analyzed with either time-series or cross-sectional data. Time-series data reflect changes over time and most typically are annual data on income and food consumption for a particular country; an example is given in Table 5.1. Cross-sectional data reflect the different levels of consumption and income for different units, such as households, at the time a survey was taken, usually a certain year. Table 5.2 illustrates data across households, and Table 5.3 represents data across countries. The basic data available for studying food consumption and the methods through which these data are collected are discussed in Chapter 7.

Budget Shares for Food

In analyzing the relationship of food consumption to income, the first statistic to examine is the average budget share or the proportion of income that is spent on food. Table 5.1 gives the percent of disposable (after taxes) personal income spent on food at home and away from home and the total of both categories, using the latest (revised) data for the United States. On average, 11.7% of disposable personal income was spent by families and individuals on food in 1989, 7.3% on food expenditures at home, and 4.3% on expenditures away from home.[7] The revised data in Table 5.1 show a lower level of spending for food than the older data series, primarily because more is deducted from grocery store sales for nonfood purchases, such as drugs, household supplies, pet food, and ice.[8]

Table 5.1. Food Expenditures by Families and Individuals as a Share of Disposable Personal Income, 1966–1989, United States[a]

Year	At Home[b] (%)	Away from Home[c] (%)	Total[d] (%)
1966	11.4	3.5	14.9
1970	10.4	3.6	13.9
1975	10.1	3.9	13.9
1980	9.3	4.3	13.6
1985	8.1	4.5	12.6
1989	7.3	4.3	11.7

[a]Data from Putnam, 1989a, p. 106; 1990a, p. 125.
[b]Food purchases from grocery stores and other retail outlets, including purchases with food stamps and food produced and consumed on farms because the value of these foods is included in personal income. Excludes government donated foods.
[c]Purchases of meals and snacks by families and individuals and food furnished employees since it is included in personal income. Excludes food paid for by government and business, such as foods donated to schools, meals in prisons and other institutions, and expense-account meals.
[d]Total may not add due to rounding.

As one might expect, the share of income spent on food purchased for use at home has steadily declined, whereas the share spent on food away from home has risen. However, the latter dropped slightly between 1985 and 1989, falling from 4.5 to 4.3%. Overall, the proportion of income spent on food declined from 14.9% in 1966 to 11.7% in 1989. This pattern reflects Engel's law. After removing the impact of inflation, real incomes generally rose during this period, as discussed in Chapter 3.

In the previous unrevised series data, the proportion of income spent on food could be traced back to 1930. In 1980, 16% of disposable income was spent on food; this figure was 17% in 1970, 20% in 1960, 23% in 1950, 22% in 1940, and 24% in 1930.[9] The decline in the share of income devoted to food extends back over decades and again reflects the operation of Engel's law. The effect of the revisions presented in Table 5.1 is reflected in the difference between the figures for 1980 of 16% in the old series versus 13.6% in the new one.

Americans are increasingly buying foods with more value added (i.e., more processing or packaging), which enhances the convenience of a product but also increases its cost. Even with these modifications, however, Engel's law still operates. A basic factor underlying Engel's law is the limited capacity of the human stomach and the myriad goods and services other than food that people wish to purchase with their income. Even though they spend more per unit of food, measured either in pounds or calories, the proportion of the average household's budget devoted to food continues to fall.

However, averages can hide a great deal of vital information. One economist tells of a man who stuck his arms in an oven and feet in a bucket of ice, and when asked to comment, replied that *on average* the temperature was very pleasant. Table 5.2 uses data from the Bureau of Labor Statistics' 1988 Continuing Consumer Expenditure Survey (CCES), which will be discussed in detail in Chapter 7, to examine the variation in the budget share devoted to food for households at different income levels.

Table 5.2 reveals several things—one is a dramatic demonstration of Engel's law. Although average food expenditures for all households in this survey were 13.3% of income, households with incomes over $50,000 spent just 8.5% of their income on food, whereas the poorest households with incomes under $5,000 were having to spend 82.1%. The percent for households with incomes under $5,000 may be exaggerated, however, because some sources of financial support, such as food stamps, may not be counted in their income. There is also a general problem with under-reporting income, and the "under $5,000" group includes households with negative incomes. Households with business or farm incomes might have negative incomes in a particular year, although their long-run incomes are quite substantial and hence their level of food spending much higher than their current income would suggest. In fact, a similar analysis of the 1982–1983 CCES data found that although households with incomes under $5,000 spent 65.6% of their reported income on food, their food purchases amounted to only 20.7% of their total consumption expenditures.[10]

A source of national pride, and rightfully so, is the fact that Americans on average spend a smaller proportion of their income on food than the people in any other country in the world, as shown in Table 5.3.[11] This is the result of our relatively high average income level, the operation of Engel's law, and the efficiency of the U.S. food system that produces reasonably priced food. Such international data should probably be viewed as roughly, rather than exactly, right. Conversion of different currencies into dollars depends on the exchange rate, and the accuracy of the basic data varies between countries.

The pattern seen in Table 5.3 is, in general, consistent with Engel's law. As one scans down the table, the income levels decrease and the proportion devoted to food increases, but there are some exceptions. The exceptions result from the fact that other factors, which are presumed to remain unchanged when evaluating the income-food consumption relation, such as prices, do not remain constant when comparing different countries. For example, although Switzerland had a higher per capita income than the United States, the Swiss spent a substantially higher share of that income on food. This reflects the very high prices for food in Switzerland, which anyone who has traveled there can attest to.

Table 5.2. Household Expenditures for Food in Relation to Disposable Income, by Income Group, 1988, United States[a,b]

Income Group	Percent of Total Households	Average Number of Persons in Household	Food Expenditures as a Percent of Income[c]
Under $5,000[d]	8.5	1.7	82.1
$5,000–9,999	14.6	1.9	28.2
$10,000–14,999	11.6	2.2	22.5
$15,000–19,999	10.1	2.5	18.4
$20,000–29,999	17.9	2.7	15.3
$30,000–39,999	13.4	2.9	13.3
$40,000–49,999	8.8	3.2	11.9
Over $50,000	15.0	3.1	8.5
Total households	100.0	2.6	13.3

[a] Source: Putnam, 1990a, p. 125.
[b] Data are only for those households reporting at least one major source of income and thus designated as complete income reporters. This classification, however, does not account for possible under reporting of income.
[c] Percentage of income after taxes.
[d] Includes negative incomes.

Income Elasticities

In terms of the relationship between consumption and income, the single statistic that economists give more attention to than any other is income elasticity. Income elasticities reflect the responsiveness of consumption (or expenditure) to changes in income. More technically, the income elasticity gives the percent change in consumption for a 1% change in income.[12] Economists classify goods as luxuries, necessities, or inferior goods on the basis of their income elasticities. The income elasticity of a luxury good is greater than one, for a necessity it is between one and zero, and for an inferior good it is negative. Spending on luxury items rises faster than income, hence they account for a larger share of the budget at higher income levels. Expenditures on necessities increase with income, but more slowly in percentage terms, so that the share of the budget devoted to the item declines. As income rises, expenditures on inferior goods actually decline.

Table 5.3. Share of Per Capita Disposable Income Spent on Food, Beverages, and Tobacco, by Country, 1983[a]

Country	Per Capita Disposable Personal Income ($U.S.)	Food, Tobacco, and Beverages (%)
Switzerland	10,724	24.2
United States	9,935	14.1
Canada	8,510	17.3
Australia	7,812	20.1
Japan	6,915	19.5
France	6,826	19.0
West Germany	6,817	21.8
Norway	6,761	25.0
Belgium	6,515	21.1
Netherlands	6,441	16.6
Finland	5,784	25.0
Sweden	5,762	24.1
Austria	5,521	22.4
United Kingdom	5,218	18.5
Italy[b]	4,751	24.8
Spain[c]	3,762	28.8
Greece	2,933	34.8
Portugal[c]	2,340	27.3
Malta[b]	2,379	37.5
South Africa[b]	1,399	32.6
Korea[b]	1,150	46.7
Columbia[c]	1,080	33.8
Thailand [b]	571	43.2
Philippines[b]	554	51.5
Honduras[b]	475	46.3

[a] Source: Dunham, 1987, p. 31.
[b] 1982 data.
[c] 1981 data.

Table 5.4 gives the income elasticities for major food expenditure categories and is based on an econometric study of the data from the 1980–1981 CCES of the Bureau of Labor Statistics. Most foods, not surprisingly, are treated as necessities, with income elasticities between 0.1 and 0.5. This implies changes in consumption between 1 and 5% for a 10% change in the level of income. The income elasticity of 0.35 for total food implies, for example, that a 10% increase in income is accompanied by a 3.5% rise in spending on food. Food away from home and alcoholic beverages are the most responsive to income changes, with elasticities over 0.5.

A previous study, which analyzed more detailed categories of food products using data from the 1977–1978 Nationwide Food Consumption Survey of the U.S. Department of Agriculture, found a number of inferior

Table 5.4. Income Elasticities for Major Food Categories[a]

Item	Elasticity
Total food	0.35
Food away from home	0.57
Food at home	0.20
Meat, poultry, fish and eggs	0.22
Beef	0.23
Pork	0.16
Other meat	0.19
Poultry	0.11
Fish	0.38
Eggs	0.00
Cereals and bakery products	0.16
Dairy products	0.14
Milk and cream	0.02
Cheese	0.32
Other dairy products	0.21
Fruits	0.19
Fresh	0.19
Processed	0.22
Vegetables	0.24
Fresh	0.24
Processed	0.23
Sugars and sweeteners	0.17
Nonalcoholic beverages	0.13
Fats and oils	0.18
Butter	0.35
Margarine	0.08
Other	0.14
Miscellaneous	0.25
Alcoholic beverages	0.56

[a]Source: Blaylock and Smallwood, 1986, p. 13.

goods. Those foods treated as inferior goods are listed in Table 5.5 with their income elasticities, which are, of course, all negative.

The consumption of food can be measured either in quantities, such as weight in pounds or kilograms or the amount of calories, or in value or expenditure terms, such as dollars. Economists find it useful to distinguish between the responses of quantity and expenditure to income changes. Both quantity-income elasticities and expenditure-income elasticities may be separately calculated. The difference between these two responses reflects the percent change in the average price paid per unit for a product for a 1% change in income and is referred to as the quality-income elasticity.[13] Whether "quality" is the best choice of words is debatable, since it may not necessarily be correlated with price and is a somewhat subjective concept.

For many foods, the quality-income elasticity is substantial. As income rises, the percent increase in expenditure is significantly greater than in quantity for many food items. Consumers do not necessarily want to consume a greater quantity of the product, but they are willing to spend more money to get it in a more processed, convenient form, with more value added and more embodied services, or simply a better tasting product. For example, 50 years ago the per capita consumption of potatoes

Table 5.5. Income Elasticities for Foods that Are Inferior Goods[a]

Item	Elasticity
Dried vegetables	−0.71
Shortening	−0.50
Flour, other than mixes	−0.39
Baby food	−0.36
Variety meat	−0.28
Other cereals	−0.21
Sugars	−0.16
Fresh potatoes	−0.15
Fresh fruit juices	−0.14
Fruit ade beverages	−0.13
Canned vegetables	−0.10
Canned potatoes	−0.09
Processed milk	−0.08
Breakfast cereals	−0.08
Lunch meat	−0.07
Seasonings	−0.07
Fresh eggs	−0.06
Dark green, fresh vegetables	−0.05
Semicondensed soups	−0.05
Leavening agents	−0.05
Jellies, jams, preserves	−0.03
Cooking and salad oil	−0.02

[a]Source: Smallwood and Blaylock, 1981, pp. 12-18.

in the United States, measured in pounds, was much greater than it is today. However, 50 years ago most potatoes consumed were the basic fresh commodity, whereas a substantial portion of the consumption today includes processed, value-added products, such as fast-food french fries or frozen hash browns, as shown in Figure 2.13 in Chapter 2.

From one perspective, virtually the entire increase in food expenditures over the last 75 years or so in the United States reflects a quality-income rather than a quantity-income response. As noted in Chapter 2, the average daily per capita availability of calories in the U.S. food supply has changed very little over a long time. The range has been between 3,100 and 3,500 Calories from 1910 to 1987.[14] This pattern again reflects the limited capacity of the human stomach. However, during this same period, real expenditures on food, after adjustment for the effects of inflation, increased substantially. This means that Americans are spending significantly more per calorie, because they wish to consume a more varied diet, with more convenient and desirable foods.

In studying the Engel relationship, economists debate which is the most appropriate measure of income to use. This discussion has both conceptual and practical dimensions. Some economic studies suggest that consumers make their consumption decisions on the basis of their relative incomes or their permanent incomes, rather than their current household incomes. The relative income hypothesis argues that the major determinant of expenditures is the household's income relative to a prior level in the case of time-series data, or relative to the income of a reference group in the case of cross-sectional data.[15] The latter implies a "keeping up with the Joneses" effect and the former "keeping up" with your own established standard of living.

The permanent income hypothesis argues that consumption decisions are based on a household's long-run expectations with regard to its level of income.[16] Short-term, transitory changes in income do not affect consumption, only changes that are perceived to be permanent. Households can use savings and borrowing to smooth out their expenditures. The concept of permanent income has proved difficult to measure empirically, since it involves expectations. Many economists view a household's total consumer expenditures as representing an approximation of permanent income, and in fact, a better indicator than current income.

From a practical perspective, exactly how income is defined on a survey questionnaire is an important issue. In some, for example, the question concerns income for the last year, in others, the last month. In addition to the problem of misreporting due to simple memory lapse, people are understandably sensitive about responding to questions about their income, and many simply refuse to answer. In general, there is a tendency for income to be under-reported. For these reasons, the best practical alternative may again be to work with the household's total consumer expenditures as an indicator of income.

THE ROLE OF PRICES

Because of the key role played by prices, neoclassical microeconomics, which includes the analysis of consumer behavior, has sometimes been called "the theory of price."[17] Prices, in our essentially free market economy, have a central role in determining what is produced, how it is produced, and for whom it is produced—questions that must be answered by any functioning economic system. Our specific interest here is in the influence of prices on consumer food demand.

Economists distinguish between the overall price level and relative prices, a distinction not always made by the typical person. If the prices of all consumer products were to rise equally, by say 5%, the relationship of different product prices relative to one another would remain unchanged. There would, in truth, be no relative price effect, only an impact on the real purchasing power of consumers' incomes, which would decline by 5% in real terms. However, typically the prices of various products increase at different rates, and some even decline occasionally. For example, if rather than beef and poultry prices each increasing by 5%, the price of one increased by 2.5% and the other by 7.5%, their relative price relationship has changed. One product has become more expensive relative to the other. Price analysis concentrates on the effect of such relative or real price changes, adjusted for the change in the overall rate of inflation.

Food prices, particularly changes in relative prices between substitute products, can have a major impact on consumption patterns. The major shifts that have occurred in the consumption of beef, veal, pork, and poultry can be related to changes in their relative prices, as shown in Table 5.6. The per capita consumption data in Table 5.6 reflect the supply available at the retail level for consumption and are derived using a food balance sheet or disappearance approach (described in Chapter 7). Between 1960 and 1970, poultry prices increased the least, and pork prices increased the most; during that period, poultry consumption rose by 41% while pork consumption changed very little. The price increase for beef was between that of pork and poultry. In line with beef's higher income elasticity (Table 5.4), beef consumption rose by 25% between 1960 and 1970 as real income increased.[18]

During the 1970s, the relative increases in prices for the three products were quite different from those in the preceding decade. Pork, with a lower price increase, became a more attractive buy than beef, and poultry's much smaller price increase made it a much more attractive buy than beef or pork. Partly in reaction to these relative price changes, consumption of beef declined by 10%, pork rose 10%, and poultry increased 25% between 1970 and 1980.

During the five years from 1980 to 1985, the pattern of relative price changes changed again. Although they varied during the period, beef prices stood at the same level in 1985 as in 1980. Pork prices increased by 21% and poultry prices by 13%. Given these price changes, not surprisingly, beef consumption rose by 3 pounds per capita, whereas pork consumption fell by 6 pounds. Poultry consumption, however, increased by another 10 pounds, suggesting that by the 1980s noneconomic factors, such as health concerns and a desire for convenience, were having a major impact on poultry demand.

Some economists believe that all the shifts in red meat and poultry consumption in the United States have been determined by changes in relative prices and real incomes. One group of researchers concluded that "an overwhelming part of the variation in U.S. meat demand can be explained by changes in retail prices and consumer incomes."[19] After taking into account the impact of demographic changes, they stated "the alleged importance of changes in other factors (such as health related concerns) affecting meat demand would appear to be minor," a position they modified by the end of the 1980s.[20]

Other economists disagree with the extreme position. Although price and income effects certainly have had a major impact, some of the shift from red meat to increased poultry consumption must be attributed to health concerns related to red meat and the impact of the myriad brand-name, value-added, convenience-oriented poultry products that have appeared. These and other factors, including demographic characteristics and lifestyle changes discussed in Chapters 3 and 4, have influenced consumers' fundamental preferences.

This debate is important because if the decline in beef consumption has primarily resulted from the effect of prices, then the beef industry

Table 5.6. Meat and Poultry: Annual Per Capita Consumption and Prices, 1960–1985[a]

	Annual Consumption (lb)[b]				Consumer Price Indexes (1960 = 100)[c]			
Foods	1960	1970	1980	1985	1960	1970	1980	1985
Beef and veal	69	87	78	81	100	130	293	293
Pork	60	62	68	62	100	141	255	309
Poultry	34	48	60	70	100	101	178	202

[a]Data from USDA, Economic Research Service, 1981; Putnam, 1989a.
[b]Retail weight.
[c]For ease of comparison, consumer price index figures were recalculated from a 1967 = 100 base to a 1960 = 100 base.

should focus on reducing production and marketing costs to maintain or expand its market. However, if the shifts in consumption are the result of preference changes related to health concerns and lifestyle, the beef industry needs to alter the product. It needs to provide consumers the choice of leaner meat made available in more convenient forms.[21]

Price Elasticities

Economists focus on price elasticity as a statistic that reflects the responsiveness of consumption to price changes. Price elasticities are analogous to income elasticities but relate quantity consumed to price, as opposed to income. More specifically, the own-price elasticity of demand indicates the percent change in demand (quantity consumed) of a product that occurs because of a 1% change in the product's price.[22]

Own-price elasticities should, in most cases, be a negative number. This means that as price rises, consumers do the logical thing and buy less of the product, and when it falls they buy more. Estimated own-price elasticities for food products typically fall between 0 and −1.0, with most between 0 and −0.5.[23] This means that the percent change in consumption is substantially less than the change in price.

Table 5.7 gives the own-price elasticities from a major study that used sophisticated statistical procedures and annual data from 1953 to 1983 for the United States. Out of approximately 40 food items, only 12 items show a substantial change in quantity consumed in reaction to a change in their prices with an elasticity of more than 0.5 in absolute magnitude. Those items are beef and veal, pork, other meats, chicken, turkey, evaporated and dry milk, oranges, grapes, tomatoes, fruit juice, canned peas, and canned fruit cocktail. For example, if beef prices were to double (increase by 100%), beef consumption would fall by 62%, all else remaining unchanged.

The notion of substitutes and complements plays an important role in the economic analysis of food consumption patterns. Consumers quite freely make substitutions among products, such as beef, pork, and poultry, that can play approximately the same role in the diet. Most products are sufficiently different to not be perfect substitutes for one another. Other products, such as spaghetti and tomato sauce, typically are eaten together and function as complements to each other.

The prices of substitutes and complements can affect the consumption of each other. For example, if the price of spaghetti were to rise, it would likely depress not only spaghetti sales, but also the purchase of tomato sauce. On the other hand, as we have seen, if the price of beef rises relative to the price of poultry and pork, this will not only depress beef consumption, but is also likely to increase the sales of poultry and pork. These are referred to as cross-price effects. Economists define cross-price elasticity as the percent change in the consumption of one product when the price of another product changes by 1%. Although somewhat of a simplification, basically cross-price effects are positive between substitutes (beef price goes up, poultry consumption increases) and negative between complements (spaghetti price rises, tomato sauce sales fall). Many products are neither substitutes nor complements, but independent, and the cross-price effect is nil.[24]

Table 5.8 gives the cross-price elasticities for beef and veal, pork, and chicken. The cross-price elasticities are all positive, as expected with substitutes. The largest cross-price elasticities are for the effect of a change in beef or pork prices on chicken consumption. If beef prices were to rise by 10%, for example, chicken demand would increase by 2.9%. Chicken price changes have little effect on beef and pork consumption. The blank spaces in the diagonal would be the own-price elasticities, which were already given in Table 5.7.

Price elasticities such as those derived from aggregate time-series data for the United States reflect the average response of all consumers. The actual responses of specific consumers to the price change of a

Table 5.7. Own-Price Elasticities for Food Categories[a]

Commodity	Elasticity	Commodity	Elasticity
Beef and veal	−0.62	Lettuce	−0.14
Pork	−0.73	Tomatoes	−0.56
Other meats	−1.37	Celery	−0.25
Chicken	−0.53	Onions	−0.20
Turkey	−0.68	Carrots	−0.04
Fresh and frozen fish	0.01	Cabbage	−0.04
Canned and cured fish	0.04	Other fresh vegetables	−0.21
Eggs	−0.15	Fruit juice	−0.56
Cheese	−0.33	Canned tomatoes	−0.38
Fluid milk	−0.26	Canned peas	−0.69
Evaporated and dry milk	−0.83	Canned fruit cocktail	−0.73
Wheat flour	−0.11	Dried beans, peas, and nuts	−0.12
Rice	−0.15	Other processed fruits and vegetables	−0.21
Potatoes	−0.37		
Butter	−0.17	Sugar	−0.05
Margarine	−0.27	Sweeteners	0.00
Other fats and oils	−0.22	Coffee and tea	−0.19
Apples	−0.20	Ice cream and other frozen dairy products	−0.12
Oranges	−1.00		
Bananas	−0.40		
Grapes	−1.38		
Grapefruits	−0.22	Nonfood	−0.99
Other fresh fruit	−0.24		

[a]Source: Huang, 1985.

particular product or a change in their income may vary considerably from these estimates. In particular, research has shown that lower income consumers are typically more responsive to price changes than those with higher incomes.[25] Rosenberger demonstrated, for example, that the price elasticity for milk was substantially higher in absolute magnitude (a larger negative number) for lower income households than for those with higher incomes.[26] This result is consistent with common sense and with economic theory. Higher income households can afford to be less sensitive to price changes; poorer households are under more pressure to look for the best buys.

The Consumer Price Index

The Consumer Price Index (CPI) calculated by the Bureau of Labor Statistics of the Department of Labor provides the most readily accessible data on prices, including those for food. The CPI is a measure of the average change in prices over time for a fixed market basket of goods and services for a representative sample of consumers.[27] The CPI for all items is the most widely used measure of the general rate of inflation in the U.S. economy. In addition, separate indexes are determined for major expenditure categories, such as food, housing, and apparel, and for about 200 detailed items, which include many food products.[28]

Indexes show price changes relative to a designated base or reference period, which is always denoted as 100. The base period for the CPI was changed to 1982-1984 = 100, beginning with the release of data for January 1988. Previously, the base period used for many years was 1967 = 100. In Table 5.9, the CPI for food for 1989 was 125.1. This means that food cost 25.1% more in 1989 than it did in the base period of 1982-1984. Changes in the CPI for a specific food category, such as poultry in Table 5.10, reflect the variation in the price of that product.

The CPI is now available for two representative groups of U.S. consumers. The CPI-W for urban wage earners and clerical workers has been calculated for over a half-century and represents the buying habits of about 32% of the civilian noninstitutional population within

Table 5.8. Cross-Price Elasticities for Beef, Pork, and Chicken[a]

Commodity	A Price Change of 1% in		
	Beef	Pork	Chicken
Percent change in sales of			
Beef and veal	...	0.11	0.06
Pork	0.19	...	0.09
Chicken	0.29	0.26	...

[a]Source: Huang, 1985, p. 46.

the United States. The newer and more widely used CPI-U relates to all urban consumers and represents the expenditure pattern of about 80% of the U.S. civilian population.[29] The expenditure pattern of each of these groups is determined by the CCES of the Bureau of Labor Statistics. This survey collects data on the consumer expenditures of households and is used to determine the goods and services that are included in the CPI market basket as well as the relative importance of each item in terms of its share of total expenditures. The CPI currently reflects the spending patterns in the 1982–1984 CCES. Before that, the 1972–1973 Consumer Expenditure Survey was utilized.[30]

The basic price data used to derive the CPI are collected by sending enumerators out in 91 areas of the country to some 24,000 retail stores and other establishments.[31] The Point-of-Purchase Survey of the Bureau of Labor Statistics, which collects data from about 4,000 households nationwide on where they purchase over 130 categories of items, is used to select and weight the various establishments where price data

Table 5.9. Consumer Price Index for Major Categories, 1966–1989[a,b]

Year	All Items	All Items Less Food	Food	Food at Home	Food Away from Home
1966	32.4	32.3	33.8	35.2	29.7
1967	33.4	33.4	34.0	35.1	31.2
1968	34.8	34.9	35.2	36.2	32.8
1969	36.7	36.8	37.1	38.0	34.8
1970	38.8	39.0	39.2	39.9	37.4
1971	40.5	40.8	40.4	40.8	39.4
1972	41.8	42.0	42.1	42.7	40.9
1973	44.4	43.7	48.2	49.6	44.1
1974	49.3	48.0	55.1	57.0	49.8
1975	53.8	52.5	59.8	61.7	54.4
1976	56.9	56.0	61.6	63.0	58.1
1977	60.6	59.6	65.5	66.8	62.5
1978	65.2	63.9	72.0	73.8	68.2
1979	72.6	71.2	79.9	81.8	75.9
1980	82.4	81.5	86.8	88.3	83.4
1981	90.9	90.4	93.6	94.8	90.9
1982	96.5	96.3	97.4	98.0	95.8
1983	99.6	99.7	99.4	99.1	99.9
1984	103.9	104.0	103.2	102.7	104.2
1985	107.6	108.0	105.6	104.2	108.3
1986	109.6	109.8	109.0	107.3	112.5
1987	113.6	113.6	113.5	111.9	117.0
1988	118.3	118.3	118.2	116.6	121.8
1989	124.0	123.7	125.1	124.2	127.4
Increase from 1966 to 1989, %	282.7	283.0	270.1	252.8	328.9

[a]Data from Putnam, 1989a, pp. 96-97; 1990a, pp. 115-116.
[b]Index for all urban consumers. 1982–1984 = 100.

Table 5.10. Consumer Price Index for Major Food Groups, 1966-1989[a,b]

Year	Meat	Poultry	Fish	Eggs	Dairy Products	Fats and Oils	Fruits and Vegetables		Cereals and Bakery Goods	Sugar and Sweets	Non-alcoholic Beverages
							Fresh	Processed			
1966	38.2	52.4	25.6	62.4	38.3	...	32.2	34.2	33.2	25.7	23.2
1967	37.2	49.0	26.4	52.2	39.9	37.0	32.3	34.0	34.0	26.5	23.1
1968	38.0	50.6	26.9	56.2	41.3	36.6	35.4	35.9	34.1	27.4	23.5
1969	41.5	53.4	28.4	66.1	42.6	36.8	35.9	36.2	35.1	28.9	24.1
1970	43.7	53.2	31.2	65.5	44.7	39.1	37.6	37.1	37.0	30.5	27.0
1971	43.4	53.5	34.4	56.5	46.1	42.7	39.1	39.5	38.7	31.6	28.0
1972	48.1	54.2	37.5	56.2	46.8	43.1	41.4	41.0	39.0	32.0	28.0
1973	59.9	76.0	43.1	83.6	51.1	46.7	48.8	44.3	43.4	34.0	30.0
1974	61.1	72.1	49.7	83.9	60.7	66.3	52.6	58.0	56.5	51.7	35.9
1975	66.2	79.7	53.8	82.3	62.6	73.5	53.7	60.7	62.9	65.3	41.3
1976	66.3	76.4	60.2	89.9	67.7	64.2	55.1	62.3	61.4	57.8	49.4
1977	64.9	76.9	66.6	87.0	69.5	70.8	62.6	64.3	62.4	60.8	74.4
1978	77.0	84.8	72.9	82.3	74.2	77.5	70.7	71.0	68.0	68.3	78.7
1979	90.1	89.1	80.0	90.1	82.7	83.7	76.0	77.2	74.9	73.6	82.6
1980	92.6	93.6	87.5	88.6	90.9	89.2	81.7	82.5	83.8	90.5	91.3
1981	96.0	97.4	94.7	95.8	97.4	98.8	91.6	92.4	92.2	97.6	95.2
1982	100.6	95.7	98.1	93.2	98.7	96.0	96.6	97.4	96.5	97.4	97.9
1983	99.5	96.9	99.3	97.6	99.9	97.3	96.3	98.3	99.5	99.3	99.7
1984	99.8	107.2	102.4	109.0	101.2	106.5	106.9	104.2	103.9	103.1	102.2
1985	98.8	106.2	107.5	90.9	103.1	108.9	109.7	107.0	107.9	105.7	104.2
1986	102.0	114.2	117.4	97.2	103.3	106.5	113.0	105.3	110.9	109.0	110.4
1987	109.6	112.6	129.9	91.5	105.9	108.1	126.8	109.0	114.8	111.0	107.5
1988	112.2	120.7	137.4	93.6	108.4	113.1	136.1	117.6	122.1	114.0	107.5
1989	116.7	132.7	143.6	118.5	115.6	121.2	147.7	125.0	132.4	119.4	111.3
Increase from 1966 to 1989, %	205.5	153.2	460.9	89.9	201.8	227.6[c]	358.7	265.5	298.8	364.6	379.7

[a] Data from Putnam, 1989a, p. 97; 1990a, p. 116.
[b] Index for all urban consumers. 1982-1984 = 100.
[c] Calculated from 1967 through 1989.

are gathered. The selection of specific items in the stores is based on the sales experience of that store in which the item is priced. The average annual retail prices for specific food items collected by the Bureau of Labor Statistics are also made available.[32]

The CPI is published monthly for a number of major cities, for urban areas of various sizes, and as a national city average for the United States.[33] An important point to remember, though, is that an index for a particular city reflects changes over time in that specific area and cannot be used to compare price levels in different locations. For example, the CPI-U for food away from home for December 1988 was 115.3 for Chicago and 118.5 for Detroit. It cannot be inferred from this comparison that food away from home cost more in Detroit than Chicago; only that it had increased more since the base period in the second city than in the first (18.5% vs. 15.3%), because the price level was converted to 100 in 1982–1984 in each city.[34]

Table 5.9 gives the CPI-U indexes with the new base of 1982–1984 = 100 for major categories from 1966 through 1989. The bottom row gives the percent change in price between 1966 and 1989 for each category. For example, the all-items CPI increased by 282.7% between 1966 and 1989. Overall food prices, as reflected in the food CPI, increased by less than this amount. As shown in the last two figures of the bottom row, the price of food at home increased less than the overall rate of inflation, whereas the price of food away from home rose by more than the general inflation rate between 1966 and 1989. This dichotomy reflects the fact that more of the cost of food away from home is attributable to labor costs, and labor costs rose more rapidly than the cost of other factors.

Table 5.10 shows the CPI-U indexes from 1966 through 1989 for major food groups. Again, the bottom row provides the overall increase between 1966 and 1989. The percent changes in the prices of the various categories are strikingly different for several items. The relatively low increase in poultry prices has already been discussed as a factor in the increased consumption of poultry. However, fish prices rose by over 460% and fish consumption increased significantly during this period. In fact, rising consumer demand was a factor driving fish prices up. On the other hand, egg prices rose only 90%, and egg consumption fell. In this case, the declining demand was a factor holding prices down. Fresh fruits and vegetables, sugar and sweets, and nonalcoholic beverages are other categories with above-average price increases and rising per capita consumption (see Chapter 2). Nonalcoholic beverage prices rose by the second largest percentage after fish.

Table 5.11 compares the annual inflation rates for all items and for food based on changes in CPIs. The annual rates are given for 1960 through 1989, and at the bottom of the table the average rates for five-year periods are shown. Over the long run, there is a high correlation between the general inflation rate and increases in food prices. The major factors pushing up food prices are the general inflationary pressures on costs added after the product leaves the farm. Some 75% of the cost of food is added after products leave the farm.[35] Food prices are affected by the costs of processing, transporting, and retailing. The beginning of Chapter 11 provides a more complete discussion of this topic.

Table 5.11. Annual Percent Changes in Consumer Price Index, 1960–1989[a]

	Category	
Year	All Items	Food
1960	1.6	1.0
1961	1.0	1.3
1962	1.1	0.9
1963	1.2	1.4
1964	1.3	1.3
1965	1.7	2.2
1966	2.9	5.0
1967	2.9	0.9
1968	4.2	3.6
1969	5.4	5.1
1970	5.9	5.5
1971	4.3	3.0
1972	3.3	4.3
1973	6.2	14.5
1974	11.0	14.4
1975	9.1	8.5
1976	5.8	3.1
1977	6.5	6.3
1978	7.7	10.0
1979	11.3	10.9
1980	13.5	8.6
1981	10.4	7.9
1982	6.1	4.0
1983	3.2	2.1
1984	4.3	3.8
1985	3.6	2.3
1986	1.9	3.2
1987	3.6	4.1
1988	4.1	4.1
1989	4.8	5.8
1960–1965	1.3	1.4
1965–1970	4.2	4.0
1970–1975	6.8	8.8
1975–1980	8.9	7.7
1980–1985	5.5	4.0

[a]Data from U.S. Department of Commerce, Statistical Abstract, 1988a, p. 445; 1990a, p. 468; and Dunham, 1990, p. 3.

However, since the basis of the food system is agricultural production, food prices retain a unique volatility. Fluctuations in basic commodity prices due to weather and foreign demand can have a dramatic short-term impact, especially on certain food prices. This fact is clearly shown in Table 5.11 in 1973 and 1974, a period of worldwide scarcity for the major grains, when U.S. exports to the Soviet Union and other countries were booming. The general inflation rate was 6.2% in 1973, whereas food prices increased by 14.5%. In 1974, general inflation was 11.0% and food prices rose by 14.4%. The Nixon administration tried price controls and even embargoed the export of soybeans to slow down the price increases.

The general rate of inflation was significantly reduced by the recession in 1981-1982. From 1979 through 1985, the annual increases in food prices were less than the general inflation rate, and food prices were a moderating influence on the overall rate of inflation. When the inflation rate goes over 5-6%, it begins to become a significant public concern. If the drought of 1988 had been repeated in 1989, food prices would have shot up and become a major issue, as they were during 1973-1974. It has been widely assumed that consumers are particularly sensitive to food price increases because food is a necessity and is purchased frequently. Recent research has found, however, that consumers' expectations about the effect of inflation on future well-being are not influenced any more by changes in food prices than in general prices.[36]

GENERAL IMPLICATIONS

This chapter demonstrated how our understanding of consumer food behavior is enriched by both the conceptual framework and empirical evidence provided by economics. Even in a society as wealthy as the United States, income and prices still have a major influence on food consumption patterns. Although the budget share devoted to food in the United States has fallen to a relatively low level when compared with those of most other countries and our own past, food remains a major category of consumer expenditure and one that is purchased more frequently than any other consumer product. Most foods are treated as necessities, which is to say their income elasticities are positive but less than one.

The own-price elasticities for most food commodities are negative but inelastic. The effect of price changes on demand is greater when there are more close substitutes for the product. However, at the level of brand-name products, brand loyalty may reduce the price responsiveness of consumers. Consumers may be willing to pay more for one brand of a particular product because they are convinced, rightly or wrongly, that it has desirable attributes and that quality and price are correlated. Substantial shifts have occurred in the relative prices of various food categories over time as a result of prices increasing at different rates.

There are also limitations to what can be explained by traditional economic analysis. Economics deals with only a subset of the various factors that affect food consumption patterns. When economists place too much faith in the powers of their discipline, claiming that economics can explain virtually all of human behavior, professionals in other disciplines are understandably aggravated. Recent additions to the economic approach, which extend the range of economic explanations, will be discussed in the next chapter. However, even with these more powerful economic tools, much of food consumption behavior remains to be explained by other factors of human behavior and marketing psychology.

Economic analysis is better at explaining aggregate behavior, both in terms of consumers and products. Economics is more effective at providing an understanding of the actions of groups of people, or a typical or "representative" consumer, than a specific individual's behavior. Economic factors generally do quite well at explaining the average level of consumption of a commodity, such as beef, for the entire population of the United States. However, economics cannot explain why one individual consumer eats four times as much beef as another one, yet both have the exact same income, education level, and ethnic background and are similar in terms of other identifiable socioeconomic factors.

Furthermore, economics does a better job of explaining consumer behavior for more aggregate commodities. Economics will better explain the differences between consumers in total food expenditures than in expenditures on dairy products alone. Likewise, the explanation will be more satisfactory for dairy products than for just cheese and better for cheese than for a specific cheese, say blue cheese. Why one individual likes blue cheese or sardines and another would not touch them likely has little to do with economics. Moreover, traditional economic analysis has virtually nothing to say about why a consumer chooses one particular brand of a product rather than another, other than that there might be a price difference that could be a factor. In fact, almost all the empirical work on consumer food demand by economists has been done at a commodity level rather than at the level of brand-name products.

Economics has little to say about the formation of consumer tastes and preferences or why and how they change. Some economists believe that "tastes neither change capriciously nor differ importantly between people."[37] This argument depends heavily on the aggregation of tastes into fundamental human needs and values that endure over the very long run. A list of such factors would include biological motivations, such as hunger and thirst, and also social and psychological factors, such as the desire for a sense of self-worth and belonging.

If less general motivations are considered, one can argue that they are changeable. Some economists believe that the major purpose of the billions of dollars spent each year on advertising consumer goods, including food products, is to influence consumer choices. John Kenneth Galbraith is perhaps the most well known economist who argues that consumer tastes are molded by advertising. "These (advertising and promotional activities) cannot be reconciled with the notion of independently determined desires, for their central function is to create desires—to bring into being wants that previously did not exist."[38]

The stability of tastes over time and their similarity among consumers depends to a large extent on the level at which consumer preferences are specified. There is remarkable constancy in the most basic human needs and wants, such as the need for nourishment and shelter and the desire for good health, love, acceptance, fulfillment, and happiness. On the other hand, preferences for specific consumer products, such as a McDonald's Big Mac, would seem to be quite fluid and malleable. The two economic models introduced in the next chapter specify the desideratum that enter the consumer's utility function at a more basic level than the traditional neoclassical, microeconomic model of the consumer presented in this chapter; hence preferences in that context are less subject to change.

The Food Consumer: New Economic Perspectives

CHAPTER 6

Time has value and its value affects consumers' decisions. Households produce many goods and services for their own consumption. Products are viewed as the sum of their attributes. Information changes consumer choices and welfare. These four important ideas have been incorporated into economic theory, extending its usefulness for explaining and predicting consumer behavior.

The model originally proposed by Gary Becker and called the "new household economics" integrates the concept of household production and the value of time into economic analysis.[1] Kelvin Lancaster's model introduced the idea that products are composed of a bundle of attributes or characteristics. These characteristics, not the good itself, are what satisfy consumer needs and wants.[2] Lancaster's approach seems to be very much in line with the way people in food marketing and product development think about products.

Both of these models have had a major impact on the economic analysis of consumer behavior. In terms of food consumption, the Becker model enhances our understanding of everything from the popularity of microwave ovens to the importance of basic cooking skills. The Lancaster model provides new insights into consumer demands as diverse as the potential market for fat substitutes, such as Simplesse, and the uproar that ensued when Coca-Cola was reformulated, causing the company to bring back old Coke as Coca-Cola Classic three months later.

In recent years more attention has been focused on the importance of information. Since consumers are almost never perfectly informed about the products they purchase and consume, increased information can improve consumer decisions and consumer utility (satisfaction). Acquiring information, however, is a time-consuming, and hence costly, activity. A typical supermarket carries over 30,000 individual products, which suggests that being a fully informed consumer would be an impossible undertaking. Even being a well-informed food consumer is a significant task. Our understanding of consumer behavior, and particularly the impact of advertising, can be enhanced by analyzing the role of information and its acquisition by the consumer.

BECKER'S THEORY:
THE IMPORTANCE OF CONVENIENCE

The traditional economic model of the consumer views people as receiving utility directly from the consumption of the products and services they purchase. In the Becker model, the actual consumables that satisfy human wants and needs are produced in the household by a production process that combines purchased goods with household members' time and household and human capital. A steak dinner prepared and eaten at home provides an example. The raw, uncooked meat purchased at the supermarket does nothing to satisfy our hunger until someone takes the time to cook it, using a broiler, range, or grill and their cooking skills.

Furthermore, it takes time to do the grocery shopping, and probably an automobile (household capital) is needed for transportation to the supermarket. The meat is likely stored in a refrigerator or freezer (household capital). Preparation of the meal also involves preparing other items to accompany the steak, setting the table, and then cleaning up afterward. Even buying a hamburger at a fast-food outlet can be viewed in this context. Time is required for travel and some form of transportation is likely used, such as an automobile, which takes some skill to drive. Again, purchased products are being combined with time and household and human capital to produce the actual meal.

Such activity is similar in many respects to the production process that typically occurs in a factory. Various inputs are combined using capital (equipment and machinery) and labor to produce a product. Each production process can be carried out with various degrees of efficiency. Greater efficiency or productivity yields more output for a given amount of inputs or reduces the inputs required for a given output. The microwave oven can be viewed as a significant efficiency-enhancing technological advance because it can reduce the time, and perhaps the energy, required to cook many foods.

Economists apply the term human capital to the skills and abilities of people. Human capital is much like physical capital (machinery) in that it can be improved through investment (in education and training) and it may deteriorate or become obsolete over time. Human capital affects the quality of the time input and can raise productivity in the household, as well as in the workplace. A skilled cook can produce a more appetizing meal with the same basic ingredients than someone with less training and experience in cooking (less human capital). This also represents an increase in efficiency.

In addition to the traditional monetary budget constraint, which requires that a household's expenditures not exceed the money available to spend, Becker also applied a time constraint. The time constraint simply recognizes that the allocation of household members' time to various activities cannot exceed 24 hours in a day. The basic allocations of time typically considered are work in the labor force, household production activity, and leisure. Additional time categories can be added to these three without changing the basic analytical implications of the model.

Time has an economic value because it is limited. An individual's wage rate is the best practical measure of that person's opportunity cost or value of time. An opportunity cost is what must be foregone by making one choice rather than another. People who choose to work only part time in the labor force, or not at all, are foregoing the wage or salary they could have earned. For those not employed in the labor force, the wages they would be able to earn if employed are considered the relevant opportunity costs of their time. Potential wages are largely dependent on a person's age, education, employment experience, and other factors that affect human capital.[3]

The budget and time constraints are combined into a single "full income" constraint. The household's *full income* equals the sum of any nonlabor income, such as rent or interest payments, and the total time allotment of each household member valued at his or her opportunity cost of time. This full income represents the total resources available to the household and is allocated to leisure, household production activities, and labor force activity. The latter generates *cash income* used by the household to purchase goods and services. Economic theory tells us that to achieve maximum efficiency, a person should allocate time so that its value in different activities is equal, although there may be factors in the "real world" that interfere with this process, such as minimum or maximum hours that one can work per week on a job.

The Impact of Time Costs

With the Becker model, the demand for a particular good is affected not only by its price, the price of other goods, and by the household's income (full income), but also by the value of time. The *full price* of something comprises both the cash expenditures and the time costs to make the item consumable. The full price of a home-cooked dinner includes not just the obvious expense of the purchased ingredients, but also the opportunity cost of the time spent preparing the meal. Likewise, the full price of a fast-food hamburger includes not just the out-of-pocket cost, but the value of a time component. If the nearest fast-food outlet is 50 miles away, the full price of one of their hamburgers would be very high indeed because of the transportation costs and the opportunity cost of the necessary travel time.

If the full price of something is composed of a direct (expenditure) component and an indirect (time) component, a useful distinction can be made between the expenditure intensity and the time intensity of various consumables. The *time intensity* of something can be defined as the ratio of its time costs to its full price and the *expenditure intensity* as the ratio of the direct purchase price to the full price. The two concepts are the inverse of each other. In terms of food, at the most time-intensive, least expenditure-intensive extreme are home-grown products, followed by food prepared from scratch, such as bread baked at home, and then home cooking in which some prepared foods, such as store-bought bread, are used. At the time-saving (expenditure-intensive) end of the spectrum are convenience foods, such as frozen dinner entrees that can be heated in a microwave oven, meals from fast-food outlets or a deli counter, and perhaps the least time-intensive, because little more than a telephone call is required, delivered meals.[4]

Life seems to become steadily more hectic for many Americans. Many feel dollar rich and time poor as real incomes rise, yet the demands on their limited available time escalate.[5] Scarcity is relative; as we become materially more wealthy and the demands on our finite time increase, time becomes relatively more scarce and hence of greater value. A television commercial for cellular telephones showed people driving up to what looked like the drive-through lane at a fast-food outlet. Instead of ordering food, however, they quite desperately tried to buy some time. One person wanted just two hours; another wanted to buy a day. As many good commercials probably do, this one may have struck a responsive chord in many people.

As discussed in Chapters 1 and 3, the labor force participation rate for women now is well over 50%, and over 70% for married women 35–44 years old. The time pressures on these women are enormous because they not only work in the labor force but continue to do most of the work inside the home (household production activity), particularly the cooking and food shopping. Given this environment, it is easy to understand why three-fourths or more of the households in the United States own a microwave oven and why convenience has become an increasingly important attribute for food products.

Fast Food and Convenience Food

The impact of the value of time on various aspects of food consumption has been studied extensively. These studies have found strong evidence indicating that as the value of time rises, particularly for women, households consume more food away from home, especially fast food, and demand more convenience in the food consumed at home.[6] Potential wages or earnings in these studies were estimated based on factors such as age and education and used as a measure of the opportunity cost (value) of time. Prochaska and Shrimper reported that expenditures on food away from home rose from 1.8 to 5.9% (depending on the region of the country) for urban households when the potential wage of the employed female household head rose by 10%.[7] Others found that an increase in the value of the food manager's time (typically the female household head) increased fast-food and other commercial away-from-home expenditures more than traditional restaurant expenditures.[8] These results should not be surprising, since many sit-down restaurant meals may take more time than cooking at home and are generally far more expensive.

Hull, Capps, and Havlicek looked at different types of households and convenience food.[9] They found that where married women were full-time homemakers, the higher the value of their time, based on their potential wage in the labor force, the more the household spent on convenience food. When the primary meal preparer was an employed woman, expenditures on complex and manufactured convenience foods rose as her wage rose. Complex convenience foods were defined as multiple-ingredient, highly prepared foods, such as bakery products. Manufactured convenience foods, such as carbonated soft drinks, have no home-prepared counterpart.

LANCASTER'S MODEL: FOODS AS BUNDLES OF CHARACTERISTICS

Lancaster's approach to consumer theory was originally referred to as the technology of consumption.[10] A more appropriate name is probably the attributes or characteristics approach. He saw products as containing basic characteristics or attributes that satisfy consumer needs and wants. Consumers aim to attain the attributes they most desire, given their personal tastes and preferences. The demand for products is derived from the demand for attributes. The technology of consumption treats goods as inputs and attributes as outputs. A single good may, and probably will, have more than one attribute and that attribute can typically be obtained from more than one good.

A fresh apple, for example, has certain nutritional and sensory attributes. The nutrient content of an apple could be determined in the laboratory by food scientists. The nutrient composition of most foods, for at least the major nutrients, are readily available.[11] The sensory attributes are probably more important to most consumers and include color, texture, flavor (taste and aroma), temperature, and overall appearance. Lancaster saw the relationship between goods and attributes as an objective, not a subjective one. This means that although one person likes a tart apple and the other likes a sweet one, they could agree on whether a particular apple was tart or sweet. A purely objective way to establish the relative tartness or sweetness of an apple would be to measure the pH level and sugar content in laboratory tests. A product may also have a unique attribute found in no other product, which might be termed "appleness," for example.

This model has several important implications that enhance our understanding of consumer behavior. First, improvements in the technology of consumption can occur if more of the desired output (attributes) can be obtained from the same input (goods). An example would be food preservation or cooking techniques that preserve more of a food's nutrients and sensory qualities. Second, if consumers are misinformed about the attribute content of products, their consumption pattern may be inefficient. With the same expenditure, they would be able to obtain more of the desired attributes if they were better informed. A person who has been told by a physician to go on a low-fat and low-cholesterol diet will not be very effective at achieving this goal without accurate knowledge of the nutrient composition of foods. More generally, the Lancaster model emphasizes the importance of consumer information, and in particular provides a theoretical justification for the ingredient and nutrition labeling of food products.

Third, Lancaster's model provides a framework for evaluating the demand for new consumer goods. The traditional economic theory of the consumer is virtually worthless for analyzing the potential demand for a new product, since it has not previously entered consumers' preferences (utility functions). A new food product can now be viewed as a bundle of attributes of which most, if not all, are shared with existing products. Products are new in the sense that they contain new combinations of attributes, but consumers already have well-formed preferences in relation to basic attributes.

Attributes and Food Products

The concept of attributes plays an important role in product development and marketing.[12] An attempt is made to identify those attributes most desired by consumers and embody them in products. As convenience has become an increasingly important product characteristic for many consumers, more and more food products are developed and marketed that stress this attribute. However, consumers do not want to sacrifice taste and other sensory attributes in order to gain convenience. The goal, therefore, is to develop products that are less work to prepare, which now typically means microwavable, and also preserve the other desired attributes of the original product. A recent television ad for a new fast-cooking rice exemplified this idea. The ad claimed that the new rice cooked in only five minutes, but tasted, and even "fluffed," just like the rice that took 20 minutes to cook.

This desire of consumers to have only a few, or even a single, attribute modified without changing other product characteristics poses a challenge to food scientists. For example, consumers want the low-calorie version of a product to taste just like the original. One of the reasons that the sales of low-sodium products have been held back is because they unavoidably taste different from the original product, which contains more salt. The potential market for fat substitutes, such as Simplesse and Olestra, will probably be enormous if they can be incorporated into products without altering the sensory characteristics.

Products are developed with certain characteristics and then marketed by emphasizing those attributes to appeal to specific market segments. Products can be categorized by their various attributes or characteristics.[13] Various combinations of attributes can be thought of as creating a product space or niche; this space may be occupied by a product or remain empty. Figure 6.1 shows four product spaces for fluid milk based on fat content. At one time, all but the whole milk space were empty, but each niche now is filled with a product to appeal to a different market segment.

In Figure 6.1, the product space is defined by only one attribute, fat content, and is, therefore, one-dimensional. Figure 6.2 shows how two attributes create two dimensions that result in four product spaces.[14] For example, product D would be a caffeine-free, diet cola. Most product spaces will have several dimensions, depending on the number of important attributes to consider. Product spaces are filled when

	Whole Milk	2% Fat	1% Fat	Skim Milk

Figure 6.1. Product spaces for fluid milk based on fat content.

	Regular	Caffeine-Free
Regular	A	B
Diet	C	D

Figure 6.2. Two-dimensional product spaces for cola drinks.

companies judge that there is a market segment to which the product will appeal that will generate a sufficient demand for the product to be profitable.

Attributes are used to compete for market share and to differentiate the products of one producer from those of other producers. Regular Pepsi, for example, traditionally had a slightly sweeter taste than regular Coca-Cola (now Classic). The major reason Coca-Cola reformulated its flagship product in 1985 was to better compete with the sweeter-tasting Pepsi.[15]

Product proliferation is one result when companies move to fill product spaces. Given the competitive environment of the food industry, if a company does not introduce a product to fill an empty space, a competitor likely will. A firm that has a successful product with a large market share will want to develop products to fill adjacent niches for the following reasons: 1) to appeal to new consumers (different market segments), 2) to leave fewer spaces open for competitors to fill, 3) to gain economies of scale from advertising and promoting the brand name, and 4) to expand the retail shelf space occupied by its products, leaving less space for competitors.[16]

Extending a product line by altering one or more product attributes typically can be done at substantially less cost and less risk of failure than developing and marketing a totally new product. These forces help explain the enormous proliferation of products with only minor attribute differences that has occurred in product lines such as soft drinks and breakfast cereals.

Product attributes are not necessarily all physical but may also be psychological. One goal of advertising and sales promotion is to create a certain brand image to enhance the differentiation of a product from its competitors.[17] The development of a brand image is typically based on the physical attributes of the product and beyond that attempts to create a particular perception of the product that will embody certain psychological attributes. The importance of psychological characteristics is particularly evident in the television advertisements for many products.

Sometimes a company may be more successful at creating brand identity than it realizes. Again, the reformulation of Coca-Cola in 1985 provides a vivid example. Within three months, Coca-Cola decided to reintroduce the old formula, calling it Coca-Cola Classic, while still keeping the new sweeter Coke on the market.[18] Although taste testing had indicated that more consumers preferred the sweeter cola flavor, Coca-Cola overlooked the powerful psychological aspects of the brand image they had created. Coca-Cola has one of the strongest brand images of any consumer product in history, which has generated an extremely strong product loyalty among consumers.

Hedonic Prices: Valuing Attributes

Fred Waugh was probably the first economist to notice that there is a measurable relationship between the price of a product and its characteristics or attributes.[19] He observed that the retail price of fresh vegetables varies with the physical attributes consumers associate with product quality. For example, the price of a bunch of asparagus is affected by factors such as the number and size of the stalks and the proportion of each stalk that is dark green, an indication of tenderness when cooked.

The concept of a relation between a product's price and its characteristics has evolved into what economists call the hedonic price model. This model can be used to estimate the value consumers place on an additional unit of a particular attribute. Hedonic price models have been widely applied to everything from automobiles to breakfast cereals. One study estimated the marginal value consumers place on 16 different nutrients based on the retail prices and nutrient composition of 31 food products, mostly meat and dairy products.[20] The results suggested that consumers placed a value of 1.7 cents on an additional gram of protein, for example. Suppose two products had exactly the same nutrient composition, except one contained 10 more grams of protein per pound. Consumers would be willing to pay 17 cents a pound more for the higher protein product.[21] A major problem with valuing nutrient content is that most consumers focus on nonnutrient characteristics, such as convenience and sensory attributes, and have only a vague notion of the nutrient composition of food products.

Other researchers have introduced nonnutrient characteristics into hedonic analyses. One study of breakfast cereals included such factors as the package size, the type of processing (flaked, shredded, granulated, etc.), the class of cereal (traditional, "kids' stuff," and high nutrition), whether the cereal was ready-to-eat or required cooking, and the type of grain (corn, wheat, oats, etc.).[22] They found, for example, that if two traditional cereals had exactly the same characteristics, but one was made from rice and the other another grain, consumers would be willing to pay more for the rice cereal. For "kids' stuff" cereal, a higher value was placed on mixed grains than single-grain products.[23]

In this study, which used data from 1972 through 1976, fiber content was treated as a negative factor, which reduced a product's value. This would almost certainly not be true today. Consumers have been bombarded with advertisements and other information stressing the importance of dietary fiber and the high fiber content of many breakfast cereals. This points out that the relative importance consumers place on different product characteristics can change substantially over time and that different consumers will value various attributes differently.

BEING INFORMED: VALUABLE BUT COSTLY

Information is valuable but costly to acquire. With improved information, consumers can better match product characteristics with the attributes they desire and thus gain more utility with the same dollar expenditures. With more complete knowledge of the prices of a particular product at different retail outlets, and the trade-off between price and quality among items in a product group, such as frozen dinner entrees, consumers may save money without sacrificing satisfaction or increase their utility without spending additional money.

On the other hand, the collection and evaluation of information, which economists refer to simply as information search, is costly. To become useful for decision making, the relevant data or raw information must be sought out, mentally evaluated, and retained by the consumer. More specifically, the information search and consumer decision-making process can be broken into several stages: 1) recognizing a need for information, 2) seeking out relevant information, 3) evaluating the information, 4) making a purchase decision, and 5) evaluating the product after its purchase and use.[24]

Information Search

The primary cost of the search for information is the consumer's time. In fact, consumer information can be thought of as a household (consumer)-produced commodity. The major inputs required to produce information are time, human capital (prior knowledge), information sources (either free or purchased), and transportation costs, if the products must be evaluated by visiting various stores in person to collect reliable information. An information search process is not necessarily as overt or well organized as this may sound. In only rare cases would a consumer decide to specifically allocate a certain amount of time to the information search for a particular product, such as a new refrigerator or new car. More typically, information search occurs in conjunction with some other activity, such as reading the newspaper and glancing at the advertisements, watching the unavoidable commercials on television, or grocery shopping and seeing a new product by chance.

What determines how much information consumers should or do collect? George Stigler, who went on to win a Nobel Prize in economics, wrote a key paper on this topic.[25] He said consumers should gather additional information up to the point where the cost of acquiring the information equals the expected value of the additional information. The value is measured in terms of the expected reduction in price from the search for a lower price, or in terms of increased utility (satisfaction) from other product characteristics. Like all economic decisions, it is a matter of balancing benefits and costs. If the expected returns exceed the costs, more information would be economical; if the reverse, too much has been invested in information search.

Factors that raise the value of information or lower the cost of acquiring it will increase the amount of information it is economically efficient to acquire. The higher the price of a product, the longer its durability, or the larger the quantity to be purchased, the greater is the value of information. This helps explain why someone grocery shopping for a family of six is more likely to seek out bargains than a person buying for a one- or two-person household. Furthermore, as the budget share for food becomes as small as it is for many American families, shoppers become less concerned with searching for better food buys. The returns on information are also affected by the amount of variation in price and quality among products and retail outlets. If every grocery store in a metropolitan area sold a particular product for the exact same price, there would be no return associated with a search for a lower price.

If information search is thought of as a production process, the efficiency of that process may be improved by education or experience (human capital). With increased education, the cost of search should decrease because "information can be assimilated more quickly and more accurately."[26] A positive correlation has been observed between educational level and the prepurchase search for information for specific goods.[27] However, higher educational levels are usually associated with higher incomes, which have an offsetting effect. Higher incomes raise the opportunity cost of time, which could offset and might override the increased efficiency of information search.[28]

Relevant experience should also increase the efficiency of the search by reducing the time required to obtain information. Most people can do their weekly grocery shopping much more quickly at a supermarket where they have shopped many times before than at an unfamiliar store where they never, or only occasionally, shop. In one, shoppers know where most of the items they wish to purchase are located; in the other, they may spend a great deal of time looking for products. This explains why most consumers do not switch grocery stores readily.[29]

An important aspect of information is that knowledge tends to become obsolete. The store with the best buy on a product this week may not be the same as last week. The most economical place for a particular family to grocery shop may differ from month to month. In addition, new products are continually introduced and the attributes of existing products change. This creates a need for a continuous search for information.

Those who advocate that the solution to a particular consumer problem is simply more or better information are being naive. People simply do not have the time to become as well-informed as they might like or as some would advocate they ought to be. If the policy objective is to raise the level of public knowledge about a product or consumer issue, the way to achieve that goal is to increase the perceived benefits or value of the information or to decrease the costs of acquiring information.

For example, most people are much better informed now concerning the link between diet and health and how they might improve their diets than they were a few years ago. This has occurred because people have come to perceive a high return associated with such information, since the public has repeatedly heard authoritative sources stress the role of diet in major chronic diseases. At the same time, the costs of becoming better informed have been greatly reduced. The basic information concerning desirable dietary changes (such as decreased fat consumption), have been widely and repeatedly disseminated in the mass media, so that public awareness has become almost unavoidable. By 1989, the Food Marketing Institute found in its annual survey that 58% of consumers considered fats a serious health hazard and another 38% something of a hazard. As recently as 1985, only 42% considered fats a serious health hazard.[30]

Information Overload

Terms such as "information overload," "information anxiety," and "overchoice" have begun to be used to describe the situation faced by consumers. A recent Soviet immigrant to the United States was quoted as saying, "In Russia, you stand in line for half an hour to buy beer. Then you have one choice, if they have beer that day. Here, you spend 30 minutes deciding which beer to buy."[31] The grocery shopper walking down the aisles of an American supermarket is confronted by a bewildering array of product alternatives to choose from. "Product proliferation exacerbates the costs of gathering information on numerous market alternatives."[32] Some consumers are overwhelmed by so many choices and, consequently, find shopping very stressful.[33]

Most consumers deal with this situation by resorting to what Linder referred to as "the rationale of growing irrationality" to conserve their time and perhaps their sanity.[34] To make rational use of time, consumers resort to making seemingly "irrational" decisions that are not as well-informed or carefully considered as might seem desirable. Anyone who spent the time to carefully consider all the alternatives before picking each and every item for the grocery cart would be in the supermarket for hours, if not all day. To avoid the time needed to make "rational" or well-informed decisions, many consumers rely on habits (buying what they have before), visceral or gut reactions, or other simple rules of thumb. Many consumers rely on brand name, for example, as a signal or clue to given product attributes or quality.[35] A signal or clue is any single piece of information that helps predict other information.

If consumers become overloaded with too much information, decisions may be worse than with less information. Consumers are forced to try to filter masses of data to extract the important information but risk overlooking significant factors.[36] Our ability to acquire information is limited by our mental processing and retention ability, the technical knowledge increasingly required to evaluate the information, and the time required.[37] Many consumer products today are sufficiently complex that considerable technical expertise is required to evaluate them. Ingredient lists on food labels for many processed foods contain chemical names that the average consumer has never heard of, for example. They represent data that cannot be processed into information by most consumers.

Information and Food Products

Three types of goods have been identified on the basis of when information about them is best gathered: search goods, experience goods, and credence goods.[38] Consumers can access the quality or attributes of a *search good* before purchase. For example, consumers will typically conduct a substantial information search before purchasing a major durable good, like a refrigerator. Information about the attributes of an *experience good* cannot be accessed until the product is actually used. Experience goods are usually relatively inexpensive products that are purchased frequently. Consumers are unable to evaluate the quality or attributes of *credence goods* even after they are consumed. Therefore, they must rely on product claims made by others.

Food is basically an experience good. There is ultimately no substitute for actually tasting (experiencing) the product. Most advertising for new food products is directed toward persuading the consumer to try the product.[39] This factor also helps explain the widespread use of free samples in supermarkets, particularly to promote new products.

However, many goods, including food, frequently have properties associated with all three categories—search, experience, and credence. Consumers typically know a considerable amount about a food product, even a new product, before they purchase it. They know of its existence; they can see its appearance, and they likely know something about its ingredients and its price before making a purchase. As such, food is a search good.

In addition, food also contains some of the properties of a credence good. Even after eating a particular food product, consumers will probably not be able to fully access all its attributes. The consumer has to depend on experts to evaluate the nutritional and health effects. For example, consumers cannot detect the presence of possible carcinogens nor evaluate their long-term impact on health. Consumers who buy organic produce generally have to simply trust that they are, in fact, buying what is claimed.

Information search and product choice are somewhat different for food than they are for most other consumer goods. Because groceries are bought frequently and many small individual items are usually purchased, grocery shopping tends to conform to repetitive buying patterns.[40] In addition, food purchases obviously reflect a household's underlying food consumption habits, which typically change slowly. For these reasons, most food consumers may engage in little information search immediately before purchase, such as reading ingredient and nutrient labels, but instead rely on "the accumulation of knowledge over time from a myriad of information sources, including experience."[41]

Some studies suggest that nearly half of supermarket purchases result from impulse decisions, with the figure as high as 60% for some categories, such as frozen foods.[42] However, these estimates may represent a significant overestimate depending on the definition of impulse purchasing utilized. There are four types of impulse decisions: 1) pure impulse, which breaks a normal buying pattern; 2) reminder impulse, in which an in-store stimulus reminds the shopper of a product need; 3) suggestive impulse, when the shopper sees a product for the first time and wants it; and 4) planned impulse, when the consumer deliberately makes in-store decisions to take advantage of price discounts, coupons, and specials.[43]

Some shoppers make quite complete grocery shopping lists. Others may use only partial lists for infrequently purchased items they might otherwise forget or not write a list at all. However, that does not mean food purchases not on a grocery list are actually unplanned, particularly in the sense of impulse purchase categories 1 and 3.

Because of the limitations of consumer information search, particularly concerning "credence" attributes, the government has intervened in many circumstances to establish product standards called *standards of identity,* which set specific performance, ingredient, processing, and quality requirements for food.[44] The U.S. Food and Drug Administration (FDA) is responsible for insuring the safety of all foods and drugs except meat, fish, poultry, and their products, which are the responsibility of the U.S. Department of Agriculture. Both agencies use standards of identity and inspection programs to keep unsafe products from being marketed. Consumers do not have the technical capability to assure the safety of their food anymore.

Labeling

Ingredient and nutrition labeling were controversial topics in the 1970s and now have become so again. The food industry argues that labeling regulations would be too costly, and consumer advocates argue that they would be a great boon to making nutritionally sound, healthy food choices. Regulations established in 1973 by the FDA established a largely voluntary system for nutrition labeling. Ingredient labeling was required when a product did not have a standard of identity, unless it was required in the standard. Nutrition labeling was voluntary unless the product was enriched or fortified or made a nutritional claim.[45]

Subsequent studies found that most consumers did not regularly read the ingredient and nutrition labels while grocery shopping.[46] In the Food Marketing Institute's 1990 survey of food shoppers, 36% reported always reading the ingredient and nutrition labels when buying packaged foods. Another 45% said they sometimes read the nutrition labels, and 49% reported always reading the label for information on ingredients and nutrition when buying the product for the first time. Over 70% said they always check the expiration date.[47]

Consumers typically use a broad array of food and nutrition information sources; to look only at how often they read labels before purchasing is too narrow a focus. The use of label information can also occur after purchase. For example, more than a few of us have probably read the information on a cereal box label while we ate a bowl of cereal in the morning. Such postpurchase information can be important because of its possible effect on future food purchases.

In addition, other benefits may be generated by mandatory ingredient and nutrition labeling. Nutrition labeling, even if not directly used by consumers, may nevertheless encourage the production of more nutritious products, increase consumer confidence in the quality of food and in the food industry, and satisfy the consumer's right to know.[48] These nonuse benefits may explain why consumers indicate a strong desire for information when questioned in surveys, even if they do not regularly use the information in making purchases.[49]

Nutrition labeling became a hotly debated topic again in the late 1980s, along with the issue of health claims. The report on nutrition labeling by the National Academy of Sciences and the Nutrition Labeling and Education Act of 1990 were discussed in Chapter 2. In addition, the FDA introduced a sweeping set of newly proposed regulations to govern food labeling in 1990 that would generally require mandatory nutrition labeling. Nutritional labels would be required on every packaged food product that is a "meaningful source of calories." Food sold by restaurants, bakeries, and other small businesses would be excluded, as would spices and bite-size foods. However, supermarkets would need to make nutritional information available for fresh produce and seafood by such means as posting labels or distributing booklets to shoppers.[50]

The new labeling regulations would require that information be included on the levels of cholesterol, saturated fat, and dietary fiber per serving, and also the calories from fat. With these four additions, the need to provide nutritional information on thiamin, riboflavin, niacin, and one of the two protein listings would be dropped. The intention is to give more attention to nutrients and other food components that have been linked to chronic diseases and less to those associated with particular nutritional deficiencies, which are increasingly rare in the United States. Strict new definitions would be established for such claims as "cholesterol-free," "low cholesterol," or "reduced cholesterol." Cholesterol-free could be used only if the product contained fewer than two milligrams of cholesterol per serving, fewer than five grams of total fat, and fewer than two grams of saturated fat per serving. The proposals would also create definitions for standardized serving sizes for many food products. In the past, food companies have been able to set whatever serving sizes they chose on food labels.

The proposed regulations also allow for the display of a second label or "nutritional profile" below the required label. This profile would be optional because not all food packages would have room for it. The nutritional profile would give the percentage of the daily values recommended for consumption of certain nutrients and food components contained in a serving. See Chapter 2 for details on the nutrient values for the Reference Daily Intakes (RDIs) and Daily Reference Values (DRVs) to be used as the basis for the percentages on the labels. The label would have to include information on fat, saturated fat, cholesterol, carbohydrates, fiber, and sodium.[51]

Earlier, the FDA set off a lively debate when it proposed ending its policy prohibiting food companies from making health claims concerning their products on package labels.[52] Instead, the FDA would establish guidelines for regulating the content of health messages. The information on the label would have to be truthful and not misleading, based on valid scientific evidence, and consistent with generally recognized nutritional principles.[53] These guidelines could easily be open to sharply different interpretations, though.

A carefully worded message by the Kellogg Company concerning the possible health benefits of its bran cereals prompted the FDA to reconsider its long-standing policy against health claims. The message pointed out that a high-fiber, low-fat diet might reduce the risk of some kinds of cancer and that bran cereals are high in fiber. The FDA's proposed policy revision may be viewed as opening an important new avenue for educating the public about nutrition and health issues.

However, the policy may also be quite susceptible to misuse. For example, when some studies, but not others, found oat bran could lower blood cholesterol levels, it became a very "hot" food-marketing tool. More and more product labels featured prominent statements that they contained oat bran. However, nutritionists pointed out that the amount contained in many products was too little to have a significant impact on blood cholesterol levels and that oat bran could not make food, which for example might be very high in saturated fat, healthful.[54]

Price Information

The value of information can be most directly measured for product prices. The prices of specific consumer products frequently vary considerably from store to store, even within fairly small geographic areas. In this situation, the return on information gained by shopping around is the reduction in the price paid for the product.

Table 6.1 shows the variation in price for certain food products among seven grocery stores in the Minneapolis–St. Paul metropolitan area. For several years, Elaine Asp has collected comparative price data on the ingredients of a traditional Thanksgiving dinner for a local television station. Prices of 28 different products were collected in 1988, although only seven are shown in Table 6.1. The last row in the table gives the price of the entire market basket of 28 items for each store. Store A is an upscale superstore and store B an upscale supermarket. Stores C and D are conventional supermarkets. Stores E, F, and G are warehouse or super warehouse stores. These store definitions are discussed in Chapter 11.

Table 6.1. Price Variation for Thanksgiving Dinner Grocery Products[a] (Dollars per Unit)

Product	Grocery Store							Average
	A	B	C	D	E	F	G	
Butterball turkey (14 lb)	18.06	16.66	15.26	13.86	13.86	13.72	13.72	15.02
Land O Lakes butter (1 lb)	2.15	2.19	2.09	1.99	1.85	1.84	1.84	1.99
Potatoes (5 lb)	1.69	1.59	1.59	1.59	1.49	1.39	1.18	1.55
Celery (1 stalk)	0.99	0.69	0.79	0.79	0.79	0.69	0.69	0.78
2% milk (1/2 gal.)	0.99	0.99	1.00	1.02	1.02	0.99	0.99	1.00
Stove Top Stuffing	1.16	1.23	0.99	1.19	0.99	0.99	0.99	1.08
Cool Whip	1.06	1.15	1.09	0.79	0.87	0.87	0.79	0.95
Total for 28 products	52.98	51.49	50.81	47.68	44.28	43.11	42.57	47.56

[a] All grocery stores were located in the Minneapolis–St. Paul metropolitan area. Prices were collected in October 1988.

The product with the least price variation was milk, with a range of only $0.99–1.02 per half gallon. The dispersion in prices is considerably greater for most of the other products, particularly the more highly processed, brand-name products. Stove Top Stuffing prices ranged from $0.99 to $1.23 and Cool Whip varied from $0.79 to $1.15. Most products cost least in the warehouse stores and most in the upscale stores, as might be expected. The total cost of the 28 items for Thanksgiving dinner varied from $42.57 at one warehouse store to $52.98 at the upscale superstore.

Table 6.2 shows the variation in price for several products at two fast-food chains at three different locations in the Minneapolis–St. Paul metropolitan area. The price variation among these products is probably greater than most people would imagine for items being sold by the same fast-food chain and which are so highly standardized.

In one sense, price dispersion is a reflection of ignorance on the part of consumers.[55] If consumers were fully informed, they would all buy at the store with the lowest price, assuming that the product is completely homogeneous (exactly identical) and transportation costs are equal. The end result would be a single price for a product at all the retail outlets in a given market area.

However, even for the completely standardized products in Tables 6.1 and 6.2, absolute homogeneity (similarity) does not exist if the location and characteristics of the retail establishment are included. A hamburger selling for $1.65 at a fast-food outlet only three blocks from your home and one for $1.45 at an outlet three miles away are differentiated by location. The more expensive one is the more economical purchase because of the reduced transportation and time costs.

The identical product purchased at two different stores may also be differentiated by the characteristics of the stores themselves. For example, warehouse stores usually provide fewer services than conventional

Table 6.2. Price Variation for Fast-Food Products[a] (Dollars per Unit)

Product	Store			Average
	1	2	3	
Fast-food chain A				
Regular hamburger	0.63	0.72	0.68	0.68
French fries	0.61	0.59	0.61	0.60
Milk shake	0.90	0.85	0.85	0.87
Fast-food chain B				
Regular hamburger	0.65	0.62	0.68	0.65
French fries	0.61	0.56	0.63	0.60
Milk shake	0.85	0.79	0.94	0.86

[a]The fast-food outlets were within a few miles of each other in the Minneapolis–St. Paul metropolitan area. Prices were collected in March 1988.

supermarkets and certainly fewer than most upscale markets. Many grocery shoppers are quite willing to pay more for the same products if they receive more service and do not, for example, have to bag and carry out their own groceries.

Several studies by economists have published comparative price information for supermarkets in a specific area in the local newspaper(s). The effect on price level and dispersion were then measured. One study, which used the metropolitan areas of Ottawa-Hull in Canada as the test city and Winnipeg as the control, found that average prices fell, price dispersion among stores was reduced, and consumer satisfaction improved.[56]

In another study in four U.S. cities, the average cost of the market basket declined relative to costs in the control cities while prices were being published, but the dispersion of prices was not affected. Although consumers felt the information was reliable and useful, they did not change their store patronage.[57] In both projects, consumers were able to easily obtain comparative price information from the newspaper, which otherwise would have entailed an expensive, time-consuming information search; thus, the cost of the information search was substantially reduced.

Advertising

Advertising both informs and attempts to persuade consumers.[58] Some types of advertising have more information, whereas others have a stronger persuasive message. Newspaper and in-store advertisements by grocery stores typically focus on providing information. They tend to concentrate on product specials and price discounts. On the other hand, the television advertising of brand-name, manufactured food products typically has a largely persuasive message. Because of the "experience good" nature of food, the aim of much food advertising is to persuade the consumer to try (experience) the product.

Americans are exposed to such an enormous volume of advertising, it is easy for them to become cynical about its lack of informational content. However, even advertisements that are almost totally persuasive in their orientation usually supply some useful information. If nothing else, advertising serves to identify potential sellers (stores) and product alternatives. It is frequently through advertising that consumers become aware of new products, and given the thousands of new food products introduced annually, this represents a useful function.

Advertising expenditures in the food marketing system reached record levels of $11.5 billion in 1988.[59] Food processors are the largest advertisers in the United States, generating more than 20% of all direct consumer advertising. In 1987, food processors spent $5.4 billion on advertising in seven media. Breakfast cereals are the most advertised product in the United States. Television advertising, at $4.3 billion, amounted to 83% of all advertising expenditures by food processors.[60] Food industry advertising is further discussed in Chapter 11.

Because television viewing is a particularly passive activity requiring little involvement, viewers become passive recipients of advertising messages. Television advertisements need to be repeated frequently because of the low viewer involvement.[61] Most television advertisements for food products and other consumer goods have little factual information. They frequently attempt to relate the product to "the fulfillment of basic human needs, such as love, acceptance and happiness."[62] The desired result is to cause a subconscious change in viewers' attitudes that ultimately affects their purchase decisions.

The effectiveness of food advertising may be overestimated. Most people are quite skeptical of the claims made in food advertisements. Only 16% of the respondents in a survey by Consumer Network, Inc., a research firm, said food advertisements were "very honest," whereas 52% called them "somewhat honest" or "dishonest." The most frequent complaints concerned nutritional information that is misleading, claims that exaggerate the good taste and ease of preparation, and overuse of words such as "new" and "improved." Some people gave as examples advertisements that stress a cereal's high fiber content but do not mention the product's sugar or salt content, or advertisements for cooking oil that focus on the health benefits of reduced cholesterol but then show a high-fat product like fried chicken. One consumer said that "food ads are sneaky . . . they use words so as not to lie, but to deceive."[63]

The Federal Trade Commission is charged with maintaining certain standards in advertising. The commission is supposed to prevent false or deceptive advertising and may require advertisers to document any claims they make.[64] However, some would argue that the interpretation and enforcement of these standards has become quite lax. The situation with regard to advertising might still be typified as one of "caveat emptor," which translates from Latin as "let the buyer beware" and means that consumers need to protect themselves from the unscrupulous.

Some recent research suggests that the impact of television advertising, in particular, may be overestimated. Gerard Tellis, a University of Iowa professor, used television meters and store scanner data to track the TV watching and purchases of a 200-person sample in the city of Eau Claire, Wisconsin. He found that, for the two consumer products studied, television advertisement had "a very minimal effect on purchases."[65] In-store displays and coupons did have a major impact on consumer purchases. However, this research must be extended to larger samples and other products, and be duplicated by other researchers, before its conclusions can be fully accepted.

Advertising raises the issue of the malleability of consumer tastes again and the concept of consumer sovereignty. Consumer sovereignty is the notion that consumers freely choose what products they buy and hence what is produced. However, advertising and other promotional techniques may allow producers to influence consumers to want what they have chosen to produce.[66]

GENERAL IMPLICATIONS

This chapter has explored the economics of household production, the value of time, product attributes, and information. Each of these factors affects the decisions of food consumers. In particular, Becker's model of the household and time allocation provides a theoretical framework that can help explain the growing importance of convenience in food products.

Food products are being viewed as bundles of attributes or characteristics by processors and marketers, and most importantly, by consumers themselves. The desire for convenience relates to an attribute. Most consumers would like the sensory characteristics of a product to remain unchanged while it becomes quicker and easier to prepare. They do not want the microwave version of the product to taste different from what they are accustomed to. Food scientists are increasingly being asked to design foods with specific attributes.

With the enormous proliferation of product alternatives, the greater complexity of many food products and their myriad ingredients, and the strong evidence linking diet and health, food information has become ever more important to consumers. At the same time the value of information has risen, the cost associated with the time needed to become well informed has also increased. The private and public benefits from truth in labeling and advertising imply a continued role for government regulation of information about the attributes of food.

Data: Where We Get the Facts

CHAPTER 7

Information about the food consumption, eating patterns, and food purchasing behavior of consumers is becoming more important now than ever before to all components of the food industry and distribution system. According to Don Peppers of Lintas:USA, a New York ad agency, "The marketing battleground is shifting at an extremely rapid pace to the information battleground."[1] Sources of food consumption, purchase, and expenditure data are increasing; they include not only traditional sources such as governmental agencies, universities, and trade associations, but also a growing number of private consumer information firms in market research, marketing, and advertising, as well as research foundations.

Access to food consumption and expenditure data and the quality of the data differ with the source.[2] Accessibility depends on whether data are considered in the public domain or proprietary. Data generated by governmental agencies and universities are in the public domain for anyone to access and are considered to be of high quality. Those generated by private firms or by individual businesses for their own use are proprietary. Access is generally restricted and the data may vary considerably in quality, depending upon the sampling, collection, and statistical methods used. Data from consumer information companies, for example, are accessed only by subscribers and individual firms that purchase them, and data generated by individual businesses for their own use are seldom accessible to anyone else. Data generated by trade associations and research foundations may not be strictly proprietary since limited access by industry and the research community may be permitted, but the data are not in the public domain either. The inaccessibility of proprietary food consumption and expenditure data excludes them from data bases used by government and university researchers.

Interpretation and appropriate use of food consumption and expenditure data require that the user understand the data from each source. Peter Drucker, a widely read business consultant, said, "Information is data endowed with relevance and purpose. Converting data into information thus requires knowledge."[3] This chapter includes a review of major sources of time-series data and cross-sectional data for food consumption (food quantities) and expenditures (dollar amounts spent for food) for the United States. Methods used to collect data and their characteristics, accuracy, uses, and limitations are discussed. The data sources discussed in this chapter have been widely referenced in other chapters, so to avoid repetition, examples of the data are not presented here.

TIME-SERIES FOOD CONSUMPTION AND EXPENDITURE DATA

Time-series data show trends in food consumption or food expenditures over time, usually in years. They are generated by governmental agencies and are in the public domain. They usually are summarized from national food supply data already used for other purposes by the U.S. Department of Agriculture (USDA) and other agencies.

The Economic Research Service (ERS) of the USDA has the responsibility for developing three annual data series that provide time-series data for food consumption and expenditures:[4] the Per Capita Food Consumption series, the Index of Per Capita Food Consumption series, and the Total Food Expenditure series.[5] Data from both the ERS and the Human Nutrition Information Service of the USDA are used to estimate nutrients for the Nutrient Content of the United States Food Supply series. Both the ERS and the U.S. Department of Commerce report the percentage of disposable personal income spent for food.

Per Capita Food Consumption Data. Consumption, when discussing food, may mean "quantities of food purchased, quantities of food used to prepare meals, or quantities of food eaten."[6] Per capita consumption data were first published by the USDA in 1941 and have been issued annually since then.[7] Later, a historical data series, first published in 1949, tracked per capita food consumption from 1909 to 1948 and provided data for the study of long-term trends in food and nutrient consumption.[8] Although food production data date back to the 1860s, the need for a consumption component in U.S. national food supply data was not recognized until the 1930s and early 1940s when the need for planning to avoid agricultural surpluses and shortages was recognized and food needs for the World War II years had to be estimated.[9]

The Per Capita Food Consumption series, published by the ERS in the annual statistical bulletin *Food Consumption, Prices, and Expenditures,* is the only data source that provides estimates of the quantities of food available for consumption by the U.S. population.[10] Estimates for this data series are made for over 200 foods each year using supply and utilization balance sheets that show commodity flow from production to utilization (Figure 7.1).[11] This is the "balance sheet" approach to estimating per capita food consumption. Sources of the commodity data for the balance sheets include the USDA's National Agricultural Statistics Service and Agricultural Marketing Service, current industrial reports and foreign trade data from the Census Bureau, other governmental agencies, and private organizations such as trade associations.

To determine total food available for consumption in the United States, also called disappearance data, estimates of total nonfood utilization (as feed, seed, and for industrial uses), exports, shipments to territories, and ending stocks, are subtracted from the total annual food supply (from farm production, imports and inshipments from territories, and beginning stocks) as shown in Figure 7.1. To express consumption on a per capita per year basis, total food available for consumption (disappearance) is divided by Census Bureau estimates of the U.S. population on July 1. Personnel in the Armed Forces overseas are included for commodities shipped overseas in substantial amounts.[12] Quantities for per capita food consumption data for most foods are reported by the ERS on a retail weight equivalent basis, that is, weight as sold in retail stores.[13] Food consumption trends based on these time-series data are

The Supply and Utilization Commodity Flow

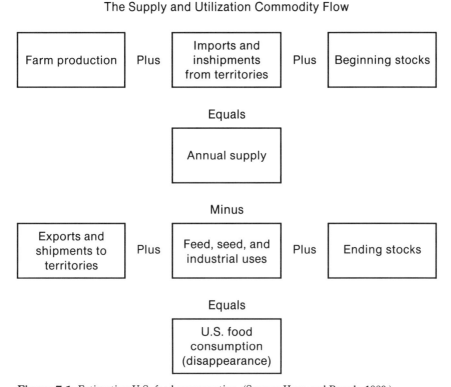

Figure 7.1. Estimating U.S. food consumption. (Source: Harp and Bunch, 1989.)

presented in Chapter 2 in Figures 2.1–2.6 and 2.9–2.15 and are discussed in the text of that chapter.

It is important to remember that time-series food consumption data only tell us whether Americans are consuming more or less of various foods over time.[14] Because these data are aggregated for the entire United States, they cannot be used to estimate consumption by region or by population subgroups based on socioeconomic or demographic subdivisions of the population. A major limitation of time-series data is that they overestimate actual consumption. Food not actually eaten by people, such as food eaten by pets, and food losses from spoilage and waste in processing, distribution, retailing and marketing, food service establishments, and the home, are included in the figures. On average, these data imply per capita food consumption is about one-third higher than is indicated by surveys of individual intake. Other limitations include a lack of data for processed products, inaccurate retail weight conversion factors, periodic changes in the data available for vegetables and fruits, and the inability to account for changes in the quality attributes of the food and in the composition of the population.[15]

Index of Per Capita Food Consumption. The index of per capita food consumption shows changes in the amounts and kinds of food consumed at the retail level.[16] This price-weighted index not only indicates the economic importance of foods, but also includes consumer preferences and the costs of production and marketing.[17] Besides measuring quantity changes in consumption, this index also indicates quality changes, such as shifts from low- to high-priced foods.

Changes in the quantity of high-priced foods have a greater effect on this index than quantity changes in low-priced foods. Price weighting also overcomes the effect that the decreased weight of highly processed foods, with little or no waste or refuse, would have on the data series. An example would be the shift in poultry retailing from whole birds to parts, such as boneless chicken breasts. Highly processed foods, because of their price, increase the index, even though in some instances the quantity of food may be decreasing.

The Index of Per Capita Food Consumption is calculated using retail price weights based on what consumers pay for food at the retail level. Retail prices in a base period and quantities of food in retail weight equivalents in a given year are used to calculate the index. When the same base period for retail prices is used for several years, changes in the index show changes in food quantities consumed from one year to the next. The base period for calculating the food consumption index is selected by the Office of Management and Budget according to the policy for federal statistics. This index and all other statistical indexes published at the same time by the federal government use the same base period. Currently, the base period designated is 1982–1984, which is set equal to an index of 100. Because the index is still computed using 1977–1979 average retail prices, interim conversion procedures are used to convert the index to the 1982–1984 base period.

Nutrients in the U.S. Food Supply. Estimates of the amounts of food energy and 25 nutrients available in the U.S. food supply per capita per day are published by the Human Nutrition Information Service of the USDA in the Nutrient Content of the United States Food Supply series.[18] Data are available from 1909 on.[19] The nutrient content of food available for consumption (disappearance data) is calculated by multiplying the amount consumed per capita per year for each food (retail weight basis), obtained from the ERS, by the most recent data for nutrients in the edible portion (per pound basis), obtained from the Nutrient Data Research Branch of the Human Nutrition Information Service. These data are then converted to a nutrients per capita per day basis. Data are also reported as the percentage of each nutrient contributed by the 13 major food or commodity groups designated in the ERS food consumption data.

Users of these data must remember that the data for nutrients available from the food supply cannot be used to derive nutrients in food actually ingested by individuals. In general, nutrients in the food supply overestimate actual consumption because they include nutrients lost during processing, marketing, or cooking.

Food Expenditure Data. Time-series food expenditure data for all food consumed are now available from the ERS in the Total Food Expenditure series, which estimates expenditures for food in the United States[20] This includes all expenditures for the consumption categories shown in Figure 7.2.[21]

Food expenditures are estimated using three different methods: 1) retail sales, 2) commodity flow or value added, and 3) value of quantities at retail prices.[22] Each method provides unique data that are not available when the other methods are used. The availability of expenditure data over time also differs according to the method used.

The retail sales method, for which data are available starting in 1929, is considered "the most direct measurement of food expenditures."[23] When using this method, ERS analysts classify food expenditures into four categories: 1) food for use at home, 2) meals and snacks consumed away from home, 3) packaged alcoholic beverages for use at home, and 4) alcoholic beverages consumed away from home.[24]

Expenditure data estimated by the commodity-flow method are available for 1869, 1879, and annually since 1889. When this method is used, the margin associated with processing, wholesaling, retailing, and food service is added to the value of raw commodities from producers and from imports.[25]

Expenditure data estimated using the value of foods at retail store prices are available for selected years starting in 1940. When using this method, the total value of individual foods is determined from quantities and retail prices, with an additional margin added for food service prices if appropriate.[26] It is important that users of food expenditure data know how the methods used to make the estimates affect the resulting data. Problems with data availability affect estimates by each method and limit the methods that can be used for certain years.[27] More data are available for recent years, but the costs to obtain them and government budget decreases have become problems.

Percentage of Disposable Personal Income Spent for Food. The percentage of disposable personal income (after taxes) spent for food is estimated from food expenditure data by both the ERS and the U.S. Department of Commerce.[28] Because different techniques are used, the percentages determined by these two agencies are different, but they show similar trends in food expenditures.[29] ERS estimates are lower than those of the Department of Commerce because ERS food expenditure data for food at home excludes pet food, ice, and animal feed and subtracts more nonfood items from grocery store sales.[30] An example of ERS data

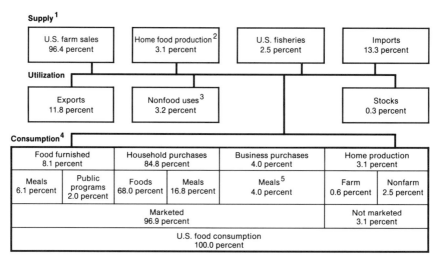

1/ Total supply is 115.3 percent of domestic consumption.
2/ Includes sport fish and game and farm and nonfarm home production.
3/ Excludes use for feed and seed.
4/ Percentage of U.S. food consumption.
5/ Business expenses for travel and entertainment.

Figure 7.2. Food sector flows, 1982. (Adapted from Manchester, 1987; Harp and Bunch, 1989.)

for food expenditures as a percentage of disposable personal income was given in Table 5.1.

The U.S. Department of Commerce Personal Consumption Expenditure (PCE) data series, used to calculate the percentage of disposable personal income spent for food, is a part of the National Income and Product Accounts issued quarterly by that agency in the *Survey of Current Business*.[31] The PCE estimates are made on a national level based on business and government sources of information. PCE estimates for food include only what was purchased by individuals and households from their own funds; they exclude foods bought for travel and entertainment using business funds and foods used in hospitals and other institutions that do not charge separately for food. Benchmark PCE estimates are made every five years. Estimates for food are made by determining the value at the manufacturing level, then adding transportation costs and markups at the wholesale and retail levels, and making adjustments for exports, imports, and inventory changes. Updates to the PCE series are made between benchmark years.

It is important to understand that these two estimates of the percentage of disposable personal income spent for food are different, and to distinguish between them. The ERS publications refer to data used to calculate this percentage as "food expenditures," "personal consumption expenditures," and "personal expenditures."[32] These data should not be confused with the Personal Consumption Expenditure data series from the U.S. Department of Commerce.

CROSS-SECTIONAL DATA ON FOOD CONSUMPTION AND EXPENDITURES

Cross-sectional data are collected from a population at one moment in time, such as a day, week, or month. Samples of households or individuals selected to represent the population being studied supply the data. Collecting data from a statistically selected "representative" sample of a population permits extrapolation of the results to the entire population.

Cross-sectional data on food consumption can be collected from households and individuals or from food purchase or product movement data in the marketplace. Cross-sectional data on food expenditures are collected from households or from retail food sales data. The data are collected using surveys or panels, or by monitoring purchases using data from electronic scanners. Because cross-sectional data are collected from households and individuals, data for specific households or individuals can be retrieved and studied separately. Cross-sectional data in the public domain are collected and generated by governmental agencies and universities. More cross-sectional than time-series data are proprietary. Most proprietary cross-sectional data are collected, processed, and sold by private consumer information firms.

Surveys of Consumers

In the United States, cross-sectional household food consumption data are collected periodically in the Nationwide Food Consumption Survey (NFCS) conducted by the USDA. Data for the money value of food used in households also are collected by the NFCS. Household food expenditure data are collected in the Continuing Consumer Expenditure Survey conducted by the Bureau of Labor Statistics. Food consumption data for individuals are collected periodically in the NFCS and in the Continuing Survey of Food Intakes of Individuals, both conducted by the USDA. Individual consumption data also are collected in the National Health and Nutrition Examination Survey conducted by the National Center for Health Statistics, U.S. Department of Health and Human Services.

Food consumption surveys provide data that can be used in many ways.[33] They provide information about how available food supplies, as reported in time-series data, are distributed to households and individuals, in terms of quantities of food and nutrients. These data also provide information used to study factors that affect food and nutrient consumption and food expenditures of households and individuals. They are used to study issues regarding food assistance programs, food economics, and food marketing, as well as to develop dietary recommendations and guidance systems.

Conducting a Survey. Planning and conducting a food consumption survey requires attention to a number of details that ensure the collection of appropriate and valid data, meaning they are a true measure of what is intended to be measured. Data must also be reliable, meaning they are reproducible or repeatable.[34] The purpose of the survey must be defined and objectives developed first, and then methods to collect the data are selected. A questionnaire, which includes questions and directions for asking them, is developed and tested before the actual survey. The survey questionnaire must be designed to ask questions that will provide the best data and to consider respondent burden—how much time and effort will be required of the survey subjects. The survey design also includes a plan for sampling the population to be studied, a time line, a budget, personnel needed, and plans for summarizing the data and preparing the final report.

Several of the methods described in different sources that have been used alone or in various combinations in surveys to collect food consumption and expenditure data from households and individuals are discussed herein.[35] These include the face-to-face or personal interview and the telephone interview, in which an interviewer obtains and records the data on forms or directly into a computer. Also included are the group-administered and mail-back questionnaires, where respondents record the data on forms and return them to the investigator.[36] Procedures for collecting data from households differ from those used for individuals, even though the names of the methods are similar. Furthermore, the same method may have more than one name, making it necessary to carefully note both the name of the method and the data collection procedure when using survey data. Some new approaches to collection of food consumption data are described in a report on survey methodology published recently by the Human Nutrition Information Service.[37]

Collecting Data from Households. Several methods are used to collect food consumption data from households to estimate the total quantity of food consumed or purchased for consumption by an entire household for a predetermined period of time. Expenditure or value data for food consumed or purchased also may be collected. The two most commonly used methods are the Food Account (also termed the Diary or Record of Food Purchases), and the Food List (or List Recall) method. Two methods used less often are the Inventory Record (or Food Record) and Weighed Consumption (or Measured Consumption).

Household food consumption data are generally used to estimate food available to the household for consumption, rather than food actually eaten. Household food expenditure data are used to estimate the monetary value of food available for consumption. If data are collected on the number, age, and gender of household members eating from the household food supply, number of meals eaten away from home, and number of guests for meals in the household during the survey period, per capita food consumption and expenditures can be calculated from household data.

When the *Food Account* method is used, a household member keeps a record of all food purchased and its cost and all home-produced food brought into the kitchen for household consumption during the survey period. The recording period depends on the survey and the complexity of the diet. Record keeping is relatively easy, therefore this method tends not to change usual household food practices. The method can be used to collect data for longer times than other methods and is relatively inexpensive to use, but its accuracy can be a problem when significant amounts of food stored in the household are used during the survey period. However, the data are accurate enough to show trends in food purchases and expenditures.

In the *Food List* method, a trained interviewer uses a list of major food items in a structured questionnaire format to help the household member most involved with food purchasing and preparation recall the kinds, quantities in market units, and prices of food used by the entire household during the survey period, which usually is the previous seven days. This method is relatively inexpensive because it requires only one visit by the interviewer and is easy for the household respondent; therefore, cooperation is usually good. Accuracy depends on how well the respondent remembers all the foods that were used and gives correct estimates of food quantities.

The *Inventory Record* method requires a trained interviewer to take a weighed inventory of foods on hand in the household at the beginning and end of the survey period, which is usually one week. A household member also keeps a daily record of food purchased or brought into the household from other sources during the period. The accuracy of this method is high, but it is time-consuming and expensive because it requires at least two visits by the interviewer and, in addition, records have to be kept by the household member.

The *Weighed Consumption* method requires that the investigator weigh the food prepared and served in the household each day. This is the most accurate method to determine food actually eaten, but also the most expensive because of the time spent in the household by the investigator. It is seldom used unless one of the other methods is unsatisfactory. The method is appropriately used in developing countries, where home food production is important, where there is little variety in number of foods consumed, and where market units for foods purchased are not standardized.

Collecting Data from Individuals. Methods used to collect food consumption data from individuals are used to estimate the amount of food consumed on a daily basis for a predetermined time. The two most frequently used methods are the 24-Hour Recall (also called the Recall) and the Food Record (also called the Diary). Other methods are the Dietary History, which includes the Food Frequency and Quantified Food Frequency, and the Weighed Intake.

The *24-Hour Recall* method requires that a trained interviewer, in a face-to-face or telephone interview, assist individuals in recalling kinds and amounts of each food consumed during the previous 24 hours. The method is inexpensive since it requires only one short interview and places minimal responsibility on the respondent. Because cooperation is ordinarily good, the method is commonly used in surveys of large numbers of individuals. The accuracy of the data depends on whether the survey day(s) represents the usual food intake of the individual and on the ability of the respondent to remember every food consumed and to accurately estimate the quantities eaten.

The *Food Record* method requires the individual being surveyed to keep a record of the kinds and amounts of all foods eaten during a specified time, usually three to seven days. Accuracy depends on the ability and willingness of the individual to assume responsibility for recording the data whenever food is eaten and to accurately estimate the quantities. Sometimes individuals may change eating patterns to avoid having to record data.

The *Dietary History* method uses a series of food records kept at intervals over months or years, or questionnaires filled in either by an interviewer or by the respondent, to estimate the usual food intake pattern of an individual over a long time. The method may or may not quantify the amount of food eaten and is time-consuming in terms of interviewer time; therefore, it is relatively expensive. It is useful in providing information on food habits as they relate to consumption and tracking changes that may be occurring in food consumption. When *Food Frequency* methods are used, a trained interviewer collects data on how often foods on a list are consumed in a day, week, month, or year, or the data may be collected using a self-administered questionnaire that contains the list of foods. *Quantified Food Frequency* methods collect estimates of quantities of food consumed along with data on how often foods are eaten, and therefore provide the most complete data on food consumption of the Dietary History methods.

In the *Weighed Intake* method, all food consumed by an individual during a specified period is weighed. Accuracy is high unless the individual discovers shortcuts to weighing and recording the data or changes eating patterns to avoid weighing the food. Even though this method is time-consuming and expensive, it is standard procedure in laboratory metabolic studies. Its use is limited mainly to research studies where the investigator does the weighing.

Panels

The *Panel* method involves continuous reporting of data by selected groups of households or individuals who are usually paid to keep a diary of food purchases and expenditures.[38] These reports usually provide monthly or quarterly data about quantities of food purchased for household use, the prices paid, and the retail food outlets where the purchases were made. A panel may have a constant or a rotating membership. Rotating panels periodically replace a certain percentage of the households with different households having similar characteristics. Panel data are more costly to obtain than typical survey data and can be thought of as providing "pooled data," that is, a time-series of cross sections.

Scanners

The use of computerized laser scanner checkout systems began in retail food outlets in the mid-1970s.[39] Scanners at the checkout counter "read" the Universal Product Code (UPC) symbol consisting of dark lines and spaces of varying widths above two sets of numbers on package labels. The right half of the symbol with its numbers identifies the manufacturer and the left half identifies the product and package size. Connection of the scanner to a computer enables the computer to display the product name, description, and price on a screen at checkout and also to print that information on the cash register receipt.

When scanning data are saved, the scanner data bases created become electronic versions of customer cash register receipts that have been entered into an electronic journal.[40] Data bases such as these monitor retail purchases and product movement of UPC-coded food items for manufacturers, and provide up-to-the-minute sales information about specific products.[41] The scanning of food products increased from 21% of the dollar grocery volume in the United States in 1981 to 62% in 1988.[42] Scanner data have characteristics similar to both time-series and cross-sectional data. The data exist over time and across cross-sectional units, which are individual food stores, at any one time, and are aggregated over each store's customers.[43] According to Schiller, "The installation of checkout scanners in most of the nation's supermarkets has brought with it an avalanche of data, more timely and specific than any available before."[44] Marketers now can obtain weekly data for each item in each size, and some data are available from individual stores.[45] Although the volume of scanner data is intimidating, progress is being made in processing and using the information it contains.[46]

SOURCES OF CROSS-SECTIONAL DATA

This section briefly reviews the major sources of cross-sectional data in the United States. The primary government surveys include the NFCS, the Continuing Survey of Food Intakes of Individuals, the National Health and Nutrition Examination Survey, and the Continuing Consumer Expenditure Survey. In addition, the private sector is collecting increasing amounts of cross-sectional data and making growing use of innovative collection techniques.

Government Surveys

Nationwide Food Consumption Survey. The NFCS is conducted by the USDA approximately every 10 years to assess changes in food consumption patterns in the United States[47] Food consumption and expenditure data were collected from households in 1935–1936, 1942,

1948, and 1955, and from both households and individuals in 1965–1966, 1977–1978, and 1987–1988.[48] A multistage, stratified area probability sample of households is drawn for these surveys that is designed to produce a sample representative of the U.S. population.

The number in the sample differs among the surveys. In 1987–1988, the goal was to survey about 6,000 households representative of all income strata, including approximately 15,000 individuals from those households, and an additional 3,600 low-income households, including approximately 10,000 individuals from those households. Household data were collected for seven days by the Food List method. Individual data were collected for three days using a 24-Hour Recall by the interviewer for the first day and then a two-day Food Record kept by the respondent. The questionnaire also collected demographic and socioeconomic information about the households and individuals who participated in the survey.

Household and individual consumption data from this survey are reported as quantities of foods and amounts of food energy (calories) and 27 nutrients. The household data collected do not show the distribution of food among household members, but per capita consumption can be estimated. Household data indicate food used in the household and include food that may have been wasted. This is referred to as "economic consumption." Individual data estimate food actually eaten by individuals at home and away and are called "physiological consumption." In addition, the money value of the foods used in the household is reported.

Continuing Survey of Food Intakes by Individuals. The CSFII was started by the USDA in 1985 and continued in 1986.[49] It was designed to complement the data collected at 10-year intervals in the NFCS by surveying food consumption practices and the nutritional adequacy of food intakes of selected population groups between NFCS surveys. Such information may help to discover early indications of dietary changes and facilitate responses in economic, nutritional, and educational policies. In 1985 and 1986, the nationally representative core group surveyed consisted of a stratified area probability sample of women in all income strata ages 19–50 and their children, ages 1–5, and low-income women 19–50 years old and their children ages 1–5. The 1985 survey also included men 19–50 years old.

Data were collected using the 24-Hour Recall method six times a year (every two months) to obtain better information on the usual food intakes of the respondents. The first visit was a face-to-face interview and the remaining five contacts were telephone interviews. Personal interviews were conducted for subjects not having telephones. Demographic and socioeconomic data were collected for each household. Consumption of quantities of food, food energy, and 27 nutrients and dietary components were reported in five CSFII 1985 series publications and in four CSFII 1986 series publications issued from 1985 to 1989.[50,51]

National Health and Nutrition Examination Survey. NHANES is conducted by the National Center for Health Statistics of the Department of Health and Human Services to assess the health and nutritional status of the U.S. population.[52] Three surveys have been conducted and a fourth is in progress. Data were collected for persons ages 1 to 74 years in 1971–1975 for NHANES I, for persons ages 6 months to 74 years in 1976–1980 for NHANES II, and in 1982–1984 for Hispanics (HHANES). Data collection for persons 2 months and older for NHANES III began in September 1988 and will continue for about six years. A stratified, multistage, probability sample of the U.S. population was drawn to obtain a representative sample for each of these surveys. The sample size differs among the surveys. The goal for NHANES III is to survey approximately 40,000 individuals at 88 locations across the United States.

Data are being collected by interview and physical examination in mobile examination centers moved to designated locations for specified times. The interviewer collects demographic, socioeconomic, dietary, and health-related information. Dietary intake data are collected using the 24-Hour Recall method. The interviewer uses a computerized dietary data collection system to specify detailed food descriptions from data supplied by the respondents and to help respondents accurately recall food quantities. The physical examination portion includes medical and dental examinations, anthropometric (body) measurements including height and weight, and laboratory tests of blood and other biological specimens. Data from this survey will be used to estimate the prevalence of major diseases, nutritional problems, and risk factors for disease. Data on foods and nutrients consumed by the subjects will be used to identify and follow nutrition-related risk factors and to provide information for studies of the relationships between diet, nutritional status, and health.

Continuing Consumer Expenditure Survey. The CCES is conducted by the Bureau of the Census for the Bureau of Labor Statistics, U.S. Department of Labor, to collect household expenditure data (including data on food) needed to revise the Consumer Price Index.[53] Consumer expenditure data have been collected approximately every 10 years in surveys in 1888–1891, 1901, 1917–1919, 1934–1936, 1941–1942, 1950, 1960–1961, and 1972–1973. Starting in 1979, a continuing survey was initiated because rapidly changing economic conditions created a need for more up-to-date data than was available in the 10-year surveys. CCES data are now published quarterly and annually. An example of cross-sectional data for household food expenditures was given in Table 5.2. The data are collected from a national probability sample of households that represents the total civilian noninstitutional population and a portion of the institutional population.

Food expenditure data are collected by the Food Account method in both the Interview Panel Survey and the Diary Survey. The Interview Panel Survey collects data on large purchases from a panel of approximately 5,000 households once each quarter. The only food data collected are for aggregate food expenditures, at home and away from home. Data are collected from a household for five consecutive quarters, and then it is dropped and replaced by another household. The rotation is designed so 20% of the sample is dropped and a new group added each quarter, making it a continuous survey.

The Diary Survey collects data from another sample of approximately 5,000 households each year. Respondents record detailed data for two consecutive one-week periods for small, frequently purchased items (including food) that are difficult to recall. The Diary Survey provides considerable detail on specific categories of food-at-home expenditures. A major use of CCES food expenditure data is in selecting and weighting the food items for the market basket used to calculate the Consumer Price Index (described in detail in Chapter 5). The USDA's Economic Research Service also uses CCES diary survey data in its statistical bulletins.

National Nutrition Monitoring System

The collection and distribution of food consumption and expenditure data are done through the National Nutrition Monitoring System (NNMS).[54] The system was developed in response to a congressional mandate to the USDA and the U.S. Department of Health, Education and Welfare (which has since been reorganized into the U.S. Department of Health and Human Services) in the 1977 Food and Agriculture Act, which called for a comprehensive nutritional status monitoring system.[55] The mandated proposal for such a system was submitted to Congress in 1978 and in 1981 was followed by the Department of Health and Human Services-USDA Joint Implementation Plan for a Comprehensive National Nutrition Monitoring System.[56] Another report, sent to Congress in 1987, summarized progress and new goals, and presented plans for the system until the middle of the 1990s.[57] However, there still is no law in place that officially establishes a system, and funding for NNMS activities is not well organized.[58] The system, summarized in Table 7.1, will follow the food continuum from the producer to the consumer and involve many governmental agencies.[59] Several data sources reviewed in this chapter are components of the NNMS. The Bureau of Labor Statistics has also initiated a long-term project to combine data from various household surveys conducted by different government agencies.[60]

Consumer Panels at Universities

Household consumer panels have been established at some universities to collect food consumption and expenditure data.[61] Among them are the Griffin (Georgia) Consumer Research Panel, the Puerto Rico Panel, and the Panel Study of Income Dynamics at the University of Michigan. Data from all these panels are in the public domain. The Griffin Consumer Research Panel was established by the Georgia Agricultural Experiment

Table 7.1. Major Components of the National Nutrition Monitoring System[a]

Category and Activity	Department and Agency[b]	Interval
Food supply data	USDA-ERS	Yearly
	USDA-HNIS	Yearly
Food demand studies	USDA-ERS	Continuous
Nutrient composition of foods		
Nutrient Data Bank	USDA-HNIS	Continuous
Nutrient Composition Laboratory	USDA-ARS	Continuous
Total Diet Study	DHHS-FDA	Yearly
Food consumption practices and dietary status		
Nationwide Food Consumption Survey	USDA-HNIS	Every 10 years; latest: 1987–1988
Continuing Survey of Food Intakes of Individuals	USDA-HNIS	Latest: 1985 and 1986
National Health and Nutrition Examination Survey III	DHHS-NCHS	Every 10 years; latest: 1988–1994
Total Diet Study	DHHS-FDA	Yearly
Vitamin and Mineral Supplement Survey	DHHS-FDA	Continuous
Health and nutritional status		
National Health and Nutrition Examination Survey III	DHHS-NCHS	Every 10 years; latest: 1988–1994
Coordinated State Surveillance System	DHHS-CDC	Continuous
National Health Interview Survey	DHHS-NCHS	Yearly
Food marketplace surveillance		
Food Labeling and Package Survey	DHHS-FDA	Every 2 years
Nutrition information and education	USDA	Continuous
	DHHS	Continuous
Dietary knowledge and attitudes of the public		
Health and Diet Survey	DHHS-FDA	Every 1–2 years
Methodological development	USDA, NIH, FDA, CDC	Continuous

[a]Data from Forbes and Stephenson, 1984; Forbes, 1988a; Sims, 1988a; Woteki et al, 1988b.
[b]ARS = Agricultural Research Service, CDC = Centers for Disease Control, DHHS = Department of Health and Human Services, ERS = Economic Research Service, FDA = Food and Drug Administration, HNIS = Human Nutritional Information Service, NCHS = National Center for Health Statistics, NIH = National Institutes of Health, USDA = U.S. Department of Agriculture.

Station. Data were collected from 120 households by mail-in diaries from 1974 through June, 1981. The Puerto Rico Agricultural Experiment Station established a household panel in 1977 to collect continuous data for studying food demand. The Survey Research Center in the Institute for Social Research at the University of Michigan established a panel of some 5,000 households in 1968 to study income dynamics and changes in the economic status of households, including household expenditures for food at home and away from home and food stamp program participation. This panel has provided a rich source of longitudinal data, with the data now available for many consecutive years.

Trade Associations and Consumer Magazine Surveys

Trade associations sponsor surveys of consumers periodically to obtain data about specific trends in food consumption and expenditures. The following are some examples of these surveys.

The Food Marketing Institute has sponsored consumer attitude surveys annually since 1974 to identify consumer trends in shopping, food buying, and food preparation behavior, and attitudes toward supermarkets, nutrition, food safety, and other issues pertaining to consumers and the supermarket.[62] Certain survey questions are the same from year to year in order to track trends over time, and others are modified or added to reflect current issues and concerns. A sample of approximately 1,000 supermarket shoppers is surveyed by telephone each year. Random-digit dialing techniques are now used to select a sample that represents the total U.S. population. Selection criteria require that respondents be heads of households with primary or equally shared responsibility for food shopping and have shopped for groceries in the past two weeks.

The Food Marketing Institute joined with *Better Homes and Gardens* magazine in 1987 to commission surveys annually for five years to study how the role of food in households is changing. The first survey reported in 1988 studied food patterns and meal consumption, and the second in 1989, titled "Dinnertime USA" studied how Americans eat dinner. Data were collected in approximately 750 telephone interviews of respondents from households with the desired characteristics, revealed by screening questions. These surveys provide data about food preparation and consumption in the home.

Supermarket Business magazine conducts an annual Consumer Expenditures Study to follow food consumption from one year to the next in terms of changes in retail food sales in all outlets and through grocery stores only. Data are also collected from various other sources including manufacturers, processors, packers, marketers, management companies, advertising agencies, government agencies, market research firms, trade associations, wholesalers, and retailers.

Private Consumer Information Companies and Market Research Firms

Private market research companies provide proprietary panel data that is sold on a fee basis to processors, manufacturers, and marketers.[63]

Household Panels. The Market Research Corporation of America operates two panels that collect consumer data. The National Consumer Panel collects data from households and the Continuous Menu Census Panel collects data from individuals. In the National Consumer Panel, which was established in 1939, each household supplies weekly household purchase data from a diary and is rewarded with trading points for gifts. The present panel is a national probability sample of approximately 7,500 households. Panel data for purchases of food and nonprescription drugs are summarized weekly and monthly. The data are summarized according to demographic characteristics and region every six months.

National Purchase Diary Research, Inc. has a specialized household panel called the Chain Restaurant Eating-out Share Trend (CREST) reporting on the purchase of food away from home.[64] Every two weeks the reporting sample, which is not a probability sample, includes 10,000 households, approximately 30,000 individuals, and approximately 45,000 meals. The data, which are extremely detailed, are collected by mailed diaries.

Panels of Individuals. The Continuous Menu Census conducted by the Market Research Corporation of America was started in 1957. It collects 14-day diaries of every food and beverage eaten at home and away from home by respondents in 500 households each quarter.[65]

Panels of Retail Food Stores. The A.C. Nielsen Service operates a continuous panel of approximately 1,300 retail stores that supply sales data every 60 days for an estimated 1.5 million households through an audit data system.[66] The data are summarized for individual products by brand, package size, and average retail price across geographic regions.

Scanner Information Systems. Scanner data are available from retail food stores or food dealer associations and are summarized and sold by private consumer information companies.[67] Nielsen Marketing Research, for example, buys scanner-derived sales data from 3,000 stores in the United States.[68] Several panels of households have been established whose purchases are scanned to provide food purchase data.[69]

The selected households use a panel identification card and shop at participating stores equipped with scanners. The identification card tells the computer which household is making the purchase. Demographic data on the household have been collected and coded previously. At checkout, the cashier uses the card to trigger a data collection system on the computer that saves the food purchase data. Examples of companies that sell scanner panel data include Information Resources Incorporated,

The Test Marketing Group, A.C. Nielsen Co., and the National Planning Data Group.[70]

The use of scanners benefits consumers by providing faster checkout and retailers by lowering labor costs, but the value of scanner data is greater than either of these benefits.[71] Though "most marketers are only beginning to exploit this information, they are getting a better feel for exactly what a price cut, coupon blitz, store display, or discount to the retailer actually does for sales and profits."[72] Scanner data also reveal how effective displays and newspaper advertisements are. For example, "Nestlé Foods Corp. learned that a combination of store displays and newspaper advertisements resulted in huge volume increases for its Quik chocolate drink."[73] Bill McNair, speaking for Nielsen Marketing Research, says that "a good scanner-analysis system . . . shows . . . how sales respond to pricing, how much merchandise is in stock, and how shelves should be arranged."[74] Capps and co-workers recently designed a management information system for supermarkets that incorporated use of scanning data in managerial decision making.[75] The use of scanner data for demand analysis also has been explored by Capps.[76] Scanner data are beginning to be used to measure price elasticity and to estimate own-brand elasticity and cross-price elasticity of foods.[77]

Problems associated with scanning data include how to summarize the large volume of information collected, how to overcome the lack of demographic information in a scanner data base (when it is not specifically collected), how to obtain purchase information for items that do not have a UPC code, how to motivate firms selling food to allocate the resources needed to analyze and make better use of the information scanning data provide, and how to speed up the processing and analysis of scanning data.[78] Scanning data, despite their limitations, are an important component of the more complex single-source data systems to be discussed next.

Single-Source Systems and Electronic Data Collection. Single-source data systems are one of the newest types of marketing data developed and sold to marketers by consumer information companies and market research firms. Single-source research is "a numerically oriented methodology" that is "one of the hottest trends in marketing."[79] "Single source systems that directly link consumers' exposure to advertising and promotions with what they buy could provide the elusive link between marketing efforts and consumer activity."[80]

Most prominent in descriptions of single-source data are the electronic monitoring techniques used to collect new types of data from panels of households to discover how advertising and promotions affect consumer purchases.[81] These techniques include people meters on television sets, rather than interviews, to monitor household exposure to TV advertising messages; portable scanning wands used in the home to record UPCs of foods purchased, which replace manually recorded paper diaries; and household identification cards used in the store at checkout to activate data collection systems that link in-store scanner data of purchases with panel households.[82] "Buyergraphics" is the term coined by the Arbitron Ratings Company applied to charts based on these sources of information.[83]

Single-source data, according to Dick Nelson of Campbell Soup Company, are "changing the way we think about marketing. The levels of analysis are far beyond a few years ago."[84] Campbell's used single-source data to position Souper Combo microwavable frozen soup and sandwich packages among competing products when they were first introduced on the market.[85]

But single-source data systems developed by consumer information companies and market research firms do much more than monitor the activities of households selected to participate on panels. "A single-source system records each marketing signal that impacts a household either directly (in-home) or indirectly (via the retailer), traces the route and medium these signals took to impact that household, and partitions the household's purchase behavior in a way that links it with signal content."[86] The objectives of such a system include measuring the effects of price and promotions on consumer behavior in the store and at home and analyzing how consumption is affected by marketing strategies and the characteristics of households in a geographic area.[87]

Single-source systems available now, which have been developed from components of older, less integrated systems, use similar data but different techniques to integrate the data. Examples of the new systems are Infoscan, developed by Information Resources Incorporated; Scantrack, developed by the A.C. Nielsen Company; and Samscan developed by SAMI/Burke Incorporated, a Control Data subsidiary. The latter is linked to in-home scanner data collected by a household panel for ScanAmerica, which was developed by another Control Data subsidiary, the Arbitron Ratings Company.[88]

All these systems collect most of their data from in-store scanners and household panels in selected cities. In 1989, Infoscan, which grew out of BehaviorScan, collected data from 2,400 stores and 70,000 households in 49 cities, with all households having scanner identification cards and 10,000 households having television people meters. Scantrack collected data from 2,600 stores and 40,000 households in 50 cities, with 15,000 panelists having in-home scanner wands, 2,500 of these having television people meters, and another 8,000 having scanner identification cards. Samscan collected data from 2,100 stores and 12,000 households in 5 cities, from warehouse withdrawals for 15,472 stores, and from

1,000 ScanAmerica household panelists with in-home scanners and television people meters.[89]

Problems associated with the collection and use of single-source data include the time and expense to summarize and interpret the huge quantities of data, the accuracy of in-store and in-home scanning because of items missed; the cost, limited availability, and use of electronic people meters; the extent of household cooperation that introduces sample bias; and the effectiveness of TV advertising in influencing buyer behavior.[90] According to Robert Schindler of the Graduate School of Business at the University of Chicago, single-source systems "might overwhelm managers with information."[91] Campbell Soup's Dick Nelson agrees that "finding the staff time to fully analyze the data is a problem."[92] Robert Schindler further states "In general, just having information is not enough. You have to know how to use it. More accurate data are not necessarily going to produce more effective marketing."[93]

GENERAL IMPLICATIONS

Future trends in retail decision making will include the development of a complete retail management expert system.[94] This will first involve merging single-source systems and geo-demographic systems (such as Vision, see Chapter 4), which will then be linked with totally integrated localized systems that contain a data base of information about shoppers at one store. These customer data bases will enable food marketers to become proactive marketers rather than reactive retailers.[95] Market basket models will be developed to assist in the management of space in a retail store, and space management models will be developed to assist suppliers in meeting demands of retailers. Finally, all of these components will be integrated into an expert system for retail management.

These massive data bases can potentially be used to better meet consumers' needs and serve their preferences. There is a suspicion, however, that they could be used to target manipulative advertising to unsuspecting consumers or to invade the privacy of individual lives. The balance in the use and abuse of such data will need to be watched.

A problem in data collection is the growing number of people who are refusing to participate in government household surveys. This can affect the validity of the data collected—whether or not they represent the population being sampled. People are becoming more cynical and skeptical and wish to maintain their privacy. In addition, with the increased labor force participation of women and the rising time pressures faced by many people, an increasing number are unwilling to devote the time (which may be several hours) to participate in a major survey.

Government agencies that collect survey data will need to explore ways to reduce the burden on respondents through the use of new techniques and technologies.

Finally, appropriate interpretation and use of food consumption and expenditure data depend on how well users understand the characteristics and limitations of the data. Time-series and cross-sectional data each have unique properties that have been described in this chapter. Of special interest are the government sources of these data that are supplied to the business and research communities annually or at specified time intervals and the new sources of proprietary data being developed in the private sector by the emerging consumer information industry.

Older Americans and Their Food Habits

CHAPTER 8

By 2030, the number of elderly in the United States will double. More than 64.6 million people, making up at least 21% of the population, will be over age 64, and 12% of the population will be over age 74.[1] By the second half of the 21st century, almost half of the people in the United States will be over age 50. As stated in the 1987 Economic Report of the President, "No other demographic change will influence the nation in the next 50 years as much as this 'graying' of America. Every American and every facet of the society will be affected."[2]

Populations are aging around the world. Between 1980 and 2020, the number of elderly (over age 64) in westernized countries will grow 66%. In developing countries, especially in Asia, this population will grow by more than 200%.[3] The increase in the elderly population in the United States is illustrated in Figure 8.1. The median age in the United States increased from 23 in 1900 to 33 in 1991 and is projected to reach 42 by 2050.

Two factors important to increases in the number of elderly in the United States are the 1946–1964 baby boom and improved life expectancy. The first of the baby boomers will reach age 65 in 2011, and the last will reach age 65 in 2029. A bulge in the elderly population due to the baby boom generation will start in about 21 years and continue for at least 21 years thereafter.

Improved life expectancy has resulted largely from better prenatal care, postnatal care, nutrition, and health care. For example, the rate of death due to coronary heart disease began to decline in the 1960s and had fallen by half by 1990. Over half of this drop is attributed to a decline in smoking and fewer people with high blood pressure or high cholesterol.[4] Figure 8.2 illustrates the increase in life expectancy at birth in the United States for four population groups since 1900. For all groups, the greatest rates of increase were due to a decline in infant mortality early in the 20th century. The United States has not made significant progress in reducing infant mortality since 1950 and now ranks 17th among the world's nations, with 10 infant deaths per 1,000 live births.[5]

The longer people live, the longer they are expected to live. Table 8.1 compares 1900 and 1986 estimates for the ages to which four population groups were expected to live at birth and at age 5, 30, 65, and 80. The gains in the average expected lifetime were greatest for nonwhites at all ages up to 65, when the gains for white women were greater.

This chapter explores the trends in income and lifestyles of the elderly. Some common patterns of food consumption emerge among the aging, but diversity continues, especially between the poor and the increasingly affluent, and between the young-old and the old-old.

A PROFILE OF THE ELDERLY

A little over half (52%) of those aged 65–74 were married couples in 1986; 29% were women living alone, 9% were men living alone, and 1.5% were living in a nursing home or other group facility. Among those over age 74, 33% were married couples, 44% were single women, 11% were single men, and 6% were in a group facility.[6] Of those over age 85, 70%

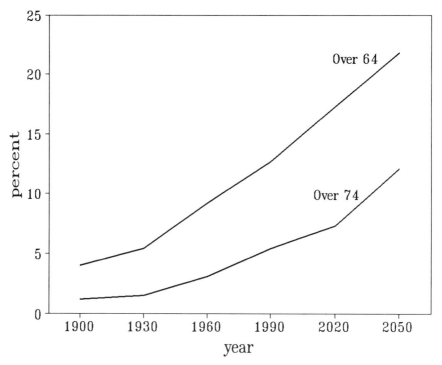

Figure 8.1. Percentage of the population over ages 64 and 74, from 1900 to 2050. (Data from Duensing, 1988, p. 11.)

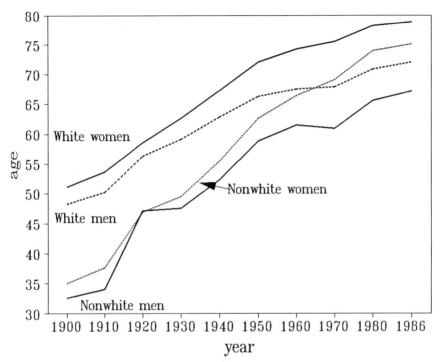

Figure 8.2. Life expectancies at birth, by race and gender, for the United States, from 1900 to 1986. (Data from the U.S. Department of Health and Human Services, National Center for Health Statistics, 1988a, 1988b, 1988c.)

Table 8.1. Life Expectancy of Four Population Groups, United States, 1900 and 1986[a] (Average Age of Expected Death at Birth and Later, with Percent Increase Over Time)

	Men			Women		
Age	1900	1986	Percent Increase	1900	1986	Percent Increase
White						
Birth	48.2	72.0	49.3	51.0	78.8	54.3
5	59.4	72.8	22.5	61.0	79.6	30.4
30	64.9	74.2	14.4	76.4	80.1	4.8
65	76.5	79.8	4.3	77.2	83.7	8.3
80	85.1	86.9	2.1	85.5	88.8	3.8
Nonwhite						
Birth	32.5	67.2	106.5	35.0	75.1	114.3
5	50.1	68.6	37.0	49.0	76.3	55.6
30	59.3	74.7	26.1	60.7	77.1	27.0
65	75.4	79.1	4.9	76.4	82.7	8.2
80	85.1	87.1	2.3	86.5	88.9	2.8

[a]Data from U.S. Department of Health and Human Services, National Center for Health Statistics, 1988a, 1988b, 1988c.

were female, 52% still owned their own homes, 30% lived alone, and 23% lived in a group residence.[7] In 1987, two-thirds of nursing home residents were over age 80, 90% were white, and one-third had no immediate family.[8] The average age of the 1.5 million nursing home residents is rising. With a growing number of people older than 80, or even 100, the need for nursing home care is expected to rise but not as rapidly as the demand for retirement residences, where people can live independently and have access to company, care, and dining facilities.[9]

The proportion of elderly who lived with their children declined from 31 to 9% between 1950 and 1970 and will decline further after 2000.[10] Southeast Asians and Hispanics are exceptions; about one-quarter of these elderly women live with their adult children.[11] Retiring women will have fewer children to live with, only 1.8 children on average by 2020. One-fourth of women age 65 in 2020 will have no children at all. Since women outlive their husbands by an average of 16 years, they need to find or retain suitable housing that allows them an independent and healthy lifestyle.[12] This is increasingly possible with rising incomes and life expectancies.

In 1989, over three-fourths of the elderly owned their homes; most continue to live in them. When asked where they would really like to live, half of retired persons responded to a 1989 poll that they would prefer to live with their children, in apartments, or in retirement communities.[13] Contrary to popular perception, housing costs take a large percentage of the elderly's income, mostly because their incomes are low. The average 1983 equity in homes owned by the elderly was $59,000.[14] In 1987, those aged 65–74 spent 31% of their income on housing, and those over age 74 spent 37%.[15]

Economic Status

At age 80, Pablo Picasso is reported to have said, "Age only matters when one is aging. Now that I have arrived at a great age, I might as well be 20." Growing old is not what it used to be. Although the median income of elderly householders is still about half that of the general population, their spending power has been increasing at a more rapid pace. Between 1967 and 1984, the percent increase in income of the elderly, after adjusting for household size, was almost 55% compared with 27% for those under 64.[16] Figure 3.15 in Chapter 3 illustrates this point. Between 1970 and 1987, real average income of the elderly rose absolutely, from $13,907 to $17,827 (in 1983 dollars), and relatively, from 54 to 63% of overall average household income.[17] The distribution of income among elderly households is, however, still skewed towards the lower end. Over half had incomes under $13,000 in 1987 compared with 28% for all households. Only 6–7% of the elderly had incomes over $50,000 compared with 20% for all households.[18]

Among the elderly households, those with the least income were single women. In the mid-1980s, 44% of households with members over age 74 were single women. Their median income was $7,314—only 65% of that for all households over age 74.[19] In 1987, almost 20% of widows lived in poverty.[20] Even though there are 4.8 million more elderly women than men, fewer women (10.6 million) received Social Security income than men (11.8 million in 1985). The average benefit paid to women was 76% of that paid to men.[21]

About three-fourths of the differences in income between elderly men and women can be explained by pension income. In 1984, only 55% of workers participated in employer-sponsored pension plans. Half of the working men and 39% of the women had vested pension plans. Workers earning over $36,000 a year were more than twice as likely to participate in employer-sponsored pension plans or private plans, such as individual retirement accounts or 401K plans.[22] Currently, in many pension disbursement plans, all income stops at the death of the retired worker. New regulations about pension disbursements specify that lifetime payments must be deliberately chosen over a joint survivor plan, making it more likely that future widows and widowers will continue to receive pension incomes after their spouses die.[23]

On a per capita basis, the income of elderly families is higher than that of other families, mostly because family size is smaller. In 1983, per capita income for the elderly living in families averaged $9,080, 101% of that for nonelderly family members ($8,960), an increase from 94% in 1970. For elderly, unrelated individuals per capita income was 59% of that for younger, unrelated individuals ($10,040 vs. $16,900), an increase from 47% in 1970. The relative income status of the elderly has improved by almost any measure one chooses to use.[24]

Improvement in the economic status of the elderly is due, in large part, to increased Social Security benefits. In 1950, 16% of the elderly received retirement benefits from Social Security; in 1985, 94% received such benefits. Between 1970 and 1983, the annual value of these benefits increased 46%, while wages and salaries increased only 7%.[25]

Net worth peaks between the ages of 55 and 64. Median net worth was $73,664 for households in that age group in 1987 (Table 3.4, Chapter 3). After age 64, median net worth was $60,266, but the average was over $250,000. This implies a concentration of wealth among the elderly; only 14% of elderly households had more than the average net worth. About 43% of the elderly's wealth is in private savings, with 18% in pensions.[26] Contrary to life cycle models of savings, accumulated wealth diminishes very slowly after retirement.[27]

Enhanced economic status of the elderly, as a group, has occurred despite two major trends that could have led them into poverty. The first is that men have been retiring earlier, diminishing lifetime earnings. In recent times, the average man spent 15 years in retirement. Eighty percent of men retired voluntarily, unless they retired before age 62. Then, only 44% retired voluntarily. The rest retired because of a health condition or were laid off, fired, or bought out.[28] Tables 3.6 and 3.7 in Chapter 3 show that men over the age of 45 have decreased their labor force participation since 1970. In contrast, women's labor force participation rates have increased. For men employed in the labor force aged 60-64, the probability of retiring between ages 65 and 69 increased from 0.37 to 0.53 between 1957 and 1987. This probability, known as the "retirement hazard rate," is now about the same for men (0.53) and women (0.57).[29] The lifetime labor force participation rates of men and women are converging. Women's earnings have tended to hold up the incomes of older people as have indexed Social Security payments.

The second trend that could have caused diminished economic status is increased longevity, which increases the number of years over which retirement income must be spread. Greater wealth and indexed Social Security income have helped alleviate this problem, and longer working lives will likely secure more income for the elderly in the future.

The Golden Generation

Increased economic status of the elderly has manifested itself in a rich market for products and services for older Americans. Many marketers think of the "golden generation" as starting at age 50.[30] The first baby boomers will be 50 in 1996. There are already noticeable changes in advertising that targets older people. New names and acronyms appear. For example, grown-up, mature people are known as "grumpies"; wealthy older people as "whoopies"; retired affluent professionals as "rappies"; and the mature, active, free, indulgent, and affluent are known as the "Golden Mafia."[31]

Products and services to enhance the lifestyle of older people appear frequently. The wealthiest of all age groups, those aged 50-64, will soon be the largest population group. They spend about 7% more than average households on all goods and services and 14% more on food. Older Americans spend less on food in restaurants, even though they have more leisure time to eat out.[32] This is partially explained by their eating out at inexpensive places. For example, McDonald's, a relatively inexpensive restaurant, did 30% of its business with those over age 50 in 1989.[33]

Researchers and marketing analysts have puzzled over a useful way to segment and, therefore, target the elderly market. A frequently used segmentation is the "mature," ages 55-64; the "young-old," ages 65-74;

and the "old-old," over age 74.[34] Some speculate that the biggest differences are between those still working and those retired, and that age is simply representative of other major changes in lifestyle that accompany empty nests and retirement.

One study found that young adults spent discretionary income acquiring possessions, whereas those between 40 and 60 spent discretionary income on "catered experiences"—activities allowing active participation and enjoyment, such as sports, travel, and artistic, cultural, and culinary events. Those over age 60 spent money on "being experiences" that highlighted their sense of well-being, identity, and intelligence—experiences like interpersonal relationships, philosophical introspection, and enjoyment of nature. They traveled to meet new friends and to broaden their minds.[35] Over 80% of luxury travel is done by people over age 55. Seventy-eight percent of people over age 60 have traveled out of the United States; most of them have visited at least 24 different states. Travel increases directly with income, education, and age,[36] and travelers experience new foods and acquire new tastes.[37]

Older consumers expect products to be functional. They want products that reinforce their status with their peers and products and services that provide gateways to other pleasurable experiences. They are sensitive to value; price matters only as it relates to affordability.[38]

Older Americans, now and in the future, are the healthiest, wealthiest, and longest living people in history. Expenditures by those over age 64 rose from 2.5% of the gross national product in 1960 to 5.9% in 1982 and are continuing to climb.[39] Their preferences are felt in the marketplace, not least of all in the market for food. They are not a homogeneous group, however. A nationwide survey of 600 elderly found that half could be classified as "nutrition concerned." These people still cooked most meals and rarely snacked throughout the day. One-third were classified as "fast and healthy." They used convenience foods but were concerned about fat and sodium. They also had the highest median income ($21,593). The rest were called "traditional couponers" who distrusted advertising and were not interested in convenience or new information about food.[40]

OLD FOOD HABITS MEET NEW FOOD NEEDS

Aging bodies need fewer calories. As the body ages and physical activity slows, muscle mass is lost and often replaced by fat. Fat tissue burns fewer calories than muscle, so fewer calories are needed to maintain body weight. Consequently, the elderly eat less food, or, at least, fewer calories. It is estimated that elderly men and women need 15–20% fewer calories than when they were age 35, given equal amounts of physical exercise.[41] For every decade past age 20, caloric needs decrease 2-8%.[42] A study at Tufts University found that elderly men ate 600 fewer calories per day than men age 35; elderly women ate 300 fewer calories than women age 35. Both represent a decline of almost 25% in calorie consumption.[43] As the population ages, aggregate per capita consumption of calories should decline.

Food Expenditures

As far back as 1960, research showed that, all other things being equal, aggregate food expenditures tend to decline as the population ages.[44] This is consistent with the declining incomes and lowered caloric requirements of the elderly and with their tendency to eat less food away from home.

Regardless of retirement age, food expenditures tend to decline after retirement. This decline averaged 14%, but was greater (33%) for those under age 62 who retired involuntarily. For those over age 62 with Social Security income, the decline was less—between 4 and 13%.[45] Social Security income acts as a buffer against a decline but will not stop it.

The decline in food expenditures for households of the elderly (in 1984 dollars) is illustrated in Table 8.2. Between ages 64-74 and age 75 and older, household expenditures on food in grocery stores declined 40%; expenditure on food away from home declined 67%.[46] Food expenditures increase as a percentage of household budgets, however, since food expenditures decline only half as fast as incomes decline among the elderly.[47]

For the future, four factors suggest an increase in food expenditures by the elderly, even though they will still spend less on food than their younger counterparts. First, the number of single, elderly householders will more than double in the next 45 years.[48] Those who live alone do

Table 8.2. Food Expenditures and Aging[a] (Average Annual Expenditures of Households, in 1984 Dollars)

Expenditures	All Households[b]	Households Headed by Older Americans			Average[c] for All Ages >54
		55-64	65-74	75+	
Total	20,862	22,264	15,038	10,718	17,144
Total on food	3,280	3,602	2,714	1,865	2,900
Food at home	2,300	2,536	2,027	1,518	2,129
Grocery store	2,164	2,412	1,929	1,462	2,029
Convenience store	136	124	98	55	99
Food away from home	980	1,065	687	348	772

[a] Data from Lazer and Shaw, 1987; U.S. Department of Labor, Bureau of Labor Statistics 1989b.
[b] In all households, the average number of persons was 2.6, for ages 55-64, 2.5; for ages 65-74, 1.9; for ages 75+, 1.6; and for all over age 54, 2.1.
[c] These figures are weighted averages that take into account the different sized households in different categories.

not realize economies of scale in food purchases, so they spend more per person than larger households. Second, they will be demanding smaller or single-serving packages, which cost more per unit of edible food but are also convenient and cut down on food waste in the household. Third, the rising incomes and wealth of the elderly foretell higher per capita food expenditures. Caloric intake is 100–200 calories per day lower for low-income elderly.[49] As low incomes rise, more food is usually consumed. Fourth, demand for convenience and services will increase—services in the form of food packaging, ready-to-heat or ready-to-serve food, meals eaten away from home and meals delivered to the home.

Shopping

Food shopping is a major activity for many elderly people. In 1978–1979, the shopping behavior of a subset of elderly, mostly white, women, who were predominantly urban and Protestant, was analyzed. They went to the grocery store once or twice a week. Four out of 10 saw grocery shopping as a pleasant activity; 35% received food stamps. Their average expenditures were $55 per trip to the grocery store and $7 per occasion on food away from home. Their food dollar was spent on various foods in the following percentages: meat and meat substitutes (25%), vegetables (12%), fruits (12%), milk and milk products (11%), beverages (12%), and flour products (6%).[50] These results differ somewhat from food expenditures by the elderly during 1972–1973.[51] In the earlier period, across the nation, the elderly spent less on fruits and vegetables and more on milk, flour, and cereal products.

In rural America, over 51% of the elderly went to the grocery store at least twice a week. They usually spent about half an hour in the store; fewer than half drove their own cars to the store. Attitudes towards shopping explained less than 4% of the frequency or duration of the trips to the grocery store, implying that these were necessary trips.[52] Opportunities for home-delivered food at a reasonable price may expand, but the social function of shopping should not be underestimated for the elderly.

In one midwestern state, 10% of the elderly reported difficulty in grocery shopping.[53] Difficulties arose from diminished physical strength needed for handling carts, lifting heavy loads, or reaching and stooping. Failing eyesight made it harder to read labels. Although some studies found that the elderly responded positively to businesses that provided comfort needs such as places to sit, transportation, convenient rest rooms, delivery services, and clear, large labels, other studies found these amenities to be less important. The special needs of elderly shoppers are discussed further in Chapter 11 in the food retailing section. What is distinctive about elderly consumers is that they are more likely to make joint decision purchases (if married), use more printed media for information (relative to electronic media), and resent firms that remind them they are old. Many do not acknowledge senior citizen discounts or other "senior" benefits because they do not perceive themselves to be as old as they are.[54]

Health Concerns

Expenditures on food away from home by the elderly were found to be inversely correlated with high "nutritious-healthful" scores.[55] This implies that those who have strong attitudes about nutrition and health are more likely to eat at home. Those elderly who rated high on "social activity" scales spent more on groceries. It was found earlier that those who had high social participation had significantly better diets.[56] Low incomes, physical inability, and loneliness contributed to poorer diets.[57] In fact, recent research on gerontology suggests that many of the conditions thought to characterize old age, not counting degenerative diseases such as Alzheimer's, are the result of poor nutrition and little exercise. Those who have active physical and intellectual lives and believe that they matter to other people have been found to largely escape signs of senility altogether.[58]

Health-related food problems that increase with age are those related to excess calories and fat in the diet. With increased evidence that fat, especially saturated fat, increases the chances of heart disease and decreases life expectancy, we can expect that an aging population will decrease fat consumption. It is difficult to say exactly what the effect will be, however, because although people become more risk averse during middle age, they tend to take greater chances as they get older.[59]

Diet studies show that over half of the elderly consume the Recommended Dietary Allowances for seven specified nutrients. Food intakes were most likely to be low in calcium, magnesium, and vitamin B-6. Those elderly who met the Recommended Dietary Allowances for nutrients spent more for food at home, ate larger quantities of food, ate a greater number of foods, and selected foods with higher nutrient-to-calorie ratios.[60] Since the need for calories diminishes with age but the need for vitamins and minerals apparently does not, the need for nutrient-dense foods and low-calorie foods will increase. Noncaloric sweeteners and fat substitutes will probably find a good market among the elderly.

The National Institute on Aging found that 16% of those over age 65 and one quarter of those over age 74 had nutritionally poor diets. Single, elderly men were most likely to have poor diets.[61] This was mainly due to inexperience in food preparation and lack of motivation. Other health-oriented food considerations are related to special diets for common diseases, such as high blood pressure or osteoporosis. Eating solid foods was reported to be a problem for 6% of elderly over age 65 and 14% of those over age 85.[62]

The improved longevity and health of the elderly do not necessarily go hand in hand. Although the "young" elderly (those under 75) tend to be healthier and more active, once they reach 85, the older they are, the more likely they are to be physically disabled and ill. Dementia illnesses are estimated to strike 1% at age 65, 2.5% at age 70, 5% at age 75, 12% at age 80, more than 20% at age 85, and more than 40% at age 90. Of those aged 74–84, 6% live in nursing homes, compared with 22% of those over age 85.[63] The amount of food sold to and served in group quarters for the very old is likely to increase.

Debilitating diseases and other aging conditions are now thought to be unique to some cohorts that share similar historical experiences. New generations of elderly may produce new patterns of health and disease. For example, it is hypothesized by gerontologists that osteoporosis is a generational artifact—characteristic of a cohort of older women who, as young girls, rarely exercised and did not develop full bone strength.[64] Many of the now accepted features of aging may disappear over the next 20 years, to be replaced by new ones and new food habits.

Consumers accept the knowledge that diet may play a role in lengthening life and slowing down the aging process. In a telephone survey, the elderly were found more likely to engage in dietary behavior associated with better health (Table 8.3). One-third to two-thirds of the elderly reported taking vitamin and mineral supplements. Those who did had more income and education.[65] In fact, good health generally increases with income and education. The prevalence of chronic

Table 8.3. Percentage of Elderly Versus Nonelderly Complying with Health-Improving Behaviors[a]

Behavior[b]	65 and Over (%)	Under 65 (%)
Exercise regularly	23	36
Avoid salt	65	50
Avoid fat	74	52
Consume fiber	69	58
Avoid cholesterol	58	40
Avoid sugar	60	50
Consume calcium	58	49
Consume vitamins and minerals	68	62
Maintain recommended weight	25	23
Moderate or no alcohol	91	88

[a] Adapted from Bausell, 1986.
[b] All comparisons show those age 65 and over were significantly different from those under age 65 at a statistically significant level of ($P < 0.001$), except for the last three entries.

conditions peaks after age 75 for upper income groups compared with a peak at ages 55–64 for lower income groups.[66]

"We are on the cusp of an era where the healthy, active, older adult will choose foods that help maintain good health."[67] If that is true, then food processors and retailers have a clear signal about important marketing strategies. Enthusiasm for this should, perhaps, be tempered by the results of a recent survey of retired people who were asked if they would be willing to pay extra for foods low in salt, cholesterol, sugar, fat, or calories. Eighteen percent were willing to pay more, 60% were not.[68] Eighteen percent of 35 million people is still a market of 6.3 million willing to pay more for modified, "healthful" foods. That is a good-sized market niche, but far from the whole market. This, again, points out the diversity in the food market, even among the elderly.

Types of Foods

Elderly people were found to eat more than average amounts of fresh fruits and vegetables, cereals, bakery products, poultry, pork, and oils. They ate less than the average amounts of red meat, milk, soft drinks, prepared foods, and alcohol. They ate less food away from home.[69] Those over age 74 ate substantially less beef, citrus, legumes, nuts, and beverages, but more noncitrus fruits and juices.[70] In 1977–1978 one study found that significantly more people over age 50 than younger adults ate the following foods: fruits, vegetables, whole grain breads, crackers, breakfast cereals, milk, eggs, desserts, coffee, and tea.[71]

In a recent study, those who were especially aware of diet and health linkages ate more whole wheat bread, frozen fish, lean beef, winter squash, margarine, tea, and low-fat (2%) milk.[72] A New York Times poll showed that 30% of the elderly did not eat snacks; of those who did, 38% ate sweets and ice cream (compared with 53% of those aged 18–29), and 27% snacked on fruit, juices, and vegetables (compared with 15% of those aged 18–29).[73] The 10 most popular foods for those over age 64 were reported to include low-fat low-calorie low-cholesterol cheese, canned roast beef hash or canned beef, nondairy cream substitutes, dried fruits, sugar substitutes, canned stews, canned pineapple, and cottage cheese.[74]

Food Away from Home

Virtually all studies of food expenditures show that the elderly spend less money and a smaller percentage of their food budget on food away from home.[75] This is consistent with the overall propensity of the elderly to eat less, which conforms with their lower relative incomes, needs for special diets, and concerns about how diet affects health. It is inconsistent with increased leisure time and a propensity to look for activities that consume time and provide for social contacts. The elderly have typically consumed items that use time and allow them to get out of the house. For example, one study found that older Americans prefer to go out to movies rather than stay home to watch them on a VCR. They turn shopping into exercise and pleasure; they prefer bank tellers to automated teller machines because of the personalized interaction, and they want products that are uncomplicated and require little effort to use.[76] These results suggest that eating out in restaurants should be attractive as a way to get out of the house, to receive personal service, and, potentially, to contact friends and neighbors. It also implies that new home cooking technology, or foods prepared or packaged in new and complex ways, may not be readily adopted by the elderly.

Observing numerous elderly people eating out and socializing leads one to look beyond the message given by average expenditures on food away from home. Eating out is highly dependent on income and on marital status. Upper income, single, elderly men and women spent 44 and 25%, respectively, of their food budgets on food away from home in 1972. Single, elderly men and women with lower incomes spent only 11 and 15%, respectively.[77] Little variation was found in the number of meals eaten away from home among various age groups, although they did decline slightly after age 55.[78] Others predict that an aging population will be very good for the restaurant business.[79] The jury is out, but the elderly will probably be eating away from home more in the future.

HELP FOR THE NEEDY

In 1987, 12% of people over age 64 lived in households where the income was under the poverty line. This contrasts with a 30% poverty rate for the elderly in 1967 and 43% in 1959.[80] (The poverty income guidelines for 1989 are given in Table 9.2 in Chapter 9.) Most of the elderly in poverty were living alone; three-fourths were women and one-third were minorities. Of those over age 64, 7% of men and 12.8% of women were in poverty. Of those over age 85, 15% of men and 20% of women were in poverty except for black women, 47% of whom lived in poverty.[81]

One of the main reasons for a decrease in poverty among the elderly is the Social Security system. In 1983, a couple's benefit was $744 per month, 48% more than the "poverty line" for an elderly family of two. On the other hand, the average widow's benefit was $393 per month, 98.9% of the poverty line for a single, elderly person.[82] Ninety percent of federal outlays for the elderly have no eligibility criteria based on income from other sources. This means that the really poor may not be helped as much as if they were targeted for help, but it also means that the average aid to the elderly is much greater than it would otherwise be. Much of the income-in-kind includes Medicaid and Medicare. In 1983, Medicare spent $1,800 per elderly person on medical care. If the income-in-kind is added to the cash income of the elderly, the poverty rate drops from 12% to between 3.3 and 9%, depending upon how the income-in-kind is valued.[83] Adding the value of food stamps and housing benefits reduces the poverty rate by only about 2%, regardless of how it is valued.

Many elderly who are not below the poverty line are close to it. Twenty-one percent of those over age 65 fell below 125% of the poverty line in 1986; 42% fell below 200% of the poverty line.[84] Therefore, almost half of those over age 65 in 1986 had incomes of less than $10,510 for an individual or $13,260 for a couple. This amounted to 65% of the average income for all single-person households and 45% of the average income in all two-person households.[85] People in these income brackets have been called the "'tweeners."[86] Tweeners do not live in poverty, but their incomes are less than twice the poverty line. They are at risk of falling into poverty at any time, mainly because they lack access to housing subsidies and other in-kind help that their poorer counterparts receive. They also have few resources from which to generate additional income.[87]

The Older Americans Act established the Elderly Nutrition Program in 1972 to provide at least one hot meal per day, five days a week, to people over 60 and their spouses (regardless of age). In 1987, it served some 230 million meals.[88] These meals must provide one-third of the Recommended Dietary Allowances for specified nutrients. Federal money is provided to subsidize the serving of these meals in group dining facilities in urban and rural settings throughout the country. Studies have found that those who participate in this program improve their nutritional status.[89]

Another food program designed for the elderly poor is the Expanded Nutrition Program. It delivers meals to about 3% of the home-bound elderly over age 74.[90] These meals contribute 50–60% of the daily nutrients to recipients.[91] The number of meals served increased 12% in 1975 and 37% in 1987. As more older, elderly people live alone at home, this service is likely to expand further.[92] A large number of services for the single elderly living at home will likely be in demand at all income levels, including such services as home-delivered meals, homemaker assistance, and home nursing services.

Food stamps are also available to the elderly who are poor. Seven percent of those over age 64 received food stamps in 1983, at a face value of $482 annually.[93] Food stamps have been found to significantly increase the amount of food eaten at home, thereby improving the nutrition of the elderly.

GENERAL IMPLICATIONS

The number of older people in the United States and around the world is increasing rapidly. The great bulge in the numbers over age 65 will not start until 2011, but the over age 50 market will swell by 1996. This age group is the richest of all age groups, and it is healthier and more active than ever.

Implications for food consumption are mixed. The elderly spend more per capita on food, but less per household. They need fewer calories, so their demand for food is expected to decline. Their food expenditures will likely increase as they travel more, eat out more, and purchase more convenience foods and more foods that cater to special health concerns than in the past. They are known to consume less meat, milk, citrus, legumes, nuts, and beverages than younger people.

As lives are extended through improved diet and health care, new patterns of living and eating will evolve. More very old people will live in group facilities, increasing the demand for institutional food. Still more will need food or meals delivered to private homes. Most will be self sufficient and demand quality food to eat at home and away from home.

The Forgotten Poor
and Their Food Problems

CHAPTER 9

Ours is a society in which time is becoming a scarcer resource than money, and many food consumers are willing to pay a premium for quality, variety, and convenience. However, millions of Americans do not share in this abundance. For many individuals and families, just getting enough to eat is still a common problem. The program, "Hunger in America," shown on public television in December 1989, chronicled the lives of four families for whom hunger was a problem.

Brian Fuller and his wife operated a small dairy farm in Stevens County, Washington. They had three daughters. In 1989, they earned $7,200, which was less than half the poverty level for a family of five. After they had covered bills that must be paid, they had little money left for food. Some nights dinner might be just cheese and soup, and there were times when there was literally nothing in the refrigerator.

The Craigs were a black family who lived in Green County, Alabama. Mr. Craig made $25 per day working on a farm when work was available. There were eight children living at home in a house without indoor plumbing. They typically ran out of food stamps before the end of the month, and having enough for the family to eat was a frequent worry.

The Spences, who lived in Minneapolis, Minnesota, had recently lost their home after Mr. Spence lost his job. They were getting by on welfare payments and food stamps. One of their young sons admitted to going to school hungry sometimes; when asked how that made him feel, he said, "sad."

The Castros were a Hispanic family who worked as farm laborers in California's Central Valley. The older children frequently worked in the fields along with their parents. The pay was $4.25 an hour. The Castros could not afford to buy the very vegetables they helped to raise, and in winter, when there was little work, they could not afford to buy meat.

The Fullers, the Craigs, the Spences, and the Castros are typical of the 32 million people living in poverty in this country. Although they may not be facing severe malnutrition and such outright starvation as occurs during famines in Africa, many have serious food and nutrition problems. Furthermore, the poor and their plight seem to have become largely invisible to, and easily forgotten by, those who are more well-off and living in society's mainstream.

The magnitude and nature of the problems of hunger and poverty in the United States are described in this chapter. The specific nutrition and nutrition-related health problems of the poor and the major government food assistance programs, such as the Food Stamp Program, the National School Lunch Program, and the Special Supplemental Food Program for Women, Infants, and Children are then discussed. We also review the widespread private food assistance initiatives to help the poor through emergency feeding facilities and food shelves. The chapter closes with a discussion of some moral and economic arguments for addressing the food and nutrition problems of those who are poor.

HUNGER AND POVERTY

In the late 1960s, public concern about the widespread problem of hunger in the United States was aroused by the attention given the issue by the Citizens' Board of Inquiry report, the CBS television documentary, "Hunger, USA," and Nick Katz's 1969 book, *Let Them Eat Promises: the Politics of Hunger in America.*[1] The Poor People's March in Washington, D.C. was another factor that raised the public consciousness. In addition, those who accompanied the fact-finding missions to depressed areas in the rural South and elsewhere, including the late Senator Robert Kennedy and other politicians, were strongly affected by what they saw. In some of the worst situations, they were shocked to find children suffering from severe malnutrition and actual starvation. Senator George Murphy, a Republican from California, was dismayed at what they found: "I didn't know that we were going to be dealing with the situation of starving people and starving youngsters."[2]

Action was taken to address the problem of hunger. The White House held a conference on Food, Nutrition, and Health in 1969 to address the issue, and the Senate Select Committee on Nutrition and Human Needs was formed.[3] The major response by the federal government was a substantial expansion in funding for the domestic food assistance programs, particularly food stamps, during the 1970s. By the late 1970s, the situation had greatly improved and significant progress had been made in reducing the occurrence of hunger in the United States.[4] In the 1980s, many argue that conditions deteriorated and that hunger again emerged as a serious national problem.[5]

The Physician Task Force on Hunger in America concluded in 1985 that "hunger in America is a national health epidemic."[6] They found that "hunger is now more widespread and serious than any time in the last ten to fifteen years" and "perhaps never in the past half century has hunger in this nation spread so quickly."[7] The Physician Task Force estimated that some 20 million Americans, 12 million children, and 8 million adults were affected by hunger.[8]

Hunger

Hunger can be an ambiguous term, however, and different meanings may be applied by those who claim it is widespread and those who minimize the problem.[9] The President's Task Force on Food Assistance suggested two basic definitions. Medically, hunger is defined as "a weakened, disordered condition brought about by prolonged lack of food."[10] This clinical definition relates to extended nutritional deprivation and the resulting physiological effects. With this definition, hunger implies malnutrition (undernourishment). On the other hand, in common usage, hunger may simply mean "the inability, even occasionally, to obtain adequate food and nourishment."[11] It is the experience of not being able to get enough to eat and being unsatisfied. In this case, hunger can be a concern even if there are no clinical symptoms of malnutrition. Hunger may be a social problem, even if the deprivation is not prolonged enough to cause observable implications for nutrition and health.

The President's Task Force, using the clinical definition of hunger, found that there was "no evidence that widespread undernutrition is a major health problem in the United States," except perhaps among the homeless.[12] They did find evidence that some people had difficulty obtaining food but found it "impossible to estimate the extent of that hunger."[13] They could not document the amount of such hunger caused by income limitations.

For many low-income individuals and families, it may be more relevant to think of the problem as a lack of "food security."[14] An absence of food security is typified by difficulty in obtaining a sufficient quantity or the necessary quality of food. Providing enough food for their families is a reoccurring worry, and sometimes they may not have enough to eat. These households may have many demands placed on what few financial resources they do have. The situations of the families described in the introductory section of this chapter reflect typical food security problems faced by many of the poor.

The time near the end of the month is a particular problem for many poor families. They have used up all their food stamps, if they receive them, and have little or no cash remaining. There may be little left to eat in the house and they may be reduced to eating the cheapest foods they can find. Macaroni and cheese is typical of the cheap staples that may be eaten with greater frequency towards the end of the month. "They get full off rice and butter and sugar," was how Joyce Wiltz, a welfare mother in Houston, described what her children ate after she had used up their monthly food stamp allotment.[15] The demands placed on private food shelves typically reach a peak toward the end of the month.

Most poor families spend their food budgets quite wisely. The evidence suggests lower income households are more efficient food shoppers and obtain more nutrients per dollar's worth of food than those with higher incomes. For example, according to data from the 1977–1978 Nationwide Food Consumption Survey, households with incomes below $5,000 obtained 1,280 Calories, 45 grams of protein, and 470 milligrams of calcium per dollar's worth of food used at home, compared with 1,140 Calories, 41 grams of protein, and 440 milligrams of calcium for households with incomes of $20,000 and above.[16]

The Poor

There is a strong association between the occurrence of hunger and poverty. Lack of food security and inadequate diets among the poor are primarily a direct result of inadequate income to buy sufficient food. In addition, the link between poverty and hunger may be indirect and "part of a complex of problems, including a lack of information, physical and mental illness, addiction to drugs and alcohol," and other factors.[17]

Table 9.1 gives the number of persons and the percentage of the population below the poverty level in the United States from 1960 to 1988. The determination of the poverty level is explained in the next section. In 1960, almost 40 million Americans, 22.2% of the population, were living below the poverty line. By 1966, the number of people under the poverty line had fallen by over 10 million persons and was down to 14.7% of the population. The number reached a low of 24.5 million people in 1978, which was just 11.4% of the population. This significant progress against poverty was the result of a growing economy, the government's antipoverty programs, particularly those initiated under Lyndon Johnson's Great Society and War on Poverty, and inflation indexing of Social Security benefits for the elderly.

During the economic recession in the early 1980s, the number of people living in poverty rose by over 10 million, reaching 15.2% of the population by 1983. Even during the late 1980s, when the U.S. economy enjoyed one of its longest periods of prosperity in history, the proportion of the population living in poverty remained distressingly high.

Primarily because of increased Social Security payments, the rate of poverty has declined most sharply among senior citizens. In 1970, 24.6%

of people aged 65 and over were officially poor. By 1987, this figure had fallen to 12.2%, lower than the rate of 13.4% for the overall population, as shown in Table 9.1.[18] Senior citizens are now proportionately less poor than the rest of the population.

However, the rate of poverty among children under age 18, in what is one of the richest countries on earth, reached 20.0% in 1987, up from 14.9% in 1970. Even more shocking is that nearly half of all black children (45.1%) were living in poverty; for children in Hispanic families, the figure was 39.3%.[19]

It is useful to distinguish between different categories of the poor: 1) the traditional poor, such as single-parent households with a historically high rate of poverty, 2) the new poor, who are individuals and families experiencing an extended period of unemployment and reduced income, and 3) the homeless, who are individuals without a permanent address.[20] An additional category now being identified is the working poor. The problems and availability of assistance programs are different for these three groups.

Of the traditional poor, about half of all households headed by women with dependent children are below the poverty line. Some two-thirds of these families receive Aid to Families with Dependent Children and Medicaid benefits, and an even higher proportion participate in the Food Stamp Program. In terms of the new poor, about one-fifth of households

Table 9.1. U.S. Population Below the Poverty Level[a]

Year	Number (Millions)	Percent
1960	39.9	22.2
1966	28.5	14.7
1970	25.4	12.6
1975	25.9	12.3
1976	25.0	11.8
1977	24.7	11.6
1978	24.5	11.4
1979	25.3	11.6
1980	29.3	13.0
1981	31.8	14.0
1982	34.4	15.0
1983	35.3	15.2
1984	33.7	14.4
1985	33.1	14.0
1986	32.4	13.6
1987	32.3	13.4
1988	31.9	13.1

[a] Source: U.S. Department of Commerce, Bureau of the Census, 1990a, p. 458.

that experience unemployment fall into poverty. Because they have assets, they may be ineligible for assistance such as food stamps.[21] For this reason, they may turn to privately run food shelves. They also have fixed payments, such as mortgages, which may leave little money left to buy food.

Homelessness is the most extreme form of poverty. A few days before Christmas in 1989, there was a picture in the newspaper of a homeless man covered by a blanket huddled over a steam grate. He was within sight of the national Christmas tree in front of the White House in Washington, D.C., in weather with a below-zero windchill.[22] In a survey of 27 cities, the Mayors' Task Force on Hunger and Homelessness found that 24% of the homeless were employed and that the homeless include an increasing number of families with children, who have lost their homes.[23] The homeless population in the United States has been estimated to be at least 500,000 on any given day. As many as 2 million people may be homeless at some time over the course of a year.[24] Most efforts to help the homeless are local and many are private, nongovernment initiatives.

The working poor hold part-time or part-year, or even full-time, year-round, low-wage jobs, but still earn so little that their household incomes are below the poverty level. Working 40 hours a week, 52 weeks a year at the minimum wage of $3.35 an hour in early 1990 generated an annual income of $6,968, which was below the poverty level for any household of two or more persons.[25] Under the new law, the minimum wage was raised to $4.25 an hour in April 1991.

For many people, poverty is temporary. However, for others it is a persistent, chronic condition. Based on an analysis of data that traced the economic circumstances of the same families over many years, researchers found that one out of four Americans lived below the poverty line at some point in the 1970s. However, less than 10% of those falling into poverty were persistently poor during 8 or more of the 10 years, and more than half were poor for 2 years or less. Many people slip into poverty as the result of the economic adversity that may accompany a divorce or the loss of a job, for example. Most manage to climb back out of poverty in a fairly short time.[26]

The same study also found that 2.6% of the population were poor for more than 7 years. The persistently poor have limited job opportunities and become heavily dependent on welfare. This group has been referred to as the "underclass." They are isolated from mainstream society and basic economic opportunities. More recent studies have found the problem of persistent poverty growing worse in the United States. Over one-fifth of blacks living in big cities were living in poverty for the entire 10 years from 1974 to 1983.[27]

Defining Poverty

The purpose of measuring poverty is to identify families and individuals who do not have sufficient economic resources to achieve a minimally acceptable standard of living. The poverty income guidelines for 1989 are given in Table 9.2. The poverty level rises from $5,980 for a single individual to $20,260 for a family of eight. The current poverty index is based on a family's food needs. This method of measuring poverty was first proposed by Mollie Orshansky of the Social Security Administration in 1964 and was adopted as the official government measure of poverty in 1969. The basic concept of the Orshansky poverty index is to define as poor any household that would have to spend more than one-third of its income to purchase a minimum, nutritionally adequate diet.

Based on an analysis of the USDA's 1955 Household Food Consumption Survey, Orshansky found that the typical household of at least three persons was spending about one-third of its income on food. She then multiplied USDA's 1961 Economy Food Plan by three to determine the poverty threshold. The Economy Food Plan provided a low-cost food basket for families of different sizes and composition and for individuals by age and gender. The plan met their nutritional needs for selected nutrients in terms of the Recommended Dietary Allowances (RDAs) being used at that time. It reflected the actual food use of low-income households. The poverty guidelines are updated annually to reflect changes in the Consumer Price Index, which measures the overall rate of inflation.[28] The Orshansky poverty index suffers from a number of limitations and is in some ways quite arbitrary. However, it was available when there was a great need for an official poverty measure. Since its adoption, it has served as the standard for measuring our relative progress or lack of progress against poverty in the United States.

Table 9.2. 1989 Poverty Income Guidelines[a,b]

Size of Family	Poverty Guideline ($)
1	5,980
2	8,020
3	10,060
4	12,100
5	14,140
6	16,180
7	18,220
8	20,260[c]

[a] Source: Federal Register, 1989.
[b] For all states, except Alaska and Hawaii.
[c] For family units with over eight persons, add $2,040 for each additional person.

The poverty guidelines relate to total annual money (cash) income before taxes. Noncash or in-kind benefits, such as Medicare, Medicaid, food stamps, school lunches, and housing assistance, are not included. These include many of the government's major antipoverty programs. The federal government now calculates an alternative measure of poverty, which includes the value of noncash benefits.

Two different methods are used for valuing the noncash benefits: a market value approach and a recipient or cash equivalent approach. The market value of a noncash benefit is what it would cost if purchased in the private market. The recipient or cash equivalent value is the amount of cash that would make the recipient just as well-off. The recipient or cash equivalent value is typically smaller than the market value of an in-kind benefit, because the recipient would prefer a smaller amount of cash that could be spent as he or she chose. The proportion of the population in 1987 below the poverty level was only 8.5%, counting all noncash benefits using the market value approach, and 11.0% using the recipient or cash equivalent approach, rather than the 13.4% given for 1987 in Table 9.1.[29]

NUTRITION AND HEALTH PROBLEMS OF THE POOR

This section looks at specific nutrition and nutrition-related health problems of the poor. Evidence is examined from the USDA's 1977–1978 Nationwide Food Consumption Survey (NFCS), the 1986 Continuing Survey of Food Intake by Individuals (CSFII), and the National Health and Nutrition Examination Survey conducted in 1976–1980 (NHANES II). These data sources allow us to compare the nutrient intake and the nutrition-related health problems of the poor with the rest of the population. More recent data were not yet available.

Nutrient Intake

Table 9.3 gives the percentage of the population, by poverty status and race, who consumed less than 70% of the RDA for food energy and 12 other major nutrients. The proportion receiving less than 70% of the RDA is a better indicator of potential nutrition problems than the average or mean percent of the RDA consumed for a nutrient.

Calorie intakes were more likely to be below 70% of the RDA for food energy for both whites and blacks who were below the poverty level. In addition, blacks were more likely than whites in both income groups to consume less than 70% of the RDA for Calories. Even though the caloric intakes of approximately 40% of those below the poverty level were low, being overweight was, and is, a problem for many of the poor.[30]

For the remaining 12 nutrients in Table 9.3, a higher proportion of the population below the poverty level had intakes lower than 70% of the RDA. However, for most nutrients the differences were quite small. It was not indicated in the available reports whether any of the apparent differences shown in Table 9.3 between those below and above the poverty level were statistically significant.[31] The concept of statistical significance relates to whether the differences perceived in the sample can be reasonably presumed to be true for the entire population, which the sample represents, or whether they are just a matter of chance.

Nutritional deficiencies for women and children are given in Table 9.4 for 1986. The information is from the USDA's CSFII, which sampled only two specific subgroups in the population on a regular basis: women 19–50 years of age and their children 1–5 years old.[32] The percentage with nutrient intakes less than 70% of the RDAs are given for women and children in households with incomes at or below 130% of the poverty level, and for those over 130% of the poverty level. These particular income levels are used because they are the ones available in the published USDA reports.[33]

For food energy and each of 15 other nutrients shown in Table 9.4, a larger proportion of low-income women consumed less than 70% of the RDAs. The differences for some nutrients were small. However, from 8 to 20% more women with low incomes had low intakes of calcium,

Table 9.3. Percent of the Population with Nutrient Intakes Less Than 70% of the Recommended Dietary Allowances by Poverty Status and Race[a] (1977–1978)

Nutrient[b]	Below Poverty		Above Poverty	
	White	Black	White	Black
Food energy (Calories)	37	43	31	39
Protein	5	5	3	3
Calcium	45	56	40	56
Iron	35	39	32	34
Ascorbic acid	32	26	26	24
Vitamin A	37	37	31	30
Thiamin	18	16	17	16
Riboflavin	13	16	11	17
Niacin	15	14	9	9
Vitamin B-6	55	52	50	50
Vitamin B-12	21	22	14	17
Phosphorus	11	17	7	12
Magnesium	42	56	36	53

[a] Source: U.S. Department of Health and Human Services, Public Health Service, 1986, pp. 251-279; based on the U.S. Department of Agriculture's 1977–1978 Nationwide Food Consumption Survey, three-day individual data.
[b] 1980 Recommended Dietary Allowances were used.

ascorbic acid, vitamin A, riboflavin, niacin, vitamin E, and magnesium. Although 54.6% of the women in households with income at or below 130% of the poverty level consumed less than 70% of the food energy (Calorie) RDA, as will be shown later, many low-income women are overweight.

A larger proportion of the children in low-income households consumed less than 70% of the RDA for food energy and each of the other nutrients, with the exception of iron. The differences between the two income groups were greatest for food energy, vitamin A, vitamin B-6, magnesium, and zinc. For iron, 40.8% of low-income children consumed less than 70% of the RDA, but more higher income children (44.8%) underconsumed iron. Again, it was not indicated whether these apparent differences are statistically significant.

Nutrition-Related Health Problems

Many health problems that are either directly or indirectly related to poor nutrition are more prevalent among the poor.[34] Figures 9.1 through 9.6 examine specific health and nutrition conditions of particular concern among the low-income population. These figures are based on data from NHANES II conducted from 1976 through 1980.

Excessive weight is a critical health problem among low-income women. Figure 9.1 clearly shows that the percent of overweight women is far

Table 9.4. Percent of Women and Children with Nutrient Intakes Less than 70% of the RDA by Poverty Status (1986)[a]

	Women 19–50 Years		Children 1–5 Years	
Nutrient[b]	0–130% Poverty	Over 130% Poverty	0–130% Poverty	Over 130% Poverty
Food energy	54.6	46.1	15.8	7.6
Protein	8.3	4.8	0.8	0.0
Calcium	55.9	46.8	19.4	16.6
Iron	81.5	78.0	40.8	44.8
Ascorbic acid	36.4	25.3	7.5	6.6
Vitamin A	51.9	34.3	11.1	2.2
Thiamin	25.6	19.5	0.6	0.0
Riboflavin	29.0	18.1	1.7	0.4
Niacin	16.7	8.5	2.8	1.3
Vitamin B-6	80.5	73.2	12.0	6.4
Vitamin B-12	24.7	17.3	3.1	1.1
Vitamin E	61.3	41.2	33.2	30.7
Folacin	89.6	87.0	8.7	6.0
Phosphorus	15.7	9.3	6.1	1.4
Magnesium	69.2	52.8	10.2	2.3
Zinc	79.8	77.3	40.5	34.8

[a] Source: U.S. Department of Agriculture, Human Nutrition Information Service, 1988b, pp. 70-77, and 1989, pp. 78-85.
[b] 1980 Recommended Dietary Allowances used.

higher among those below the poverty level than those above it. Nearly 50% of poor women ages 35–44 and more than half of those ages 45–54 were overweight. A person was defined as overweight who was at or above the 85th percentile in terms of their weight in relation to their height, with the mean weight for height determining the 50th percentile.[35] Pregnant women were not included. Being overweight increases the risk of certain diseases, such as hypertension and diabetes, and can be correlated with increased morbidity and mortality.[36] Excessive weight is not a particular problem among low-income men and, in fact, the percentage of men who are overweight is lower among all age groups over age 35 for those below the poverty level.[37] Table 2.12 in Chapter 2 shows the overweight share of men and women from various ethnic groups.

Iron deficiency is a particular problem among certain portions of the low-income population. The NHANES II survey used several biochemical indicators to diagnose impaired iron status in the blood.[38] Figures 9.2 and 9.3 show impaired iron status by gender, poverty status, and age. As can be seen, the problem was most serious for boys 3–5 years old, teenage girls ages 12–17, and women 25–54 in households below the poverty level. Nearly 14% of boys age 3–5 living in poor households suffered

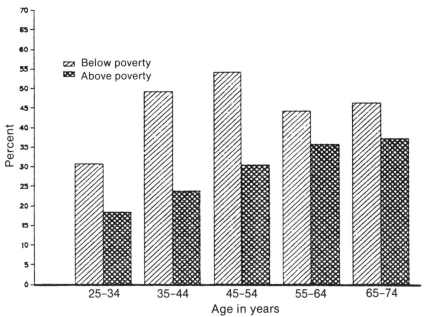

Figure 9.1. Percent of overweight women, by poverty status and age. (Reprinted from U.S. Department of Health and Human Services, Public Health Service, 1986, p. 60.)

from an iron deficiency as opposed to about 4% in households above the poverty level. The prevalence of iron deficiency was generally high for women 25-54 years of age but was even higher for those below the poverty level. In addition, 20.6% of infants 1-2 years of age in poor households suffered from impaired iron status, compared with only 6.7% of infants in nonpoor households. In its most serious form, iron-deficiency anemia can lead to abnormal, small, pale red blood cells.[39]

For other nutrient intakes, evidence of vitamin C depletion was most common for those living below the poverty level, especially among poor adult men who were smokers.[40] Based on blood samples, 20% of men ages 55-74 who were poor had a low serum vitamin C level compared with only about 6% for those not poor.[41]

Growth charts are based on the distribution of heights and weights of children by age and gender in a healthy, reference population. A particular child's height and weight can be compared with that of the reference population reflected in the growth chart. The impacts of racial and ethnic differences on children's growth rates are minor compared to the effects of diet and health-related factors.[42]

A normal pattern of physical development and growth is characteristic of healthy, well-fed children.[43] A nutritionally adequate diet is necessary

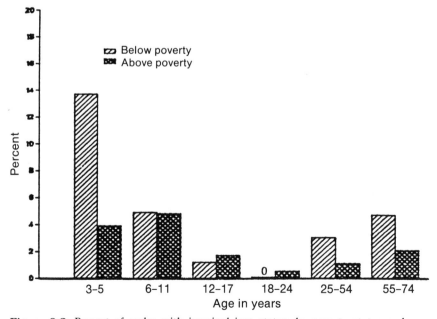

Figure 9.2. Percent of males with impaired iron status, by poverty status and age. (Reprinted from U.S. Department of Health and Human Services, Public Health Service, 1986, p. 174.)

for a child's development, but other factors that affect the child's health are also important. If a child's height is less than it should be for his or her age, this is called "stunting". "Wasting" is the term used when a child's weight is too low in relation to his or her height. The former is an indicator of a child's long-run or chronic nutritional and health status. The latter reflects a child's short-run or current nutritional and health status. Figure 9.4 shows the percentage of children below the fifth percentile of height based on the National Center for Health Statistic's growth chart. At the fifth percentile, a child would be significantly stunted. He or she would be shorter than 95% of the children in a healthy population of the same age and gender. Children living below the poverty level consistently suffer a higher incidence of stunting than those above poverty. The most extreme difference is shown for girls 2–5 years old, with over 14% of those below the poverty line below the fifth percentile, whereas about 5% in nonpoor households fell below the fifth percentile.

Poverty did not have a consistently significant effect on a child's weight in relation to his or her height, except for boys ages 6–9. About 7% of those in poor households were below the fifth percentile of weight for height as opposed to only 2% among the nonpoor.[44]

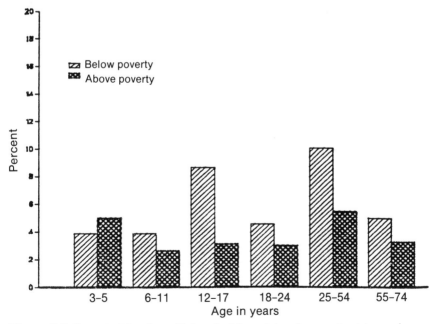

Figure 9.3. Percent of females with impaired iron status, by poverty status and age. (Reprinted from U.S. Department of Health and Human Services, Public Health Service, 1986, p. 174.)

For every age group shown in Figure 9.5, the percentage of people diagnosed as having diabetes in the NHANES II survey was higher for those below than for those above the poverty line. Diabetes is a condition involving the inadequate production of insulin by the pancreas and an inability to metabolize glucose in the bloodstream. Genetic factors are believed to play a dominant role in the onset of most cases of diabetes. However, research suggests that overeating, combined with a lack of physical activity and excess body weight, may be associated with many cases of diabetes.

Overall, the incidence of diabetes was 12.9% for the poor and 6.8% for the nonpoor. However, the correlation between poverty and diabetes may be largely indirect. Blacks, who are disproportionately poor, also suffer from a higher rate of diabetes (11.2%) than whites (7.0%). Furthermore, 13.4% of overweight people were diabetic, compared with 4.9% for those who were not overweight. As was shown in Figure 9.1, low-income women are more likely to be overweight and could thus be expected to have a higher incidence of diabetes.[45]

Unavoidably, this discussion understates the seriousness of the nutrition and nutrition-related health problems of the poor. The samples

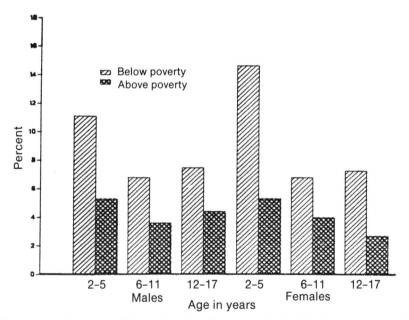

Figure 9.4. Percent of children below the fifth percentile of height for their age on the growth chart of the National Center for Health Statistics, by poverty status, sex, and age. (Reprinted from U.S. Department of Health and Human Services, Public Health Service, 1986, p. 213.)

for the major surveys (the 1977–1978 NFCS and NHANES II) did not include individuals without a permanent address (the homeless) or American Indians living on reservations.[46] These two groups suffer from a high incidence of extreme poverty and serious malnutrition. The sampling plan of future surveys should be expanded to include these important, high-risk population groups.

FOOD ASSISTANCE PROGRAMS

The origin of federal food assistance programs can be traced back to farm support laws enacted during the Depression of the 1930s. The legislation was designed more to dispose of agricultural surpluses than to meet the food and nutrition needs of people, but the food distribution to the poor was a welcome help to most of the recipients anyway.[47] A commodity distribution program was established that distributed surplus agricultural commodities directly to the needy. In 1939, 13 million Americans received such food supplements.[48] A food stamp program and a school lunch program were initiated in 1939 and a school milk program in 1940. Many of these programs were curtailed or reduced during World War II, which was accompanied by soaring demand for agricultural

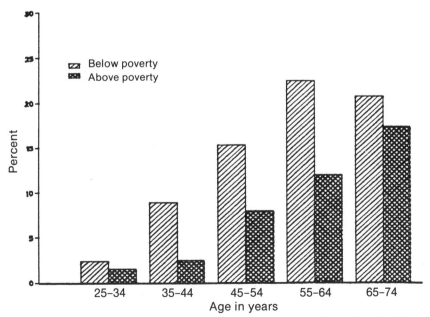

Figure 9.5. Percent of adults with diabetes, by poverty status and age. (Reprinted from U.S. Department of Health and Human Services, Public Health Service, 1986, p. 203.)

products and a robust economy. The initial food stamp program, for example, was discontinued in 1943.[49]

The commitment to funding food and nutrition assistance was greatly expanded in the 1970s in response to the concerns about widespread hunger in the United States. In addition, the primary emphasis shifted from disposing of surplus agricultural commodities to assisting low-income people with their food needs. The federal government's expenditures on food assistance programs rose from $1.1 billion in 1969 to $11.2 billion in fiscal year 1979 (FY 79), largely due to a substantial expansion in the coverage of the Food Stamp Program.

In the 1980s, during the Reagan administration, with a tax cut and greatly expanded expenditures on national defense, there was significant pressure to reduce, or at least hold down, spending on domestic programs. President Reagan, in his 1982 State of the Union Address, proposed replacing the major federal food assistance programs with cash block grants to the states.[50] The federal government's spending on food assistance programs, in current dollars, continued to grow during the 1980s anyway, increasing from $14.2 billion in FY 80 to $21.2 billion in FY 88.[51] However, government expenditures for food stamps in FY 82 were reduced by 12% and for child nutrition programs by 24% below the levels they would have reached without budget reduction measures enacted in 1981.[52] Furthermore, between FY 83 and 88, although spending on food programs rose 9.9%, the Consumer Price Index increased 18.4%. Therefore, in real terms or constant dollars, expenditures for food assistance fell by fully 8.5%.[53]

Federal expenditures and the average monthly participation in FY 88 (when available) are given in Table 9.5 for the various food assistance programs. Food stamps were the largest program by a substantial margin, with federal outlays of over $12 billion and an average of almost 19 million recipients. The Special Supplemental Food Program for Women, Infants and Children was one of the few programs to expand significantly in recent years and now accounts for the third largest allocation of food assistance dollars. In 1982, food stamps were replaced with a nutrition assistance block grant in Puerto Rico. Over half of the island's population participates. Monthly participation averaged 1.4 million in FY 88.[54]

The next five programs listed in Table 9.5 are child nutrition programs that operate through our nation's schools and child care centers. The National School Lunch Program had the second highest expenditures. Over 24 million children participated on average, with slightly less than half receiving free or reduced-price meals. The Child Care Food Program provides cash and commodity assistance to child care centers and to family day care homes. The School Breakfast, Summer Food Service, and Special Milk programs are additional child nutrition programs that operate through the schools.[55]

The last five programs involve the distribution of commodities. The Temporary Emergency Food Assistance Program provides surplus agricultural commodities to needy persons. The Charitable Institutions Program provides surplus commodities to charitable organizations that serve meals to the needy. The Commodity Supplemental Food Program operated through 18 state agencies and one Indian tribal organization in FY 88, serving the elderly, women, infants, and children. The Needy Family Program now operates only on Indian reservations and on our Pacific Island territories, which prefer food commodities to food stamps. The Nutrition Program for the Elderly supplies cash and commodities to senior citizen centers that provide meals and to the Meals-On-Wheels program for the homebound.[56]

Several federal programs that provide food assistance but which are not run through the U.S. Department of Agriculture (USDA) Food and Nutrition Service are not listed in Table 9.5. The Expanded Food and

Table 9.5. Government Food Assistance Programs: Federal Cost and Participation[a] (Fiscal Year 1988)

Programs	Federal Government Costs[b] (Dollars, in Millions)	Participation[c] (Thousands)
Food stamps	12,341	18,700
Special Supplemental Program for Women, Infants, and Children	1,801	3,593
Nutrition assistance block grant, Puerto Rico	879	1,430
Child nutrition programs		
National School Lunch	2,920	24,200[d]
Child Care Food	618	1,251
School Breakfast	484	3,690[e]
Summer Food Service	136	1,577[f]
Special Milk	19	NA[g]
Commodity distribution programs		
Temporary Emergency Food Assistance	633	NA
Charitable Institutions	154	NA
Commodity Supplemental Food	62	213
Needy Family	62	137
Nutrition Program for the Elderly	150	NA
Total[h]	21,211	

[a] Source: U.S. Department of Agriculture, Food and Nutrition Service, 1989.
[b] Includes state administrative matching funds and other program costs.
[c] Average monthly participation unless otherwise indicated.
[d] 9.8 million are free, 1.6 million reduced price, and 12.8 million paid.
[e] 3.03 million are free, 180,000 reduced price, and 470,000 paid.
[f] Participation in July.
[g] Not available.
[h] Not all programs are shown, so categories do not add up to the total.

Nutrition Education Program (EFNEP) operates through the Agricultural Extension Service. The program educates low-income families on efficient food purchasing and preparation and on nutritional needs. The Community Food and Nutrition Program helps local and state governments coordinate private and public food assistance. The Emergency Food and Shelter Program provides federal funds to assist the homeless. An estimated 46% of the funds are used to provide meals.[57]

The Food Stamp Program

The current Food Stamp Program was initiated on a pilot basis during the Kennedy Administration in 1961. The program was permanently authorized in 1964 for states wanting to take part, and in 1974 Congress passed legislation that required all states to offer food stamps.[58] The objective of the program, as declared in the Food Stamp Act of 1977, is to "permit low-income households to obtain a more nutritious diet."[59] Food stamps are a vital support for many low-income families. One example is Delaine Lee, an unemployed, single mother living in rural Minnesota, who said "I wouldn't make it without the food stamps. That's plain and simple."[60]

Monthly allotments of coupons that can be used to purchase food at grocery stores are issued to eligible households. Congress reformed the program so that after 1979 all eligible households received their coupon allotment for free. Before that time, most households had to purchase their allotment at some fraction of the face value of the coupons. The Food Stamp Program operates through the public assistance agency in each state and the local county welfare offices, which certify the eligibility of applicants and issue stamps. The federal government, through the USDA's Food and Nutrition Service, covers the entire cost of the coupons and at least half of the states' administrative expenses. Overall policies and procedures are set at the federal level. The eligibility criteria and benefit levels are standardized nationally.[61]

To be eligible to receive food stamps, a household's gross monthly income may not exceed 130% of the official poverty guidelines for their household size. Also, after being allowed certain deductions, such as a standard deduction of slightly over $100 for most households, and a deduction for excess shelter expenses, the household's net income may not exceed the monthly poverty income level (divide the levels in Table 9.2 by 12 to get the monthly poverty levels). Households with an elderly or disabled member need only meet the net income criteria. Households receiving public assistance or Supplemental Security Income, a welfare program for the low-income elderly, are automatically eligible.[62] There are also limits on the assets a household may hold. A household, for example, cannot own a car worth more than $4,500, unless it is needed for employment, or have more than $2,000 in cash and liquid assets, unless the householders are elderly.[63] If not employed, householders must fulfill a work registration requirement.

The food stamp (coupon) allotment is affected by a household's size and income. Households with more members receive a larger coupon allotment, but more income reduces their benefits. The allotment is reduced by 30% of the household's net income. This reflects the idea that a family should spend 30% of its own income on food. The maximum allotment, as of October 1989, for a household with no net income, was $99 per month for a single person, $182 for two, $260 for three, $331 for four, on up to $596 for eight, and then $75 more for each additional person.[64] The monthly food stamp allotment averaged $49.77 per person in FY 88, which works out to about 55 cents per meal.[65]

The maximum food stamp allotments are based on the Thrifty Food Plan, which replaced the Economy Food Plan as the USDA's lowest cost food plan. It is one of four USDA food plans discussed in Chapter 2. The maximum food stamp allotment was 100.65% of the cost of the Thrifty Food Plan in FY 89 and that will rise to 103% in FY 91.[66] The Thrifty Food Plan purports to provide a nutritious diet that reflects the food consumption patterns of low-income households. Its objective is to conform as much as possible to the actual consumption patterns of low-income households in order to meet the nutrient goals and cost limit established for the plan.[67] However, households that do not plan meals and grocery shop carefully, or lack the necessary nutrition knowledge or cooking skills, would have difficulty achieving a nutritional diet with the food expenditures allowed under the Thrifty Food Plan.[68]

Empirical research studies have found that households receiving food stamps increase their total food purchases by 25–35 cents for each dollar's worth of food coupons received.[69] This means the $12 billion of food stamps issued in FY 88 increased total food sales by $3–4.2 billion, which is fairly minor as a factor in the total food market. The reason the increase is not dollar for dollar is that food stamp households typically substitute coupons for some of the cash they spent on food prior to joining the program, a decision that is completely legal and logical. For example, a family that was spending $400 per month for food before, after joining the program and receiving $200 worth of coupons, may purchase $460 of food, but now needs to spend only $260 of their cash income on food.

The same studies show, however, that food stamps are far more effective at increasing the recipient households' food expenditures than cash payments. The food purchases of low-income households typically only increase by 5–10 cents for each additional dollar of cash income.[70] They face many other pressing demands on their very limited financial resources. An analysis of the 1977–1978 NFCS data for low-income households found that those receiving food stamps had more nutritious diets than households that were eligible but not participating in the program. The stamp recipients consumed significantly more of each nutrient studied, but the total effect was quite limited.[71]

A major criticism of the Food Stamp Program is that the program is not utilized by a large proportion of those eligible.[72] It has been estimated that between 30 and 60% of those households that are eligible over the period of a year do not participate in the program.[73] Some are unaware of their eligibility; others want to avoid the hassle of applying or the stigma of using food stamps. A federally funded outreach program aimed at increasing participation was eliminated in 1982.[74]

Arguments have been made for eliminating the use of food stamps and simply providing assistance in the form of cash. The various reforms of the program have reduced its impact on expanding food demand and improving nutrition. Food stamps have literally become a substitute for a national income maintenance program.[75]

Participation in the Food Stamp Program increased by 1.3 million people between May 1989 and May 1990 and reached over 20 million for the first time since 1985.[76] A marked increase in the number of recipients is typical during periods of weakness in the economy. Enrollment in other welfare programs, particularly Aid to Families with Dependent Children, also rose during this period. Besides a general economic slowdown, administrative factors may have contributed to the rise in food stamp enrollment. For one thing, the application form was significantly shortened in some states.

Food Stamp Program expenses rose sharply in FY 1990. Based on a predicted participation level of 18.1 million, the Bush administration had originally requested $13.3 billion for food stamps for FY 90. Congress appropriated $14.8 billion and then had to add another $1.2 billion to keep the program funded. The House passed an appropriation of $18.1 billion for food stamps for FY 91. Depending on the length and depth of the economic downturn, food stamp participation and expenditures could climb considerably higher.[77]

Other Major Government Programs

The Special Supplemental Food Program for Women, Infants, and Children (known as WIC) was started as a pilot program in 1972 and then officially established in 1974. Its goal is to improve the nutrition and health of pregnant, breast-feeding, and postpartum women and their infants and children under age five. The program is run through some 8,000 local health clinics and is aimed at those who are at nutritional risk because of inadequate income. To be eligible, household income cannot exceed 185% of the poverty guidelines.

Most clinics now give vouchers to participants that can be used to purchase specified foods at grocery stores. A few clinics distribute the food directly or arrange for home delivery. The authorized foods are designed to fulfill nutrient needs that have been found lacking in the target population. Milk, cheese, eggs, fruit or vegetable juice containing vitamin C, dried beans and peas, peanut butter, iron-fortified breakfast cereal, infant cereal, and iron-fortified infant formula are included among the approved food items. The foods are individually prescribed and mothers receive nutrition education. Monthly food benefits averaged $33.32 per participant in FY 88.[78] WIC is not an entitlement like food stamps and other of the food assistance programs; this means that there have not been sufficient funds to cover all those who have been determined eligible and in need of the program. Coverage is provided on a priority basis with the highest priority given to pregnant women, then infants up to a year old. These two groups typically receive complete coverage.

The extensive nutrition and medical data collected as part of the program have been used to evaluate its impact. The evaluation studies have found the program to be highly effective. Program participants had improved intakes of a number of important nutrients, including iron and vitamin C. In addition, the program resulted in an increase in average birth weights and a decrease in preterm births and neonatal mortality.[79] Largely because of its proven effectiveness, the WIC program has been able to obtain increased funding in recent years. Funding increased from $949 million in FY 82 to $1.8 billion in FY 88, shown in Table 9.5.

The National School Lunch Program was first authorized in 1946. This program helps support food services in elementary and secondary schools and in child care centers, with cash and commodity distributions. Cash payments are based on the number of meals served, and are higher for those meals provided free or at reduced cost. Schools are also given government-owned, surplus commodities. The household income of a child's family must be below 130% of the poverty level for him or her to be eligible for free lunches and below 185% of the poverty figure for reduced-price meals. In FY 88, some 4.03 billion meals were provided at 90,600 sites, with 47.5% either free or at reduced price.[80] A typical price in 1989–1990 for a full-priced lunch was $1.00 in elementary school and $1.20 in secondary school.[81]

The goal of the school lunch program, as written in the original legislation, is "to safeguard the health and well-being of the nation's children, and to encourage the domestic consumption of nutritious agricultural commodities and other food."[82] However, the nutritional quality of the meals provided by the program has been criticized, particularly for containing too much fat, sodium, and sugar.

Another issue is whether to provide meals that children will like, and hence eat, or ones that will develop good nutritional habits. Studies have found that about 15% of the food served in a typical school lunch remains uneaten and ends up in the trash.[83] The proportion wasted was even higher for some highly nutritious foods, such as carrot sticks.[84] In order to provide foods the students like, more and more "fast-food" products are showing up in school lunch meals.[85] They are popular with a generation of children who frequently go to McDonald's or Burger King. Even school lunch menus are being consumer-driven.

An evaluation based on data from the 1977–1978 NFCS found the program had a significant positive impact on the nutrient consumption of participating children, and particularly low-income children.[86] Children ages 6–11 who participated in the school lunch program, had higher intakes of calcium, iron, riboflavin, and vitamins A, B-6, and C.[87]

The Temporary Emergency Food Assistance Program was established in 1981 as a mechanism for distributing surplus government inventories, particularly dairy products, to low-income households. This is the program behind the cheese give-aways. Other commodities that have been distributed are honey, rice, butter, nonfat dry milk, cornmeal, and flour. The food is distributed free to the recipients, who are supposed to meet eligibility standards established by the states. The value of the program's distributions declined nearly 30% between FY 87 and 88 because of the reduced availability of surplus commodities.[88]

Private Initiatives

During the 1980s there was a sharp increase in the number of people seeking food assistance from private, nongovernment organizations. The two basic forms of private assistance are "food shelves," which provide basic grocery products free to needy families, and feeding facilities or "soup kitchens" which serve free meals to the destitute. The 303 food shelves operating in Minnesota, for example, filled over 1.2 million requests in 1987, representing an increase of about 600% since 1982.[89] Furthermore, it has been said that there are now more soup kitchens in the United States serving more meals to more people than at any time since the Depression of the 1930s.[90] The number of providers of free meals in New York City jumped from 30 in 1981 to 500 in 1987.[91]

Food shelves are run by churches, social service agencies, or free-standing organizations. Their budgets are usually small, and they heavily depend on volunteers for labor and on donated food and money. They typically provide clients with a supply of groceries designed to last their families three to seven days. Eligibility is determined by each food shelf, but usually no one who says their family is in need is turned away. Clients must, however, normally live within a given geographic area. Families might have been limited to one visit per month in the past, but in some places, increased demand has forced food shelves to limit users to four to six visits per year.

A survey of food shelf users in Minnesota found that 63% were families with children under 18 years of age, and 25% had jobs. Over half were not receiving food stamps, and the most common reason given was they thought their families were not eligible. However, income data suggested that many of them were eligible.[92] Many users would be classified among the "new poor." Demand on food shelves is particularly heavy towards the end of the month, when many food stamp recipients have exhausted their resources.

Food banks act as warehouses, collecting and distributing food to affiliated food shelves. A major function of the food banks is to solicit donations of food products from major food manufacturing and distribution companies. Second Harvest, with headquarters in Chicago, is a national network of food banks. In 1985, it distributed 152.2 million pounds of food donated by 256 food companies to 205 member food banks throughout the United States[93]

The feeding programs that provide free meals often serve as a last resort for those who have fallen through the social welfare "safety net." The population served by these free-meal providers contains a high proportion of homeless people. Many of these soup kitchens try to help their users with additional needs, such as finding housing and clothing and, sometimes, child abuse and alcoholism problems.[94] Most soup kitchens operate on a shoe string. Much of the work is performed by volunteers.

These private initiatives can be viewed from two perspectives. One is as a healthy indicator of the ability of private charity and volunteerism to reduce overdependence on government welfare programs. The other views them as an indication of the large number of poor and hungry and the serious inadequacy of the government's safety net. There are limits to the role that can be played by private programs. What they can do best is fill gaps left by the government programs, responding to emergency needs and special local requirements.

However, the private programs are becoming a long-term food source for many individuals and families.[95] Those who run the private programs find the demand threatens to overwhelm their very limited resources. Robert Andersen, who helped start the Rainbow Kitchen, a free-meal operation in Homestead, Pennsylvania, said, "I'm afraid we're becoming the substitute for a long-term solution."[96] Two additional problems of the private efforts are the wide differences between areas in their availability and the unreliability of charitable donations. Food assistance must continue to be treated as primarily a government responsibility. Private programs can reasonably be expected to shoulder only a limited portion of the burden. Dolores Patrick, the Rainbow's director, said, "Our dream is to go out of business" for lack of a need.[97]

GENERAL IMPLICATIONS

Americans have mixed feelings about government welfare programs that assist the poor. This includes the food programs, and particularly, food stamps. Many find their cost objectionable and incidents of fraud and misuse prompt outrage. However, Americans are also a charitable, compassionate people, and when the situation of specific individuals is described, such as the Spences or the Fullers at the beginning of this chapter, most people would likely favor helping them. A political consensus has emerged, however, that social welfare programs should contain strong work incentives and job training support, which reflects the widespread belief that able-bodied adults should work to support themselves.

Current government programs, including those involving food assistance, reflect the belief that certain types of consumption—those related to nutrition, health, and education—are more meritorious than others. Society is more concerned about the level of inequality in the distribution of such merit goods than the distribution of income. Access to adequate food might be thought of as a fundamental right, since a lack of food means, in the extreme, to be deprived of life. There is no basis for making ethical judgments among different consumption patterns for most goods. However, food consumption levels can be evaluated against nutrient requirements, dietary guidelines, and health status.

The economists' concept of human capital offers another perspective on food assistance. The productivity of our economy depends on the skills and knowledge of the work force. As Theodore W. Schultz, a recipient of the Nobel Prize in economics, noted, "Much of what we call consumption constitutes investment in human capital," especially expenditures on education, health, and nutrition.[98] The human capital argument is particularly strong for children. A child's nutritional status can affect his or her physical and mental development and educational achievement. If our nation is to have a highly productive labor force that can compete in the world economy of the 21st century, it depends on our investments in the education, health, and nutrition of today's children.

Food Safety:
A Growing Concern

CHAPTER 10

Food safety is a growing concern for many consumers. Americans have come to take a bountiful food supply for granted, but many are worrying about the safety of their food and its impact on their health. In early 1989, two widely publicized food safety incidents occurred within a short time: the public outcry over use of Alar (daminozide) on apples, and the Chilean grape tampering scare, in which some imported grapes were found to be laced with cyanide.[1] During the Chilean grape incident, one mother in Oregon became so concerned that she called the state highway patrol to ask them to stop her daughter's school bus and remove the grapes from her lunch.[2] However, anyone who thinks food safety concerns are a recent phenomenon should read Upton Sinclair's famous book, *The Jungle* (1906), which describes scandalous conditions in the meat-packing industry around the turn of the century before federal meat inspection was introduced.[3]

Everyone, including consumers, producers, processors, and politicians, would support the position that the United States should have an adequate, reliable, wholesome, nutritious, high-quality, reasonably priced, and safe food supply. No one would claim to be in favor of unsafe or unwholesome food. The controversy begins with the interpretation of these goals, including food safety, and the actions taken or not taken to achieve them.

This chapter first looks at food safety from various perspectives— consumers', producers', and others. The basic food safety legislation in the United States and the policy formulation process are briefly reviewed. Later, two key elements required for making sound food safety decisions are discussed: estimating the risk involved and establishing an acceptable level of risk. Consumers' perceptions of the riskiness of an activity or product are frequently quite different from the actual hazard involved and there are factors that can explain this divergence. The issue of food safety is also related to the degree of trust and confidence consumers have in the food industry and the government regulatory process. The

Table 10.1. Consumer Food Safety Concerns[a,b]

| Factor | Percent Rating as a Serious Hazard | | | | | 1989 Rating (%) | | | |
	1984	1985	1986	1987	1988	Serious Hazard	Something of a Hazard	Not a Hazard At All	Not Sure
Residues, such as pesticides and herbicides	77	73	75	76	75	82	13	3	3
Antibiotics and hormones in poultry and livestock	NA[c]	NA	NA	61	61	61	26	6	7
Nitrites in food	NA	NA	NA	38	44	44	38	5	13
Irradiated foods	NA	NA	37	43	36	42	24	10	24
Additives and preservatives	32	36	33	36	29	30	59	8	4
Artificial coloring	26	28	26	24	21	28	48	19	5

[a] Source: Food Marketing Institute, 1989a, p. 54 (used by permission).
[b] May not add to 100% due to rounding.
[c] Not asked.

role consumer information can and should play in food safety issues is also addressed. In the last section, several food safety topics of particular current interest are discussed, including pesticide residues, foodborne pathogens, seafood inspection, food additives, and safety concerns related to new technologies.

VARIOUS PERSPECTIVES ON FOOD SAFETY

For most consumers, food safety may be a growing, but at most times still a largely latent concern. In the January 1989 Food Marketing Institute's survey of food shoppers, people were asked how confident they were about the safety of the food in supermarkets. Twenty-three percent of respondents were completely confident, 58% mostly confident, 15% somewhat doubtful, 2% very doubtful, and 2% not sure.[4] When a list of specific food safety concerns was read to them, however, a large proportion of respondents identified several issues as posing a serious hazard. Table 10.1 gives detailed responses for 1989 and traces the percentage who believed each factor was a serious safety hazard back to 1984, the first year the Food Marketing Institute survey began asking this question. The specific question asked was, "I'm going to read a list of food items that may or may not constitute a health hazard. For each one, please tell me if you believe it is a serious health hazard, somewhat of a hazard, or not a hazard at all."[5]

According to the results in Table 10.1, the most worrisome food safety concern for consumers was pesticide and herbicide residues, followed by antibiotic and hormone use, nitrites, irradiation, additives and preservatives, and then artificial colors. In a 1980 Louis Harris poll, 81% of the respondents felt that society was exposed to a greater risk from chemicals than 20 years earlier.[6] The greatest food safety concern of consumers "is that suspected or known cancer-causing chemicals are being used in food production and processing, with unknown long-run health risks."[7] This helps explain why consumers rank pesticide and herbicide residues as such serious health hazards. Consumers expect government to treat food safety as a high priority issue and to act to ensure the safety of food. In a 1983 survey of consumers in Kansas, 90% agreed that food safety should be a high government priority.[8]

The hazard posed by microbial contamination is usually quite far down on most consumers' lists of food safety concerns.[9] This ranking is quite different from the priorities that food safety experts place on various issues. The professional staff of the Food and Drug Administration (FDA) considers microbiological contaminants to be the major health hazard associated with food, followed by malnutrition and diet-related factors related to degenerative diseases; environmental contaminants such as

PCBs (polychlorinated biphenyls), dioxin, and mercury; naturally occurring toxins in foods; pesticide residues; and then food additives.[10]

Some consumer advocates and some people in the food industry hold quite extreme views on the food safety issue. Various consumer and environmental groups think that government regulations are irresponsibly ignoring chemicals that pose insidious health threats.[11] This was the position of the Natural Resources Defense Council regarding Alar.[12] The Council believes food safety regulation has been overly influenced by commercial agriculture and the food industry.[13] The government regulatory system is seen as inadequate and the agricultural and food industries as unresponsive to safety concerns, and in particular, unwilling to cut their use of toxic chemicals.[14]

On the other side of the food safety issue are many in the food industry who complain about over-regulation to the point where costs are increased with only marginal returns to safety. They argue that the elimination of all food-related risks is not possible, either economically or technically. They find regulatory procedures, particularly for the approval of new pesticides and additives, to be unduly complex and time-consuming. The approval process for a new pesticide can take up to 6 years and that for a new food additive, up to 10 years.[15] The cost to bring a new chemical such as these to market may range from $30 to $50 million.[16] Many in the industry believe that the hazards are exaggerated and the public's anxieties unduly inflated by the more extreme consumer advocates and the media. Public policy ends up being made more on the basis of political expediency than scientific facts.[17] Not surprisingly, given these divergent viewpoints, food safety concerns can become highly charged public policy issues.

FOOD SAFETY REGULATION AND THE POLICY PROCESS

Early in this century, the public's concern about food safety was aroused by several events. In addition to Sinclair's *The Jungle,* Wiley's poison squad had a major impact.[18] Harvey Wiley was chief of the Bureau of Chemistry in the U.S. Department of Agriculture. He used a squad of volunteers to test the safety of various foods they had purchased. The testing frequently required eating the food, since today's laboratory procedures did not exist. Many problems were found. At about the same time, the New York City Health Commission found that more than 50% of the 4,000 milk samples it tested were adulterated. The milk was diluted by water, and chalk or plaster of Paris had been added.[19]

In 1906, Congress passed the Pure Food and Drug Act and the Meat Inspection Act. The former stated that the food that moved in interstate commerce was to be safe, but it was not a very effective regulation. No fines or penalties were established.[20] The latter set up a federal meat inspection system. Most importantly, these laws established that the federal government has a responsibility and a legal right to ensure a safe and wholesome food supply.[21] The FDA, created in 1931, was ineffective until after the passage of the Federal Food, Drug and Cosmetic Act in 1938. This law gave it the authority to fine and imprison violators.[22] Originally, the FDA was part of the USDA, but in 1953 it was transferred to the Department of Health, Education and Welfare, now the Department of Health and Human Services. The Miller Pesticide Amendment, under which the pesticide residue on food is regulated, was added to the Food, Drug and Cosmetic Act in 1954.

The Poultry Products Inspection Act was enacted in 1957 and gave that responsibility to the USDA. The 1958 Food Additives Amendment placed the burden of proving that an additive was safe on the manufacturer before introducing it rather than on the government (or consumers) after introduction.[23] This stance represented a fundamental shift in entitlements (rights) from manufacturers to consumers, and helped set the stage for future regulation and litigation of product safety issues. The 1958 amendment also contained the well-known Delaney clause, which will be discussed in detail later.

Four other laws that have had an effect on food safety issues are the 1960 Color Additives Amendment, which regulates coloring additives; the 1966 Fair Packaging and Labeling Act, which regulates advertising on packaged items including food; the 1970 Egg Products Inspection Act, which regulates egg processing plants; and the 1971 Freedom of Information Act, which opened government actions to public scrutiny.[24] In addition to these major pieces of legislation, there are many other federal and state statutes relevant to various aspects of food safety regulation.[25]

The food safety regulation system is far more complex than just the passage of laws by Congress. Specific agencies in the executive branch are given the authority to implement laws within the guidelines established by legislation. Implementation requires much more specificity than is contained in the legislation. A vast number of specific rules and regulations have been promulgated under the various laws by the agencies involved, principally the FDA and USDA.[26] Proposed rules and regulations must be officially announced in the *Federal Register,* a daily record of the executive branch of government. A period of time is allowed for receiving comments concerning the proposal, and frequently formal public hearings are held.[27] The proposed rule or regulation may be dropped or modified before it is finalized. The complicated process of implementing and enforcing the laws passed by Congress gives the executive agencies and departments, and the civil servants in them, far more power and influence than most people realize.

DECIDING WHAT IS SAFE

Donald Kennedy, a past commissioner of FDA and president of Stanford University, suggests that two elements are required for sound food safety decisions: an objective estimate of the risk involved and a policy judgment about the acceptable level of risk.[28] The first is primarily a scientific issue and the second a public policy issue. Individual consumers cannot objectively determine their exposure to hazards in the food supply, nor can policymakers. Both must rely upon scientists to make these assessments. Sound food safety policy decisions require accurate estimates of the level of risk involved. In speaking about his experience as FDA commissioner, Kennedy said that many times, decisions must be made "when the data are not as good as you would like."[29] In many cases, the toxicity information upon which policy is based is lacking or inadequate. As Kennedy also said in reference to possibly hazardous substances, "we live in a world full of suspicion but woefully short on verification."[30] The other fundamental food safety issue is lack of consensus on an acceptable level of risk. How much risk, if any, are we as a society willing to accept to receive the benefits associated with the hazard?

Estimating the Risk or Hazard

We have made enormous advances in our ability to detect trace amounts of substances. Using current chromatographic separation and purification procedures and high-resolution mass spectroscopy, amounts as small as parts per trillion can be measured.[31] In fact, this very ability to detect infinitesimally small quantities has contributed to many of the dilemmas faced in food safety regulation. As Donald Kennedy said in testimony before a Senate committee, "we can detect more than we can evaluate, and measure more than we can understand."[32] Kennedy has characterized the current methods of estimating the risk consumers face from exposure to a possible hazard as primitive compared with the advances in hazard detection capability.[33]

Animal tests, typically using mice or rats, are the primary means for assessing the toxicity or health risks of a substance. Typically, tests are conducted for acute, subacute, and chronic toxicity.[34] The first step is to estimate the exposure level in terms of the consumption in a typical diet on a per unit of body weight basis, based on the amount of the substance that occurs or would occur in foods. The acute toxicity level is determined by giving increasingly larger doses to the test animals until the dose is lethal. An important concept used by scientists, which most consumers are unaware of or overlook, is that virtually every substance is toxic at some level of exposure; it is simply a matter of the dose.[35] Familiar substances, such as salt or water, are poisonous "if taken in excess or in the wrong manner."[36] A corollary to this concept is that substances may also have a minimum or threshold level below which there is no effect, either harmful or beneficial.[37]

The subacute tests involve giving animals a substance daily over a period of time to study the health effects and establish the no-effect dose or minimum-effect dose, which is just below the level at which there are physiological effects.[38] The no-effect or minimum-effect dose is then usually divided by a factor of either 100 or 1,000 to determine the acceptable daily intake for humans, which is expressed on a per unit of body weight basis.[39]

The chronic tests, which are how the risk of cancer is evaluated, check for long-term harmful effects and typically involve a small number of animals over a period of years.[40] The dose given is usually many times the acceptable daily intake for humans on a per unit of body weight basis. Otherwise, very large numbers of animals might have to be tested to establish results, for example, for a one-in-a-million response at low exposure. Mathematical models are used to extrapolate from the high-dose animal results to the low-exposure situation for humans.[41]

Other animal tests are conducted to determine the effect of the substance on birth defects or mutations.[42] The testing of possibly hazardous substances using human subjects is, in most cases, ethically unacceptable. Scientists can use epidemiological studies to look at samples from particular human population groups over long periods to attempt to identify health risks. However, it is always difficult in such studies to determine whether associations actually reflect causation or are just spurious or coincidental.[43]

There are many problems in extrapolating from the results of animal tests to humans.[44] The doses given to test animals are massive compared with the actual or expected level of human consumption.[45] In addition, a basic difficulty is that there are metabolic differences between the test animals and humans, and other differences in chemical responsiveness may exist.[46] Thalidomide, which caused major birth defects in Europe, is a tragic example of the limitations of animal tests. At a dose level of 4 grams per kilogram of body weight per day, no birth defects were found in tests on rats. However, a dose level of only about one ten-thousandth of that amount (a single dose of 0.5 milligrams per kilogram) could cause terrible birth defects when taken by women at certain stages of their pregnancy.[47]

Two recent developments in risk assessment and management should be mentioned. The Hazard Analysis Critical Control Point (HACCP) concept is gaining widespread use in industry to assess and control risks in processing food products. The approach first involves determining the risks. Control points are then set up in the processing to monitor each risk area and ensure that it remains within acceptable limits. Some advocate the adoption of HACCP in public policy risk assessment and control.[48]

Ames, Magaw, and Gold developed a Human Exposure–Rodent Potency (HERP) index to evaluate the relative risks from a variety of chemicals that may be carcinogenic.[49] They argued that animal test results should not be used to estimate absolute human cancer risks. The index values provide a relative ranking of the cancer-related risks of various chemicals based on their carcinogenicity to rodents and estimated human exposure. Rodent potency is based on the dose of the chemical needed to produce tumors in half of the test animals. Ames and co-workers concluded that the risks of cancer from normal exposure to pesticide residues and food additives are minor compared with that from levels of naturally occurring carcinogens in food and the environment.[50]

In the future, alternative methods such as cell and tissue cultures and computer modeling may reduce the need to rely on animal tests. Gary Flamm, director of the FDA Office of Toxicology Science predicted that "large animal tests for carcinogenicity will be all but passé in the next 10 to 15 years."[51] With research advances, scientists will be able to identify "biomarkers" for cancer potential that will require the use of smaller groups of animals for shorter periods of time.

Establishing an Acceptable Risk Standard

As Sandra Archibald states, "food safety is governed by a patchwork of safety standards defined in a multitude of laws that have evolved over time to meet a variety of needs."[52] The risk standard in effect is related to how a substance enters the food supply rather than to the actual health risk it presents. Figure 10.1 presents the major risk standards currently in use, from the zero-tolerance, zero-risk principle of the Delaney clause to the risk benefit approach of the Federal Insecticide, Fungicide and Rodenticide Act (FIFRA). In fact, one of the major criticisms of the current system of food safety regulation is the inconsistency of the risk standards applied.[53]

Delaney was a congressman whose wife died of cancer, who quite understandably took a particular interest in cancer-related health and safety issues.[54] The Delaney clause was attached to the Food Additive Amendment of 1958 to the Food, Drug and Cosmetic Act.[55] It states that "no additive shall be deemed to be safe if it is found to induce cancer when ingested by man or animal, or if it is found, after tests which are appropriate for the evaluation of the safety of food additives, to induce cancer in man or animal."[56]

The Delaney clause applies specifically to food additives. Much of the controversy concerning it relates to judging the appropriateness of a test, since most of the evidence of carcinogenicity comes from animal tests. The concept of zero tolerance appeals to much of the public. Many consumers object to the presence of even very small amounts of hazardous substances in food.[57] Although it may be naive, they do not see why any hazardous substance should be in food. In a survey of Kansas consumers, 63% felt that the government should try to eliminate all health risk from the food supply, and 70% agreed that the government should not allow carcinogenic chemicals in food.[58]

The Delaney standard of zero tolerance has become less workable as the ability to detect minute quantities of a substance has increased. When the Delaney clause was enacted in 1958, laboratory equipment could detect 100 parts per billion of a substance, which meant that any amount less than that was, for practical purposes, equal to zero since it could not be measured. Increased detection capabilities, to as little as parts per trillion, have created a policy dilemma. One part per trillion is the equivalent of a single grain of sugar in an Olympic-sized swimming pool.[59] The detection limitations of the past effectively set a de minimis standard because infinitesimally small traces of a substance could not be measured.[60] However, explicitly setting de minimis standards is far more complicated.

The term "de minimis" comes from a legal argument: *de minimis non curat lex,* which is Latin for "the law does not concern itself with trifles." This legal concept suggests that very small amounts or very small risks can be ignored, and courts should be reluctant to apply a statute to enforce literally pointless results.[61] A de minimis standard of one in 1 million was used in the California Birth Defects Prevention Act (SB 950), Figure 10.1. The Environmental Protection Agency (EPA) announced that it intends to use a de minimis standard to register pesticides with a low-level cancer risk, after being urged to do so by a National Academy of Sciences panel.[62] The FDA appears to be moving in the direction of a de minimis standard and away from a zero-tolerance concept.[63] The de minimis standard currently being applied is one in one million (10^{-6}), which means the hazard should not cause more than one additional death per one million people over their lifetimes.[64]

Under California's recent Safe Drinking Water and Toxic Enforcement Act, better known as Proposition 65, a no-significant-risk standard of one additional death per 100,000 people (10^{-5}) over their lifetimes was adopted.[65] The complexity of applying the de minimis and the no-significant-risk standards should not be underestimated. They require estimating exposure to a hazardous substance and extrapolating to human response from animal test results.[66] Clearly the degree of uncertainty that surrounds such dose-response estimates will typically be considerable. The level of risk is also likely to vary among individuals because it depends on exposure and is influenced by differences in individuals' genetic predispositions to cancer or sensitivity to other hazardous substances.[67] De minimis and no significant risk are applied as actuarial risk standards.

A risk-benefit approach is mandated by the Federal Insecticide, Fungicide, and Rodenticide Act, which regulates pesticide residue on fresh agricultural products. This approach allows the environmental and health risks to be offset by the economic benefits.[68] The justification for a risk-benefit standard is that pesticides are supposedly essential to ensuring an adequate food supply, and some residue is unavoidable.[69]

More generally, a risk-benefit approach focuses on balancing the risks and benefits to society from an activity or the use of a substance.[70] Some find this approach ethically unappealing or unacceptable, since the major risks typically involve placing a monetary value on human health and life. A lack of necessary data to carry out rigorous quantitative analyses of risks and benefits is another problem. It leads to conflicting advice and public confusion.[71] In addition, the people bearing the greatest health risks are frequently different from those receiving the greatest benefits.

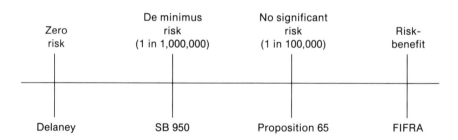

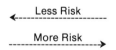

Figure 10.1. Various risk standards allowed in different legislation: the Delaney clause of the 1958 Food Additives Amendment; the California Birth Defects Prevention Act (SB 950); the Safe Drinking Water and Toxic Enforcement Act (Proposition 65); and the Federal Insecticide, Fungicide, and Rodenticide Act (FIFRA). (Reprinted from Archibald et al, 1988b.)

For example, the greatest risk from the use of pesticides falls on agricultural laborers.

The cost-benefit approach is related to the risk-benefit approach, but is somewhat different in that it compares the benefits to society from reducing a risk to the costs involved in its reduction.[72] Again, this involves placing a value on reduced pain and suffering and the saving of human lives. A risk-benefit or cost-benefit approach does introduce the important concept of trade-offs. Greater safety is not free. Producing more of it will require reducing something else. Sometimes, the cost of giving up a possibly hazardous product or activity would be quite minor, whereas at other times it would be substantial. Alar appears to be an example of the former, since completely discontinuing its use has had little effect on the quantity and quality of the apple crop.[73] Alar acted as a growth regulator that helped to keep apples from falling off the tree and increased their storability.[74]

Consumers themselves seem to apply risk-benefit criteria when the benefits are obvious and substantial. For example, most of us choose to drive or ride in automobiles, although we know that tens of thousands are killed and seriously injured in car accidents every year. However, the automobile gives us a highly valued mobility. When the FDA, following the Delaney clause, moved to ban saccharin in 1977 because it was linked to urinary bladder cancer, public outcry caused Congress to pass legislation putting a moratorium on the ban. Instead, warning labels on food containing saccharin were required.[75] Many consumers, particularly diabetics and those with weight problems, saw a significant benefit to the availability of saccharin, one of the few low-calorie sweeteners on the market at that time.

In the final analysis, the amount of risk society will tolerate is decided by the political policy process.[76] "We decide as a matter of public policy how much risk we are prepared to tolerate."[77] The politics of public policymaking is the means by which risks and benefits are ultimately balanced in our system of government. Major food safety decisions will remain political because costs and benefits cannot be measured precisely and inevitably entail value judgments.

The political process can be frustrating. There is frequently a long lag between the initial awareness of a problem and the implementation of a policy. The political process is far more responsive to a crisis or exposé, as demonstrated by the Alar issue, than it is to problems that are not the focus of media and public attention.[78] A public policy decision is typically the result of compromise that reflects the impact of various special interest groups in relation to their political influence. The protection of consumers is but one factor influencing policy decisions concerning food safety issues.[79]

PERCEPTIONS OF RISK

There is often a wide divergence between people's perception of the riskiness of a certain activity or product and the actual statistical probability of injury or harm. Feelings about flying and driving provide a good example. Flying provokes outright fear in some and mild anxiety in others, but most people give little thought to the dangers of driving. However, the fatality rate per 100 million passenger miles for travel by automobile was over 30 times the similar fatality rate for scheduled airlines during 1983-1985.[80] The adage about the most dangerous part of an airline trip being the drive to and from the airport is basically true, but most of us do not feel that way. A similar gap exists between the perception of risk and the actual hazard involved for many food safety concerns. Understanding what factors heighten or reduce the public's perception of risk is important.

Why are some actions or products perceived as being so much more dangerous than they actually are, whereas the reverse holds true for others? Table 10.2 lays out some of the factors that typically are related to people finding a particular risk either more or less acceptable. Lowrance, who wrote a widely referenced book on this subject, differentiated between the scientific measurement of risk (hazard), which is objective, and the judging of safety or the perception of risk, which is subjective.[81] In some recent studies, the terms hazard and outrage have been used to refer, respectively, to the objective and subjective dimensions of risk.[82]

Factors on the left-hand side of Table 10.2 are related to less concern about a particular statistical probability of risk, whereas those on the right side are associated with a heightened sense of danger. For example, risks borne voluntarily (driving an automobile) are perceived to be less dangerous than those borne involuntarily (pesticide residues on food). The willingness of people to bear a risk is also influenced by their

Table 10.2. Factors Influencing the Perception of Risk[a]

Decreased Perception of Risk	Increased Perception of Risk
Risk assumed voluntarily	Risk borne involuntarily
Effect immediate	Effect delayed
No alternatives available	Many alternatives available
Risk known with certainty	Risk not known
Exposure is an essential	Exposure is a luxury
Encountered occupationally	Encountered nonoccupationally
Common hazard	"Dread" hazard
Affects average people	Affects especially sensitive people
Will be used as intended	Likely to be misused
Consequences reversible	Consequences irreversible

[a] Source: Lowrance, 1976, p. 87 (used by permission).

perceptions of the benefits of the activity or product. The lower the perceived benefits, the lower the tolerance for the resulting risk.[83]

A close examination of the factors in Table 10.2 that are related to an increased sense of risk can help us understand why the public reacted so strongly to the Alar issue.[84] First, the consumption of apples and apple products with Alar residue was definitely involuntary. The effect was delayed, since the risk involved the possibility of cancer, which would occur years later. There were lots of alternatives. Consumers could quite easily reduce their consumption of apples and apple products or give up eating them altogether. There is more of an attitude of "grin and bear it" if the risk involves something with no alternatives that is viewed as essential or is related to earning a living.

There was considerable disagreement about the risk posed by Alar. The Natural Resources Defense Council said it was high. The apple industry claimed Alar posed no hazard and apples treated with the chemical were completely safe. The EPA said Alar might pose a risk, but not a sufficient one to warrant an immediate ban. Consumers usually worry more about such uncertain and involuntary risks than about those that are known but voluntarily accepted.[85] In the latter case, the individual's sense of control, naive though it may be, makes the risk more acceptable.

Furthermore, the claims against Alar involved the most dread disease of all, cancer, and the Natural Resources Defense Council claimed that because of their relatively high consumption of apple products, the risk was greater for children. Children are an especially sensitive group, because parents, in particular, and the larger society rightly have a strong protective feeling toward them. When a food safety issue brought together apples, cancer, and children, a strong public reaction should have been expected. In addition, the public's willingness to accept any risks posed by Alar was very low because they perceived its benefits to be very minor.

The attention the media give to a safety-related issue has a strong impact on the public's perception of the risk involved.[86] One of the reasons that most people are more anxious about flying than they are about driving is that every airline disaster is a major news story. On the other hand, the typical automobile fatality is usually reported in a short story in the back of the newspaper and not covered on television at all. Likewise, the Alar issue and the grape tampering incident received extensive coverage in the media. Each in its turn was for several days a front page newspaper story and covered near the beginning of both national and local television news programs. With such media saturation, the intensity of the public concern generated should not have been surprising.

THE ISSUE OF CONFIDENCE AND TRUST

Food safety issues are related to the level of trust and confidence consumers have in the food industry and in the ability of the government regulatory process to protect them. Food safety is mostly a credence attribute, one which must be accepted on trust, since consumers cannot evaluate most hazards themselves. There has been an erosion in the public's confidence in both the food industry's and government's ability to ensure the safety of the food supply.[87] An increasing number of consumers believe the federal government is failing to regulate the food supply to keep it safe.[88]

The technical and regulatory complexity of many food safety issues makes them difficult to explain to consumers. In addition, the credibility of experts has eroded. The public has less faith in experts' risk assessments. This loss of public confidence makes it more difficult for government and industry to deal with specific food safety issues. Both need to work to regain the public's trust. Loss of public confidence in the government's ability to deal with food safety issues is giving rise to some private initiatives. Some supermarkets in California and other states, for example, have begun to do their own testing for chemical residues and certification of fresh produce.[89]

Such widely publicized cases as the Alar controversy not only affect the sales of specific products but increase consumer concern about the safety of all food. The Food Marketing Institute's annual survey of food shoppers was taken in January 1989.[90] In response to the question, "How confident are you that the food in the supermarket is safe?," 81% of respondents were completely or mostly confident. The Alar issue then hit in late February and the grape tampering episode in early March. The Food Marketing Institute did a follow-up survey and asked the same question again in mid-April.[91] Those completely or mostly confident in the safety of the food supply had fallen 14 percentage points, to 67%. By late April, when surveyed once again, the figure had recovered to 73%.

Major food safety incidents damage public confidence in the food industry and government even more, if handled improperly. The apple producers' initial reaction was to take out full-page newspaper advertisements saying that Alar posed no health danger. They misread the nature and the depth of the public concern and came across as stonewalling and not being sufficiently concerned about a serious issue. The EPA's response perplexed many and eroded the public's confidence in government's role as a safety watchdog. The spokesperson for the EPA said that although Alar was considered unsafe and announced the agency's intention to ban it, that process could take at least 18 months.

The EPA said Alar was not sufficiently dangerous to require immediate action.[92] However, a typical consumer cannot see why an unsafe product should not be withdrawn immediately, as Alar eventually was.

The producer's response to a food safety issue can be very important for both limiting lost sales and maintaining credibility with the public.[93] Disputing the seriousness of the problem, as in the initial reaction of the apple producers to the Alar issue, may only serve to focus public attention on the issue, heighten the level of uncertainty, and harm the credibility of the industry. When a major food safety issue arises, the public wants to know that the seriousness of the problem has been recognized and appropriate action has been taken. One of the most damaging effects on credibility occurs when statements are made that later have to be retracted.[94]

CONSUMER INFORMATION AS A REMEDY

Some argue that the best approach to food safety issues is simply to provide the relevant information to consumers and allow them to make their own decisions concerning behavior and products.[95] However, others argue that, whereas consumer information has an important role to play in food safety issues, it is not a panacea. When consumers were asked who they most rely on to ensure the safety of the food they buy, 41% answered themselves, whereas only 20% said the government, 14% food manufacturers, 10% food retailers, and 8% consumer organizations.[96]

Relying on well-informed consumers to make their own food safety decisions is appealing for several reasons. This approach appeals to the American concept of freedom of choice, as well as to the tenets of economic theory. Some see government intervention in terms of health and safety regulations as moving in the direction of impinging on individual liberty.[97] Although both smoking and drinking impose extremely high health and economic costs on individuals and society, government did not succeed in banning alcoholic beverages in the 1930s and is unlikely to ban either cigarettes or alcohol in the foreseeable future.

The second argument supporting the information approach relates to economic efficiency. Because individuals differ in their attitudes towards risk and their willingness to pay to reduce risk, the imposition of a single level of safety by government regulation will be inefficient. It is more efficient to allow consumers to adjust their own behavior and product purchases in terms of their own risk preferences.[98] With government regulations and safeguards, there is also some evidence that consumers engage in offsetting behavior, known as moral hazard. Some of the impact of improved automobile and highway safety, for example, has been offset by people driving faster.[99]

A purely informational approach would require large amounts of time for consumers to become adequately informed, likely more time than most people would be willing to commit.[100] Since time is a limited resource with an opportunity cost, as discussed in Chapter 6, the information approach imposes large costs on consumers, which is also inefficient. The issue of information overload is relevant. Increased use of warning labels on products, for example, carries a danger of overkill, with consumers no longer paying attention to them.[101] This problem has been referred to as the "cry wolf" dilemma, which is an analogy to the fable in which the little boy sounds a false warning several times and is then ignored when the threat of a wolf is real. The ubiquitous warning labels that say, "This product may be hazardous to your health," go virtually unnoticed by most people, as they consume alcohol, cigarettes, and products with saccharin.

Furthermore, the technical expertise necessary to evaluate many food safety issues is simply beyond the level of the typical consumer. If the experts and the regulators cannot decide what to do about a complex food safety issue, it is totally unreasonable to expect the average consumer to be able to make such a decision.[102] When a regulation is written that bans a product, the government regulators can be viewed as assuming consumers would not use the product if they were fully informed.[103] Consumers can view a ban as information about the product's risks to their health. It reduces their decision costs.

A strict information approach would also tend to discriminate against certain vulnerable groups, such as some of the elderly, the less educated, the illiterate, and those who do not understand English, who would have particular difficulties evaluating the information. The safety-related message might also be distorted by the impact of special interest groups.[104] The consumer can, as in the case of Alar, receive several conflicting messages concerning the safety of a food product or substance. For all these reasons, consumer information by itself has an important, yet limited role to play as a remedy for food safety concerns. It is in the interest of individual consumers and society to delegate safety assessments and regulation to government agencies and expect them to act judiciously. Safety is partly a public good that can best be ensured by government action.

Appropriate government action depends on the seriousness of the hazard and the ability of consumers to detect or be informed about that hazard prior to consumption. Figure 10.2 shows a continuum of food quality and safety factors from imminent, lethal hazards on the left, to desirable characteristics on the right; moving from left to right, the need for strict government regulation decreases and the possibility to "privatize" decisions through information increases.[105]

Consumers want two major types of information. One type describes the product, its ingredients, nutrient composition, chemicals used in the product's production, and the type of packaging material. The other type informs consumers of any potential risks associated with the product's consumption. Consumers would like to know the nature of the hazard and its probability.[106] Current laws and regulations do a better, although far from complete, job of providing consumers with the descriptive type of information.

CURRENT FOOD SAFETY ISSUES

Several major food safety issues are of considerable current interest. These include concerns about the safety of pesticide residues, microbiological contamination, food additives, seafood, and new technologies.

Pesticide Residues

Pesticide residues have become a major food safety concern for many consumers. In a national survey of adults taken by *Newsweek* magazine in early 1989, 38% said they "are more worried that the food they eat may be contaminated by pesticides or other toxic chemicals."[107] Seventy-three percent thought fewer pesticides and chemicals should be used

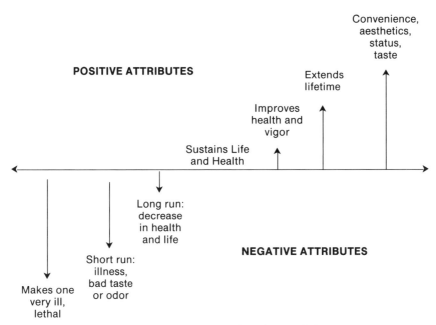

Figure 10.2. Continuum of food quality and safety characteristics.

even if higher prices resulted. About 50,000 pesticide products that contain more than 600 chemical ingredients are in current use.[108] However, a a very small number of these account for most of the total pounds of pesticides used.[109] The EPA ranked pesticide residues as the third worst environmental cancer risk, after occupational exposure to chemicals and indoor radon.[110]

However, even given this, the consensus among scientific experts seems to be that pesticide residues pose a fairly low cancer risk, particularly relative to other major risk factors like smoking. They point out that the overall health hazard for consumers from pesticides used in accordance with good agricultural practices is small.[111] The FDA found no residue at all on 57% of 14,492 food samples taken in 1988, and fewer than 1% had illegally high residues.[112] In addition, the FDA annually conducts the Total Diet Study as a final check on the safety of the food supply. Over 200 food items that would be included in a typical American's diet are purchased. The items are then prepared as they might be for a normal home-cooked meal (washed, peeled, baked, etc.) and then analyzed for pesticide residues, industrial chemicals, and toxic elements. The findings have consistently been within the government safety guidelines.[113]

In fact, the more serious health hazard associated with pesticides is faced by farmers and agricultural laborers.[114] There were 1,065 confirmed cases of pesticide-related occupational illnesses in California in 1986.[115] Another serious problem is ground water contamination, which will be discussed in Chapter 11.[116]

The EPA is responsible for setting the permissible tolerance levels for pesticide residues. The monitoring and enforcement of those levels is under the authority of the FDA.[117] Many of the pesticide chemicals that were already on the market when the EPA was first given the responsibility to regulate them under the Federal Insecticide, Fungicide, and Rodenticide Act in 1972 would not meet the standards applied to new pesticides. An amendment to the act required the EPA to reevaluate old pesticides. However, the reevaluation process has been extremely slow. In 1988, Congress directed the EPA to complete the reevaluations by 1997.[118]

One of the criticisms of the regulations has been the inconsistency in the treatment of old and new pesticides. Getting approval for a new pesticide is a time-consuming and costly process for a chemical company. Frequently though, newer pesticides are far safer than the older ones that are on the market. On the other hand, removing an old pesticide from the market is typically a lengthy process for the government. Public hearings are usually required and there may be legal challenges that can delay action.[119] As with food additives, there has been a basic change in the entitlement to safety that changes the burden of proof. Charles Benbrook of the National Academy of Sciences characterized the situation as, "new pesticides are guilty until proven innocent and old pesticides are innocent until proven guilty."[120]

Other major criticisms of the EPA's evaluation of the safety of pesticides include its failure to examine the additive or cumulative effect when several chemicals are used on the same crop. In addition, the EPA evaluates only the active ingredients in a pesticide, not the inert ingredients used to dilute and stabilize the active agents, which may also be toxic.[121] In October 1989, the Bush administration sent a proposal to Congress that would streamline the procedure to remove hazardous pesticides from the market. Some environmental and consumer groups opposed certain features of the President's proposal such as the risk standard to be used, and federal preemption that would prevent states from having stricter regulations than the federal government. As of mid-1990, Congress had not yet taken action.[122]

The adoption of integrated pest management and alternative agricultural techniques by farmers hold out the hope that the use of pesticides could be sharply reduced.[123] The possibility of using biotechnology to develop pest-resistant crop varieties adds to this hope. Realistically, if consumers want a reduction in the use of pesticides, they will need to abandon their demand for blemish-free produce. A recent survey by the Georgia Experiment Station found that although 50% of consumers wanted pesticides banned, less than 20% said they would accept produce with insect damage.[124] Organically grown products (discussed further in Chapter 11) make up about 1% of the fresh produce sold in grocery stores but about 4% of the value of all fresh produce sales.[125]

Many people are shocked when they first learn about the FDA "food defect action levels" which set limits for such things as insect parts and eggs and rodent hairs and excreta in food products. A one-pound box of macaroni, for example, can contain up to nine rodent hair fragments.[126] The FDA says these defect levels pose no health hazard and most of the foreign matter is microscopic, so it is unnoticed. Such natural defects unavoidably get into foods as they are raised, harvested, stored, and processed. The alternative to setting such defect levels would be to use more pesticides.

Microbiological Food Contamination

Since foods are naturally perishable, in the absence of preservation they tend to become contaminated by bacteria, yeasts, molds, and viruses that may cause illness and even death.[127] The occurrence of foodborne illness in the United States is vastly underreported.[128] In many cases, the victims do not associate their symptoms with the food they recently ate and assume they are suffering from some type of flu. Most recover in a few days without seeing a doctor.

However, the seriousness of the health problem posed by microbial food contamination should not be underestimated. Because most of the cases go unreported, there is a wide range of estimates of the number of cases of foodborne illness. Estimates range from several million to over 200 million cases per year in the United States.[129] The number of deaths from food contamination is estimated at 9,000–12,000 per year.[130] The costs to society in terms of health care costs and lost productivity from such illness were recently estimated to be $4.8 billion per year.[131]

Foodborne bacteria can cause two basic types of illness: infections and intoxications. The former is caused by consuming a foodborne microorganism that then infects the human body. The latter results from eating something that contains a toxin that was produced by microorganisms growing in the food.[132] *Salmonella, Staphylococcus aureus,* and *Clostridium perfringens* are the microorganisms currently responsible for the largest number of foodborne illnesses in the United States.[133]

Salmonella, which is the name given to a group of almost 2,000 related bacteria strains, is the most widespread food contamination problem. Some 37% of the confirmed cases of foodborne illness reported between 1977 and 1982 were caused by *Salmonella* species.[134] Salmonellosis is an infection caused by *Salmonella.* Its severity depends on the number of bacteria ingested. The symptoms for people who become infected are similar to the flu and may include diarrhea, an upset stomach, fever, and headache. The symptoms usually last from three to five days.

The Department of Agriculture estimates that about one-third of the chickens headed for consumer tables are contaminated by salmonellae.[135] Some critics argue that the contamination rate is even higher and that the majority of birds are contaminated when they leave some of the processing plants with careless sanitary procedures.[136] The *Salmonella* bacteria are in the fecal matter of the chickens and can be easily spread through the slaughter, evisceration, and washing processes.

Salmonellae are not only a problem in poultry. The source of an outbreak of salmonellosis in Minnesota in the summer of 1989 was determined to be mozzarella cheese.[137] Consumers have also been warned not to eat foods that contain uncooked eggs, such as homemade mayonnaise, eggnog, cookie dough, and desserts containing uncooked eggs, because the bacteria have been found inside unbroken eggs.

Staphylococcus aureus is considered the second most common cause of foodborne illness. When the bacteria reproduce in sufficiently large numbers in a food product, enough toxin is produced to cause a reaction when consumed. The illness usually occurs within a few hours and typically symptoms are chills, abdominal cramps, nausea, vomiting, and weakness. The bacteria are commonly present in the nose, throat, hair, and skin of many healthy people. They are spread by unsanitary food handling, and improper refrigeration permits bacterial growth. The most frequent problems occur in cooked protein foods that are handled after cooking. Some common examples are tuna, chicken, ham, and potato salads.[138] *Clostridium perfringens* is another microorganism common in the environment. Outbreaks of illness that have diarrhea as the major symptom are connected with improper food preparation and storage. Protein foods are again the most common source of contamination.[139]

The bacterium *Clostridium botulinum* produces a toxin that causes botulism, which is a very serious disease. The majority of botulism outbreaks have been traced to home-processed foods, particularly home-canned low-acid foods, such as certain vegetables. Recently, unusual products such as oil-packed garlic have been implicated in outbreaks. The botulinum toxin is one of the most poisonous substances known. An amount of botulinum toxin equal to an aspirin tablet would be enough to kill the entire population of a city the size of Los Angeles.[140]

Campylobacter jejuni, Listeria monocytogenes, Escherichia coli O157:H7, and *Shigella* have been referred to as the "emerging pathogens" because increasingly they are found to be the source of foodborne illnesses.[141] *Campylobacter* contamination may now be the leading cause of diarrhea in the United States.[142] The most serious outbreak of listeriosis occurred in 1985 when 142 persons became ill from contaminated cheese from a plant in California. Half were mothers and their infants, and the mortality rate was 30%.[143] *Yersinia enterocolitica* and four species of *Vibrio* are other sources of foodborne illness. Some microbiological food contamination is also related to long-term health risks. Aflatoxin is a toxin produced by a mold that may grow on some foods, such as corn and peanuts. Aflatoxin is a potent carcinogen in animal tests, and tolerance levels have been set to limit exposure to it.[144]

The fact that the average consumer is probably unfamiliar with many of these foodborne pathogens reinforces the argument that the public is not well informed about microbiological food contamination as a food safety issue. The problem may be worsening because of changing food supply and consumption patterns.[145] Two examples are the increased consumption of raw seafood at sushi bars and the greater consumption of imported foods, which may be processed under less sanitary conditions than domestic ones. A particular concern is the increasing popularity of fresh prepared foods, at deli counters for example, and fresh refrigerated foods.[146] Both must be treated with the necessary care to avoid contamination.

Most incidents of foodborne illness could be prevented. The Centers for Disease Control (CDC) has estimated that some 94% of the cases of foodborne disease in the United States are due to lax sanitary practices in the home or in food service establishments.[147] Douglas Archer, director of the FDA's microbiology division, said that consumers, not the food industry, are to blame for most cases of foodborne illness.[148] Proper cooking and refrigeration would prevent most such illnesses. For example, cooking thoroughly at high enough temperatures kills the *Salmonella* bacteria in meat or poultry. In addition, proper sanitary food preparation procedures need to be followed to prevent cross-contamination to other foods from contaminated countertops, cutting boards, knives and other utensils, and even hands.[149]

An increasing number of consumers are ignorant of, or overlook, the basic procedures that should be followed in home food preparation to minimize the risks of foodborne illness. A survey found that 32% of consumers let cooked chicken cool to room temperature before refrigerating, which is not advised.[150] This problem is related to a general decline in cooking skills and food preparation knowledge. Consumer education is clearly an important part of addressing the considerable health problem of foodborne illnesses.

Seafood Inspection

Currently, there is no mandatory federal inspection program for fish and other seafood as there is for meat and poultry. About 75% of the seafood in the United States has not been inspected.[151] Some of the documented stories about the practices of unscrupulous fishermen and processors in the industry are shocking—for example, the harvesting of shellfish at night from sewage-polluted waters by oyster bootleggers in Florida.[152] Another example was the totally unsanitary practices in one Port Bolivar, Texas, seafood packing plant, in which there was no hot water to sanitize equipment, the toilet did not work, the place was swarming with flies and infested with cockroaches, and "workers hauled trash and cooked crab meat around on the same cart."[153]

According to the CDC, there were 171 cases of foodborne illness for every billion pounds of seafood eaten in the United States, as opposed to 102 cases for poultry and 57 for beef and veal.[154] Much of the credit for originally focusing attention on what she called the "great American fish scandal" belongs to Ellen Haas of Public Voice for Food and Health Policy, a consumer advocacy organization.[155] A voluntary Commerce Department program inspected only 11% of the seafood in 1987, and the Food and Drug Administration inspects only a tiny portion of the seafood imported into the United States.[156] To keep the issue in perspective, it should be recognized that the major problems exist in only a very small portion of the $30 billion-a-year seafood industry.[157]

Seafood consumption in 1988 fell slightly to 15 pounds per person, down from 15.2 in 1987, which represented the first decline since 1982.[158] This drop was partly in response to rising prices but may also be partially attributable to safety concerns. Sufficient attention has been focused on the problem so that Congress is expected eventually to pass a law that sets up a comprehensive, mandatory seafood inspection program. This legislation stalled in Congress over disputes about who should do the checking and how it will be financed.[159] Meanwhile, the FDA and National Marine Fisheries Service have given notice of their proposed intention to jointly start a voluntary, fee-for-service inspection program that would employ a HACCP approach to enhance existing seafood inspection programs.[160]

Food Additives

Food additives are substances added to foods in minor amounts, either intentionally to improve nutrition, quality, or shelf life, or unintentionally as a result of production, processing, storage, or packaging.[161] Over the years, many of the major food safety controversies have involved additives, such as DES (diethystilbestrol), a synthetic growth hormone fed to cattle; cyclamates and saccharin, both synthetic sweeteners; two food dyes, violet no. 1 and red no. 2; and sodium nitrite, a preservative used in cured meat, like ham and hot dogs.[162] Perhaps the major current issue concerning food additives is the Delaney clause itself, which has already been discussed in some detail.

Many additives have been designated as Generally Recognized as Safe (GRAS). This category includes substances that are nontoxic when "used in the food supply under normal manufacturing processes."[163] The GRAS list was originally composed in 1958 when the Food Additive Amendment was passed. However, it has since been modified, and the FDA has thought it necessary to test many of the additives that were on the original GRAS list.[164] Recall that the original additives were considered safe until proven otherwise. As a result of this testing, some old compounds have been banned. One of the GRAS categories that is being tested, for example, is synthetic chemicals that have been in long use in the food supply prior to 1958. Additives not on the GRAS list, which are not known to be carcinogenic, are evaluated on a risk-benefit basis and placed in the regulated food additives category, for which the amounts that can be used are specified.[165]

An important fact that is frequently overlooked is that foods may contain naturally occurring substances that are toxic and carcinogenic. For example, raw cabbage, lettuce, and spinach contain small amounts of 3,4-dibenzopyrene, which has been linked to gastric cancer.[166] Comfry herb teas contain symphytine, a known carcinogen. Barbecuing fat-containing meats produces benzopyrene, which is a suspected carcinogen. If the natural food supply contains these risks, some question why standards for food additives should be particularly strict. The counterpoint is that if a normal diet poses some risk from low exposure to naturally occurring toxic and carcinogenic substances, then additives that may be toxic should be tightly controlled so as not to unnecessarily add to the body's burden.[167]

New Technologies

New technologies—in particular, food irradiation and biotechnology—which are just reaching the point of commercial applications, are running into consumer resistance. The FDA has certified the safety and approved the use of several specific products or applications. In March 1990, the FDA gave its approval to the first genetically engineered food product for humans, an enzyme called rennin used in making cheese.[168] Previously, rennin was extracted from calves' stomachs, but genetic engineering produces it both more cheaply and in purer form.

The FDA in spring 1990 also approved the irradiation of poultry to kill salmonella and other disease-causing microorganisms.[169] However, given consumers' reservations about irradiation, the poultry industry indicated it is unlikely to start using this technology.[170] The FDA previously approved the limited use of irradiation on spices, pork, and some fruits and vegetables for several purposes.[171] The little use that is currently made of this technology in the United States is primarily for spices and ingredients mixed into other foods that do not require an identification label indicating they have been irradiated. However, the FDA lacks reliable information on the use of irradiation by food processors and does not have an inspection program for irradiation facilities.[172]

Cobalt 60, a man-made radioisotope that has been used in hospitals for years, is typically employed to generate the gamma rays that are used in food irradiation.[173] The process does not make the food radioactive; in fact, it is difficult to tell whether food has been irradiated. Some experts do have concerns about the chemical changes in the food that may occur with irradiation, given that the molecular structure may be affected.[174] Others are concerned about the hazards of transporting the necessary radioactive materials to and from irradiation plants around the country.

Biotechnology has been defined as "the application of scientific and engineering principles to the processing of materials by biological agents to provide goods and services."[175] It can be more simply defined as the use of living organisms to modify existing products.[176] Hence, fermentation is a biotechnology, and humans have been applying it for centuries to make cheese, wine, beer, and other alcoholic beverages. Even leavened bread is based on biotechnology. Genetic engineering is truly new and specifically involves the development of techniques for manipulating genes.[177]

A major controversy has surrounded bovine somatotropin (BST), also called bovine growth hormone, a product of genetic engineering. Tests suggest it can boost cows' milk production from 10 to 25%.[178] Four major pharmaceutical companies have invested over $300 million developing BST.[179] The gene that produces BST is extracted from the pituitary glands of slaughtered cows and is spliced into the DNA of *E. coli* bacteria. The *E. coli* are fermented and multiply rapidly. After the bacteria die, the BST is separated and purified. This process allows the growth hormone to be produced on a large scale.[180]

The FDA has approved the product for tests and asserts that milk from treated cows is safe. BST is simply a synthetic version of a naturally occurring hormone. Milk from cows injected with BST cannot be identified from other milk. In addition to consumers who are leery of genetically engineered products, major opposition has come from dairy farmers who worry about the economic impact of a sharp increase in milk supplies. In 1989, several major supermarket chains and the largest dairy cooperative in the nation said they would refuse to sell milk from cows treated with BST.[181] Both the Minnesota and Wisconsin legislatures passed bills in 1990 that placed a temporary moratorium on the use of BST by dairy farmers in their states. In April 1990, the FDA decided to delay for at least a year the approval of BST for general use to wait for more data on the effectiveness of the hormone and its effect on cows.[182]

Why have these new technologies generated such strong safety concerns among consumers? Table 10.2, presented earlier in this chapter, provides some important insights. Irradiation, biotechnology, and genetic engineering are all associated with many of the factors on the right-hand side of Table 10.2, which increase the perception of risk. Risks would be borne involuntarily, alternatives are available, the risks are uncertain, none of the technologies are absolutely essential, and all involve nonoccupational risks for consumers. Given the complexity of the technologies, they might be misused. That the effect would be delayed, a dread hazard is involved, and the consequences might be irreversible also affect the extent of consumer worry about the potential carcinogenicity of irradiated food or specific biotechnology products.

Furthermore, the very complexity and sophistication of these technologies pose difficulties for consumer acceptance. Many consumers lack the level of science education necessary to understand the fundamentals of how irradiation and genetic engineering work; and what people do not understand, they tend to fear. These technologies also face unique liabilities in terms of consumers' perceptions. In the aftermath of Three Mile Island and Chernobyl, public resistance to nuclear power has been high and the effect has carried over to anything related to radiation, including food irradiation.[183] As in some science fiction fantasy, genetic engineering may generate fears that some gene manipulation may run amok, creating some deadly new virus or bacteria.

As discussed earlier in this chapter, consumers are more willing to accept a risk when the benefits are clear. Consumers, so far, do not see persuasive benefits to either food irradiation or BST. In comparison, even though microwave ovens use a technology that few consumers have more than a superficial understanding of, the benefits in terms of increased convenience have been so attractive that consumers seem to feel very comfortable with the technology and have few safety worries. Consumers may even be too complacent regarding microwave cooking. There are some suggestions that small amounts of possibly carcinogenic chemicals from some packaging materials may migrate into the food heated in a microwave.[184]

There is also the commonplace, and often overlooked, hazard of burns associated with microwave cooking, which is a particular risk for children. In a recent survey, 65% of the parents indicated that they let their children, ages 4-12, use the microwave. Many of these children are too young to read or follow directions and should not be operating a microwave oven. People, and especially children, have received severe burns from the steam from microwave popcorn bags and similar closed packages, and from the boiling portions of unevenly heated foods, either eaten or spilled on themselves accidentally. Additional hazards are posed by melted plastic containers, hot susceptor packages, arcing and fires, and contamination from foodborne pathogens surviving in raw parts of unevenly cooked foods.[185]

Another interesting comparison can be made between BST and PST (porcine somatotropin). PST is a genetically engineered growth hormone for hogs. Recent consumer surveys suggest the public may be more receptive to the use of PST, since it could yield a benefit that consumers value, leaner pork products.[186] Tests have found that when PST is administered to hogs, the pork is 30-40% leaner, although breeding can produce similar results.[187]

Consumers do not perceive a benefit from BST. No one is claiming the milk will be any better, just that it will not be any different. Production efficiency would be increased, but consumers probably are doubtful that retail milk prices would be much lower. They may be right, given government dairy policy and a chronic excess supply. All this suggests that the biotechnology industry may have made a crucial strategic error. They might have been well advised to have pushed for the approval of the commercial use of PST first, rather than BST. The controversy over BST and the delay in its commercial application may slow the adoption of other genetically engineered products.

Other Current Issues

There are several other food safety issues that should at least be briefly mentioned. These include the current meat and poultry inspection system and its proposed revision, food tampering and adulteration, safety related issues concerning food imports and exports, the level of funding and staffing of the federal regulatory agencies, and the relationship between federal and state regulatory activity.

Insuring the safety and overall quality of meat and poultry is the responsibility of the Food Safety and Inspection Service of the U.S. Department of Agriculture. The inspection system has become overburdened and outdated. Inspectors have been expected to examine every meat or poultry carcass.[188] However, that inspection has usually been very cursory, relying on the inspector's sight and smell, with only a few seconds to make each evaluation.[189] Only occasional spot tests have been conducted for bacterial and chemical contamination. A 1985 National Academy of Sciences report recommended the establishment of a traceback system, monitoring critical points, and more checking for higher risk problems, such as *Salmonella*.[190]

The Department of Agriculture has proposed a major revision of the inspection system, which would rely heavily on self-inspection by the industry and sharply cut the number of federal inspectors.[191] A HACCP approach would be implemented.[192] Government inspectors would visit plants with good records only occasionally and concentrate inspections in those with chronic problems. This proposal has been met with considerable controversy. Critics are particularly concerned about the pressures to overlook questionable practices or products that plant employees checking quality control might face.[193]

Food tampering and adulteration are rare, but particularly disturbing, food safety issues. The most well-known food tampering incident is, of course, the Chilean grape episode. According to a follow-up analysis, the grape tampering probably occurred in the United States, not in Chile.[194] Many packaged foods are now sold in tamper-resistant containers. However, most of these are probably not tamper-proof and protecting many food products from tampering, such as fresh meat and produce, is far more problematic. Tampering is really a form of terrorism and is as difficult to prevent as other terrorist acts when the perpetrators do not care if innocent people are harmed.

The two most well-known recent incidents of food adulteration in the United States involved infant apple juice and orange juice. In each case, the food processing company purposefully substituted cheaper ingredients for the apple or orange juice and thus engaged in fraud. However, in both cases the substitute ingredients, such as beet juice, were completely safe. Perhaps the worst adulteration incident in recent history occurred in Spain in 1981. Nearly 700 people were killed and thousands more were injured when rapeseed oil tainted with aniline dye and intended for industrial use was sold as cheap olive oil for human consumption.[195]

Assuring the safety of imported foods should be a high priority concern. Fruit and vegetable imports have increased sharply in recent years. Between 1980 and 1986, the value of fruit imports tripled and vegetable imports doubled, according to a General Accounting Office (GAO) study.[196] In addition, 8.5% of the U.S. red meat supply is imported, which includes some 40% of the ground beef sold in this country.[197] The use of agricultural chemicals and drugs elsewhere is regulated by each country's own laws and may not be ones accepted here. Food imported into this country is subject to our regulations concerning chemical residues.[198]

The GAO found the violation rate for imports to be substantially higher than for domestic products.[199] Moreover, detailed up-to-date information about the chemicals and drugs used overseas is lacking and if a substance is not used here, typically no tests are made for it.[200] The personnel inspecting imported food products are also spread too thinly to do an adequate job, which reflects the general underfunding of food inspection activities.

A related issue, which is likely to become increasingly important, is the relationship between food safety regulations and international trade policy. The United States claimed the European Economic Community's (EEC) January 1989 ban on beef imports containing growth hormones was a pseudosafety issue enacted as a nontariff barrier to trade.[201] Americans may, however, underestimate the sincerity of Europeans' safety concerns regarding growth hormones. They had already been banned in Europe for European producers.[202] The General Agreement on Tariffs and Trade (GATT), negotiated among numerous trading countries, forbids health and safety regulations on imports that act as barriers to trade unless they legitimately protect the health and safety of local consumers. Free trade agreements put a heavy burden on establishing that legitimacy and proving that the standards are not set primarily to protect local industries.[203]

A rather unglamorous, but quite crucial food safety issue, is the level of funding and staffing of the government regulatory agencies, particularly the FDA and USDA's Food Safety and Inspection Service (FSIS). For food safety laws to be effective, they must be backed up by enforcement. This takes adequate funding for those agencies to carry For food safety laws to be effective, they must be backed up by enforcement. This takes adequate funding for those agencies to carry out their responsibilities. There is reason to believe that a lack of funding has undercut the effectiveness of the FDA and FSIS. The number of FSIS meat and poultry inspectors was cut from 8,400 to 7,200 between 1979 and 1989. They are responsible for over 6,000 meat and poultry processing plants in the United States.[204]

The FDA, which has only some 1,000 inspectors, suffered a 15% reduction in its field staff in the 1980s.[205] In addition to its food inspection responsibilities, the FDA is also responsible for drugs, medical devices, and radiation-emitting products like microwave ovens. The pesticide staff at the EPA was also reduced during the 1980s.[206] Frank Young, the FDA commissioner, was quoted as saying to a Senate committee, "If you want me to do this job, give me the resources. It is a cruel joke to pass over 20 bills requiring more work and then decrease the resources."[207] In a hopeful sign, the Bush administration's budget proposal for fiscal year 1991 contained a marked increase in funding for the FDA and allowed for an increased staff level.[208]

Jurisdiction over the regulation of food safety and quality is shared by the federal and state governments.[209] The federal government has broad powers under the Constitution to regulate goods that move in interstate commerce. In areas of regulation where Congress has passed legislation, federal law can typically preempt state action by stating that intent. Where federal regulation and preemption do not exist, states have the right to take action under their general police power to protect the health and safety of their citizens.[210]

When federal laws are perceived to be inadequate, there is pressure for states to step in with their own regulations, as happened with Proposition 65 in California, an initiative passed by the state's voters in November 1986. Proposition 65 proposed that foods sold in California have warning labels if they contain chemicals demonstrated to cause cancer or birth defects.[211] Proposition 128, commonly referred to as "Big Green," appeared on the California ballot in the November 1990 election, but it did not pass. "Big Green" covered a broad range of environmental issues; one of its measures would have phased out all agricultural pesticides that cause cancer or birth defects.[212]

A patchwork of different state-by-state food safety regulations would fragment the national food marketing system, reduce efficiency from economies of scale, and lead to higher food costs. To avoid this possibility, the federal government must not abdicate its responsibility to provide leadership on food safety issues and to take action to address major concerns. Most of the important food safety issues are best addressed at the national level, rather than state by state. This point is agreed upon by most consumers and food industry people alike.

GENERAL IMPLICATIONS

Much of the acute concern about food safety generated by the Alar and grape tampering episodes dissipated over several months. In the January 1990 Food Marketing Institute survey of consumers, confidence in the food supply had recovered to nearly the same level as a year earlier, before the two incidents. Seventy-nine percent indicated they were completely or mostly confident that the food found in supermarkets was safe, compared with 81% in January 1989.[213] Consumers' underlying awareness of and sensitivity to food safety issues remain high, however. Furthermore, there are certain to be cases in the future when particular food safety issues or incidents again become major news stories.

Both food safety and quality concerns have become increasingly important. They can be viewed as normal goods, and perhaps even luxury goods. As defined in Chapter 5, the demand for a normal good increases as income levels rise and the demand for a luxury grows faster than the growth in income. People are, of course, concerned about their health. Moreover, they attach disutility to things or events that produce anxiety. With rising incomes and better information, food safety and quality are more in demand.

Food safety and quality concerns have also increased in importance in other high-income societies, such as Japan and Western Europe. For example, in Great Britain recently there was a furor over the possible safety concerns posed by BSE (bovine spongiform encephalopathy), commonly called "mad cow" disease.[214] BSE is a neurological disorder that affects the cow's brain. When the disease was identified in a cat, concerns were raised that humans could also contract it. These disclosures caused a sharp drop in British cattle sales and almost caused a major trade dispute within the EEC when France and Germany initially moved to ban British beef.[215]

Many of us seem to have the perception that we face more risks and live in a more dangerous world than in the past. Such anxieties may be partially attributable to the complex, technologically advanced nature of modern society. It may be worth reminding ourselves that most of us can expect to live longer, healthier lives than ever before. Although there is certainly room for improvement, the existing laws and regulatory system are perhaps given too little credit for the level of safety the food supply already offers.

The Food Industry: An Overview and Implications of Consumer Trends

One of the things that makes a major impression on many foreigners who visit the United States for the first time is our supermarkets. They are amazed by the abundance, variety, and quality of foods that most of us take for granted. Boris Yeltsin, the well-known Russian politician, returned to the Soviet Union from his first trip to the United States in 1989 with rave reviews about the standard of living in this country. In a major speech to 20,000 supporters, he specifically remarked: "Their supermarkets have 30,000 food items. You can't imagine it."[1] Most people in the Soviet Union have had to wait in lines to buy even basic food staples, which frequently are of very poor quality. Many of the products that we routinely buy in grocery stores would be viewed as unheard of luxuries in many parts of the world. When McDonald's opened its first fast-food outlet in the Soviet Union in January 1990 in Moscow, it was mobbed by customers eager to try a "Beeg Mak" (Big Mac) and "kartofel-free" (french fries).[2]

Some aspects of the food industry in the United States can perhaps be criticized, but overall the total system that produces, stores, processes, distributes, and sells food to consumers is truly an American success story. As shown in Figure 11.1, the food system is composed of several intermediary sectors that link producers and consumers. Our food system is a marvel of efficiency and responsiveness to the consumer compared with those of most other countries in the world.

A brief overview of the U.S. food system, including various components of the cost of food, is provided in the first section of this chapter. The major sectors of the food industry—farming, processing and manufacturing, wholesaling, and retailing—are covered in the remaining sections. The retailing discussion covers both the food store segment (the at-home market) and the food service segment (the away-from-home market). After a short overview of the structure of each sector of the industry, the implications of the various consumer trends discussed earlier in this book and other important emerging issues are examined.

A BRIEF OVERVIEW OF THE FOOD SYSTEM

With the old saying in mind that a picture may be worth a thousand words, we present several figures that give a broad overview of the total food industry or food system in the United States. The first two graphs (Figures 11.2 and 11.3) indicate the value added to the domestic economy and the employment generated by the various major sectors in the total food and fiber system. By presenting data for both 1975 and 1988, the growth of the various sectors can be compared.

On the basis of input-output analysis, the total food and fiber system was estimated to have contributed $727 billion to national income in

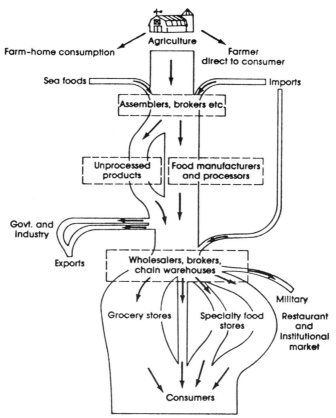

Figure 11.1. The food system. (Reprinted from National Commission on Food Marketing, 1966.)

1988, which represented 14.9% of the total value added in the domestic economy. *Value added* measures the net contribution of an economic sector to the national economy and is determined by subtracting the value of the inputs used by a sector from the market value of the final goods and services produced. The total value added in the food and fiber system has steadily risen over time. However, its relative contribution to the national economy has gradually declined as other parts of the economy have grown more rapidly. For example, in 1975, the food and fiber system accounted for 20.4% of the total value added in the economy, 5.5 percentage points more than in 1988.[3]

Figure 11.2 shows that the largest sector in terms of value added was transportation, trade, and retailing ($239.2 billion in 1988). This sector also grew the most between 1975 and 1988. Farming grew the least. The agricultural input sector that provides goods and services to farming, such as agricultural chemicals and machinery, might also be included

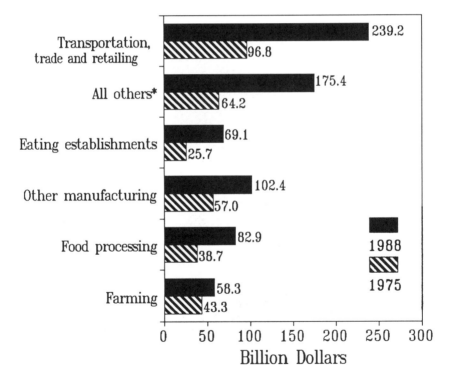

Billion Dollars

*Includes other services, mining and forestry

Figure 11.2. Value added to the domestic economy by the food and fiber system in 1975 and 1988. (Data from U.S. Department of Commerce, Bureau of the Census, 1990a, p. 637.)

as part of the total food and fiber system. However, the input sector is not typically included in the food and fiber system in government publications, and is not included in Figures 11.1–11.3.

The food and fiber system provided jobs to 19.6 million workers in 1988 and 20.2 million in 1975. There were several years in between in which employment climbed to almost 22 million. The food and fiber system accounted for 16.1% of total employment in 1988, down from 21.5% in 1975.[4] The argument might also be made here that these figures represent an undercount because the agricultural input sector is excluded.

As shown in Figure 11.3, the largest generator of jobs is the transportation, trade and retailing sector of the industry, with 6.5 million workers. With increasing productivity, employment in the first three sectors—farming, processing, and other manufacturing—declined between 1975 and 1988, even as their output and value added rose. Employment in farming declined by a million people as labor productivity in agriculture continued its long upward trend. Labor productivity indexes

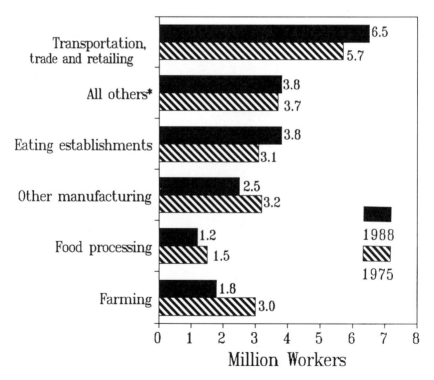

Million Workers

*Includes other services, mining and forestry

Figure 11.3. Employment in the food and fiber system in 1975 and 1988. (Data from U.S. Department of Commerce, Bureau of the Census, 1990a, p. 637.)

nearly doubled for the farm sector between just 1982 and 1987.[5] Fewer and fewer labor hours are needed in farming to produce the required level of output.

Figure 11.4 indicates the distribution of consumer food expenditures between the marketing system and farmers for the years 1978–1988. The *food marketing bill* reflects the difference between total consumer expenditures for all domestically produced food products and what farmers received for the equivalent farm commodities.[6] The marketing bill, which is calculated annually, provides a measure of the marketing margin for food, also called the farm-to-retail price spread.

The farm value share of total consumer expenditures for domestic foods, which was 41% in 1950, declined to 33% by 1965 and to only 25% by 1988. Some might conclude that this trend in the farm share represents something unfair and perhaps even a little suspicious. However, the basic explanation is simple. Consumers have demanded more convenient, and hence more highly processed food products, and shifted to eating more food away from home. Therefore, more and more of the value and costs of the final retail-level products are added after the basic commodities leave the farm. In addition, food marketing costs have risen more rapidly than farm-level costs, particularly because of increased labor costs.[7]

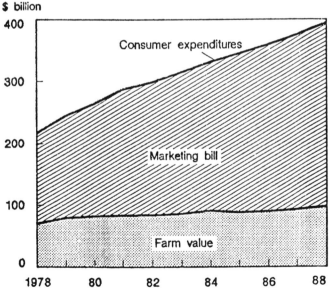

Figure 11.4. Distribution of consumer food expenditures between the marketing system and farmers: 1978–1988 (using preliminary data for 1988). Data are for domestically produced farm foods purchased by U.S. consumers for consumption, both at home and away from home. (Reprinted from Dunham, 1989, p. 39.)

More generally, as shown in Figure 11.5, the farm value as a proportion of the consumer food dollar is much lower for food purchased and consumed away from home than for that consumed at home (16% vs. 30%). Food service (preparation and service) accounted for 60% (60 cents out of every $1.00) of the cost of food away from home. Processing accounted for 31% and retailing 23% of the cost of at-home food purchases. The farm value share also varies considerably for different products, and whereas it was only 7% for white bread, it was 62% for eggs.[8]

Figure 11.6 provides more detailed information on the various cost components of the food marketing bill. Labor costs took 34.5 cents of the average dollar spent on food at home and away. Labor costs in 1988

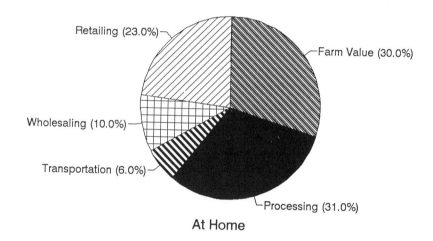

Retailing (23.0%)
Farm Value (30.0%)
Wholesaling (10.0%)
Transportation (6.0%)
Processing (31.0%)

At Home

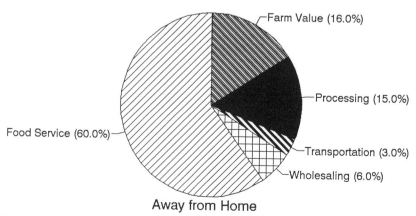

Farm Value (16.0%)
Processing (15.0%)
Food Service (60.0%)
Transportation (3.0%)
Wholesaling (6.0%)

Away from Home

Figure 11.5. Where the average food dollar went in 1988, both at home and away from home. (Reprinted from Dunham, 1989, p. 39.)

were $136 billion.[9] The cost of containers and packaging totaled $32 billion, which averaged about 8 cents of every dollar spent on food. The value of the farm products, labor, and packaging, together accounted for over two-thirds (67.5%) of the total costs for food. Other categories shown in Figure 11.6 include intercity transportation, depreciation, advertising, energy, profits, and rent.

FARMING

A brief overview of the changing structure of farming and current agricultural policy in the United States is provided in this section. Some of the implications for farming of the trends discussed earlier in this book appear next. Particular attention is given to the increase in contract farming, production for specialty markets, commodity promotion activities, and to the growing importance of environmental, health, and food safety concerns for agricultural policy and farming. A short discussion of fishing and aquaculture is also included.

The Structure of Farming and Agricultural Policy

There are approximately 2.2 million farms in the United States, down from a peak of 6.8 million in 1935.[10] However, the total area farmed has changed very little and is still about 1 billion acres.[11] As recently as 1950, 15% of the population resided on farms.[12] Now, only about 2%

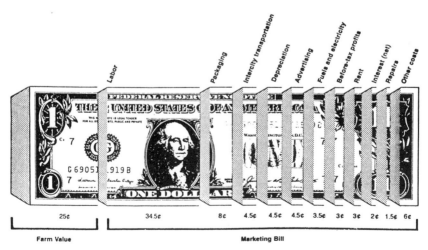

Figure 11.6. What the average dollar spent on food paid for in 1988, including food at home and away from home. Other costs include property taxes and insurance, accounting and professional services, promotion, bad debts, and many miscellaneous items. (Reprinted from Dunham, 1989, p. 39.)

Table 11.1. Distribution of Farms, Cash Receipts, Total and Off-Farm Income by Farm Sales Class, 1988[a]

Farm with Annual Sales	No. of Farms	Percent of All Farms	Percent of Total Cash Receipts	Average Total Cash Income[b] ($)	Average Off-Farm Income ($)	Percent of Income from Off Farm	Percent of Direct Government Payments
<$10,000	1,030,000	46.9	2.4	28,980	29,640	102.3[c]	3.8
$10,000–39,999	525,000	23.9	7.3	27,280	20,100	73.7	14.3
$40,000–99,999	320,000	14.6	13.6	39,920	14,680	36.8	24.9
$100,000–499,999	293,000	13.3	40.0	104,590	17,270	16.5	48.4
≥$500,000	30,000	1.4	36.6	800,030	28,230	3.5	8.4
All farms	2,197,000	100.0	100.0	50,790	23,530	46.3	100.0

[a] Source: U.S. Department of Agriculture, Economic Research Service, 1989c.
[b] Total cash income includes net farm income plus off-farm income.
[c] Off-farm income is more than 100% of total cash income because they lose money on farming (net farm cash income is negative).

of the population lives on farms. The U.S. Department of Agriculture (USDA) currently defines the farm population as all persons living in rural places with $1,000 or more of agricultural sales in a reporting year. There has been a trend towards a bimodal distribution of farms, with a small number of large operations producing a large share of the agricultural output and a large number of small operators who earn most of their income from off-farm sources.

Table 11.1 shows that less than 15% of farms had sales of $100,000 or more, but they accounted for 76.6% of all cash receipts from farming in 1988. Moreover, the 30,000 farms with sales of $500,000 and above had more than 30% of the cash receipts alone. On the other hand, there were just over 1.5 million farms with annual sales below $40,000. About 93% of the total cash income of these small operations came from off-farm sources. Farms with sales under $10,000 received 102% of their total cash income from off-farm sources. This figure exceeds 100% because they actually lost money on their farming operations, as reflected in a negative net farm income.

Recently the percentage rate of decline in the number of farms has been greatest for intermediate size farms. These farm operators frequently have found their farm income was inadequate and had to consider either increasing the size of operations or combining farming with off-farm employment.[13] The number of corporate farms has been increasing and reached 50,000 by 1985. However, nearly 90% of these were family-held corporations formed primarily for management and tax purposes and are very similar to other large family farms in their operation.[14]

In the mid-1930s, the average income for farm families was just over 50% of the average income for all American families. It reached 70% of the overall average family income by 1950, and pretty well pulled even by 1970. It shot well above the average family income in the commodity boom of the early 1970s and then fell to 76% of the average in 1981 during the farm crisis of the early 1980s. By the late 1980s, farm family income had again climbed and was 20% above the average family income in 1988. Although far more variable from year to year, the average farm family's income appears to have surpassed the average income of nonfarm households.[15] There are, however, disadvantaged farm families living in poverty just as there are disadvantaged families in the rest of the population.

Government intervention in agriculture is universal among countries, and the United States is no exception. Widespread government efforts to support agricultural commodity prices began in the 1930s during the Great Depression. The political support to maintain sizable government farm programs has existed ever since. The fundamental problem is that the productive capacity of American farms exceeds the effective demand from domestic and foreign markets.[16] It has been considered politically unacceptable to allow farm commodity prices to fall to a level that would clear the markets, although U.S. farm policy legislation is moving in a more market-oriented direction. Because of its dependence on the weather, agricultural production also suffers from a high degree of variability, and hence uncertainty and risk, as was again made evident in the drought that occurred in the United States in 1988. That drought caused the largest one-year decline in world grain stocks ever recorded.[17]

The core of U.S. agricultural programs is a system of loan rates and target prices, primarily for the major grains, like wheat and corn. The loan rate establishes a commodity price floor. On the other hand, if the market price falls below the target price that has been set, the government pays the farmer the difference. This difference between the market price and the target price is known as a deficiency payment.[18] To participate in these programs, farmers must follow certain requirements, typically involving land set-asides to reduce total output. The major impact of these programs on consumers is that they pay higher taxes, or the federal deficit is larger. Food prices are more stable, albeit possibly at a higher level in the short run, but, in the long run, prices could be lower than they would otherwise be. The argument that stabilizing farm prices and incomes leads to lower consumer food prices hinges on the idea that decreased risk and uncertainty lead farmers to invest in more modern and efficient technology, which in turn decreases production costs and increases output.[19]

Since the percent of income needed to purchase food in the United States has fallen steadily since the 1930s, this argument has some plausibility, but exceptions can be found. For example, dairy, peanut, and sugar support programs push up both the farm and retail prices of these commodities.[20] Marketing controls on some fruits and vegetables tend to raise their retail prices, but ordinarily ensure a steady, high quality supply.[21] These marketing orders are still controversial, though. Some claim they waste good food, make nutritious food unaffordable to the poor, and restrict entrepreneurship in farming.

Federal expenditures on farm commodity programs reached a peak of $25.8 billion in 1986 but have fallen to about half that level or less in the last few years.[22] During the current period of large federal budget deficits, spending for farm programs has come under increased scrutiny, especially by urban legislators. The programs are particularly criticized for their inflexibility and distributional impact. As can be seen in the last column in Table 11.1, the relatively small number of large producers receive a disproportionately large share of the benefits, a consequence of their producing a large share of the output.

It can be debated whether the farm programs should be viewed as a food security policy, which helps create a healthier, more stable farm economy and ensures ample food supplies, or as a welfare program, which basically transfers income from taxpayers to farmers, who now have higher family incomes than nonfarmers.[23] The U.S. government has worked through the latest multilateral negotiations under the General Agreement on Tariffs and Trade (GATT) to reduce farm support programs and subsidies worldwide. The ultimate goal, stated by the U.S. negotiating team, is to eliminate all "trade-distorting" subsidies, although governments could still make direct income payments to farmers.[24]

There was discussion in the late 1970s during the Carter administration, when Bob Bergland was Secretary of Agriculture and Carol Foreman was an Assistant Secretary, of establishing an integrated food and nutrition policy, which would encompass policy measures affecting supply, demand, and market structure. The government would start with a set of nutrition guidelines, and food and agricultural policy would then be based on those objectives.[25] However, this approach was met with resistance by the farm lobby, and the approach to food and agricultural policy continues to be dominated by producers' concerns and determined largely by political considerations.[26]

In addition to its basic price support policies, the government also finances agricultural research and extension activities. Current government expenditures on agricultural research are somewhat over $1 billion per year.[27] Studies have found the return on this investment to be high. It has been strongly argued that these expenditures should be substantially increased. The argument for this public support of agricultural research is that consumers are the ultimate beneficiaries of increased productivity achieved through agricultural research.[28]

Aquaculture. Fish farming or aquaculture, which involves the production of fish and shellfish on special farms, has increased rapidly in the last two decades.[29] Total U.S. aquaculture production reached 721 million pounds in 1987, with a value of $613 million, up from 203 million pounds in 1980.[30] The types of fish and shellfish produced by aquaculture in the United States are primarily high-value species that include catfish, crawfish, freshwater prawns, clams, mussels, oysters, shrimp, Pacific salmon, and trout. Over 40% of the oysters and almost all of the catfish, crawfish, and rainbow trout in the United States are provided by private aquaculture.[31] Catfish are the most important single product, with 372 million pounds produced in 1987 and a value of $277 million.[32] Catfish farming is largely concentrated in several southern states.

Most fish and shellfish are still obtained by harvesting the natural supply, primarily from the ocean. Some 14.6 billion pounds of fishery products were used in the United States in 1988, 10.5 billion for human food and 4.1 billion for industrial use. The domestic catch provided about half of the total, or 7.2 billion pounds, and imports 7.4 billion.[33] Canned tuna fish production alone had a value of $960 million in 1988, and the value of all processed fishery products was $5.4 billion.[34] Although aquaculture still provides only a relatively small portion of the total supply, it is rapidly growing in importance as the demand for fish and shellfish increases and as the sustainable harvests from the natural supply of various species are reached, or in some cases even exceeded through overfishing.

Farming:
Implications and Current Issues

In today's consumer-oriented marketplace, agricultural producers and their organizations need to be attentive to changes in consumer demand and position their products to respond to consumers' wants and needs. Farmers should not view these changes as threats, but as potentially profitable opportunities. These arguments are obviously more pertinent the closer the link between producer and consumer. They apply more directly to fresh produce than to feed grains. However, even the latter are strongly affected by way of changes in meat consumption. For an increasing number of farmers, the key to higher profits lies more in marketing than in production. Promotion activities, niche markets, product differentiation, and contract and specification buying are becoming increasingly important.[35]

One of the responses to changing consumer preferences is an increase in the number of brand name fresh products—fruits, vegetables, and meat.[36] Food processors, retailers, producer cooperatives, and in some instances large growers, as with lettuce, are introducing brand name lines of fresh products. An attempt is made to differentiate the brand name product on the basis of convenience, attractiveness, and consistent quality. This differentiation, in turn, increases the need for farmers to raise a reliably high-quality product.

With the segmentation of the consumer market, as discussed particularly in Chapter 4, opportunities for products aimed at specialized, "niche" markets have increased. Some consumers are willing to pay a premium for products such as free-range chickens, natural beef raised without antibiotics or hormones, or wild game meat that is raised for sale. Ethical considerations are also beginning to affect some consumers' choices. An example is "Pastureland Farms" pork, which was introduced in two Minneapolis–St. Paul supermarket chains in 1990. Pastureland was approved by the Animal Welfare Institute. The animals are raised in roomy bedded pens and allowed to roam outside, rather than being crowded into close, confined quarters.[37] How large the market is for such ethically oriented products remains to be seen.

One of the specialized markets that receives the most attention is for organic products. Organic refers to produce that is grown without chemical pesticides or synthetic fertilizer and is distributed without artificial preservatives or dyes.[38] Some 15 states have begun organic certification programs, and the 1990 Farm Bill contains federal guidelines. In Minnesota, for example, fields must have been chemical-free for three years to qualify.[39] Organic farming is no longer limited to just small producers or hobbyists. A number of large California vegetable producers have converted at least a part of their fields to organic production.

Sales of organic products amount to over $3 billion annually. However, less than 1% of the agricultural produce in the United States is currently raised organically.[40] The actual magnitude of the market is unclear. In surveys, a majority of consumers say they would buy organic products if available and almost half state they would pay a premium.[41] However, actual product sales indicate consumers are resistant to paying a premium and retailers have experienced some difficulties with organic products.[42] This is not the first time that consumers have said one thing, but in fact done something else. One explanation for their seeming inconsistency is that, while there is a lack of a clear definition for organic food, consumers think of it as the ultimate in natural, fresh, and safe food. If it turns out to look worse or store poorly, they quickly return to more familiar nonorganic products.

In terms of the possible impact of major health-related changes in diet, research has shown that if all American consumers had adopted the *Dietary Goals for the United States* as described in Chapter 2, the impact on farmers would vary greatly, depending on the commodity. The results of a simulated change in American diets between 1981 and 1986 showed that crop farmers would have generally benefited from higher farm prices and incomes. Livestock and egg producers would have faced declines in quantity demanded, farm prices, and incomes. Poultry, wheat, and rice farmers would have benefited from increased demand, but corn growers would have been adversely affected mainly because of a decline in the demand for pork, and subsequently for feed corn, and due to a decline in sweetener consumption. Overall, net farm income would have fallen slightly and the cost of government farm programs would have increased, mainly due to dairy price supports. Consumers' food costs would have declined, primarily because crop foods are generally cheaper than animal foods, and a shift away from consumption of animal foods makes for a lower-cost diet.[43]

Science and technology increasingly provide the ability to modify the attributes of agricultural products to match consumers' preferences. The beef and pork sold today are leaner than in the past. Breeding and feeding programs have made a difference.[44] The effort to develop a lower cholesterol egg seems to be achieving some success.[45] Advances in biotechnology and genetic engineering will greatly enhance our ability to redesign plant and animal products to contain attributes desirable to consumers.[46] As mentioned in Chapter 10, for example, tests show that the use of the growth hormone PST (porcine somatotropin) can produce leaner pork.

A recent study for the National Academy of Sciences emphasized that government policies regarding grades, standards, and labeling may act as barriers that retard the response of producers to changing consumer preferences, particularly for less fat in meat and dairy products.[47] The current grading system rewards meat producers for marketing fatter animals. The highest grade of beef (prime) has the highest fat content. The pricing system for milk is still based partly on butterfat content, even though consumers have shifted towards low-fat and nonfat dairy products and research efforts are underway to reduce the fat and cholesterol content in milk products.

Agricultural commodity groups are increasingly engaging in promotional activities. The dairy, beef, egg, turkey, and pork producers all have used national television and print advertising campaigns to try to boost the sales of their products. Most consumers have probably become familiar with the slogans: "Milk—it does a body good," "Beef—real food for real people," and "Pork—the other white meat." The beef campaign has, for example, stressed that moderate-size servings of beef can fit into a low-fat, low-cholesterol diet. These promotional campaigns were all made possible by legislation passed by Congress that establishes a "checkoff," or flat rate tax, which is subtracted from the farmer's sales price. For example, the beef checkoff imposed in 1985 was one dollar on each animal sold. The dairy checkoff raised $211 million in 1987 and the one for beef raised $82 million.[48] The funds may be used to finance education, research, and promotion campaigns and are administered by independent boards composed primarily of farmers.

In addition to dairy, pork, and beef, there have been checkoff-financed promotional campaigns for a number of other crops, and several other commodity groups have asked Congress to establish checkoff programs for them. There are critics of these programs. Major criticisms are that the checkoff is not voluntary, but is a mandatory tax owed by all producers, and that oversight of the funds has been too lax. There are also questions about the effectiveness of the promotional activities.[49]

All in all, these checkoff campaigns are generally seen as a positive response on the part of producers to the need to promote their commodities. They represent a recognition on the part of producers of the importance of marketing, and specifically, that the market is increasingly consumer-driven. The amount of money spent on the promotion of generic commodities remains only a tiny fraction of the billions of dollars spent by the major food companies in promoting brand name food products.

As discussed in Chapter 1, there has been an increase in specification buying and contract farming. The latter relieves producers of any marketing responsibilities since they raise their crops or animals under contract to a processor, or in some cases, a retailer. This practice is widespread among chicken producers, but is also beginning to occur in pork production and may spread to beef. It has been increasing for certain crops as well, especially for the processing of fruits and vegetables. Contracting gives the processors tighter control over quantity, quality, and cost.

However, there may be some serious problems with contract production from the farmer's perspective.[50] For example, the relationship between an individual chicken producer and a major processor can be a very uneven one. The processor controls the number of chicks a farmer raises and establishes the price for the adult birds. The farmer provides the chicken houses and labor. Processors argue that producers are protected from the risks of the volatility of broiler prices. However, contracts can be broken with only very short notice and may offer little protection. The farmer still bears the risk of lost birds, which can be substantial during a heat wave. With the high rate of mergers and acquisitions among poultry processors, more and more chicken producers find themselves facing a monopsony situation with only a single processor buying poultry in their geographic area. Studies have found that prices for adult birds are higher and that producers may gross as much as 20% more in areas where several processors are competing.[51]

Environmental Concerns

Environmental considerations are likely to have an increasing impact on farming and agricultural policy in the future. Concern is growing that some current agricultural practices are damaging the environment and the resource base on which agriculture depends.[52] There is concern about the level of wind and water erosion on some farm land, the degradation of lakes and rivers from agricultural runoff, the contamination of ground water from agricultural chemicals, and the buildup of salts and other chemicals in the soil of some irrigated areas.

Food safety and environmental quality concerns become intertwined, especially regarding the use of chemical pesticides. In the first, the concern focuses on possible residues on food crops, and in the second, on the effect on the environment, and particularly the effect on groundwater. Although incomplete, a 1988 Environmental Protection Agency (EPA) survey found groundwater in 26 states contained detectable amounts of pesticides from agricultural use.[53]

The use of pesticides rose from just over 300 million pounds of active ingredients (the chemicals that actually control pests) in 1964 to about 900 million pounds in 1988.[54] Herbicides, which kill weeds, were used on only 10% of the land planted to corn, cotton, and wheat in 1952; this figure had climbed to 90–95% by 1980.[55] Many farmers are themselves now concerned about the environmental consequences of heavy use of pesticides. A poll of Iowa farmers found that 78% thought modern agriculture is too dependent on herbicides and insecticides.[56]

A recent National Academy of Sciences report, *Alternative Agriculture,* argued that government agricultural policies have discouraged environmentally desirable farming practices.[57] Government programs have encouraged monoculture, locking farmers into specific crops in order to protect their acreage base for agricultural price support purposes. Deficiency payments increase the incentives for farmers to maximize yields through the heavy application of fertilizer and pesticides. There is a push to make the farm programs more flexible, to allow more crop rotation and thus reduce the need for agricultural chemicals.[58]

Some responses to these environmental concerns are already occurring. Millions of acres have been placed in the Conservation Reserve Program, which pays farmers to remove erodible land from production.[59] There is growing interest in alternative agriculture technology. The USDA now has a Low-Input Sustainable Agriculture Program (LISA), although at a very low level of funding.[60] The definition of sustainability is somewhat ambiguous, but the core of the concept relates to agricultural practices that preserve or improve the environmental resources, particularly the soil, upon which agriculture is based, so that production may be maintained indefinitely. Sustainable or alternative agriculture emphasizes the reduced use of pesticides and synthetic fertilizer, increased reliance on crop rotation and natural manures, and an understanding of and respect for ecological processes.[61]

Many mainstream farmers are starting to reduce their use of agricultural chemicals.[62] Between 1982 and 1988, the total use of pesticides in U.S. agriculture trended down slightly.[63] Farmers are concerned about the quality of the groundwater, which their families typically use for drinking water. They are finding that a reduction in input costs can sometimes increase profitability. However, many farmers feel threatened by the attacks of environmentalists. They oppose measures that would tax the use of pesticides or tightly regulate and reduce, or even eliminate, the use of many chemicals.[64] There are concerns that consumer food prices would rise and that the competitiveness of U.S. agricultural products in world markets would suffer.[65]

Over a longer term, biotechnology may provide at least part of the answer by developing crop varieties that are pest resistant and that can fix nitrogen from the air, eliminating the need for most pesticides and fertilizers. However, some biotechnology research involves developing crops that will resist chemical herbicides better, which environmentalists believe could lead to an increase in their use.[66] Finally, there is growing environmental concern about the buildup of carbon dioxide and other gases in the atmosphere that could lead to global warming and shifting climatic patterns, which potentially would have a major impact on agricultural production.

FOOD PROCESSING AND MANUFACTURING

The major function of food processors, such as Kraft General Foods and General Mills, is to add utility and value to raw farm products.[67] The terms "food processor" and "food manufacturer" are usually used synonymously. Food processors interface with both producers and consumers. They buy commodities to be processed from farmers. Although they typically sell to food wholesalers or directly to retailers, they ultimately depend on consumers to purchase and use their products. Some are "further processors"; they add value to already-processed foods used as ingredients in their products.[68]

Food manufacturing has been defined as "activities that typically use power-driven machines and materials-handling equipment to mechanically or chemically transform raw materials into foods and beverages for human consumption."[69] Food processing and manufacturing firms are diverse. They may be large or small, corporately or individually owned, single plant or multiplant, and specialized or diversified.[70]

Processors provide important marketing functions such as new product and process development, packaging, labeling, branding, storing, transporting, and financing.[71] Processing may result in product differentiation and the derivation of several consumer products from one raw farm commodity.[72] Wheat, for example, is milled into flour, which then is used to make a variety of different baked products and other cereal-based foods. In response to the demands of consumers, processors in recent years have emphasized the development of convenience foods such as "microwavable" foods and refrigerated "fresh" foods, as well as new ingredients, new processing techniques, and new packaging materials and technologies.[73]

Several of these developments are included among the Institute of Food Technologists' list of the most important innovations in food technology in the last 50 years.[74] The top 10 innovations include aseptic processing and packaging, minimum safe canning processes for vegetables, the microwave oven, frozen concentrated citrus juices, controlled atmosphere packaging for fresh fruits and vegetables, freeze-drying, frozen meals, the concept of water activity, food fortification, and ultra-high-temperature processing of milk and other products. Other innovations lower on the list are polyunsaturated corn oil margarine, fat hydrogenation, high-fructose corn syrup, aspartame (NutraSweet), and extruded food technology. Many of these innovations are currently being used, but others have been slow in reaching the market.[75]

The Structure of Food Processing and Manufacturing

There are 47 separate food processing and manufacturing industries in the United States that, in 1988, added an estimated $88 billion in value to raw food products.[76] These industries include the processors of meat products (meat packing, poultry, eggs), dairy products, preserved fruits and vegetables, grain milling products, bakery products, sugar and confections, fats and oils, beverages, and miscellaneous foods such as fishery products, coffee, and others.[77] About 12,000 new grocery products were introduced in 1989 by these industries, including about 9,200 new food products. Of these, 1–10% were expected to succeed and only 8–9% were actually new or "significant."[78]

The food processing industry is becoming more and more concentrated, with mergers and acquisitions creating fewer, larger, and highly diversified firms. Three of the largest mergers of food processors in U.S. history occurred in 1988, including that of the Philip Morris Companies and Kraft to form the largest consumer foods company in the United States.[79]

There are two major segments of the food processing industry.[80] One is a dominant core of a few very large firms that produce popular brands and have the major portion of industry sales. The second is a competitive fringe of a large number of small firms that produce less popular brands and have a small portion of industry sales.

Food processors make significant contributions to the U.S. economy through sales to consumers, the purchase of raw products, capital investment, and labor costs.[81] Sales by the food processing industries were an estimated $340 billion in 1988, an increase of 6.5% over 1987 sales. Food processors purchased nearly $130 billion worth of raw food products in 1988, including an estimated $100 billion worth of U.S. agricultural commodities, $19 billion worth of imports of foreign agricultural commodities, and $9 billion worth of seafood and fishery products.

An estimated $8.5 billion was spent by food processors in 1988 for new plants, equipment, and plant modernization and automation, which increased efficiency and labor productivity without changing employment levels.[82] Research and development accounted for expenditures of about $1.4 billion in 1988, with processors purchasing another $1 billion worth from other industries such as packaging, computer, and machinery firms. Processors employed about 1.6 million people in 1988 and spent an estimated $30 billion on labor costs.

In the international economy, the United States is the largest importer and exporter of processed food. The value of processed food imports has generally exceeded exports. In 1988, food exports increased, helping to lower the trade deficit.[83] In addition, although foreign investment in U.S. food processing firms is somewhat greater than U.S. investment in foreign firms, the foreign subsidiaries of U.S. firms account for a substantial proportion of sales for many U.S. food processors. According to a recent USDA study, about one-fifth of the sales of a composite of 57 food companies came from overseas operations.[84] Beverage firms, principally soft drinks (Coca-Cola and Pepsi), have the largest international sales.

Food Processing:
Implications and Current Issues

Food processors are becoming consumer-oriented as they respond to consumer demands. For example, Hormel was trying to sell "to a consumer who no longer existed" before realizing that consumers wanted convenience and prepared foods rather than fresh meat that had to be cooked for a meal.[85] Processors increasingly target specific consumer groups with line extensions of successful products, which are developed to please particular consumers' preferences and needs.[86] If new product introductions continue to increase at the present rate of about 10% annually, there will be about 28,000 new food products introduced in the year 2000.[87]

Processing and packaging techniques are being developed to aid processors in providing the "fresh" foods consumers now demand. Some of the technical innovations that lengthen the shelf life of products are new cook-and-chill systems for quick chilling and quick reheating later, "sous vide" in which prepared food is vacuum packaged in plastic pouches and refrigerated, and modified-atmosphere packaging.[88] Furthermore, competition for a greater share of the food service dollar is moving back in the distribution system from the retailers to the processors who are developing and supplying packaged meals, entrees, side dishes, and desserts that require virtually no cooking or cleanup.[89]

The microwave oven has opened new product categories for food manufacturers. New food product introductions for the microwave oven reached almost 1,000 in 1989, about 10% of new product introductions.[90] Heat and eat microwave breakfasts and shelf-stable lunch items are new items in this category. Foods for the microwave oven fall into two categories: foods that formerly were cooked by other methods that are repackaged with directions for both microwave and conventional cooking, termed "dual ovenable," and microwave-only foods that are formulated and packaged especially for the microwave oven.[91] The former have turned out to be relatively unsuccessful from the quality standpoint, and the latter are more difficult to develop than expected.[92] Predictions are that dual-ovenable will be overtaken by microwave-only products in the early 1990s.[93]

Induced Innovation. In the future, improving the quality of microwave food will be extremely important for consumer acceptance. Product formulations for a growing number of microwave foods now include the use of specialized ingredients and the addition of flavors to duplicate flavors in conventionally cooked foods. There is also an increasing use of active packaging, such as susceptors to direct power to the crusts of products, to make them brown and crisp. Also, special labels are being used that direct power to designated areas of the package to overcome uneven heat distribution.[94]

Technological and institutional changes in the food industry can be attributed, at least in part, to "induced innovation."[95] The theory of induced innovation says that technical innovations may result from a change in the relative prices of inputs to the production process, and/or to shifts in consumer demand that change the ratio of product prices to costs of production. For example, because refined sugar has been more expensive than corn sweetener, soft drink producers have found ways to use corn sweetener to achieve the same taste. This technological innovation was induced by a change in relative input costs.

Likewise, the shift in consumers' preferences and increased demand for low-calorie products created an incentive to develop better noncaloric sweeteners to capture potential profits. Aspartame (NutraSweet), for example, has been an enormously profitable product. Changes in consumer preferences send signals back to processors to develop innovations that meet the demand for preferred products or product characteristics. The rush to develop microwavable products has been a response to the consumer demand for convenience.

The food industry is responding to changes in consumer attitudes and preferences with innovations in product characteristics. Consistent with long-term preferences for good health, many consumers want food with less fat and cholesterol, and some are willing to pay more for it. Consequently, several processors have stopped using animal fats or saturated vegetable fats such as palm and coconut oils. A technology has been developed to process eggs into a low-fat, low-cholesterol raw egg product (sold in liquid form), and researchers are working on the feed and biology of chickens trying to produce a lower cholesterol egg.

Meat and dairy producers are following the same path. Fast-food chains have cut down the fat in their hamburgers, started to use vegetable oils to fry foods, cut down the fat in milk shakes, and added salad entrees.[96]

The hunt has been on to develop fat-free ingredients that have the functionality and performance of fats in food products. The development of Simplesse by Monsanto's NutraSweet Company, and Olestra by Procter & Gamble, are two examples. Simplesse, which has been approved by the Food and Drug Administration (FDA) for certain uses, is now being used in a line of fat-free, frozen desserts called Simple Pleasures. Simplesse is made from milk or egg white proteins and cannot be used in foods that are heated. Olestra, a sucrose polyester made from sugar (sucrose) and fatty acids, has not yet received FDA approval. It can be used in frying and baking.[97]

By mid-1990, some 150 new fat-free food products had been introduced, including everything from Kraft's salad dressings to McDonald's muffins. Foods labeled "nonfat" or "fat free" can contain as much as 0.49 grams of fat per serving, since the FDA allows companies to round down to the nearest gram.[98] There are concerns about the nutritional implications of these foods, particularly if their heavy consumption interferes with the overall quality of the diet.[99]

More generally, food substitutes, also called alternative foods or food analogues, fall into two categories: those used in special dietary foods to decrease the intake of a certain dietary component(s), such as fat, and those that are alternatives for expensive foods. In the second category, an example is surimi, a product flavored and shaped like expensive shellfish, which was mentioned in Chapter 1. Surimi is made from minced fish from abundant but less popular species. Surimi products provide an inexpensive substitute for shellfish. Another example is textured soy protein, which is sometimes used as a substitute for meat.[100]

Consumer concerns about the impact of packaging on the environment are starting to induce innovation in the amount and type of packaging used for food. About 12% of the total solid waste now comes from food packaging.[101] Trash generated by the fast-food industry is being viewed as a major environmental problem. Foam containers used for fast food are considered especially undesirable, because they may be made with ozone-depleting chemicals. The decision was made by McDonald's late in 1990 not to use foam containers any more.[102] Degradable packaging has been one response, but its merits are questioned. Supposedly degradable materials may degrade slowly or not at all in an actual landfill environment. Source reduction, in the form of reduced packaging, and recycling are probably more promising ways to deal with excessive packaging and waste from the consumption of food. Incineration is also being more widely used, but it is controversial.

Source reduction is considered by the EPA to be the strategy that is most efficient and has the greatest potential for decreasing solid waste, because "what isn't there to begin with doesn't have to be recycled."[103] However, in reducing packaging, processors also must consider the number of roles packaging plays for a product, such as transportability, storability, preservation, and ease of preparation.[104] Recycling is the second most desirable strategy for dealing with packaging waste, according to the EPA. Recyclable materials are now replacing materials not readily recyclable in more and more food packages.[105] More generally, increased public concern, and the resulting new government regulations, will raise the costs of manufacturing processes that degrade the air or water and induce processors to seek alternative technologies. This is an example of the type of shift in relative input costs that induces innovation.

Automation. The automation of food processing plants should significantly increase their efficiency in the future with "megafactories" designed with "multiple product, flexible lines."[106] Automation can be viewed as an "induced innovation" in response to rising labor costs. For example, just-in-time inventory control, one of the "Japanese methods" of materials requirement planning, is now being introduced into some segments of the food industry.[107] This method is based on market turnover. Products are produced just in time to replace those sold, rather than on a schedule based on processing economies. The traditional U.S. method was to push products into the marketplace whether they were needed or not.

Just-in-time inventory management of ingredients reduces production costs by decreasing space and inventory needs. For example, the just-in-time system implemented for soup production at Campbell Soup Company reduced production costs 20%, space 30%, and inventory 60–70%. However, success of the just-in-time system depends on the availability of suppliers who can guarantee that their products meet specifications and who are willing to deliver raw materials to processors more frequently and in smaller quantities than they have in the past.

Automation and employee training have recently been implemented by the C & H Sugar Company to increase efficiency, decrease costs, and convert the entire plant from a "production-driven" to a "customer-driven" operation.[108] A computer-controlled, operatorless warehouse enables bar-coded pallets of product to store themselves. Multitask training of employees to broaden their equipment maintenance and production line responsibilities decreased labor needs 25% and job classifications from 117 to 7.

FOOD WHOLESALING

Wholesalers move fresh and processed food products from producers or processors to supermarkets and other food stores and to restaurants and other food service establishments.[109] Their major functions are to purchase, transport, assemble, store, and distribute food to their customers. Wholesalers are experts in buying and selling food, and they advise retailers about product availability and prices.

The Structure of Food Wholesaling

The three principal types of wholesalers in the United States are merchant wholesalers, manufacturers' sales branches and offices, and agents and brokers.[110]

Merchant wholesalers purchase and take ownership of food and nonfood items before they sell them. They are classified according to the services they offer, the variety of items they handle, and whether or not they are affiliated with food retailers. Merchant wholesalers may be either full-service or limited-function. Full-service wholesalers supply a number of services that retailers may use, such as inventory control, pricing, financial management and analysis, merchandising and advertising support, private label support, site selection, credit, and financing of new stores. Limited-function wholesalers do not supply these services.[111]

Based on the variety of items they handle, merchant wholesalers are classified as general line, limited line, or specialty wholesalers. Two new classifications that have emerged in recent years include wholesale clubs and national food service distributors.[112]

General line wholesalers include a small number of very large companies that handle a wide assortment of food and nonfood items.[113] These wholesalers are classified according to whether or not they are affiliated with retailers. Wholesaler-retailer affiliations offer the buying power of a corporate chain and the benefits of being an owner-operator of an independent store. They have put pressure on the independent wholesalers who are not affiliated with retailers, causing them to concentrate their selling to food service operations. In wholesaler-sponsored voluntary retail groups, wholesalers bring retailers together into a group and provide services in exchange for the business of the retailers, which is guaranteed. In retailer-owned cooperative groups, independent retailers purchase and operate their own wholesale facilities cooperatively.[114]

Limited-line wholesalers include a large number of smaller firms that handle only dry groceries, mainly canned foods, coffee, spices, bread, and soft drinks. Specialty wholesalers handle only one or a few products, such as dairy products, meat, poultry, fish, fruits and vegetables, or frozen foods.[115]

Wholesale clubs, such as Price Saver and Sam's Wholesale Clubs, are a new type of merchant wholesaler; they originated in the 1970s and expanded rapidly in the 1980s. They are "hybrid wholesale-retail establishments" that sell food and many other types of products, such as appliances, hardware, and office supplies. Prices are slightly above wholesale to members who may be individual consumers, small food service operators, or grocers.[116]

National food service distributors, such as Sysco, which is the largest, supply food, equipment, and services to restaurants, fast-food outlets, airlines, and food service institutions.[117] Large food service distributor groups have been growing in recent years. These groups consist of several independent wholesalers who work together to buy, market, and distribute large quantities of products. This sector also includes integrated manufacturer-distributors who have their own food service sales force and do their own advertising, distributing, and marketing.

Large processors and manufacturers maintain their own sales force at the wholesale level by staffing manufacturers' sales branches and offices. Selling is done on commission, and these offices also are responsible for storing, transporting, and marketing the products. Agents and brokers provide the sales force and marketing services primarily for small food processors, although some large processors also use them. Agents and brokers sell on a commission basis and do not actually handle or take title or possession of the products they represent.[118]

The food wholesaling industry had sales of $417 billion in 1988.[119] Of this total, merchant wholesaler sales were the largest at $240 billion or 58%; manufacturers' sales branches were at $101 billion or 24%; and agents' and brokers' sales were $75 billion or 18%. Sales in 1988, which were only 3.5% higher than in 1987, showed a small annual growth rate, probably because of more direct shipments from processors to retailers. Wholesalers employed 647,000 workers in 1988. Although wholesaler employees earned higher average hourly wages than workers in any other segment of the food marketing industry, profits of wholesale firms in 1988 were comparable to those of processors, retailers, and the food service sector.[120]

Wholesaling:
Implications and Current Issues

Major changes in food wholesaling occurred during the 1980s as a result of mergers and acquisitions and the accompanying increase in aggregate concentration.[121] The acquisition of local and regional distributors by large wholesalers is expected to continue. Increasingly, these firms will supply the financial and managerial services needed by independent retailers.[122] Large corporations control most of the assets of the industry. For example, in 1986, of the 25,000 corporate wholesalers that filed tax returns, 16% owned 88% of the industry assets. The two largest wholesalers in the United States in 1987 were Super Valu and Fleming Companies. In 1988, there were fewer mergers than in previous years, but the value and size of each were the largest ever recorded. Although the large firms control most of the assets, the small firms have the highest profits.[123] Mergers and acquisitions also have increased consolidation of wholesale clubs, and growth in this segment of wholesaling is expected to expand in the future in terms of markets, services, and products offered.

Serving larger food outlets, such as super warehouse stores and hypermarkets, creates new opportunities and problems for food wholesalers.[124] Hypermarkets, for example, have little storage space and require deliveries seven days a week, 24 hours a day, and within 12 to 24 hours of ordering to keep up with their product turnover. As the number of hypermarkets increases, wholesalers will need to provide for weekend and holiday deliveries to supply them. Some wholesalers are diversifying their services and clientele by supplying more services to different types of stores. In the future, general line food wholesalers are also expected to build more retail stores to operate themselves.[125]

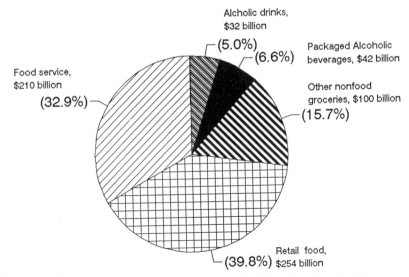

Figure 11.7. Sales by the food marketing system in 1988. (Data from U.S. Department of Agriculture, Economic Research Service, 1989b.)

Electronic ordering and delivery services are increasing the efficiency of wholesalers by enabling customers to place orders directly to the wholesaler using computers.[126] Direct store delivery, which involves transporting products directly from producers or processors to retailers, is another development that increases efficiency in distribution. To minimize losses from product failures in the supermarket, wholesalers are charging "flop fees" to remove products from the warehouse when they have not met a minimum sales goal within three months.[127]

FOOD RETAILING

The last step in the food marketing chain is the retailer who markets food to individual consumers. Final sales by the food marketing system to consumers reached $638 billion in 1988.[128] Food retailing today includes two main segments: food stores and food service. As shown in Figure 11.7, retail food (food store) sales were $254 billion in 1988, with another $100 billion in sales of nonfood groceries. Food service sales were $210 billion. The distinction between these two markets is diminishing, however, with many food stores now including delis and restaurants and many food service establishments offering take-out services and home delivery. In fact, take-out-to-eat (TOTE) food is the fastest growing market segment.

Food store retailers act as the purchasing agents for consumers. They must remain closely attuned to consumers' preferences.[129] According to Robert O. Aders of the Food Marketing Institute, "The supermarket is a miracle that happens every day. It is a miracle of quality, convenience, low cost and abundance."[130] Retailers' control of store shelf space, and their use of product movement information from scanning data to make decisions about what items they will carry, now give them considerable power over producers, processors, and wholesalers—power that processors formerly had over retailers through national brand marketing.[131]

Food store retailers buy thousands of food products from wholesalers and sell them in consumer-size quantities.[132] They are responsible for attractively displaying products in the store, monitoring the inventory, storing perishables properly, furnishing information about food availability and prices to consumers through advertising, and providing a variety of in-store services depending on the type of store.[133] In-store services, which are a form of nonprice competition, range from nutrition advice and recipes to check cashing and bottle redemption.[134]

Customers increasingly demand service and choices in the supermarket. Working women and men have little time to shop and cook; they want "more prepared food for the microwave. They want pharmacies, post offices, in-store restaurants, and caterers. And they want it all under one roof."[135] According to Tim Hammonds of the Food Marketing Institute, "We (supermarkets) are competing with just about any retail outlet that you can think of."[136] Convenience for the consumer is one of the major goals of food retailing. Convenience has two components; ease of purchase and ease of preparation, both of which are important in the products and services offered by retailers.[137]

The Structure of Food Store Retailing

Food retailing in the United States began with general stores in small settlements. As settlements grew, separate grocery stores developed. In the mid- to late-1800s, low-price, high-volume chains were formed that, along with independents, were service-intensive, depending on clerks to fill orders and offering home delivery and credit. In 1916 the first self-service, cash-and-carry store opened. One-stop shopping began in the 1920s and the first supermarket opened in 1930.[138]

It may be helpful to define the major components of the food store segment of food retailing. A food store is defined as "a retail outlet with at least 50% of sales in food products intended for off-premise consumption."[139] A food store can be either a grocery store or a specialized food store. A grocery store sells many different foods as well as nonfood items; a specialized food store sells food from only one category, such as meat and seafood, dairy products, candy and nuts, or baked products.

Grocery stores are classified as supermarkets, convenience stores, or superettes.[140] Supermarkets are cash-and-carry, self-service and partial-service food outlets offering a full line of food and nonfood items in a large number of departments. To be classified as a supermarket, sales of a food store must be at least $2.5 million annually.[141] The average supermarket now has much higher annual sales of over $7.8 million.[142] Convenience stores are small and compact and offer a limited variety of about 3,000 items that include fast-moving staple and convenience food and nonfood items along with fast foods and gasoline. They are open long hours, are easy to access, and feature quick service.[143]

Superettes are similar to supermarkets but have annual sales of less than $2.5 million.[144] The average annual sales of superettes have been increasing and now are nearly $2 million.[145] Other food stores with annual sales of less than $1 million are grouped together. They include general food stores, food cooperatives, health food stores, roadside and farmer's markets, and mom-and-pop stores.[146]

Various supermarket formats, which include conventional, extended, and economy formats, provide consumers with many alternatives for grocery shopping.[147] However, supermarkets are changing and differences among them are becoming less distinct.[148] Conventional format stores are still most prevalent. They are "relatively undifferentiated, unadorned and standardized . . . with middle-of-the-road pricing and selection."[149]

Conventional supermarkets are being converted into other formats, such as superstores, warehouse stores, or gourmet stores.[150] The extended format, which stresses a broad selection of food and nonfood products and various service departments, includes combination food and drug stores and superstores, the two formats most often developed by chain store retailers.[151] The economy format, which features low prices and less service, includes the hypermarket, super warehouse, warehouse, and limited assortment stores.[152]

Conventional supermarkets provide some specialty departments and some service. Their average size is 22,500 square feet, they carry about 12,000 items, and in 1988 they had 42.8% of supermarket sales, down 4.8% from 1986; see Figure 11.8. In 1988, 57.8% of all supermarket outlets were conventional supermarkets, down 5.1% from 1986.[153]

The combination food and drug store carries a wide variety of food and also includes a pharmacy, nonprescription drug department, a wide variety of health and beauty aids, and other nonfood general merchandise. About 25–35% of sales are from nonfood general merchandise. The size of these stores ranges from 35,000 to 45,000 square feet, they carry an average of 27,000 items, and in 1988 they accounted for 8.6% of supermarket sales.[154]

The superstore, which is the format that often develops when conventional supermarkets are expanded and upgraded, has a broad selection of food and nonfood items including specialty products and

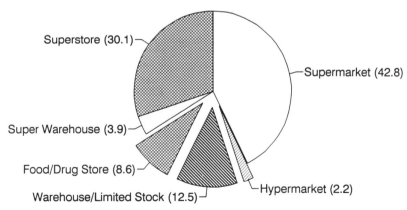

Figure 11.8. Percent of supermarket sales by type of store in 1988. (Data from U.S. Department of Agriculture, Economic Research Service, 1989b.)

perishables, offers extensive service, and ranges in size from 55,000 to 65,000 square feet in area. Superstores do over $8 million in business annually and had over 30% of supermarket sales in 1988.[155]

The hypermarket, which combines an economy supermarket and a discount department store, is the largest of the supermarkets.[156] So far, European retailers are largely responsible for the growth of this format in the United States. Hypermarkets offer a wide variety of food products, including specialized food departments, and derive up to 40–50% of their sales from general merchandise items such as housewares, small appliances, toys, sporting goods, automotive, hardware, and lawn and garden departments. They range from 100,000 to more than 200,000 square feet in area and carry an inventory of from at least 30,000 to 70,000 items.[157] Their sales in 1988 were 2.2% of supermarket sales. Hypermart*USA in Dallas, for example, is 223,000 square feet in area and has a 2,200-car parking lot, 2,000 shopping carts, and 52 checkout lanes.[158] Recently, discount retailers with experience in marketing nonfood items in high volume have begun hypermarket operations to compete with traditional food retailers.

Super warehouse stores, warehouse stores, and limited assortment stores are called "no frills" stores because they stock and shelve products in case lots, offer low prices and few services, and have lower labor costs. For example, customers bag their own groceries and store personnel handle the products as little as possible.[159]

Super warehouse stores, also called superdiscount stores, offer prices 10–20% below conventional supermarket prices, few services, and a wide variety of products that may include fresh seafood, delicatessens, in-store bakeries, pharmacies, and other special departments.[160] They vary in size from 50,000 to 140,000 square feet, and have at least $15 million in sales annually. Their sales in 1988 were 3.9% of supermarket sales. Typically, large full-service wholesalers either own or franchise these stores.[161]

Warehouse and limited-assortment supermarkets stock fewer items, fewer brands, and fewer sizes than super warehouse stores. They vary in size from 12,000 to 35,000 square feet in area and carry at least 7,500 items.[162] Limited-assortment stores are smaller, usually carrying 1,500 items or fewer, mostly dry groceries and very few perishables. Their size is less than 10,000 square feet in area. Sales by warehouse stores and limited assortment stores together amounted to 12.5% of supermarket sales in 1988.[163] The percentage of total supermarket sales by the various types of stores is summarized in Figure 11.8.

A format map locating supermarkets based on pricing policy and product variety is given in Figure 11.9. In the figure, pricing policy as represented by the price margin is shown on the horizontal axis and product variety on the vertical axis. The conventional supermarket is the store format used as the point of reference in the center where the lines cross. The different store formats are located in each of the four quadrants (A–D) according to their price and product variety characteristics. For example, the store with the most product variety is the hypermarket, and the store with least variety is the specialty food store. The stores with the largest price margins and smallest selections are the mom-and-pop stores, convenience stores, and specialty shops, located in quadrant D.

Food stores and food service establishments may either be members of a chain or an independent. A chain is "a food retailer or food service operator owning 11 or more stores or outlets," whereas an independent operator owns "10 or fewer stores or outlets."[164] Membership in a chain does not depend on dollar volume of the store.[165] Retail outlets are integrated horizontally in chains, and some chains are vertically integrated to include wholesalers and processors.[166] Chain stores may be corporately owned on a national or regional level or privately owned. Food stores that are independently owned and affiliated with a wholesaler are called affiliated independents. Unaffiliated, independently owned food stores are not associated with a wholesaler.[167]

Price and nonprice competition in food retailing has resulted in pricing strategies and merchandising practices designed to differentiate the stores and attract customers.[168] Pricing strategies used include market basket pricing and variable price merchandising. *Market basket pricing*

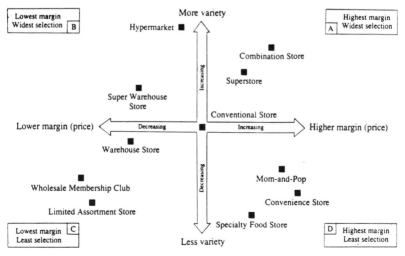

Figure 11.9. Store formats ranked by price margin and product variety. (Reprinted, by permission, from Heller, 1986.)

involves setting low prices for foods in one category and then charging higher prices, and thus a higher profit margin, for foods in another category. With this type of pricing, the prices of similar products will vary from store to store. *Variable pricing* involves the use of selective price cuts in the form of "loss leaders," selling a product below the cost to the retailer, and weekend specials, to give the store a low-price image to the consumer. Losses from pricing strategies are recovered when consumers purchase high-profit items while in the store. Retail food prices, therefore, are typically based more on consumer demand and strategy than on the price of farm commodities.[169]

Grocery store sales, at nearly $312 billion in 1988 were up 5.3% from 1987. Ninety-four percent of all food store sales were in grocery stores.[170] Specialized food store sales at $19 million in 1988 were 5.8% of all food store sales. Chain grocery stores and independents had 51.3% and 42.3% of food store sales, respectively. Supermarkets dominated the retail food market with sales of nearly $231 billion. Consumer spending in grocery stores in 1988 averaged $65.68 per household or $24.29 per capita per week.[171]

The 50-year trend toward fewer food stores continued in 1988 when the number of food stores fell to an all-time low of 234,575 outlets.[172] Of these, 70.5% were grocery stores and 29.5% were specialized food stores. Most of the stores that closed were mom-and-pop stores with annual sales below $500,000.[173] Although the number of supermarkets is lowest, their sales are highest, reflecting consumer acceptance of the wide variety of products, services, and convenient one-stop shopping that they offer. Convenience stores are the only format that have shown growth in numbers (over 6% in 1987), but their total sales are still among the lowest of all formats.[174] This growth is expected to continue but at a slower rate.[175]

Retail food stores employed over 3 million workers in 1988, up 3.9% over 1987.[176] Increases in the number of employees will continue because more food preparation and services must be provided by retailers in order to market more fresh and prepared foods. Consequently, labor productivity has been decreasing in food retailing even though several labor-saving technologies are being introduced.[177] Wages in food retailing were stable in 1988, with grocery store wage rates slightly higher per hour than those of specialized food stores. Profits as a percentage of retail food sales averaged 1% in 1987. As a percentage of stockholders' equity, average profits in the first half of 1988 were 13.2%, up from 1987 when they were 12.6%.

Mergers and acquisitions, as well as restructuring through divestitures and consolidations, have been prevalent in food retailing in recent years.[178] In 1988, the merger of American Stores Company with Lucky Stores, Inc. made American Stores the largest food retailer in the United States. Parenthetically, the investment of foreign firms in U.S. food retailing is occurring at a faster rate than the investment of U.S. firms in foreign food retailing.

Food Store Retailing: Implications and Current Issues

The trend toward fewer food stores is resulting in greater average sales per store and substantial increases in the number of items stocked.[179] New stores are getting bigger, averaging 43,830 square feet in 1986 compared with 29,056 in 1976. Kroger's new stores, for example, are 55,000 square feet or larger, and some retailers are building stores up to 60,000 square feet.[180] Large stores stock more nonfood items and have more flexibility in merchandising and ordering, including direct store delivery of items from the manufacturer.[181] In the future, more stores will use scanner and demographic data to tailor store inventories to the clientele of individual neighborhoods.[182]

Supermarkets will have a different appearance in the future; they will be more elaborate than they are now and their floor plans will change.[183] For example, delis may have separate entrances and checkouts. In-store bakeries and other specialties leased out to other operators will enable the supermarket to take advantage of their expertise and reputation.[184] Likewise, supermarkets may also sell more franchised foods, such as cookies and cinnamon rolls.

Other predictions for the future indicate that grocery stores will provide more convenience for shoppers and more one-stop shopping than ever before.[185] Supermarkets have begun to carry many of the special products formerly carried only by specialized food stores, a trend that will affect sales and the importance of both types of food stores.[186] Some supermarkets already provide a number of nonfood services that range from Federal Express drop boxes and cash machines to pet care. A variety of special departments and products may include exotic and organically grown produce, fresh pasta, and cooking classes.[187] In response to consumer concerns about food safety, some food retailers are beginning to have the produce they carry tested for chemical residues.[188]

New retailing strategies being developed by supermarkets include stores that market to specific ethnic subgroups in the population.[189] Service departments and an expanded selection of nonfood items will become more important for supermarkets in the future. Food stores in some areas are being organized specifically to enable busy customers to shop and check out quickly.[190] Self-service checkouts permitting customers to scan their own groceries are being tested in some supermarkets.[191] Home delivery, order-ahead service, and drive-through grocery pick-up will spread.[192] Pharmacies, nonprescription drugs, and financial services are growth areas. Others are produce and ready-to-heat meals in dairy, meat, and deli cases.[193]

Supermarkets and convenience stores will be strongly competing for a portion of the food service business.[194] More supermarkets will have delis, bakeries, soup bars, and salad bars (some with sit-down facilities) to supply a full meal to shoppers. Sales growth of prepared food and deli departments in supermarkets where consumers can buy salads and hot and cold entrees is predicted to be about 15% per year.[195] The sales growth rate of take-out food is predicted to be 18% compared with 6% for all foods.[196] A recent study recommended that supermarkets make their take-out food more attractive to customers by providing more ethnic and hot food choices, telephone ordering, home delivery, and drive-through windows.[197] Convenience stores will carry more sandwiches and deli foods, all made in a central commissary. Some already provide microwave ovens or grills for hot foods, and some are combining with fast-food chains.[198]

"Electronic marketing" is being introduced by food retailers to maximize in-store sales.[199] In-store electronic marketing utilizes electronic signs, kiosks containing a microcomputer and monitor with store information, monitors with video displays, and audio systems with music and sales messages. Coupon dispensers, laser printed cash register tapes, and home shopping by telephone all use computer-based systems.[200] Data collected and analyzed for use in retail food marketing include product sales data collected by in-store scanners for Universal Product Code marked products and coded identification cards used to identify customer purchases.

In 1988, about 60% of grocery store sales were processed through optical scanning systems.[201] The advantages of scanners include faster checkouts and fewer errors.[202] Scanning also is being used in inventory control, automated warehouse ordering, verification of invoices, shelf allocation, and customer check validation.[203] New developments in the use of scanning include the self-service checkouts mentioned previously. Other innovations include electronic shelf labeling and a remote shelf labeling system that is being tested by retailers in several locations. The latter enables a central computer to update shelf labels.[204] A system to interface wholesalers' and retailers' computer systems is being tested in which wholesalers can make their own price changes and retailer price changes at the store simultaneously.[205]

Scanning data and computer technology make it feasible for retailers to calculate *direct product profitability* for each item in a food store.[206] Direct product profitability has developed into an important management tool. It involves calculation of the profitability of each item in a supermarket based on labor, space, inventory, transportation, and any other costs associated with the item.

Because of the shortage of retail shelf space, "the stores dictate how much or how little space they'll give a product, and they're demanding a growing list of fees and discounts to do so."[207] Food retailers have begun charging processors "slotting allowances." These are payments for shelf space that reduce a retailer's risk of losses when accepting new products.[208] However, this added expense has the potential to prevent small companies from entering the market with their products, thus affecting consumer choices and prices. Some retailers are charging "pay to stay" fees to keep products on the shelves, fees for display space and promotions, and "failure fees" to remove unsold products from the shelves. Retailers also are requiring manufacturers to buy back unsold products at retail prices, and to do a specified amount of advertising in the local media.[209]

Generic products in plain-labeled packages and bulk foods have not been particularly successful in raising profit margins. Food retailers are now trying to increase margins and reverse the downward trend in sales of private label products by carrying upscale, high-quality private labels. They are raising the price and advertising private labels in competition with national brands.[210] Grocery store chains also are attempting to force processors to charge the same price for their products across the country, rather than continue regional pricing strategies. Many processors have set different prices regionally, depending on their marketing strategies and product sales in a region.[211]

The most frequent pet peeves food shoppers have about food retailing reveal some interesting problems.[212] They include expiration date labels that cover a label with an earlier date, higher-price labels that cover lower ones, merchandise that is not kept clean, meats that do not look fresh, long checkout lines, store employees that are not helpful, produce that is wilted or too ripe, and items that are out of stock.

The growing number of elderly shoppers will need special attention from retailers in the future. As discussed in Chapter 8, these shoppers may need help in handling groceries and grocery carts. Uncluttered aisles, benches to rest on, small-size packages, and a variety of special dietary foods also cater to their needs.[213]

Supermarkets are slowly beginning to accept credit cards for consumer convenience. However, the expense of the computer hardware and software needed to accept credit cards at checkouts and the 1% fee charged by credit card companies each time a card is used are problems for retail grocers because of their low profit margin. Also, there is opposition from those who think that food should not be purchased on credit.[214] However, buying food on credit is consistent with historical practices in small grocery stores where credit was often extended.

The Structure of Food Service Retailing

The food service segment of food retailing is defined as "the dispensing of prepared meals and snacks intended for on-premise or immediate consumption," and is composed of both commercial and noncommercial establishments.[215] Commercial establishments are open to the general public and prepare, serve, and sell meals, beverages, and snacks for profit. Noncommercial establishments prepare and serve meals and snacks as a support service, such as in educational facilities, hospitals and extended care facilities, plants and office buildings, correctional facilities, military bases, day care centers, and transportation modes including trains, cruise ships, and airplanes.

Commercial establishments include drinking places, eating places, lodging places, recreation and entertainment places, and retail hosts. Drinking places are establishments that may have food service but primarily sell alcoholic beverages for on-site consumption, such as bars, taverns, and nightclubs. Eating places sell prepared meals and snacks for on-site or immediate consumption. They are classified as establishments with "full-service menus," such as restaurants, or "limited-menu service" such as lunchrooms, cafeterias, and fast-food places.[216] Lodging places such as hotels, motels, and lodges (not including rooming and boarding houses and private residences) may supply food service. Recreation and entertainment food service includes facilities at such places as theaters, bowling alleys, commercial sports establishments, golf courses, athletic clubs, and amusement parks. Retail hosts include food service in retail establishments, such as department stores, drug stores, limited price variety stores, and miscellaneous retailers.[217]

The organization of the commercial food service industry, like that of food stores, includes local independents and chains.[218] The latter includes franchised fast-food and full-service restaurants. Food service formats include establishments with different types of menus, floor plans, and ambience. Food processors, such as General Mills, own some restaurant chains, and some chains have their own wholesaling and purchasing facilities.

There were 727,000 commercial eating establishments in 1987—one for every 2,700 people in the United States, up from one for every 7,000 people 10 years earlier.[219] On an average day, over 133 million Americans (more than half the population) purchase and eat food away from home.[220] This away-from-home food market provides more convenience and service for consumers than retail food stores.

The food service industry has grown twice as fast as food store sales in recent years, partly because incomes have been increasing and more household members are in the labor force.[221] Sales of fast-food establishments have grown most rapidly.[222] However, this growth has slowed down considerably, and the industry is now considered "flat." Increased competition is occurring, resulting in significant changes in certain segments of food service retailing.[223] Profits in the food service industry ranged from 2 to 12% of sales in 1987.[224]

In 1988, 62% of the commercial segment was made up of eating and drinking places and these had 86% of the commercial sales.[225] Eating and drinking places had sales of $126 billion and added an estimated $68 billion to the value of their food. In 1988, restaurants and lunchrooms made up about half of all separate eating places, and fast-food establishments made up the other half. Each had 42% of total commercial food service sales and 31% of all food service sales. Franchised restaurants increased in number to nearly 91,000 in 1988, up from 78,000 two years earlier, with sales of about $63 billion in 1988.[226]

Mergers and acquisitions in the commercial food service industry in 1988 numbered 74, down from 77 in 1987 and 81 in 1986. In addition, there were several leveraged buyouts. Internationally, over 6,700 franchised U.S. restaurant units operated in foreign countries in 1986. Canada and Japan had the most outlets at nearly 1,900 and 1,600, respectively. Most of the units sold hamburgers, roast beef, chicken, or pizza.[227]

Food Service Retailing: Implications and Current Issues

In 1990, restaurants were "facing the biggest slump of the decade."[228] Overall, the $60 billion fast food industry had stopped growing except for the pizza, Mexican food, frozen yogurt and ice cream outlets, and take-out and home delivery services.[229] Reasons for this lack of growth were a saturated market and an overbuilt industry that had shown little innovation. The number of women entering the labor force slowed recently, affecting the increase in eating out. The ubiquitous microwave oven, increased sales of take-out food by groceries, higher wages for labor, and changing consumer tastes, all conspired against growth in food-away-from-home sales.[230] The economic slowdown that began in 1990 and developed into a recession by year-end, also clearly had a very adverse effect on restaurant sales, especially those in the higher price category.

Demographic trends and the aging of the population also play a role since there are fewer young people and patronage of fast-food places decreases by age: 18-34 year olds ate at a fast food chain three times per month compared with two times for 35–44 year olds and once for those over age 55.[231] Eating at fast-food places appears to be dropping even among the heaviest users, the 18–34-year-old crowd. Increased concerns about diet and health also took their toll. Forty percent of consumers reported decreasing their visits in June of 1990, mostly due to publicity about the high fat and cholesterol content of the foods.[232]

Another problem facing restaurants is that families and two-career couples feel "that eating out is too much of a hassle" as microwave ovens have made even "fast food seem slow."[233] The baby boomer's tastes are shifting from less expensive fast food to higher quality, ethnic, and international cuisine. The moderately priced, ethnic sit-down restaurant with high-quality food is one of the few food service segments that is growing.[234] For example, General Mills' Olive Garden chain featuring Italian food has been adding 50 new units per year and now has reached 173 units with sales of $300 million, a fourfold increase in four years.

Responding to the competition and to consumer preferences will be the key to success in the food service industry in the future.[235] These responses will include making changes to keep old customers, attract new ones, and better provide for changes in consumer preferences.[236] Food quality and value are growing in importance, as are location, menu selection, differentiation from other establishments, special services such as a drive-up windows, and advertising and promotion campaigns.[237]

Prices are being discounted to keep customer numbers up in the short run, and in the longer run, ambience and menus "catering to America's health craze" are being used to attract new customers.[238] Franchised restaurants have responded to the increased competition from the supermarkets and hotels that have restaurants and take-out service by adding menu items, becoming more specialized, and by adding take-out services of their own. Home delivery is also increasingly being offered by restaurants, even by higher priced places.[239] Other changes being made include advertised promotions, specially priced menu combinations, and coupons and premiums.[240]

Differentiation based on premiums offered for children, called "catering to the kiddie market," is a strategy now being employed by fast-food chains to attract customers.[241] Fast food marketers are spending millions of dollars on "gimmicks, giveaways and other promotions" to attract the children of baby boomers and to compete with quick microwave meals. The fast-food outlets are all trying to catch up with McDonald's appeal to children. Arby's recently spent $1 million on its "Looney Tunes" promotion, Wendy's recently gave away 6 million plastic figurines in a promotion, and Hardee's sold about 40 million California raisin toys.[242] According to a survey reported by Wendy's, 68% of their adult customers said that their children influenced where the family ate, and of that 68%, 80% said premiums offered affected the children's selection.[243]

"Frazzled two-income families increasingly prefer the convenience of eating at home."[244] In 1989, this attitude helped to increase the take-out-to-eat (TOTE) food business to $51 billion, with an increase to $55 billion expected in 1990.[245] Part of that increase will be from the home-delivered pizza business, which is growing nearly twice as fast as the fast-food industry as a whole.[246] To satisfy consumer desires for convenience and for spending more time at home, a majority of commercial food service outlets offer take-out, including virtually all fast-food outlets. In 1988, take-out and home delivery from upscale and midscale restaurants increased by 24 and 17%, respectively.[247] Some TOTE food is assembled using already prepared food; in essence, it amounts to take-out meals taken out again.[248]

Gourmet food to go is the latest take-out trend. Typically, delivery companies contract to deliver food for upscale, white-tablecloth restaurants. The restaurant supplies the meals at a discount to the delivery service; the restaurant's waiters may even serve the meals, and the customer pays an appropriately higher price. Other home delivery services include third-party deliverers who deliver items chosen from several different restaurants. High-income households and some elderly people are the "biggest buyers of gourmet delivery."[249]

These services increase labor costs while food service outlets are trying to hold down menu prices in order to keep their customers. There are limits to what service-oriented food places can do. For example, guaranteed delivery time, promoted primarily by pizza outlets, has become controversial because of law suits filed as a result of traffic fatalities involving vehicles making such deliveries.

Food purchasing practices of the food service industry have a major impact on the food marketplace. Food quality specifications developed by food service establishments, particularly the fast-food segment, influence both the market for farm products and the processing of those products.[250] For example, McDonald's is the largest beef purchaser and purchases 7.5% of the U.S. potato crop each year. McDonald's has had a major effect on meat marketing in the United States. Food service establishments have had similar impacts on the poultry, fish, cheese, lettuce, and tomato markets.[251]

Development of new menu items by fast-food firms has begun to follow procedures similar to those food processors use to formulate new products.[252] Market research investigates consumer interest, ingredients are screened by microbiologists for food safety and by economists for cost. Time and motion studies are conducted to see how long it takes to make the new menu item and ingredient supplies are investigated. Innovation is being induced by changes in consumer demand.

Declining labor productivity has troubled the food service industry.[253] Increased competition and consumer demand for more services resulted in the addition of workers at a time of slow market growth, increasing costs, and decreasing productivity. High labor turnover of 250% per year for restaurant workers and 50% for management adds to the costs.[254]

Slow growth was reflected by an 8.2% decrease in new business starts in 1988 and a 13% increase in business failures.[255] Two factors contributing to this slow growth were less expansion in the fast-food industry and a labor shortage because there were fewer 16–24-year-olds in the population. This age group typically has been employed to staff fast-food outlets. Mothers and retirees are now being recruited for food service jobs, and McDonald's claims they are stabilizing its workforce.[256] Increases in the minimum wage from $3.35 to $3.80 per hour in 1990 and to $4.25 per hour in 1991, with the possibility of mandatory health coverage for part-time workers, puts more pressure on labor costs in the food service industry.[257]

As labor costs rise relative to capital, the food service industry will be induced to introduce new, more capital-intensive ways to produce and deliver food using less labor. Alternatively, they will have to deliver food and service for which consumers are willing to pay more in order to keep the ratio of production costs to product price down. The proliferation of vending machines, the adoption of robots in the kitchens of fast-food places, the purchase of frozen prepared entrees from food processors, and the standardization of food quality and menus in franchised restaurants all help to increase productivity. They increase the speed of service in middle-priced restaurants, allowing them to serve more customers per hour and to compete with TOTE food and microwaved meals.

Self-service in restaurants and hotels for all types of meals is becoming popular and is likely to increase because it minimizes labor costs. Advantages to the consumer are that self-service saves them time, they have more control over their own food selection, they seem to enjoy the all-you-can-eat format, and they have something to do other than sit and wait for their orders to be delivered.[258]

The use of credit cards to pay for fast-food purchases has begun in the last year or two and is expected to continue and to eventually expand nationwide.[259] Arby's, McDonald's, Wendy's, and Domino's Pizza all have done test marketing with credit card companies. In Arby's test with Visa, a new verifying device for credit cards made the transaction faster than with cash, with no customer signature required.

In this test, about 2–3% of sales were paid for by credit card, and the purchases were larger, an average of $5.50 versus $3.00 for cash transactions. In Japan, prepaid cards of different denominations are used instead of credit cards at some McDonald's outlets.

Other trends in food service retailing include site sharing, that is, two or more restaurants sharing the same kitchen and parking lot; cross-franchising, with one franchise unit operating within another; carrying unique products such as local produce or specialty desserts; issuing restaurant coupons and meal discounts; vending machines that cook and distribute french fries; rent-a-chef services where a chef comes to the home to prepare a meal for a party, or meals for the family for a week; and services that prepare and deliver ready-to-eat or ready-to-heat meals on a regular schedule, daily or weekly.[260]

Retail Food Advertising

Studies show that a large proportion of all food buying decisions are made in the grocery store.[261] More attention is being given to sales promotions, particularly in-store promotions, which include coupons, displays, special discounts, demonstrations, and food samples. Such sales promotions are becoming more important than media advertising for many products. Media advertising is aimed at building long-term brand loyalty, whereas sales promotions are aimed at the immediate sale of the product.[262] John Randazzo, a principal in a sales promotion agency, says, "Advertising tells people why they should buy a product. Sales promotion tells them why they should buy it now."[263] A recent survey of food manufacturers found that half of their advertising promotion is being done inside the store and half outside. During difficult economic times, funds are shifted from traditional advertising campaigns to sales promotions in order to keep sales volume up.[264]

New advertising techniques are being targeted at shoppers in grocery stores. This advertising includes music and advertisements over supermarket loudspeakers and advertisements on video screens. Other new types of advertising include advertisements on videocassettes on Home Video Preview, cooking contests, and sponsorship of sporting events.[265]

Food manufacturers printed 215 billion coupons in 1988, amounting to 850 coupons per capita.[266] Seven billion printed coupons, worth $2.93 billion, were redeemed by consumers, which was a redemption rate of approximately 3%. The redemption rate has been falling.[267] Given the increased participation of women in the labor force and the time crunch, which were discussed in Chapter 3, this trend should not be surprising. Fewer people have the time to clip and sort coupons; their time is too scarce and too valuable.

Electronic coupons, which are just now being introduced and are not yet widely used, come in different forms. They may be coupons printed on the back of cash register tapes, or paperless electronic coupons, which involve the automatic deduction of coupon discounts from the customer's bill at checkout.[268] Electronic couponing gives consumers the benefits of promotions without having to take time to search for, clip, and save coupons. Electronic coupons also may be targeted to individual customers, based on their actual purchases.[269] The impact of electronic couponing on newspaper advertising is not known. However, predictions are that if successful, it will decrease retailer coupons in newspapers but will have little effect on printed manufacturers' coupons.[270]

Frequent shopper programs as a form of advertising are being introduced. They provide shoppers with a "smart card" containing a computer microchip that is used to record their purchases. When shoppers buy a brand from a participating marketer, they win points toward catalog merchandise. Smart cards also supply information about consumers' demographics and buying habits for consumer data bases. In addition, they are also used in electronic couponing to automatically give customers deductions for existing coupons when they check out.[271]

Other trends in advertising and marketing that are or will be occurring include produce advertising based on claims that it is free of pesticide residues.[272] In today's micromarketing, one product will be advertised in different ways through different marketing campaigns targeted to different buyers; there will be less mass marketing.[273] Furthermore, food advertising will appear less often on network television and more on cable television, radio, and in magazines.

Most food service advertising, which is dominated by the major fast-food chains, is done on network or local television. Eating and drinking places spent $1.34 billion on advertising in 1987. The 10 biggest spenders on food service advertising were responsible for 80% of the advertising expenditures in both 1987 and the first half of 1988. Of these, McDonald's had the highest expenditures at nearly $362 million in 1987, with more than 95% being spent for television advertising.[274] As already discussed, the fast-food chains also employ a number of on-site sales promotion techniques. Other aspects of food industry advertising were discussed in Chapter 6.

All food advertising is designed to get consumers to eat the advertised product or to shop or eat at the advertised location. It is a competitive game, with very little opportunity to increase total food consumption. As discussed in earlier chapters, population growth is slowing and many consumers in the United States are overfed. Above all, those who are successful at capturing a larger share of a more slowly growing market will be the ones that can create products and services that meet consumers' changing needs and preferences.

A HISTORICAL PERSPECTIVE

The history of food and agriculture is a story of gradually shifting roles. First food production, then processing, and now, increasingly, food preparation has shifted out of the household.

Historically, men and women spent much of their time in the pursuit and preparation of food. Initially, they roamed and hunted and gathered food, eating it as they went. Sometime between 7000 and 3000 B.C., agriculture was born, probably in the Middle East and Southern Europe. As crops were planted and harvested, small villages were established. The nomadic lifestyle was no longer necessary. Animals were domesticated for meat—first goats, then pigs—and by about 5800 B.C., milk cows.[275] Farm households produced more food than they could eat and there began to be a surplus to support a nonagricultural community.

After the Industrial Revolution, the railroads "had the first and most radical influence on both the quality and quantity of food available in the cities."[276] With the capability of moving large quantities of food over long distances with relative speed, the railroads helped to commercialize agriculture and move the source of food ever further away from its consumers.

Throughout all of this, the final preparation—the cooking of food— was moving in and out of the household. Food cooked outside the home is not a thoroughly modern phenomenon. Cookshops were known in Mesopotamia in the days of Nebuchadnezzar. In London in 1183, one could buy "dishes roast, fried and boiled, fish great and small, the coarser flesh for the poor, the more delicate for the rich, such as venison and birds both big and little."[277] The primary reason for the popularity of cookshops in earlier days was a lack of cooking equipment in homes. Today, one can observe similar activity in developing countries where "street food" is common. With the advent of cookstoves, and later refrigeration, cooking and eating were centered in European and American homes. Women cooked the food eaten by their families and had considerable control over the diet and the quality of food served. As late as 1910 in England and America, restaurants were off limits to respectable women.[278]

Intermediary food processing became increasingly popular in the 19th century. For many centuries, wheat had been ground into flour at mills, far from homes where it would be used to make bread. Canning of meats and vegetables began in the early 1800s, about the same time blocks of ice started to be used to chill and preserve food.[279] As food preservation technology continued to progress, the shelf life of food increased, and food origins became increasingly distant from the place of consumption.

Now, the cooking of food is moving out of the household and into the kitchens of restaurants and other food service establishments, into supermarkets with their delicatessens, and into food processing plants. With the quest for convenience, consumers are demanding food that can be "prepared" in minutes and be tasty and safe. Issues of food quality and safety have gained importance. Even though it can be argued that the food supply is both safer and of higher quality than ever, consumers feel they have less and less control over what they eat.

Throughout history, raw food commodities have typically required a number of preparatory steps to make them ready for consumption. That has not changed, but major changes have occurred in how those steps are done and in who does them. As consumers become more affluent, they relegate those steps farther away from themselves and their homes. Possible exceptions are home vegetable gardeners and gourmet hobbyists. With an increasing amount of food preparation and assembly being done outside the home, even if it is eaten inside the home, the food industry has an ever greater role in defining food, in ensuring its quality and safety, and in responding to the preferences of individual consumers. Over time, the fundamental human concerns regarding food remain largely unchanged. People desire a food supply that is reliable and affordable, furnishes the nourishment to sustain life and health, and provides satisfaction and pleasure when consumed.

Abbreviations, Notes, and References

ABBREVIATIONS

ACORN	A Classification of Residential Neighborhoods
ARS	Agricultural Research Service
BSE	Bovine spongiform encephalopathy
BST	Bovine somatotropin
CCES	Continuing Consumer Expenditure Survey
CDC	Centers for Disease Control
CES	Consumer Expenditure Survey
CPI	Consumer Price Index
CSFII	Continuing Survey of Food Intakes by Individuals
DHEW	U.S. Department of Health, Education and Welfare
DHHS	U.S. Department of Health and Human Services
DRV	Daily Reference Value
EEC	European Economic Community
EFNEP	Expanded Food and Nutrition Education Program
EPA	Environmental Protection Agency
ERS	Economic Research Service (of the USDA)
FDA	Food and Drug Administration
FIFRA	Federal Insecticide, Fungicide and Rodenticide Act
FMI	Food Marketing Institute
FSIS	Food Safety and Inspection Service
FY	Fiscal year
GAO	General Accounting Office
GATT	General Agreement on Tariffs and Trade
GRAS	Generally Recognized as Safe
HACCP	Hazard Analysis and Critical Control Points
HERP	Human Exposure–Rodent Potency index
HNIS	Human Nutrition Information Service
LISA	Low-Input Sustainable Agriculture
NAS	National Academy of Sciences
NCHS	National Center for Health Statistics
NFCS	Nationwide Food Consumption Survey
NHANES	National Health and Nutrition Examination Survey
NIH	National Institutes of Health

313

NNMS	National Nutrition Monitoring System
PCE	Personal consumption expenditure
PDI	Personal disposable income
PRIZM	Potential Rating Index by Zip Market
PST	Porcine somatotropin
RDA	Recommended Dietary Allowance
RDI	Reference Daily Intake
SRI	Stanford Research Institute
TOTE	Take-out-to-eat
UPC	Universal Product Code
USDA	United States Department of Agriculture
VALS	Values and Lifestyles System
WIC	Women, Infants and Children (Supplemental Food Program)

NOTES

CHAPTER 1. Introduction: Major Trends in a Consumer-Driven Food System

1. U.S. Department of Commerce, Bureau of the Census, 1990a, p. 637. See Chapter 11, the section titled "A Brief Overview of the Food System," for an explanation of value added.
2. U.S. Department of Agriculture, Economic Research Service, 1989b, p. 1; Dunham, 1989, p. 33.
3. Pierson and Allen, 1988.
4. Borra, 1988.
5. Putnam, 1990a, p. 34.
6. Wall Street Journal, 1989a; also see Figure 3.1 in Chapter 3.
7. Kiplinger Agriculture Letter, 1987d; U.S. Department of Commerce, Bureau of the Census, 1984a, 1990a.
8. Mehegan, 1988.
9. Wall Street Journal, 1989a.
10. U.S. Department of Commerce, 1990a.
11. U.S. Department of Commerce, 1990a.
12. Kiplinger Agriculture Letter, 1987a.
13. Wall Street Journal, 1988d.
14. Kiplinger Agriculture Letter, 1987a.
15. Corchado, 1988.
16. Corchado, 1988; also see Figure 3.2 in Chapter 3.
17. Koten, 1987.
18. Steinburg, 1983.
19. Rich, 1987.
20. Business Week, 1987a.
21. Pillsbury, 1988.
22. Leonard, 1982.
23. U.S. Department of Commerce, Bureau of the Census, 1990a, p. 378.
24. U.S. Department of Commerce, Bureau of the Census, 1990a, p. 385; also see Table 3.8 in Chapter 3.
25. Minneapolis Star Tribune, 1988c.
26. Burros, 1988a.
27. Kiplinger Agriculture Letter, 1987b.
28. Freedman, 1989b.
29. Minneapolis Star Tribune, 1987a.
30. Becker, 1965.
31. Otten, 1988.
32. Morris, 1988a.
33. Wall Street Journal, 1988b.
34. Iggers, 1987.
35. Ver Meulen et al, 1987, p. 12.
36. Morris, 1988a.
37. Glazer, 1988, p. 229.
38. Flanigan, 1988.
39. Kiplinger Agriculture Letter, 1988c.
40. Ver Meulen et al, 1987, p. 12.
41. Food Marketing Institute, 1989a, p. 54.
42. Bruhn et al, 1988, p. 10.

43. Food Marketing Institute, 1989a, p. 52.
44. Rosewicz, 1989.
45. U.S. Department of Health and Human Services, Public Health Service, 1988.
46. National Research Council, Committee on Diet and Health, 1989a.
47. U.S. Department of Health and Human Services, Public Health Service, 1988.
48. Food Marketing Institute, 1989a.
49. St. Paul Pioneer Press, 1988a, p. 3A.
50. Minneapolis Star Tribune, 1990c; U.S. Department of Health and Human Services, Public Health Service, 1989 (see Table 2.13 in Chapter 2).
51. See Table 2.1 in Chapter 2.
52. National Research Council, Board on Agriculture, 1988.
53. Heller, 1986.
54. Guyon, 1983.
55. U.S. Department of Agriculture, Economic Research Service, 1989b, p. 1.
56. Glazer, 1988, p. 220.
57. Holusha, 1990; Jones, 1990.
58. Gallo, 1990.
59. Bremner, 1990, p. 90.
60. Borra, 1988.
61. Sheraton, 1988.
62. Iggers, 1987.
63. U.S. Department of Agriculture, Economic Research Service, 1989b.
64. Lancaster, 1966a,b.
65. Dunham, 1989, p. 39.
66. Dunham, 1989.
67. Hays, 1988.
68. Beck et al, 1989b, p. 67.
69. Minneapolis Star Tribune, 1987b.
70. U.S. Department of Agriculture, Economic Research Service, 1989b, p. iii.
71. U.S. Department of Agriculture, Economic Research Service, 1989b, pp. 46 and 81.
72. The Economist, 1988, p. 95.
73. Kiplinger Agriculture Letter, 1988e.
74. The Economist, 1989a.
75. The Economist, 1989a.
76. The Economist, 1989a.
77. Asinof, 1988.

CHAPTER 2. Trends and Traditions in the American Diet

1. Naisbitt, 1982.
2. Food Marketing Institute, 1990.
3. Hiemstra, 1968; Putnam 1989a, 1990a.
4. Hiemstra, 1968; Putnam, 1989a.
5. Hiemstra, 1968; Putnam, 1989a, 1990a.
6. Putnam, 1990a,b.
7. Kiplinger Agriculture Letter, 1989f.
8. Kiplinger Agriculture Letter, 1989e.
9. Putnam, 1990b.
10. Buse, 1990.
11. Putnam, 1990b.
12. Haidacher and Blaylock, 1988, p. 30.
13. Smith et al, 1990.

14. Smith and Yonkers, 1990.
15. Smith et al, 1990; Owen, 1990.
16. Smith et al, 1990.
17. Haidacher and Blaylock, 1988.
18. Putnam, 1990a.
19. Putnam, 1990a.
20. Haidacher and Blaylock, 1988; Putnam, 1990a.
21. Kerber, 1990.
22. Kerber, 1990.
23. Morrison, 1990.
24. Putnam, 1990a.
25. Haidacher and Blaylock, 1988.
26. U.S. Department of Health and Human Services (DHHS), Public Health Service, 1989.
27. Morrison, 1990; DHHS, Public Health Service, 1989.
28. U.S. Department of Agriculture (USDA), Economic Research Service, 1990b.
29. USDA, Economic Research Service, 1984, 1990b.
30. Park and Yetley, 1990.
31. Putnam, 1990b.
32. DHHS, Public Health Service, 1989.
33. Gould and Cox, 1989.
34. DHHS, Public Health Service, 1989.
35. DHHS, Public Health Service, 1989.
36. Hiemstra, 1968; Putnam, 1989a, 1990a.
37. Smith and Yonkers, 1990; Putnam, 1990a.
38. Business Week, 1989.
39. United Fresh Fruit and Vegetable Association, 1988.
40. United Fresh Fruit and Vegetable Association, 1988.
41. Swasy, 1990.
42. Greene, 1988.
43. Putnam, 1990b.
44. Putnam, 1990b.
45. United Fresh Fruit and Vegetable Association, 1988.
46. Greene, 1988.
47. United Fresh Fruit and Vegetable Association, 1988.
48. United Fresh Fruit and Vegetable Association, 1988.
49. Hiemstra, 1968, Putnam, 1989a.
50. Hiemstra, 1968; Putnam, 1989a.
51. Robichaux, 1989.
52. Robichaux, 1989.
53. McCarthy, 1990.
54. Putnam, 1990b.
55. Morrison, 1990.
56. Minneapolis Star Tribune, 1989e.
57. Duluth News-Tribune, 1990.
58. Charlier, 1990c.
59. Minneapolis Star Tribune, 1989e.
60. United Fresh Fruit and Vegetable Association, 1988.
61. DHHS, Public Health Service, 1989.
62. Hume, 1990.
63. Putnam, 1989a, 1990a.
64. Freundlich, 1989.
65. Minneapolis Star Tribune, 1990a.

66. Moore, T. J., 1989.
67. Freundlich, 1989.
68. Freundlich, 1989.
69. Moore, T. J., 1989.
70. National Research Council, 1989a.
71. Brody, 1990b; Consumer Reports, 1991.
72. U.S. Department of Commerce, Bureau of the Census, 1987a.
73. O'Reilly, 1989.
74. Schneider, in O'Reilly, 1989, p. 58.
75. O'Reilly, 1989.
76. National Dairy Council, 1987; Federal Register, 1990d.
77. Austin and Quelch, 1979.
78. U.S. Department of Health, Education and Welfare, 1979; National Research Council, Food and Nutrition Board, 1980; National Academy of Sciences, 1982; National Dairy Council, 1987; American Heart Association, 1988; USDA, Human Nutrition Information Service, 1990.
79. National Dairy Council, 1987, p. 35.
80. American Dietetic Association, 1986.
81. American Academy of Pediatrics, 1986; National Cholesterol Education Program, 1990.
82. National Dairy Council, 1987; Cronin and Shaw, 1988; Food Chemical News, 1990c.
83. Federal Register, 1990d.
84. Federal Register, 1990d; Food Chemical News, 1990d.
85. USDA and DHHS, 1990.
86. National Research Council, 1989b; Monsen, 1989; National Dairy Council, 1989.
87. DHHS, Public Health Service, 1988.
88. National Research Council, 1989a.
89. Federal Register, 1990d; Food Chemical News, 1990d; International Food Information Council, 1990.
90. National Research Council, 1989b; Monsen, 1989; National Dairy Council, 1989.
91. Cronin and Shaw, 1988; National Research Council, 1989b.
92. National Research Council, 1989b; Monsen, 1989.
93. National Research Council, 1989b.
94. DHHS, Public Health Service, 1988.
95. National Academy of Sciences, 1982; National Research Council, 1989b.
96. National Academy of Sciences, 1982; Nestle, 1988; Nutrition Today, 1988; DHHS, Public Health Service, 1988; National Research Council, 1989b.
97. Food Chemical News, 1990b, p. 15.
98. Food Chemical News, 1990b, p. 15.
99. USDA, Human Nutrition Information Service, Dietary Guidelines Committee, 1990; USDA and DHHS, 1990.
100. U.S. Senate Select Committee on Nutrition and Human Needs, 1977b, p. 4.
101. U.S. Department of Health, Education, and Welfare, 1979.
102. Austin and Quelch, 1979.
103. USDA, Human Nutrition Information Service, Dietary Guidelines Committee, 1990; USDA and DHHS, 1990, p. 39.
104. USDA, Human Nutrition Information Service, Dietary Guidelines Committee, 1990; USDA and DHHS, 1990.
105. American Cancer Society, 1984.
106. Minneapolis Star Tribune, 1990e; USDA and DHHS, 1990.
107. National Research Council, 1989a.
108. National Dairy Council, 1981; Haughton et al, 1987.
109. Haughton et al, 1987.

110. Haughton et al, 1987.
111. USDA, Agricultural Research Service, 1958; Haughton et al, 1987.
112. Peterkin, 1982.
113. Cleveland and Kerr, 1988.
114. Cleveland and Kerr, 1988.
115. DHHS, Public Health Service, 1989.
116. Mueller, 1989.
117. Smith and Yonkers, 1990.
118. Mueller, 1989.
119. Minneapolis Star Tribune, 1990b.
120. Food Marketing Institute, 1990.
121. Fisher, 1990.
122. DHHS, Public Health Service, 1988.
123. DHHS, Public Health Service, 1989, p. 37.
124. DHHS, Public Health Service, 1989, p. 49.
125. Minneapolis Star Tribune, 1990b.
126. Waldholz, 1990.
127. DHHS, Public Health Service, 1989.
128. DHHS, Public Health Service, 1989.
129. Minneapolis Star Tribune, 1990b.
130. Moore, T. J., 1989.
131. Monsen, 1987; DHHS, Public Health Service, 1989, p. 103. (Blood constituents are measured worldwide in SI units [Système International d'Unités]: 100 mg per deciliter of cholesterol [or high- or low-density lipoproteins] equals 2.586 SI units, or 2.586 mmol/L; 100 mg per deciliter of triglycerides equals 1.129 SI units.)
132. DHHS, Public Health Service, 1989.
133. DHHS, Public Health Service, 1989.
134. DHHS, Public Health Service, 1989, p. 48.
135. Schwerin et al, 1981.
136. DHHS, Public Health Service, 1989, p. 54.
137. Wall Street Journal, 1989d.
138. Smith et al, 1990.
139. DHHS, Public Health Service, 1989.
140. Wall Street Journal, 1989d.
141. Burckhardt, 1989.
142. DHHS, Public Health Service, 1989, p. 91.
143. Minneapolis Star Tribune, 1990b.
144. Minneapolis Star Tribune, 1989i.
145. Smith et al, 1990; Burckhardt, 1989.
146. Leonard, 1982.
147. Hirsch, 1989.
148. Mueller, 1989.
149. Hirsch, 1989.
150. Hicks, 1990.
151. Iggers, 1987.
152. Stipp, 1989.
153. Fisher, 1990.
154. Holusha, 1990.
155. Lee and Brown, 1989.
156. Minneapolis Star Tribune, 1990d.
157. Freedman, 1989b.
158. Kiplinger Agriculture Letter, 1990e.

159. Food Marketing Institute and Better Homes and Gardens, 1988.
160. Food Marketing Institute and Better Homes and Gardens, 1989.
161. DeStafano, 1989.
162. Food Marketing Institute and Better Homes and Gardens, 1989.
163. Kleinman, 1990.
164. Fisher, 1990.
165. Gorman, 1990.
166. Ostman, 1990.
167. Fisher, 1990.
168. Smithson, quoted in Burckhardt, 1989.
169. Wessel, 1989b.
170. Wessel, 1989a; Freedman, 1989a.
171. Freedman, 1989a.
172. Schwadel, 1989b.
173. Hughs, 1989.
174. Hirshman, 1978.
175. Aslop, 1989; Ingrassia and Patterson, 1989.
176. Hicks, 1990.
177. Fisher, 1990.
178. Holusha, 1990.
179. Putnam, 1990a.
180. Ackerman et al, 1990.
181. Pinstrup-Anderson, 1986.
182. Organization for Economic Cooperation and Development, 1986.
183. Korb and Cochrane, 1989.
184. British Ministry of Agriculture, Fisheries and Food, 1989.
185. Frank, 1987.
186. Lambert, 1990.
187. Lambert, 1990, p. 25.
188. Senauer et al, 1986.
189. DHHS, Public Health Service, 1989.
190. Schur, 1989.
191. Hammonds and Kozacik, 1989; Dornblaser, 1990.

CHAPTER 3. Demographic Trends Foretell Food Trends

1. Hammonds and Kozacik, 1988.
2. Conner, 1989.
3. Yaukey, 1985.
4. Blaylock and Smallwood, 1986.
5. Blaylock and Smallwood, 1986.
6. Spencer, 1986.
7. Stover, 1989.
8. Spencer, 1986.
9. U.S. Department of Commerce, Bureau of the Census, 1984c; Spencer, 1986.
10. Schlosberg, 1987.
11. Kinsey, 1987.
12. Edmondson, 1988, p. 26.
13. Batson, 1987.
14. Batson, 1987.
15. Young, 1986.
16. Schwartz, 1988.

17. Young, 1986.
18. U.S. Department of Commerce, Bureau of the Census, 1989g.
19. Exter, 1987.
20. Spencer, 1986.
21. Young, 1986.
22. Batson, 1987.
23. U.S. Department of Commerce, Bureau of the Census, 1988h.
24. Schwartz, 1988.
25. U.S. Department of Commerce, Bureau of the Census, 1988d.
26. Simon, 1989.
27. Simon, 1989.
28. U.S. Department of Commerce, Bureau of the Census, 1990a.
29. Riche, 1988a.
30. Cronin et al, 1982.
31. Pitts, 1989.
32. Blaylock and Smallwood, 1986.
33. Deveny, 1989.
34. U.S. Department of Commerce, Bureau of the Census, 1986d; Butterfield, 1991.
35. Zelinsky, 1987.
36. U.S. Department of Commerce, Bureau of the Census, 1988d.
37. U.S. Department of Commerce, Bureau of the Census, 1988d.
38. U.S. Department of Commerce, Bureau of the Census, 1988*l*, 1991.
39. U.S. Department of Commerce, Bureau of the Census, 1989d.
40. U.S. Department of Commerce, Bureau of the Census, 1988j.
41. U.S. Department of Commerce, Bureau of the Census, 1988g.
42. National Restaurant Association, 1978.
43. U.S. Department of Commerce, Bureau of the Census, 1989g.
44. U.S. Department of Commerce, Bureau of the Census, 1984f.
45. U.S. Department of Commerce, Bureau of the Census, 1984d.
46. U.S. Department of Commerce, Bureau of the Census, 1990b.
47. U.S. Department of Commerce, Bureau of the Census, 1988k.
48. U.S. Department of Commerce, Bureau of the Census, 1988k.
49. U.S. Department of Commerce, Bureau of the Census, 1989e.
50. U.S. Department of Commerce, Bureau of the Census, 1988k.
51. U.S. Department of Commerce, Bureau of the Census, 1984e; Myers, 1987.
52. Gibson, 1981.
53. Cronin et al, 1982.
54. Cronin et al, 1982.
55. Blaylock and Smallwood, 1986.
56. Young, 1986.
57. Tomlinson, 1984.
58. U.S. Department of Commerce, Bureau of the Census, 1990a.
59. U.S. Department of Commerce, Bureau of the Census, 1988c.
60. U.S. Department of Commerce, Bureau of the Census, 1990a.
61. Otten, 1990b.
62. U.S. Department of Commerce, Bureau of the Census, 1987e.
63. Riche, 1988b.
64. Wall Street Journal, 1989c.
65. U.S. Department of Commerce, Bureau of the Census, 1990a.
66. Waldrop, 1989a.
67. U.S. Department of Commerce, Bureau of the Census, 1987e.
68. Riche, 1988b.

69. Riche, 1988b.
70. Crispell, 1989.
71. Crispell, 1989.
72. U.S. Department of Commerce, Bureau of the Census, 1989c.
73. U.S. Department of Commerce, Bureau of the Census, 1987e.
74. Otten 1989a; U.S. Department of Commerce, Bureau of the Census, 1987e.
75. Rich, 1987.
76. U.S. Department of Commerce, Bureau of the Census, 1987a.
77. U.S. Department of Commerce, Bureau of the Census, 1985a.
78. Otten, 1984.
79. Stipp, 1988.
80. Riche, 1987.
81. Riche, 1987.
82. U.S. Department of Agriculture, Agricultural Research Service, 1989, p. 26.
83. U.S. Department of Labor, Bureau of Labor Statistics, 1987.
84. West and Price, 1976.
85. Price, 1988.
86. Lubin, 1986.
87. Sexauer and Mann, 1979.
88. Sexauer and Mann, 1979; Smallwood and Blaylock, 1981.
89. Kinsey, 1986a.
90. Wall Street Journal, 1989e.
91. Cutler, 1989a.
92. Paris, 1985.
93. U.S. Department of Commerce, Bureau of the Census, 1987a.
94. U.S. Department of Commerce, Bureau of the Census, 1984c.
95. Waldrop, 1989a.
96. O'Reilly, 1989.
97. Cronin et al, 1982.
98. Kiplinger Agriculture Letter, 1990a.
99. Lazer and Shaw, 1987.
100. Batson, 1987.
101. Minneapolis Star Tribune, 1987c; U.S. Department of Commerce, Bureau of the Census, 1987g, 1988e, 1988h, 1988i.
102. Batson, 1987.
103. U.S. Department of Commerce, Bureau of the Census, 1987a, 1990a, 1990d.
104. U.S. Department of Commerce, Bureau of the Census, 1990a.
105. U.S. Department of Commerce, Bureau of the Census, 1990a.
106. U.S. Department of Commerce, Bureau of the Census, 1987g.
107. Birdsall, 1972; Hinton et al, 1963; Hertzler and Owen, 1976; Hunt et al, 1976.
108. Schlosberg, 1987.
109. Levy, 1987.
110. Litan et al, 1988/89.
111. Bradbury, 1990; U.S. Department of Commerce, Bureau of the Census, 1990c.
112. Levy, 1987.
113. Congressional Budget Office, Congress of the United States, 1988a.
114. U.S. Department of Commerce, Bureau of the Census, 1990c.
115. Levy, 1987.
116. Avery and Kennickell, 1989.
117. U.S. Department of Commerce, Bureau of the Census, 1988a.
118. Levy, 1987.
119. Council of Economic Advisors, 1987, pp. 270-273.

120. Levy, 1988.
121. Browning, 1981.
122. Levy and Michel, 1986.
123. U.S. Department of Commerce, Bureau of the Census, 1987a.
124. Levy, 1988.
125. Levy, 1988.
126. Bradbury, 1990.
127. Levy, 1987.
128. U.S. Department of Commerce, Bureau of the Census, 1990c.
129. U.S. Department of Commerce, Bureau of the Census, 1986b.
130. U.S. Department of Commerce, Bureau of the Census, 1988a, 1989f.
131. Berg, 1989b.
132. Wall Street Journal, 1990.
133. U.S. Department of Commerce, Bureau of the Census, 1988a.
134. U.S. Department of Commerce, Bureau of the Census, 1988a, 1990c.
135. Levy, 1987.
136. U.S. Department of Commerce, Bureau of the Census, 1990a.
137. U.S. Department of Commerce, Bureau of the Census, 1987a.
138. U.S. Department of Commerce, Bureau of the Census, 1987a.
139. U.S. Department of Commerce, Bureau of the Census, 1987a.
140. U.S. Department of Commerce, Bureau of the Census, 1987a.
141. Stipp, 1988.
142. Noble, 1986; Rich, 1986.
143. U.S. Department of Commerce, Bureau of the Census, 1987a.
144. Berk, 1985; U.S. Department of Commerce, Bureau of the Census, 1990c.
145. St. Paul Pioneer Press, 1988b.
146. Fuchs, 1986.
147. Townsend and Riche, 1987.
148. Robinson, 1976.
149. Robinson, 1976.
150. Robinson, 1989.
151. U.S. Department of Commerce, Bureau of the Census, 1986c.
152. Wall Street Journal, 1988a.
153. U.S. Department of Commerce, Bureau of the Census, 1988f.
154. Fuchs, 1986.
155. Burros, 1988a.
156. Burros, 1988b.
157. Waldrop, 1989b.
158. Kinsey, 1983.
159. Cox, 1989.
160. McAdams, 1987.
161. Putnam, 1990a, p. 125.
162. Myers, 1987.
163. Wall Street Journal, 1989e.
164. Gibson, 1981.

CHAPTER 4. Disparate Lifestyles

1. Schiller, 1989; Deveny and Francese, 1990.
2. Schiller, 1989, p. 55.
3. Schiller, 1989.
4. Francese, 1989.

5. Francese, 1989.
6. Schubring, 1989.
7. Mitchell, 1983; Hamm, 1985; Francese, 1989.
8. National Decision Systems, 1988.
9. Hamm, 1985; Mitchell, 1983; SRI International, 1989.
10. Mitchell, 1983.
11. Mitchell, 1983.
12. SRI International, 1989; Graham, J., 1989; Riche, 1989.
13. SRI International, 1989.
14. Mitchell, 1983.
15. Mitchell, 1983, p. vii.
16. Mitchell, 1983, p. vii.
17. Mitchell, 1983.
18. Mitchell, 1983.
19. Mitchell, 1983.
20. Mitchell, 1983.
21. Mitchell, 1983.
22. Hamm, 1985.
23. Hamm, 1985.
24. Hamm, 1985.
25. Hamm, 1985.
26. Graham, J., 1989; Riche, 1989; SRI International, 1989.
27. SRI International, 1989.
28. National Decision Systems, 1987, 1988, 1989; Goel and Carnevale, 1990; Deveny and Francese, 1990.
29. National Decision Systems, 1987, 1988, 1989.
30. National Decision Systems, 1987, 1988, 1989.
31. Townsend and Riche, 1987.
32. Townsend and Riche, 1987.
33. Leonard, 1982.
34. Leonard, 1982.
35. Pillsbury Company, 1988.
36. Pillsbury Company, 1988.
37. Food Marketing Institute, 1987.
38. Schubring, 1989; Prepared Foods, 1989.
39. Sansolo, 1989.
40. Food Marketing Institute, 1987.
41. Schubring, 1989; Prepared Foods, 1989.
42. Sansolo, 1989.
43. Walsh, 1990.
44. Schiller, 1989.

CHAPTER 5. Food Economics: Insightful and Not So Arcane

1. Morris, 1988b.
2. Kuttner, 1989.
3. Stigler, 1966, pp. 1-10.
4. Burk, 1968, p. 7; Ritson et al, 1986, p. 63.
5. Burk, 1968, p. 87.
6. Tomek and Robinson, 1972, p. 17.
7. Putnam, 1990a, p. 106.
8. Putnam, 1989a, p. 6.

9. Kohls and Uhl, 1985, p. 72.
10. U.S. Department of Agriculture, Economic Research Service, 1985, p. 118.
11. Korb, 1987, pp. 18-21.
12. Tomek and Robinson, 1972, pp. 31-34.
13. George and King, 1971, p. 72.
14. Putnam, 1989a, p. 47.
15. Douglas, 1975.
16. Friedman, 1957.
17. Stigler, 1966.
18. Senauer, 1986, p. 51.
19. Haidacher et al, 1982, p. iv.
20. Haidacher et al, 1982, p. iv; Haidacher and Blaylock, 1988, p. 30.
21. Chavas, 1989.
22. Tomek and Robinson, 1972, pp. 27-31.
23. Huang, 1985; George and King, 1971.
24. Tomek and Robinson, 1972, pp. 34-36.
25. Alderman, 1986.
26. Rosenberger, 1979.
27. Wallace and Cullison, 1979; Schwenk, 1981; Blanciforti and Parlett, 1987.
28. Blanciforti and Parlett, 1987, p. 14.
29. Blanciforti and Parlett, 1987, p. 14.
30. Blanciforti and Parlett, 1987, p. 14.
31. Schwenk, 1981, p. 15; Blanciforti and Parlett, 1987.
32. Putnam, 1989a, p. 103.
33. Blanciforti and Parlett, 1987, p. 14.
34. U.S. Department of Labor, Bureau of Labor Statistics, 1989a.
35. Dunham, 1988, p. iii.
36. Van Duyne, 1982; Kinsey and Collins, 1991.
37. Stigler and Becker, 1977, p. 76.
38. Galbraith, 1958, pp. 115-116.

CHAPTER 6. The Food Consumer: New Economic Perspectives

1. Becker, 1965, 1981.
2. Lancaster, 1966a, 1966b.
3. Senauer et al, 1986.
4. Senauer, 1986, p. 55.
5. Linder, 1970.
6. Prochaska and Schrimper, 1973; Hull et al, 1983; Kinsey, 1983; McCracken and Brandt, 1987.
7. Prochaska and Schrimper, 1973, p. 601.
8. McCracken and Brandt, 1987, p. 288.
9. Hull et al, 1983.
10. Lancaster, 1966a, 1966b.
11. U.S. Department of Agriculture, Agricultural Research Service, 1976–1989.
12. Runyon, 1977, pp. 15-22.
13. Marion, 1986, pp. 249-250.
14. Runyon, 1977, pp. 18-19.
15. Maurice and Smithson, 1988, pp. 467-468.
16. Marion, 1986, pp. 249-250.
17. Runyon, 1977, pp. 20-22.
18. Maurice and Smithson, 1988, pp. 467-468.

19. Waugh, 1929.
20. Ladd and Suvannunt, 1976.
21. Ladd and Suvannunt, 1976, p. 508-509.
22. Morgan et al, 1979.
23. Morgan et al, 1979, p. 73.
24. Runyon, 1977, p. 327.
25. Stigler, 1961.
26. Feick et al, 1986, p. 179.
27. Feick et al, 1986, p. 179.
28. Feick et al, 1986, p. 179.
29. Devine and Marion, 1979.
30. Food Marketing Institute, 1989a, p. 37.
31. Krier, 1989.
32. Marion, 1986, p. 285.
33. Krier, 1989.
34. Linder, 1970.
35. Burk, 1968; Zellner, 1986, p. 12.
36. Zellner, 1986, pp. 14-15.
37. Runyon, 1977, p. 326.
38. Nelson, 1970; Eastwood, 1985, pp. 166-167.
39. Eastwood, 1985, p. 167.
40. Marion, 1986, p. 285.
41. Feick et al, 1986, p. 175.
42. Runyon, 1977, p. 342.
43. Runyon, 1977, p. 342.
44. Eastwood, 1985, p. 169.
45. Ferguson, 1990.
46. Feick et al, 1986, p. 176.
47. Food Marketing Institute, 1990, p. 43.
48. Padberg, 1977; Feick et al, 1986, p. 176.
49. Feick et al, 1986, p. 176.
50. Ferguson, 1990; Ingersoll, 1990b.
51. Ferguson, 1990; Ingersoll, 1990b; Federal Register, 1990d.
52. Shapiro, 1988.
53. Shapiro, 1988.
54. Swasy, 1989.
55. Stigler, 1961.
56. Devine and Marion, 1979.
57. Boynton et al, 1983.
58. Marion, 1986, p. 284.
59. U.S. Department of Agriculture, Economic Research Service, 1989b.
60. U.S. Department of Agriculture, Economic Research Service, 1989b.
61. Marion, 1986, p. 274.
62. Marion, 1986, p. 274.
63. Wall Street Journal, 1988c.
64. Eastwood, 1985, p. 170.
65. Lipman, 1989.
66. Galbraith, 1958, pp. 155-156.

CHAPTER 7. Data: Where We Get the Facts

1. Schiller, 1989, p. 57.
2. Raunikar and Huang, 1987.

3. Manchester, 1990, p. 1.
4. Harp and Bunch, 1989.
5. Harp and Bunch, 1989.
6. Manchester, 1990, p. 17.
7. Harp and Bunch, 1989.
8. U.S. Department of Agriculture, Bureau of Agricultural Economics, 1949; Harp and Bunch, 1989.
9. Harp and Bunch, 1989.
10. Harp and Bunch, 1989; Putnam, 1989a, 1989b.
11. Harp and Bunch, 1989; Putnam, 1989a; Manchester, 1990.
12. Harp and Bunch, 1989; Putnam, 1989a.
13. Putnam, 1989a.
14. Harp and Bunch, 1989; Putnam, 1989a, 1989b.
15. Harp and Bunch, 1989; Putnam, 1989b.
16. Harp and Bunch, 1989; Putnam, 1989a.
17. Putnam, 1989a.
18. Raper and Marston, 1988; Putnam, 1989a.
19. Raper and Marston, 1988.
20. Manchester, 1987; Putnam, 1989a.
21. Manchester, 1987; Harp and Bunch, 1989.
22. Manchester, 1987.
23. Manchester, 1987, p. 4.
24. Manchester, 1987; Harp and Bunch, 1989.
25. Manchester, 1987.
26. Manchester, 1987.
27. Manchester, 1987.
28. Manchester, 1987, 1990; Harp and Bunch, 1989; Putnam, 1989a.
29. Putnam, 1989a.
30. Putnam, 1989a; Manchester, 1990.
31. Harp and Bunch, 1989.
32. Harp and Bunch, 1989.
33. Sims, 1988a.
34. Burk and Pao, 1976; Young, 1981; Reynolds and Sponaugle, 1982.
35. Burk and Pao, 1976; Young, 1981; Sanjur, 1982; National Research Council, 1989a.
36. Reynolds and Sponaugle, 1982.
37. U.S. Department of Agriculture, Human Nutrition Information Service, 1987.
38. Rauniker and Huang, 1987.
39. Capps, 1987.
40. Schultz, 1989.
41. Capps, 1987; Hamel, 1989; Schiller, 1989.
42. Hamel, 1989.
43. Capps, 1987.
44. Schiller, 1989, p. 57.
45. Schiller, 1989.
46. McGloughlin, 1983; Hamel, 1989; Schwartz, 1989; Mayer, 1990.
47. Hama and Riddick, 1988; Peterkin et al, 1988; Sims, 1988a; National Research Council, 1989a.
48. Hama and Riddick, 1988.
49. Rizek and Posati, 1985.
50. U.S. Department of Agriculture, Human Nutrition Information Service, Nutrition Monitoring Division, 1985, 1986a, 1986b, 1987a, 1987b, 1987c.
51. U.S. Department of Agriculture, Human Nutrition Information Service, Nutrition

Monitoring Division, 1988a, 1988b, 1989.

52. Woteki et al, 1988a, 1988b; National Research Council, 1989a.
53. Garner, 1988; Harp and Bunch, 1989.
54. Brown, 1984; Callaway, 1984; Forbes and Stephenson, 1984; Ostenso, 1984; Peterkin and Rizek, 1984; Forbes, 1988a.
55. Brown, 1984; Callaway, 1984; Ostenso, 1984.
56. Brown, 1984; Ostenso, 1984.
57. Peterkin et al, 1988.
58. Brown, 1988.
59. Forbes, 1988a.
60. Garner et al, 1990.
61. Raunikar and Huang, 1987.
62. Food Marketing Institute, 1988.
63. Raunikar and Huang, 1987.
64. Raunikar and Huang, 1987.
65. Dow Diary, 1982.
66. Raunikar and Huang, 1987.
67. Capps, 1987; Schiller, 1989.
68. Hamel, 1989; Mayer, 1990.
69. McGloughlin, 1983; Mayer, 1990.
70. Capps, 1987; McGloughlin, 1983; Mayer, 1990.
71. Hamel, 1989.
72. Schiller, 1989, p. 57.
73. Schiller, 1989, p. 57.
74. Hamel, 1989, p. 39.
75. Capps et al, 1988.
76. Capps, 1987.
77. McGloughlin, 1983.
78. Capps, 1987; Hamel, 1989; Schiller, 1989; Mayer, 1990.
79. Lieb, 1989, p. 47.
80. Schwartz, 1989, p. 22.
81. Schwartz, 1989.
82. Lieb, 1989; Schwartz, 1989; Riche, 1990; Mayer, 1990.
83. Meyers, 1989; Lieb, 1989.
84. Lieb, 1989, p. 46.
85. Lieb, 1989.
86. Curry, 1989.
87. Curry, 1989.
88. Curry, 1989; Lieb, 1989; Meyers, 1989.
89. Curry, 1989; Lieb, 1989; Meyers, 1989.
90. Curry, 1989; Lieb, 1989; Mayer, 1990; Riche, 1990.
91. Lieb, 1989, p. 47.
92. Lieb, 1989, p. 47.
93. Lieb, 1989, p. 47.
94. Curry, 1989.
95. Schultz, 1989.

CHAPTER 8. Older Americans and Their Food Habits

1. Duensing, 1988.
2. Council of Economic Advisors, 1985, p. 160.
3. Plesser et al, 1988; Heller et al, 1989.

4. Stipp, 1990.
5. Fein, 1989.
6. Plesser et al, 1988; Waldrop, 1989a.
7. Plesser et al, 1988.
8. Otten, 1990a.
9. Pogrebin, 1988.
10. Council of Economic Advisors, 1985, pp. 159-186.
11. Chase, 1990.
12. Council of Economic Advisors, 1985, pp. 159-186.
13. Carlson, 1989.
14. Duensing, 1988.
15. U.S. Department of Commerce, Bureau of the Census, 1990a.
16. Hurd, 1990.
17. Hurd, 1989.
18. U.S. Department of Commerce, Bureau of the Census, 1990a.
19. Duensing, 1988.
20. Hurd, 1990.
21. Duensing, 1988.
22. Lawler, 1988.
23. Council of Economic Advisors, 1985, pp. 159-186.
24. Council of Economic Advisors, 1985, pp. 159-186.
25. Council of Economic Advisors, 1985, pp. 159-186.
26. Hurd, 1989.
27. Hamermesh, 1984.
28. Hausman and Paquette, 1987.
29. Hurd, 1990.
30. Edmondson, 1987.
31. Polman, 1989.
32. Lazer and Shaw, 1987.
33. Gerber, 1989.
34. Sherman and Shiffman, 1984.
35. Wolfe, 1987.
36. Rounds, 1988.
37. Gerber, 1989.
38. Wolf, 1987.
39. Shrimper, 1986.
40. Wascoe, 1989.
41. Munro, 1980; Diggs, 1989.
42. Brody, 1989.
43. Munro, 1989.
44. Crockett, 1960.
45. Hausman and Paquette, 1987.
46. Lazer and Shaw, 1987.
47. Shrimper, 1986.
48. Congressional Budget Office, 1988b.
49. Kohrs et al, 1989.
50. Axelson and Penfield, 1983.
51. Gallo et al, 1979.
52. Meiners and Heltsley, 1985.
53. Chase, 1990.
54. Tongren, 1988.
55. Axelson and Penfield, 1983.

56. Clancy, 1975.
57. Diggs, 1989.
58. Travis, 1987.
59. Jones-Lee et al, 1985.
60. Ingerson and Hama, 1985; Hama and Chern, 1988.
61. Brody, 1990a.
62. Chase, 1990.
63. Otten, 1984.
64. Travis, 1987.
65. Kohrs et al, 1989, p. 313.
66. Otten, 1990c.
67. Gerber, 1989, p. 135.
68. Carlson, 1989.
69. Buse and Fleischer, 1982; Salathe, 1979.
70. Shrimper, 1986.
71. Cronin et al, 1982.
72. Kohrs et al, 1989, p. 319.
73. Lawler, 1988, p. 5.
74. Sills-Levy, 1989.
75. Gallo et al, 1979; Salathe, 1979; Sexauer and Mann, 1979; Buse and Fleischer, 1982; Dunn, 1985; Shrimper, 1986.
76. Rothenberg, 1988.
77. Sexauer and Mann, 1979.
78. Dunn, 1985.
79. Kiplinger Agriculture Letter, 1990a.
80. U.S. Department of Commerce, Bureau of the Census, 1970; Lawler, 1988.
81. Otten, 1984.
82. Council of Economic Advisors, 1985, pp. 159-186.
83. Council of Economic Advisors, 1985, pp. 159-186.
84. Lawler, 1988.
85. U.S. Department of Commerce, Bureau of the Census, 1987a.
86. Smeeding, 1984.
87. Lawler, 1988.
88. Balsam and Rogers, 1988.
89. Kohrs et al, 1989.
90. Kohrs et al, 1989, p. 328.
91. Asp and Darling, 1988.
92. Balsam and Rogers, 1988.
93. Congressional Budget Office, 1988a.

CHAPTER 9. The Forgotten Poor and Their Food Problems

1. Paarlberg, 1980, pp. 101-102.
2. Physician Task Force, 1985, foreword.
3. Paarlberg, 1980, p. 102.
4. Physician Task Force, 1985, foreword.
5. Physician Task Force, 1985; Brown, 1987, p. 37.
6. Physician Task Force, 1985, p. 6.
7. Physician Task Force, 1985, pp. xxi and xix.
8. Brown, 1987, p. 37.
9. Davis and Senauer, 1986, p. 1253; Brown, 1987, p. 37.
10. President's Task Force on Food Assistance, 1984, p. 34.

11. President's Task Force on Food Assistance, 1984, pp. 34 and 36.
12. President's Task Force on Food Assistance, 1984, p. 35.
13. President's Task Force on Food Assistance, 1984, p. 39.
14. House Select Committee on Hunger, 1989.
15. Lelyveld, 1985, p. 520.
16. U.S. Department of Agriculture (USDA), Science and Education Administration, 1979a, p. 12; Senauer, 1986, pp. 52-53; U.S. Department of Health and Human Services (DHHS), Public Health Service, 1986, p. 220.
17. DHHS, Public Health Service, 1986 pp. 21-22.
18. U.S. Department of Commerce, Bureau of the Census, 1990a, p. 460.
19. U.S. Department of Commerce, Bureau of the Census, 1990a, p. 460.
20. President's Task Force on Food Assistance, 1984, pp. x-xi and 10-14.
21. President's Task Force on Food Assistance, 1984, p. xi.
22. Associated Press, 1989, p. 7A.
23. Minneapolis Star Tribune, 1989k, p. 7A.
24. President's Task Force on Food Assistance, 1984, p. xi; Minneapolis Star Tribune, 1988d, p. 17A, 1989k, p. 7A.
25. Rich, 1990.
26. Duncan, 1984, pp. 33–70.
27. Wilkerson, 1987; New York Times, 1989.
28. U.S. Department of Health, Education and Welfare, 1976, pp. xxi and 8.
29. U.S. Department of Commerce, Bureau of the Census, 1989a, p. 457.
30. DHHS, Public Health Service, 1986, pp. 2, 5-6.
31. DHHS, Public Health Service, 1986.
32. USDA, Human Nutrition Information Service, 1988a, 1988b, 1989.
33. USDA, Human Nutrition Information Service, 1988a, 1988b, 1989.
34. DHHS, Public Health Service, 1986, p. 2.
35. DHHS, Public Health Service, 1986, p. 54.
36. DHHS, Public Health Service, 1986, p. 2.
37. DHHS, Public Health Service, 1986, p. 60.
38. DHHS, Public Health Service, 1986, p. 166.
39. DHHS, Public Health Service, 1986, pp. 166-168.
40. DHHS, Public Health Service, 1986, p. 2.
41. DHHS, Public Health Service, 1986, p. 148.
42. DHHS, Public Health Service, 1986, p. 199.
43. DHHS, Public Health Service, 1986, p. 197.
44. DHHS, Public Health Service, 1986, pp. 197-199.
45. DHHS, Public Health Service, 1986, pp. 188-189.
46. DHHS, Public Health Service, 1986, p. 22.
47. Paarlberg, 1980, pp. 99-101; Jones and Richardson, 1988, p. 2.
48. Paarlberg, 1980, p. 104.
49. Paarlberg, 1980, p. 101.
50. Sims, 1988b, p. 16.
51. USDA, Food and Nutrition Service, 1989, p. 34.
52. Jones and Richardson, 1988, p. 3.
53. USDA, Food and Nutrition Service, 1989, p. 1.
54. USDA, Food and Nutrition Service, 1989.
55. USDA, Food and Nutrition Service, 1989.
56. USDA, Food and Nutrition Service, 1989.
57. Jones and Richardson, 1988, p. 6.
58. USDA, Food and Nutrition Service, 1988, 1989.
59. Allen and Newton, 1986, p. 1249.

60. Draper, 1989.
61. USDA, Food and Nutrition Service, 1988.
62. Federal Register, 1990a.
63. Davis and Senauer, 1986, p. 1256.
64. Federal Register, 1990a.
65. USDA, Food and Nutrition Service, 1989, p. 20.
66. USDA, Food and Nutrition Service, 1989, p. 3.
67. Cleveland and Kerr, 1988.
68. Allen and Newton, 1986, p. 1250.
69. Senauer and Young, 1986.
70. Senauer and Young, 1986.
71. Allen and Gadson, 1983.
72. Physician Task Force, 1985; Brown, 1987.
73. Sims, 1988b, p. 18.
74. Davis and Senauer, 1986, p. 1257.
75. Senauer, 1982, pp. 1012-1013.
76. Pear, 1990.
77. Pear, 1990.
78. USDA, Food and Nutrition Service, 1988; 1989, pp. 5-6 and 22.
79. Sims, 1988b, p. 21-24; USDA, Food and Nutrition Service, 1986.
80. USDA, Food and Nutrition Service, 1989.
81. Roseville Area Schools, 1989.
82. Allen et al, 1985, p. 29.
83. Gallo, 1978, p. 36; Paarlberg, 1980, p. 105.
84. Clark, 1981, p. 10.
85. Dean, 1989.
86. Akin et al, 1983.
87. Sims, 1988b, p. 21; Akin et al, 1983.
88. USDA, Food and Nutrition Service, 1988, 1989.
89. Food and Nutrition Forum, 1989.
90. Lelyveld, 1985, p. 20.
91. Ansberry, 1988.
92. Minnesota Food Education and Resource Center, 1985.
93. Food and Nutrition Forum, 1989.
94. Ansberry, 1988.
95. Davis and Senauer, 1986, p. 1255.
96. Ansberry, 1988.
97. Ansberry, 1988.
98. Schultz, 1961, p. 1.

CHAPTER 10. Food Safety: A Growing Concern

1. Rosewicz, 1989; Ingersoll, 1989b.
2. Beck et al, 1989a, p. 16.
3. Sinclair, 1906.
4. Food Marketing Institute, 1989a, p. 52.
5. Food Marketing Institute, 1989a, p. 54.
6. Bruhn et al, 1988, p. 9.
7. Archibald and Marsh, 1988, p. 33.
8. Kramer, 1988, p. 148.
9. Archibald et al, 1988a, p. 5.
10. Kramer and Penner, 1986, p. 21; Forbes, 1988b, p. 43.

11. Middlekauff, 1988, p. 45.
12. Beck et al, 1989a, p. 16.
13. Archibald and Marsh, 1988, p. 37.
14. Meyerhoff, 1989.
15. Burbee and Kramer, 1986, pp. 19-20.
16. Archibald et al, 1988b, p. 20.
17. Archibald and Marsh, 1988, p. 38.
18. Labuza, 1977, p. 337.
19. Paarlberg, 1980, p. 86.
20. Labuza, 1977, p. 338; Middlekauff, 1989.
21. Clancy, 1988, pp. 12-14.
22. Labuza, 1977, p. 338; Kinder et al, 1984; Middlekauff, 1989.
23. Labuza, 1977, p. 340; Middlekauff, 1989.
24. Labuza, 1977, p. 340; Middlekauff, 1989.
25. Middlekauff, 1989.
26. Labuza, 1977, p. 341.
27. Labuza, 1977, p. 341.
28. Clancy, 1988, p. 15.
29. Kennedy, 1988, p. 13.
30. Kennedy, 1988, p. 12.
31. Kennedy, 1988, p. 12.
32. Clancy, 1988, p. 15.
33. Kennedy, 1988, p. 12.
34. Labuza, 1977, p. 370.
35. Middlekauff, 1988, p. 47.
36. Sieber, 1988, p. 23.
37. Labuza, 1977, p. 381; Sieber, 1988, p. 23.
38. Labuza, 1977, p. 371.
39. Labuza, 1977, p. 371; Institute of Food Technologists, 1988, p. 121.
40. Labuza, 1977, p. 372.
41. Institute of Food Technologists, 1988, p. 121.
42. Labuza, 1977, p. 373.
43. Middlekauff, 1988, p. 47.
44. Clancy, 1988, p. 15.
45. Archibald and Marsh, 1988, p. 35.
46. Campbell, 1988, p. 34; Middlekauff, 1988, p. 47.
47. Labuza, 1977, p. 374.
48. Bauman, 1989, p. 481.
49. Ames et al, 1987; Institute of Food Technologists, 1988, p. 123.
50. Ames et al, 1987.
51. Science, 1987, p. 252.
52. Archibald, 1988b, p. 39.
53. Archibald, 1988b, p. 39.
54. Vento, 1989.
55. Labuza, 1977, p. 338.
56. Institute of Food Technologists, 1988, p. 121.
57. Kennedy, 1988, p. 9.
58. Kramer, 1988, p. 148.
59. Institute of Food Technologists, 1988, p. 123.
60. Hazlett, 1988, p. 29.
61. Institute of Food Technologists, 1988, p. 125; Dardis, 1988, p. 310.
62. Archibald, 1988b, p. 40; Dardis, 1988, p. 310.

63. Archibald, 1988b, p. 40.
64. Kennedy, 1988, p. 12.
65. Archibald, 1988b, p. 40.
66. Kennedy, 1988, p. 11.
67. Archibald et al, 1988a, pp. 5-6.
68. Archibald, 1988b, p. 39.
69. Archibald, 1988b, p. 40.
70. Dardis, 1988, p. 309.
71. Archibald, 1988a, p. 3.
72. Dardis, 1988, p. 310.
73. Rosewicz, 1989.
74. Begley and Hager, 1989, p. 20.
75. Institute of Food Technologists, 1988, p. 125.
76. Archibald, 1988b, p. 41.
77. Kennedy, 1988, p. 9.
78. Clancy, 1988, p. 12.
79. Kennedy, 1988, p. 10.
80. National Safety Council, 1987, p. 85.
81. Lowrance, 1976, pp. 75-76; Dardis, 1988, p. 308; Slovic, 1987.
82. Agriculture Canada, Food Production and Inspection Branch, 1989.
83. van Ravenswaay, 1988, p. 99; Slovic, 1987, p. 282.
84. Rosewicz, 1989; Beck et al, 1989a.
85. Slovic, 1987.
86. van Ravenswaay, 1988, p. 97.
87. Kennedy, 1988, pp. 17-18; Kiplinger Agriculture Letter, 1989c.
88. Burros, 1989.
89. McCarthy, 1988.
90. Food Marketing Institute, 1989a.
91. Food Marketing Institute, 1989b.
92. Beck et al, 1989a, p. 18.
93. van Ravenswaay and Smith, 1986, p. 15.
94. van Ravenswaay and Smith, 1986, p. 16.
95. Clancy, 1988, p. 16.
96. Food Marketing Institute, 1989a, p. 59.
97. Dardis, 1988, pp. 303-304.
98. Dardis, 1988, p. 304.
99. Dardis, 1988, p. 304.
100. Clancy, 1988, p. 16.
101. Waldman, 1989, pp. 40-41.
102. Clancy, 1988, p. 75.
103. Zellner, 1988, p. 63.
104. Clancy, 1988, p. 75.
105. Kinsey, 1990.
106. Burbee and Kramer, 1986, p. 18.
107. Begley and Hager, 1989, p. 22.
108. Beck et al, 1989a, p. 18; Vento, 1989.
109. Stimmann, 1988, p. 38.
110. Nazario, 1989b, p. B1; Vento, 1989.
111. O'Beirne, 1988, p. 183; Begley and Hager, 1989, pp. 20 and 23; Begley et al, 1989; Berg, 1989a; Nazario, 1989b; Passell, 1989.
112. Begley and Hager, 1989, p. 20.
113. Pennington, 1983; Pennington and Gunderson, 1987; Beck et al, 1989a, p. 19.

114. Benbrook, 1988, p. 31.
115. Stimmann, 1988, p. 43.
116. Stimmann, 1988, p. 43.
117. Kennedy, 1988, p. 14; Beck et al, 1989a, p. 18.
118. Beck et al, 1989a, p. 18; Vento, 1989.
119. Benbrook, 1988, p. 30; Beck et al, 1989a, p. 18.
120. Benbrook, 1988, p. 30.
121. Nazario, 1989b.
122. Kiplinger Agriculture Letter, 1989h; Minneapolis Star Tribune, 1989j.
123. Shabecoff, 1989, p. E6.
124. Minneapolis Star Tribune, 1989d.
125. Cook, 1990.
126. Minneapolis Star Tribune, 1989a.
127. Zellner, 1988, p. 55.
128. Wolf and Lechowich, 1989, p. 468.
129. Forbes, 1988b, p. 43; Roberts, 1989, p. 471; Roberts and van Ravenswaay, 1989, p. 1; Wolf and Lechowich, 1989, p. 468.
130. Forbes, 1988b, p. 43; Roberts and van Ravenswaay, 1989, p. 1.
131. Roberts, 1989.
132. Wolf and Lechowich, 1989, p. 469.
133. Wolf and Lechowich, 1989, p. 469.
134. Wolf and Lechowich, 1989, p. 469.
135. Roberts and van Ravenswaay, 1989, p. 5.
136. Kendall, 1989.
137. Slovut, 1989.
138. Wolf and Lechowich, 1989, p. 469; Labuza, 1977.
139. Wolf and Lechowich, 1989, p. 469.
140. Sieber, 1988, p. 30.
141. Food Chemical News, 1989, p. 3.
142. Food Chemical News, 1989, p. 3.
143. Wolf and Lechowich, 1989, p. 470.
144. Institute of Food Technologists, 1988, p. 122.
145. Forbes, 1988b, p. 44.
146. Freedman, 1988b.
147. Labuza, 1977, p. 253.
148. Puze, 1989.
149. Kendall, 1989.
150. Kramer and Penner, 1986, p. 21.
151. Ingersoll, 1988a.
152. Ingersoll, 1989b.
153. Ingersoll, 1988b.
154. Ingersoll, 1989a.
155. Ingersoll, 1988a.
156. Ingersoll, 1988a.
157. Ingersoll, 1988b, 1989a.
158. Putnam, 1990a, p. 72.
159. Manges, 1989; Kiplinger Agriculture Letter, 1990b.
160. Federal Register, 1990c.
161. Labuza, 1977, p. 378; Sieber, 1988, p. 28.
162. Labuza, 1977, pp. 382-388.
163. Labuza, 1977, p. 367.
164. Labuza, 1977, pp. 367-368.

165. Labuza, 1977, p. 368.
166. Labuza, 1977, p. 391.
167. Institute of Food Technologists, 1988, p. 122.
168. St. Paul Pioneer Press, 1990.
169. Federal Register, 1990b.
170. Schmickle, 1990d.
171. Rogan and Glaros, 1988, p. 833.
172. Schmickle, 1990e.
173. Rogan and Glaros, 1988.
174. Rogan and Glaros, 1988, p. 835; Brynjolfsson, 1989.
175. Bull et al, 1982; Wallace, 1987, p. 40.
176. Stucker, et al, 1986.
177. Wallace, 1987, p. 40.
178. Ingersoll, 1990c.
179. Schmickle, 1990a.
180. Stucker et al, 1986.
181. Nyberg, 1989; Schmickle, 1989b.
182. Schmickle, 1990c.
183. Rogan and Glaros, 1988, p. 837.
184. Nazario, 1990.
185. Burros, 1990b; Shapiro, 1990a.
186. Florkowski et al, 1989; Halbrendt et al, 1989.
187. Halbrendt et al, 1989, p. 153.
188. Sachs, 1989, p. 32.
189. Ingersoll, 1989a; Vento, 1989.
190. National Academy of Sciences, 1985.
191. Ingersoll, 1989a.
192. Food Chemical News, 1989.
193. Ingersoll, 1989a.
194. Ingersoll, 1989b.
195. Minneapolis Star Tribune, 1989c.
196. Minneapolis Star Tribune, 1988b.
197. Phelps, 1987; Putnam, 1990a.
198. United Fresh Fruit and Vegetable Association, 1989, p. 11.
199. Minneapolis Star Tribune, 1988b.
200. Phelps, 1987, p. 87.
201. Runge, 1989, p. 1.
202. Krissoff, 1989, pp. 34-35.
203. Kinsey and Houck, 1991.
204. Ingersoll, 1989a.
205. Beck et al, 1989a, p. 18; Vento, 1989.
206. Nazario, 1989b.
207. Beck et al, 1989a, p. 18.
208. Center for the Study of American Business, 1990.
209. Caswell, 1988, p. 129.
210. Caswell, 1988, pp. 129-130.
211. Graham, L. T., 1989; Bishop, 1990.
212. Kiplinger Agriculture Letter, 1990e; Minneapolis Star Tribune, 1989g.
213. Food Marketing Institute, 1990, p. 55.
214. The Economist, 1990b; Frankel and Mehnert, 1990.
215. Hornsby, 1990a; 1990b.

CHAPTER 11. The Food Industry: An Overview and Implications of Consumer Trends

1. Porubcansky, 1989.
2. Dobbs, 1990.
3. U.S. Department of Commerce, Bureau of the Census, 1990a, p. 637.
4. U.S. Department of Commerce, Bureau of the Census, 1990a, p. 637.
5. U.S. Department of Agriculture (USDA), Economic Research Service, 1989a, p. 52.
6. Kohls and Uhl, 1990, p. 184.
7. Kohls and Uhl, 1990, p. 185.
8. Dunham, 1988, p. 14.
9. Dunham, 1989, p. 37.
10. Wallace, 1987, p. 16.
11. Wallace, 1987, p. 16.
12. U.S. Department of Agriculture, 1988, p. 383.
13. Wallace, 1987, pp. 16-17.
14. Wallace, 1987, p. 17.
15. Kalbacher and Brooks, 1990.
16. USDA, Economic Research Service, 1990a.
17. Mitchell, 1989.
18. Kinsey, 1986b; Kramer and Elliott, 1989, p. 12.
19. Houck, 1990.
20. Kramer and Elliott, 1989, p. 12.
21. USDA, Agricultural Marketing Service, 1981.
22. Cloud, 1990b, pp. 577 and 580.
23. Cloud, 1990b, pp. 579-582.
24. Mitchell, 1989.
25. Farrell, 1978.
26. Kramer and Elliott, 1989, p. 3.
27. Schmickle, 1989c.
28. Hildreth, 1990, p. 93.
29. Martin, 1988.
30. U.S. Department of Commerce, Bureau of the Census, 1990a, p. 682.
31. Martin, 1988.
32. U.S. Department of Commerce, Bureau of the Census, 1990a, p. 682.
33. U.S. Department of Commerce, Bureau of the Census, 1990a, p. 678.
34. U.S. Department of Commerce, Bureau of the Census, 1990a, p. 683.
35 Wallace, 1987, p. 47.
36. Hammonds and Kozacik, 1988, p. 53.
37. Schmickle, 1990a.
38. Frons, 1989.
39. Hamburger and Schmickle, 1989.
40. ISI Press Digest, 1989, p. 7.
41. Hamburger and Schmickle, 1989, p. 6A.
42. Dean, 1990; Food Chemical News, 1990a.
43. Kinsey, 1990.
44. Hammonds and Kozacik, 1988, p. 52; Burros, 1990a.
45. Freedman and Ingersoll, 1988.
46. National Research Council, Board on Agriculture, 1988.
47. National Research Council, Board on Agriculture, 1988; Minneapolis Star Tribune, 1988a.
48. Cloud, 1989, p. 3047.

49. Cloud, 1989, p. 3051.
50. Charlier, 1990a.
51. Charlier, 1990a.
52. Wallace, 1987, p. 85.
53. Hileman, 1990, pp. 29-30.
54. Cloud, 1990a, p. 168.
55. Osteen and Szmedra, 1989.
56. International Herald Tribune, 1990.
57. The Economist, 1989b; Minneapolis Star Tribune, 1989f.
58. Schmickle, 1990b.
59. The Economist, 1990a.
60. Cloud and Wisenberg, 1990, p. 1187.
61. Hileman, 1990.
62. Kiplinger Agriculture Letter, 1990c.
63. Hileman, 1990, p. 31.
64. Kiplinger Agriculture Letter, 1989d, 1990c; The Economist, 1990a.
65. Kiplinger Agriculture Letter, 1989d.
66. Ingersoll, 1990a.
67. Kohls and Uhl, 1990.
68. Kohls and Uhl, 1990.
69. USDA, Economic Research Service, 1989b, p. v.
70. Kohls and Uhl, 1990.
71. Kohls and Uhl, 1990.
72. Kohls and Uhl, 1990.
73. Kohls and Uhl, 1990.
74. Food Technology, 1989.
75. Gorman, 1990.
76. USDA, Economic Research Service, 1989b.
77. Kohls and Uhl, 1990; USDA, Economic Research. Service, 1989b.
78. Gorman, 1990; USDA, Economic Research Service, 1989b; Friedman, 1990.
79. USDA, Economic Research Service, 1989b.
80. Kohls and Uhl, 1990.
81. USDA, Economic Research Service, 1989b.
82. USDA, Economic Research Service, 1989b, Kohls and Uhl, 1990.
83. USDA, Economic Research Service, 1989b, pp. 18-25.
84. USDA, Economic Research Service, 1989b, p. 23.
85. Marcotty, 1990.
86. Schiller, 1989.
87. Gorman, 1990.
88. Kiplinger Agriculture Letter, 1988d.
89. Kiplinger Agriculture Letter, 1987b.
90. Dornblaser, 1990; Lingle, 1990b.
91. Dziezak, 1987; Bjerklie, 1990.
92. Lingle, 1990b.
93. Bjerklie, 1990.
94. LaBell, 1990; Shapiro, L., 1990.
95. Hayami and Ruttan, 1971, 1985.
96. Hume, 1990.
97. Harrigan and Breene, 1989; Morrison, 1990.
98. Springer et al, 1990.
99. Morrison, 1990.
100. Food Technology, 1990; Kantrowitz, 1990; Morrison, 1990.

101. Dziezak, 1990.
102. Holusha, 1990; Javna, 1990.
103. Dziezak, 1990; Lingle, 1990a, p. 217; Thayer, 1990.
104. Lingle, 1990a.
105. Dziezak, 1990; Lingle, 1990b.
106. Gorman, 1990, p. 17.
107. Baking and Snack Systems, 1990.
108. Robe, 1990.
109. Epps, 1989; USDA, Economic Research Service, 1989b; Kohls and Uhl, 1990.
110. Epps, 1989; USDA, Economic Research Service, 1989b; Kohls and Uhl, 1990.
111. USDA, Economic Research Service, 1989b; Kohls and Uhl, 1990.
112. USDA, Economic Research Service, 1989b; Kohls and Uhl, 1990.
113. USDA, Economic Research Service, 1989b; Kohls and Uhl, 1990.
114. Kohls and Uhl, 1990.
115. USDA, Economic Research Service, 1989b.
116. USDA, Economic Research Service, 1989b; Kohls and Uhl, 1990.
117. Epps, 1989; USDA, Economic Research Service, 1989b; Kohls and Uhl, 1990.
118. USDA, Economic Research Service, 1989b; Kohls and Uhl, 1990.
119. USDA, Economic Research Service, 1989b.
120. USDA, Economic Research Service, 1989b.
121. Epps, 1989; USDA, Economic Research Service, 1989b.
122. Kiplinger Agriculture Letter, 1987b.
123. USDA, Economic Research Service, 1989b.
124. USDA, Economic Research Service, 1989b.
125. Kiplinger Agriculture Letter, 1987b.
126. USDA, Economic Research Service, 1989b.
127. Therrien, 1989.
128. USDA, Economic Research Service, 1989b.
129. Kohls and Uhl, 1990.
130. Business Week, 1987b, p. 127.
131. Gibson, 1990; Kohls and Uhl, 1990.
132. USDA, Economic Research Service, 1989b.
133. Kohls and Uhl, 1990.
134. Price and Newton, 1986.
135. Hamel, 1989, p. 36.
136. Hamel, 1989, p. 36.
137. Hammonds and Kozacik, 1988.
138. Business Week, 1987b.
139. USDA, Economic Research Service, 1989b, p. vi.
140. USDA, Economic Research Service, 1989b.
141. Heller, 1986; Litwak and Cepeda, 1989; USDA, Economic Research Service, 1989b; Kohls and Uhl, 1990.
142. Litwak and Cepeda, 1989.
143. Heller, 1986; Litwak and Cepeda, 1989; USDA, Economic Research Service, 1989b; Kohls and Uhl, 1990.
144. Litwak and Cepeda, 1989.
145. Litwak and Cepeda, 1989.
146. Litwak and Cepeda, 1989; Kohls and Uhl, 1990.
147. Heller, 1986.
148. Hamel, 1989; Litwak and Cepeda, 1989.
149. Heller, 1986, p. 30.
150. Guyon, 1983; Heller, 1986.

151. Heller, 1986; USDA, Economic Research Service, 1989b.
152. Heller, 1986.
153. Heller, 1986; USDA, Economic Research Service, 1989b.
154. Heller, 1986; Price and Newton, 1986; USDA, Economic Research Service, 1989b.
155. Heller, 1986 Business Week, 1987b; Hamel, 1989; USDA, Economic Research Service, 1989b.
156. Heller, 1986; USDA, Economic Research Service, 1989b.
157. Heller, 1986; USDA, Economic Research Service, 1989b.
158. Hamel, 1989.
159. Heller, 1986; Williamson, 1987; USDA, Economic Research Service, 1989b.
160. Price and Newton, 1986; Hamel, 1989; USDA, Economic Research Service, 1989b.
161. USDA, Economic Research Service, 1989b.
162. Heller, 1986; Price and Newton, 1986.
163. USDA, Economic Research Service, 1989b.
164. USDA, Economic Research Service, 1989b, p. v and vii.
165. Litwak and Cepeda, 1989.
166. Kohls and Uhl, 1990.
167. Kohls and Uhl, 1990.
168. Kohls and Uhl, 1990.
169. Kohls and Uhl, 1990.
170. Litwak and Cepeda, 1989; USDA, Economic Research Service, 1989b.
171. Litwak and Cepeda, 1989.
172. USDA, Economic Research Service, 1989b; Kohls and Uhl, 1990.
173. Litwak and Cepeda, 1989.
174. USDA, Economic Research Service, 1989b.
175. Kiplinger Agriculture Letter, 1987b.
176. USDA, Economic Research Service, 1989b.
177. USDA, Economic Research Service, 1989b.
178. USDA, Economic Research Service, 1989b.
179. Kohls and Uhl, 1990.
180. Hamel, 1989.
181. Kiplinger Agriculture Letter, 1987b.
182. Kiplinger Agriculture Letter, 1987c; Hamel, 1989.
183. Kiplinger Agriculture Letter, 1987c; Hamel, 1989.
184. Kiplinger Agriculture Letter, 1988a.
185. Hamel, 1989.
186. USDA, Economic Research Service, 1989b.
187. Guyon, 1983; Kiplinger Agriculture Letter, 1988d; Hamel, 1989.
188. Kiplinger Agriculture Letter, 1988d.
189. USDA, Economic Research Service, 1989b.
190. Hamel, 1989.
191. Business Week, 1987b.
192. Kiplinger Agriculture Letter, 1990d.
193. Hamel, 1989; Kiplinger Agriculture Letter, 1987c.
194. USDA, Economic Research Service, 1989b.
195. Kiplinger Agriculture Letter, 1988d.
196. Kiplinger Agriculture Letter, 1987c; Hamel, 1989.
197. Hamel, 1989.
198. Kiplinger Agriculture Letter, 1987b.
199. Schultz, 1989; USDA, Economic Research Service, 1989b.
200. Schultz, 1989.
201. USDA, Economic Research Service, 1989b; Hamel, 1989.

202. Business Week, 1987b.
203. USDA, Economic Research Service, 1989b.
204. Kiplinger Agriculture Letter, 1990d.
205. USDA, Economic Research Service, 1989b.
206. Food Marketing Institute, 1984; Business Week, 1987b.
207. Schiller, 1989, p. 62.
208. Gibson, 1988.
209. Gibson, 1988.
210. Freedman, 1988a; Gibson, 1990; Gorman, 1990.
211. Swasy and Stricharchuk, 1988; Gibson, 1988.
212. Kerr, 1989.
213. Supermarket Business, 1989.
214. Crossen, 1990.
215. USDA, Economic Research Service, 1989b.
216. USDA, Economic Research Service, 1989b.
217. USDA, Economic Research Service, 1989b.
218. Kohls and Uhl, 1990.
219. Bremner, 1989; USDA, Economic Research Service, 1989b.
220. Monson, 1990.
221. Kohls and Uhl, 1990.
222. USDA, Economic Research Service, 1989b.
223. USDA, Economic Research Service, 1989b.
224. USDA, Economic Research Service, 1989b.
225. USDA, Economic Research Service, 1989b.
226. USDA, Economic Research Service, 1989b; U.S. Department of Health and Human Services, Public Health Service, 1989.
227. USDA, Economic Research Service, 1989b.
228. McCarthy, 1990, p. B1.
229. Kiplinger Agriculture Letter, 1988b; Bremner, 1990.
230. Gibson and Johnson, 1989; McCarthy, 1990.
231. Hume, 1990.
232. Hume, 1990.
233. McCarthy, 1990, p. B1.
234. Bremner, 1990; Charlier, 1990b.
235. Bremner, 1990.
236. McCarthy, 1990.
237. Bremner, 1989; Gibson and Johnson, 1989; USDA, Economic Research Service, 1989b; Kohls and Uhl, 1990.
238. Bremner, 1990, p. 90.
239. USDA, Economic Research Service, 1989b.
240. Hirsch, 1990; McCarthy, 1990.
241. Hirsch, 1990, p. B1.
242. Moore, C., 1989.
243. Moore, C., 1989.
244. Bremner, 1990, p. 90.
245. Bremner, 1990.
246. Zellner, 1989.
247. Kiplinger Agriculture Letter, 1989a.
248. Sheraton, 1988.
249. Kiplinger Agriculture Letter, 1988b, 1989b; Schwartz and Howard, 1989, p. 42.
250. Kohls and Uhl, 1990.
251. Kohls and Uhl, 1990.

252. Koten, 1984.
253. USDA, Economic Research Service, 1989b.
254. Bremner, 1989.
255. USDA, Economic Research Service, 1989b.
256. Bremner, 1989; Gibson and Johnson, 1989.
257. Bremner, 1990.
258. USDA, Economic Research Service, 1989b.
259. Minneapolis Star Tribune, 1989b, p. 4A; USDA, Economic Research Service, 1989b.
260. Kiplinger Agriculture Letter, 1988b, 1989a, 1989b.
261. Schiller, 1989.
262. Gorman, 1990; Marinucci, 1990.
263. Marinucci, 1990, p. 3d.
264. Gorman, 1990; Marinucci, 1990.
265. Schiller, 1989.
266. Larson, 1990.
267. Wascoe, 1990.
268. Schiller, 1989; Larson, 1990.
269. Wascoe, 1990.
270. Larson, 1990.
271. Schiller, 1989; Larson, 1990.
272. Kiplinger Agriculture Letter, 1988d.
273. Schiller, 1989.
274. USDA, Economic Research Service, 1989b.
275. Tannahill, 1988.
276. Tannahill, 1988, p. 306.
277. Tannahill, 1988, p. 164.
278. Tannahill, 1988.
279. Tannahill, 1988.

REFERENCES

ACKERMAN, K., MACDONALD, S., and MILMOE, S. 1990. International trade. U.S. Dep. Agric., Econ. Res. Serv., Natl. Food Rev. 13(3):33-41.

AGRICULTURE CANADA, FOOD PRODUCTION AND INSPECTION BRANCH. 1989. Risk communication: Facing public outrage. Safety Watch 12(spring).

AKIN, J. S., GUILKEY, D. K., HAINES, P. S., and POPKIN, B. M. 1983. Evaluating school meals. Comm. Nutr. 2(1):4-7.

ALDERMAN, H. 1986. The Effect of Food Price and Income Changes on the Acquisition of Food by Low-Income Households. Int. Food Policy Res. Inst., Washington, D.C. May.

ALLEN, J., and GADSON, K. E. 1983. Nutrient Consumption Patterns of Low-Income Households. Tech. Bull. 1685. U.S. Dep. Agric., Econ. Res. Serv., Washington, D.C.

ALLEN, J., and NEWTON, D. 1986. Existing food policies and their relationship to hunger and nutrition. Am. J. Agric. Econ. 68(5):1247-1252.

ALLEN, J., MATSUMOTO, M., and TRAUB, L. 1985. Federal Food and Nutrition Programs: An Update. National Economics Division, U.S. Dep. Agric., Econ. Res. Serv. Agric. Econ. Rep. (draft). Washington, D.C., Jan.

AMERICAN ACADEMY OF PEDIATRICS, COMMITTEE ON NUTRITION. 1986. Prudent lifestyle for children: Dietary fat and cholesterol. Pediatrics 78(3):521-525.

AMERICAN CANCER SOCIETY. 1984. Nutrition and Cancer: Cause and Prevention. Spec. Rep. American Cancer Society, Washington, D.C.

AMERICAN DIETETIC ASSOCIATION. 1986. The American Dietetic Association's nutrition recommendations for women. J. Am. Diet. Assoc. 86:1663-1664.

AMERICAN HEART ASSOCIATION, NUTRITION COMMITTEE. 1988. Dietary Guidelines for Healthy American Adults: A Statement for Physicians and Health Professionals. Am. Heart Assoc., Washington, D.C.

AMERICAN MEDICAL ASSOCIATION, COUNCIL ON SCIENTIFIC AFFAIRS. 1979. Concepts of nutrition and health. J. Am. Med. Assoc. 242:2335-2338.

AMES, B. N., MAGAW, R., and GOLD, L. S. 1987. Ranking of possible carcinogenic hazards. Science 236:271-279.

ANSBERRY, C. 1988. Over at the rainbow, hunger's persistence is a growth industry. Wall Street J. June 14, p. A1.

ARCHIBALD, S. O. 1988a. Introduction. Pages 1-4 in: Regulating Chemicals: A Public Policy Quandary. Agric. Issues Center, University of California, Davis.

————. 1988b. Next steps: Looking for compromise. Pages 39-44 in: Regulating Chemicals: A Public Policy Quandary. Agric. Issues Center, University of California, Davis.

ARCHIBALD, S.O., and MARSH, R. 1988. Focusing the policy debate. Pages 33-38 in: Regulating Chemicals: A Public Policy Quandary. Agric. Issues Center, University of California, Davis.

ARCHIBALD, S. O., BRUHN, C., LANE, S., and MARSH, R. 1988a. Perspectives of consumer advocates. Pages 5-8 in: Regulating Chemicals: A Public Policy Quandary. Agric. Issues Center, University of California, Davis.

ARCHIBALD, S. O., HURD, B., and MARSH, R. 1988b. Perspectives of chemical manufacturers. Regulating Chemicals: A Public Policy Quandary. Pages 19-23 in: Agric. Issues Center, University of California, Davis.

ASINOF, L. 1988. Eating oats grows popular, but the grain is in short supply. Wall Street J. June 9, p. 1.

ASLOP, R. 1989. Brand loyalty rarely blind loyalty. Wall Street J. Oct. 19.

ASP, E. H., and DARLING, M. E. 1988. Home delivered meals: Food quality, nutrient content and characteristics of recipients. J. Am. Diet. Assoc. 88:55-59.

ASSOCIATED PRESS. 1989. Homeless for the holidays. Minneapolis Star Tribune, Dec. 23, p. 7A.

AUSTIN, J. E., and QUELCH, J. A. 1979. U.S. national dietary goals. Food Policy 4(May):115-128.

AVERY, R. B., and KENNICKELL, A. B. 1989. Rich rewards. Am. Demogr. 11(June):19-22.

AXELSON, M. L., and PENFIELD, M. P. 1983. Factors associated with food expenditures of elderly persons living alone. Home Econ. Res. J. 12:228-236.

BALSAM, A. L., and ROGERS, B. L. 1988. Service Innovations in the Elderly Nutrition Program: Strategies for Meeting Unmet Needs. Report to Am. Assoc. Retired Persons. Tufts University of Nutrition, Medford, Mass. July.

BAKING AND SNACK SYSTEMS. 1990. What does just-in-time really mean? 12(6):18.

BATSON, L. 1987. The new immigrants. Minneapolis Star Tribune, Dec. 7.

_____ . 1989. Changing the face of America. Minneapolis Star Tribune, Dec. 6.

BAUMAN, H. E. 1989. Risk assessment—Use and abuse. Cereal Foods World 34(6):480-481.

BAUSELL, R. B. 1986. Health-seeking behavior among the elderly. Gerontologist 26:556-559.

BECK, M., HAGER, M., MILLER, M., HUTCHINSON, S., HACKETT, G., and JOSEPH, N. 1989a. Warning! Your food, nutritious and delicious, may be hazardous to your health. Newsweek, Mar. 27, pp. 16-19.

BECK, M., HAGER, M., KING, P., HUTCHISON, S., ROBINS, K., and GORDON, J. 1989b. Buried alive. Newsweek, Nov. 27, pp. 66-76.

BECKER, G. S. 1965. A theory of the allocation of time. Econ. J. 75:493-517.

_____ . 1981. A Treatise on the Family. Harvard University Press, Cambridge, Mass.

BEGLEY, S., and HAGER, M. 1989. A guide to the grocery. Newsweek, Mar. 27, pp. 20-23.

BEGLEY, S., HAGER, M., and HOWARD, J. 1989. Dangers in the vegetable patch. Newsweek, Jan. 30, pp. 74-75.

BENBROOK, C. M. 1988. Critical issues related to pesticide regulation. Pages 29-32 in: Consumer Demands in the Marketplace: Public Policies Related to Food Safety, Quality and Human Health. K. Clancy, ed. Natl. Center for Food and Agric. Policy, Research for the Future, Washington, D.C.

BERG, S. 1989a. Standards for pesticide traces in food urged. Minneapolis Star Tribune, May 21, p. 3A.

_____ . 1989b. A widening gap. Minneapolis Star Tribune, Aug. 20.

BERK, S. F. 1985. The Gender Factor. Plenum Press, New York.

BEST, D. 1990. Health perceptions preoccupy product developers. Prep. Foods New Prod. Annu. 159(8):47-52.

BIRDSALL, M. 1972. Factors related to vegetable consumption of preschool children in low-income families. Ph.D. thesis, Pennsylvania State University, University Park.

BISHOP, K. 1990. Warnings on chemical hazards are upheld by California court. New York Times, Mar. 3, p. 7.

BJERKLIE, S. 1990. Microwave's next wave. Meat Poult. 36(3):30, 45.

BLANCIFORTI, L. A., and PARLETT, R. 1987. Changes in the CPI. U.S. Dep. Agric., Econ. Res. Serv., Natl. Food Rev. 36(Winter-Spring):13-17.

BLAYLOCK, J. R., and SMALLWOOD, D. M. 1981. Impact of Household Size and Income on Food Spending Patterns. Tech. Bull. 1650. U.S. Dep. Agric., Econ. Res. Serv., Washington, D.C.

_____ . 1986. U.S. Demand for Food: Household Expenditures, Demographics, and Projections. Tech. Bull. 1713. U.S. Dep. Agric., Econ. Res. Serv., Washington, D.C.

BLUESTONE, B., and HARRISON, B. 1987. American job machine has begun to sputter. Washington Post, May 17.

BORRA, S. T. 1988. A healthy diet with animal product options: What the food marketer and consumer are doing. Presented at Intercollegiate Nutrition Consortium FAN Forum,

Univ. Minnesota, St. Paul, Minn., Nov. 3. Food Marketing Inst. Washington, D.C. (mimeo).

BOYNTON, R. D., BLAKE, B. F., and UHL, J. N. 1983. Retail price reporting effects in local food markets. Am. J. Agric. Econ. 65(1):20-29.

BRADBURY, K. L. 1990. The changing fortunes of American families in the 1980s. Federal Reserve Bank of Boston. New Engl. Econ. Rev. July/Aug., pp. 24-40.

BREMNER, B. 1989. Among the restaurateurs, it's dog eat dog. Business Week, Jan. 9, p. 86.

_____. 1990. Fast-food joints are getting fried. Business Week, Jan. 8, p. 90.

BRITISH MINISTRY OF AGRICULTURE, FISHERIES AND FOOD. 1989. Household Food Consumption and Expenditure, 1988. Annu. Rep. Natl. Food Survey Committee, London.

BRODY, J. 1989. As the body ages, its needs for various nutrients changes. Minneapolis Star Tribune, June 14.

_____. 1990a. Personal health. New York Times, Feb. 8.

_____. 1990b. Margarine, too, is found to have the fat that adds to heart risk. New York Times, Aug. 16.

BROWN, G. E., JR. 1984. National nutrition monitoring system: A congressional perspective. J. Am. Diet. Assoc. 84:1185-1189.

_____. 1988. Remarks. Am. J. Clin. Nutr. 47:333-335.

BROWN, L. J. 1987. Hunger in the U.S. Sci. Am. 256(2):37-41.

BROWNING, J. 1981. How bad were the seventies? Challenge, July-Aug., pp. 47-50.

BRUHN, C., LANE, S., and WALTON, L. 1988. Perspectives of consumers. Pages 9-13 in: Regulating Chemicals: A Public Policy Quandary. Agric. Issues Center, University of California, Davis.

BRYNJOLFSSON, A. 1989. Future radiation sources and identification of irradiated foods. Food Technol. 43(7):84-89, 97.

BULL, A. T., HOLT, G., and LILLY, M. 1982. Biotechnology: International Trends and Perspectives. Organisation for Economic Cooperation and Development, Paris.

BURBEE, C. R., and KRAMER, C. S. 1986. Food safety issues for the eighties. U.S. Dep. Agric., Econ. Res. Serv., Natl. Food Rev. 33 (Spring):17-20.

BURCKHARDT, A. 1989. Cuisine concerns: How they've changed since 1969. Minneapolis Star Tribune, Oct. 4.

BURK, M. C. 1968. Consumption Economics: A Multidisciplinary Approach. John Wiley and Sons, New York.

BURK, M. C., and PAO, E. M. 1976. Methodology for Large-Scale Surveys of Household and Individual Diets. Home Econ. Res. Rep. 40. U.S. Dep. Agric., Econ. Res. Serv., Washington, D.C.

BURROS, M. 1988a. Women: Out of the house but not out of the kitchen. New York Times, Feb. 24.

_____. 1988b. It's still women's work. New York Times, Feb. 27.

_____. 1989. Food safety raises concerns. Minneapolis Star Tribune, Mar. 18, p. 1E.

_____. 1990a. Designer beef leaning on industry for consumers. Minneapolis Star Tribune, Feb. 28, p. 3T.

_____. 1990b. Packaging materials, burns and children raise fears about microwave safety. Minneapolis Star Tribune, April 8, p. 3T.

BUSE, R. C. 1990. Issues and implications for the changing demand for meat. Econ. Issues Rep. 114. Dep. Agric. Econ., University of Wisconsin, Madison.

BUSE, R. C., and FLEISCHER, A. 1982. Factors influencing food choices and expenditures. Econ. Issues Rep. 68. Dep. Agric. Econ., University of Wisconsin, Madison.

BUSINESS WEEK. 1987a. Marketing's new look. Jan. 26, pp. 64-69.

_____. 1987b. America's supermarket miracle. May 4, pp. 127-136.

_____ . 1989. The great American health pitch. Oct. 9, pp. 114-122.

BUTRUM, R. R., CLIFFORD, C. K., and LANZA, E. 1988. NCI dietary guidelines: Rationale. Am. J. Clin. Nutr. 48(suppl.):882-895.

BUTTERFIELD, F. 1991. Asians spread across the land and help change it. New York Times, Feb. 24.

CALLAWAY, C. W. 1984. National nutrition monitoring system. J. Am. Diet. Assoc. 84:1179-1180.

CAMPBELL, T. C. 1988. Food quality as measured by changes in buying behavior required for chronic disease reduction. Pages 33-35 in: Consumer Demands in the Marketplace: Public Policies Related to Food Safety, Quality and Human Health. K.Clancy, ed. Natl. Center for Food and Agric. Policy, Resources for the Future: Washington, D.C.

CAPPS, O., JR. 1987. The ultimate data source for demand analysis? Presented at the Selected Papers Session, 1987 Am. Agric. Econ. Assoc. Annu. Mtg., Aug. 2-5. Michigan State University, East Lansing.

CAPPS, O., JR., THOMAS, J. M., and LONG, D. L. 1988. Scanner Data in Managerial Decision-making. Texas Agric. Exp. Stn., College Station, Tex. Oct.

CARLSON, E. 1989. 'Graying' market may not be so golden. Wall Street J. Dec. 27.

CASWELL, J. A. 1988. Federal preemption, state regulation, and food safety and quality: Major research issues. Pages 129-137 in: Consumer Demands in the Marketplace: Public Policies Related to Food Safety, Quality and Human Health. K. Clancy, ed. Natl. Center for Food and Agric. Policy, Resources for the Future: Washington, D.C.

CENTER FOR THE STUDY OF AMERICAN BUSINESS. 1990. Regulations rebound: Bush budget gives regulation a boost. Occ. Pap. 81. The Center: St. Louis, Missouri. May.

CHARLIER, M. 1990a. Chicken economics: The broiler business consolidates, and that is bad news for farmers. Wall Street J. Jan. 4, p. A1.

_____ . 1990b. Food-chain maverick rides into a spaghetti shoot-out. Wall Street J. Jan. 29, p. B1.

_____ . 1990c. Youthful sobriety tests liquor firms. Wall Street J. June 14.

CHASE, R. A. 1990. Minority Elders in Minnesota. Wilder Research Center, St. Paul, Minn. March.

CHAVAS, J. P. 1989. On the structure of demand for meat. In: The Economics of Meat Demand, 1989. R. C. Buse, ed. Proc. Conf. Economics of Meat Demand, Charleston, NC. Oct. 20-21.

CLANCY, K. L. 1975. Preliminary observations on media use and food habits of the elderly. Gerontologist 15:529-532.

_____ . 1988. Overview of current food safety and quality issues and policies. Pages 1-26 in: Consumer Demands in the Marketplace: Public Policies Related to Food Safety, Quality and Human Health. K. Clancy, ed. Natl. Center for Food and Agric. Policy, Resources for the Future, Washington, D.C.

CLARK, A. 1981. Providing nutrition effectively: A continuing challenge. Institute for Research on Poverty, University of Wisconsin. Focus 4:3 (Spring).

CLEVELAND, L. E., and KERR, R. L. 1988. Development and uses of the USDA food plans. J. Nutr. Educ. 20:232-238.

CLOUD, D. S. 1989. When Madison Avenue talks, farm-belt members listen. Congress. Q. Nov. 11, pp. 3047-3051.

_____ . 1990a. Farmers reap a crop of scorn from anti-chemical forces. Congress. Q. Jan. 20, pp. 166-170.

_____ . 1990b. Logic doesn't always apply to multi-year farm bills. Congress. Q. Feb. 24, pp. 576-582.

CLOUD, D. S., and WISENBERG, D. 1990. House panel's sweet deal sets stage for sugar war. Congress. Q. Apr. 21, pp. 1186-1188.

CONGRESSIONAL BUDGET OFFICE, CONGRESS OF THE UNITED STATES. 1988a. Trends in Family Income: 1970–1986. U.S. Government Printing Office, Washington D.C.

———. 1988b. Changes in the Living Arrangements of the Elderly: 1960–2030. U.S. Government Printing Office, Washington D.C.

CONNER, R. L. 1989. Answering the demo-doomsayers. Brookings Rev. 7(4):35-39.

CONSUMER REPORTS. 1991. The trouble with margarine. March, pp. 196-199.

COOK, R. 1990. Organics, food safety and consumer tastes and preferences: What do they really want? Presented at the Am. Agric. Econ. Assoc. Annu. Mtg., Vancouver, B.C., Aug. 5.

CORCHADO, A. 1988. Campbell Soup is seeking to be numero uno where Goya reigns. Wall Street J. Mar. 28, p. 20.

COUNCIL OF ECONOMIC ADVISORS. 1985. Economic status of the elderly. Pages 159-186 in: Economic Report of the President—1985. U.S. Government Printing Office, Washington, D.C.

———. 1987. Economic report of the President—1987. U.S. Government Printing Office, Washington, D.C.

COX, M. 1989. Staying at home for entertainment. Wall Street J. Nov. 22.

CRISPELL, D. 1989. Three's a crowd. Am. Demogr. 11(Jan.):34-38.

CROCKETT, J. A. 1960. Population change and the demand for food. Pages 456-495 in: Demographic and Economic Change in Developed Countries. Natl. Bur. Econ. Res., Princeton. Princeton University Press, Princeton, N.J.

CRONIN, F. J., and SHAW, A. M. 1988. Summary of dietary recommendations for healthy Americans. Nutr. Today 23(6):26-34.

CRONIN, F. J., KREBS-SMITH, S. M., WYSE, B. W., and LIGHT, L. 1982. Characterizing food usage by demographic variables. J. Am. Diet. Assoc. 81:661-673.

CROSSEN, C. 1990. Putting plastic on the checkout lanes: More supermarkets accept credit cards. Wall Street J. Feb. 5. p. B1.

CURRY, D. J. 1989. Single source systems: Retail management present and future. J. Retailing 65(1):1-20.

CUTLER, B. 1989a. Bachelor party. Am. Demogr. 11(Feb.):22-26, 55.

———. 1989b. Meet Jane Doe. Am. Demogr. 11(June):25-27.

DARDIS, R. 1988. Risk regulation and consumer welfare. J. Consumer Affairs 22(2):303-318.

DAVIS, C. G., and SENAUER, B. 1986. Needed directions in domestic food assistance policies and programs. Am. J. Agric. Econ. 68:1253-1260.

DEAN, L. S. 1989. Fast food finds place in school. Minneapolis Star Tribune, Apr. 23, p. 1T.

———. 1990. Organic produce. Minneapolis Star Tribune, Sept. 12.

DE STAFANO, L. 1989. Mirror of America. Minneapolis Star Tribune, Nov. 8.

DEVENY, K. 1989. Marketing. Wall Street J. Nov. 1.

DEVENY, K., and FRANCESE, P. K. 1990. Shrinking markets: Finding a niche may be the key to survival. Wall Street J. Mar. 9, p. R29.

DEVINE, G., and MARION, B. W. 1979. The influence of consumer price information on retail pricing and consumer behavior. Am. J. Agric. Econ. 61:228-237.

DHHS. See U.S. Department of Health and Human Services.

DIGGS, M. 1989. Seniors' diets often fail to meet nutritional needs. Minneapolis Star Tribune, July 7.

DIXON, J. E. 1987. The changing marketplace: Food prepared away from home but intended to be eaten at home. Cereal Foods World 32:431-432.

DOBBS, M. 1990. Slow food capital Moscow now enjoying tasty Bolshoi Maks. St. Paul Pioneer Press, Feb. 1, 1990, p. 4A.

DORNBLASER, L. 1990. Take the 'F' train. Prep. Foods New Prod. Annu. 159(8):70-74.

DOUGLAS, E. 1975. The Economics of Marketing. Harper and Row, New York.

DOW DIARY. 1982. Changes in eating habits. Fall:4-5.

DRAPER, N. 1989. LBJ's legacy: He didn't win war on poverty, but he cut casualties. Minneapolis Star Tribune, Sept. 3, p. 1A.

DUENSING, E. E. 1988. America's Elderly: A Sourcebook. Rutgers Univ. Center for Urban Policy Research, Rutgers, NJ.

DULUTH NEWS-TRIBUNE. 1990. Survey says Americans drinking less wine. Jul. 7.

DUNCAN, G. J. 1984. Years of poverty, years of plenty: The changing economic fortunes of American workers and families. Inst. for Social Research, University of Michigan, Ann Arbor.

DUNHAM, D. 1987. Food spending and income. U.S. Dep. Agric., Econ. Res. Serv. Natl. Food Rev. 37(Yearbook):24-33.

_____ . 1988. Food Cost Review 1987. Agric. Econ. Rep. 596. U.S. Dep. Agric., Econ. Res. Serv., Washington, D.C.

_____ . 1989. Food Cost Review 1988. Agric. Econ. Rep. 615. U.S. Dep. Agric., Econ. Res. Serv., Washington, D.C.

_____ . 1990. Food Costs from Farm to Retail in 1989. Agric. Info. Bull. 593. U.S. Dep. Agric., Econ. Res. Serv., Washington, D.C.

DUNN, W. 1985. The meat and potatoes of eating out. Am. Demogr. 7(Jan.):35.

DUXBURY, D.D. 1990. 1990s consumers say no to fats—Health & convenience top trends. Food Process. 51(July):92-100.

DZIEZAK, J. D. 1987. Microwavable foods—Industry's response to consumer demands for convenience. Food Technol. 41(6):51-62.

_____ . 1990. Packaging waste management. Food Technol. 44(7):98-101.

EASTWOOD, D. B. 1985. The Economics of Consumer Behavior, Allyn and Bacon, Boston.

ECONOMIST, THE. *See* The Economist.

EDMONDSON, B. 1987. Inside the empty nest. Am. Demogr. 9(Nov.):24-29.

_____ . 1988. American hot spots. Am. Demogr. 10(Jan.):24-30.

EPPS, W. 1989. Food wholesaling. U.S. Dep. Agric., Econ. Res. Serv., Natl. Food Rev. 12(2):25-32.

EXTER, T. 1987. How many Hispanics? Am. Demogr. 9(May):36-39, 67.

FARRELL, K. R. 1978. Statement of purpose. Agricultural Food Policy Review: Proceedings of Five Food Policy Seminars. U.S. Dep. Agric., Econ. Stat. Coop. Serv. ESCS-AFPR-2, Sept., pp. 1-2.

FEDERAL REGISTER. 1989. USDHHS. Annual update on the poverty guidelines. 54(31):7097-7098, Feb. 16.

_____ . 1990a. USDA, FNS. Food stamp program: Maximum allotments and income eligibility standards. 55(7):887-889, Jan. 10.

_____ . 1990b. USDHHS, FDA. Irradiation in the production, processing and handling of food. 55(85):18538-18544, May 2.

_____ . 1990c. USDHHS, FDA and USDC, NOAA. Seafood inspection. 55(124):26334-26339, June 27.

_____ . 1990d. USDHHS, FDA. Food labeling. 21 CFR Parts 101 and 104. 55(139):29476-29486, July 19.

FEICK, L. F., HERRMANN, R. O., and WARLAND, R. H. 1986. Search for nutrition information: A probit analysis of the use of different information sources. J. Consumer Affairs, 20:173-192.

FEIN, E. B. 1989. A time to be born, a time to die. Minneapolis Star Tribune, Aug. 16.

FERGUSON, R. 1990. FDA moves to rewrite food labels. Wall Street J. July 13, p. B1.

FISHER, A. B. 1990. What consumers want in the 1990s. Fortune, Jan. 29, pp. 108-112.

FLANIGAN, J. 1988. Surgeon General's report on diet is a sign of the times. Minneapolis Star Tribune, Aug. 5, p. 2D.

FLORKOWSKI, W. J., HUANG, C. L., and GOGGIN, B. 1989. Attitudes Towards Porcine Somatotropin: A Consumer Survey of the Atlanta Metropolitan Area. Georgia Agric. Exp. Stn. Res. Rep. 570.

FOOD AND NUTRITION FORUM (FAN). 1989. Minnesota food banks. In: Food Access: Exploring Issues and Affecting Changes. Background Reading for FAN Forum III. University of Minnesota, St. Paul, July 12-13.

FOOD CHEMICAL NEWS. 1989. Foodborne illness increasing, CDC researcher reports. Aug. 28, pp. 3-4.

_____ . 1990a. Retailers finding organic produce not profitable, study says. Feb. 26, pp. 55-56.

_____ . 1990b. 'Healthy American diet' recommended by 9 health organizations. May 28, p. 15.

_____ . 1990c. FDA to use recommended calorie allowances as basis for DRVs. June 25, pp. 70-73.

_____ . 1990d. FDA nutrition labeling regulations to be finalized in 2 years. Oct. 29, p. 39.

FOOD MARKETING INSTITUTE. 1984. Productivity. 1984 Food Marketing Facts. The Institute, Washington, D.C.

_____ . 1987. Trends Update, 1987: Consumer Attitudes and the Supermarket. The Institute, Washington, D.C.

_____ . 1988. Trends: Consumer Attitudes and the Supermarket, 1988. The Institute, Washington, D.C.

_____ . 1989a. Trends: Consumer Attitudes and the Supermarket, 1989. The Institute, Washington, D.C.

_____ . 1989b. Consumer confidence in food safety. Unnumbered insert in: Trends: Consumer Attitudes and the Supermarket, 1989. The Institute, Washington, D.C.

_____ . 1990. Trends: Consumer Attitudes and the Supermarket, 1990. The Institute, Washington, D.C.

FOOD MARKETING INSTITUTE AND BETTER HOMES AND GARDENS. 1988. A Study of Food Patterns and Meal Consumptions. Joint Publ. by Opinion Research Corp. FMI, Washington, D.C.

_____ . 1989. Dinnertime USA. Joint Publ. of Survey by Opinion Research Corp. FMI, Washington D.C.

FOOD TECHNOLOGY. 1989. Top 10 food science innovations 1939–1989. Food Technol. 43(9):308.

_____ . 1990. Fat substitute update. Food Technol. 44(3):92-97.

FORBES, A. L. 1988a. 1987 ASCN public policy forum—Federal monitoring of the nation's nutritional status. Am. J. Clin. Nutr. 47:318-319.

_____ . 1988b. Microbiological contamination of food. Pages 43-44 in: Consumer Demands in the Marketplace: Public Policies Related to Food Safety, Quality and Human Health. K. Clancy, ed. Natl. Center for Food and Agric. Policy, Resources for the Future: Washington, D.C.

FORBES, A. L., and STEPHENSON, M. G. 1984. National nutrition monitoring system: Implications for public health policy at FDA. J. Am. Diet. Assoc. 84:1189-1193.

FRANCESE, P. 1989. On to the future. Am. Demogr. 11(1):20-21.

FRANK, J. D. 1987. European Community Consumers Food Consumption and Expenditure Patterns. Food Policy Research, University of Bradford, Bradford, England. March.

FRANKEL, M., and MEHNERT, D. 1990. Panic over mad cow disease. Newsweek (Int. ed.), June 4, p. 46.

FREEDMAN, A. M. 1988a. Supermarkets push private-label lines. Wall Street J. Nov. 15, p. B1.

——. 1988b. As fresh refrigerated foods gain favor, concerns about safety rise. Wall Street J. Mar. 11. p. 19.

——. 1989a. Most consumers shun luxuries, seek few frills but better service. Wall Street J. Sept. 19.

——. 1989b. The microwave cooks up a new way of life. Wall Street J. Sept. 19, p. B1.

FREEDMAN, A. M., and INGERSOLL, B. 1988. Egg producers try to halt product's slide. Wall Street J. Nov. 14, p. B1.

FREUNDLICH, N. 1989. Blood pressure is rising in the cholesterol debate. Business Week, Oct. 9, p. 128.

FRIEDMAN, M. 1957. A Theory of the Consumption Function. Natl. Bur. Econ. Res., Gen. Ser. 63.

FRIEDMAN, M. 1990. Twenty-five years and 98,900 new products later. Prep. Foods New Prod. Annu. 159(8):23-25.

FRONS, M. 1989. Just what is organic food—And is it safe for you? Business Week, Sept. 25, p. 232-233.

FUCHS, V. R. 1986. Sex differences in economic well-being. Science 232:459-464.

GALBRAITH, J. K. 1958. The Affluent Society. Houghton Mifflin, Boston, Mass.

GALLO, A. 1978. National school lunch program: Plate waste and innovative lunches. Natl. Food Rev., U.S. Dep. Agric., Econ. Stat. Coop. Serv. 3(June):35.

GALLO, A. E. 1990. The Food Marketing System in 1989. U.S. Dep. Agric., Econ. Res. Serv. Agric. Info. Bull. 603.

GALLO, A. E., SALATHE, L. E., and BOEHM, W. T. 1979. Senior Citizens: Food Expenditure Patterns and Assistance. U.S. Dep. Agric., Econ. Stat. Coop. Serv. Agric. Econ. Rep. 426. Washington, D.C.

GARNER, T. I. 1988. Methodological issues for today and tomorrow. Fam. Econ. Rev. 1(3):2-5.

GARNER, T. I., HOGARTH, J. M., MILLER, R. D., PASSERO, W., and SEDRANSH, N. 1990. Data comparability among federal household surveys. Paper presented at 2nd Int. Conf. on Research in the Consumer Interest, Am. Council Consumer Interests, Snowbird, Utah. Aug. 7-9.

GEORGE, P. S., and KING, G. A. 1971. Consumer Demand for Food Commodities in the United States with Projections to 1980. Giannini Foundation Monogr. 26. University of California, Davis.

GERBER, J. 1989. How the aging explosion will create new food trends. Food Technol. 43(4):134-150.

GIBSON, L. D. 1981. The psychology of food: Why we eat what we eat when we eat. Food Technol. 35(2):54-56.

GIBSON, R. 1988. Space war: Supermarkets demand food firms' payments just to get on the shelf. Wall Street J. Nov. 1, p. A1.

——. 1990. Grocer's private labels go from lowly to lofty. Wall Street J. Feb. 14. p. B1.

GIBSON, R., and JOHNSON, R. 1989. Big Mac, cooling off, loses its sizzle. Wall Street J. Sept. 29, p. B1.

GLAZER, S. 1988. How America eats. Congress. Q. Editorial Res. Rep. Apr. 29, pp. 218-231.

GOEL, U. P., and CARNEVALE, M. L. 1990. Devouring the data. Wall Street J. Mar. 9, p. R30.

GORMAN, B. 1989. New products: What's your next move? Prep. Foods New Prod. Annu. 1989. 158(8):16-21.

_____ . 1990. New products for a new century. Prep. Foods New Prod. Ann. 159(8):16-18, 47-52.

GOULD, B. W., and COX, T. L. 1989. Determinants of the demand for food fats and oils: The role of demographic variables and government donations. Staff Pap. 313. Dep. Agric. Econ, University of Wisconsin, Madison.

GRAHAM, J. 1989. New VALS 2 takes psychological route. Advertising Age, Feb. 13, p. 24.

GRAHAM, L. T. 1989. Warning: Proposition 65 may be harmful to your business. Cereal Foods World 34(6):473-475.

GREENE, C. 1988. A new look for supermarket produce sections. U.S. Dep. Agric., Econ. Res. Serv., Natl. Food Rev. 11(4):1-5.

GUYON, J. 1983. Supermarkets change to lure more shoppers. Wall Street J. Nov. 14, p. 27.

HAIDACHER, R., and BLAYLOCK, J. 1988. Why has dairy product consumption increased? U.S. Dep. Agric., Econ. Res. Serv., Nat. Food Rev. 11(4):28-32.

HAIDACHER, R., CRAVEN, J. A., HUANG, K. S., SMALLWOOD, D. M., and BLAYLOCK, J. R. 1982. Consumer Demand for Red Meats, Poultry, and Fish. U.S. Dep. Agric., Econ. Res. Serv. Staff Rep. AGES 820818.

HALBRENDT, C., STERLING, L., GEMPESAN, C., FLORKOWSKI, W., and HUANG, C. L. 1989. Public attitudes in the northeast region toward recombinant porcine somatotropin. J. Food Distr. 30(1):153-164.

HAMA, M. Y., and CHERN, W. S. 1988. Food expenditures and nutrient availability for elderly households. J. Consumer Affairs 22(1):3-19.

HAMA, M. Y., and RIDDICK, H. A. 1988. Nationwide food consumption survey. Fam. Econ. Rev. 1988(2):24-27.

HAMBURGER, T., and SCHMICKLE, S. 1989. From co-op to corporation, organic farming is growing into big business. Minneapolis Star Tribune, Mar. 29, p. 1A.

HAMEL, R. 1989. Food fight. Am. Demogr. 11(3):37-39, 60.

HAMERMESH, D. S. 1984. Consumption during retirement: The missing link in the life cycle. Rev. Econ. Stat. 66(1):1-7.

HAMM, L. 1985. Marketers fine tune food products. U.S. Dep. Agric., Econ. Res. Serv., Natl. Food Rev. 29:25-26.

HAMILL, P. V. V., DRIZD, T. A., JOHNSON, C. L., REED, R. B., ROCHE, A. F., and MOORE, W. M. 1979. Physical growth: National Center for Health Statistics percentiles. Am. J. Clin. Nutr. 32:607-629.

HAMMONDS, T. M., and KOZACIK, J. 1988. Consumer preferences and the American farmer. Forum Appl. Res. Public Policy 3(2):49-54.

HANDY, C., and KAUFMAN, P. 1988. Food retailing. U.S. Dep. Agric., Econ. Res. Serv., Natl. Food Rev. 11(2):28-35.

HARP, H., and BUNCH, K. 1989. Major Statistical Series of the U.S. Department of Agriculture, Vol. 5. Consumption and Utilization of Agricultural Products. Agric. Handb. 671. U.S. Dep. Agric., Econ. Res. Serv., Commodity Econ. Div., Washington, D.C.

HARRIGAN, K. A., and BREENE, W. M. 1989. Fat substitutes: Sucrose esters and Simplesse. Cereal Foods World. 34(3):261-267.

HAUGHTON, B., GUSSOW, J. D., and DODDS, J. M. 1987. An historical study of the underlying assumptions for the United States food guides from 1917 through the basic four food group guides. J. Nutr. Educ. 19(4):169-175.

HAUSMAN, J. A., and PAQUETTE, L. 1987. Involuntary early retirement and consumption. Pages 151-175 in: Work, Health and Income Among the Elderly. G. Burtless, ed. Brookings Inst., Washington D.C.

HAYAMI, Y., and RUTTAN, V. W. 1971. Induced innovation in agricultural development.

Staff Pap. P71-1. Dep. Agric. Econ., University of Minnesota, Minneapolis–St. Paul.

———. 1985. Agricultural Development. Johns Hopkins University Press, Baltimore, Md.

HAYS, L. 1988. New packages may yield fresher produce. Wall Street J. Oct. 18, p. B1.

HAZLETT, T. 1988. Perspective of regulators. Pages 28-33 in: Regulating Chemicals: A Public Policy Quandary. Agric. Issues Center, University of California, Davis.

HELLER, P. S., HEMMING, R., and KOHNERT, P. W. 1989. Aging and social expenditures in the major industrial countries, 1980–2025. Int. Monetary Fund, Occ. Pap. 47. Washington, D.C.

HELLER, W. H. 1986. A new look at store formats. Prog. Grocer 65(12):29-34.

HERTZLER, A. A., and OWEN, C. 1976. Sociologic study of food habits—A review. J. Am. Diet. Assoc. 69:381-384.

HICKS, R. 1990. Consumer Food Trends for the 1990s. Agriculture Canada, Ottawa.

HIEMSTRA, S. J. 1968. Food Consumption, Prices and Expenditures. U.S. Dep. Agric., Econ. Res. Serv. Agric. Econ. Rep. 138. Washington, D.C.

HILDRETH, R. J. 1990. Legitimacy and support for extension: A public policy issue. Pages 90-100 in: Increasing Understanding of Public Problems and Policies—1989. Natl. Public Policy Educ. Committee, ed. Farm Foundation, Oak Brook, Ill.

HILEMAN, B. 1990. Alternative agriculture: A special report. Chem. Eng. News, Mar. 5, pp. 26-40.

HINTON, M. A., EPPRIGHT, E. S., CHADDERDON, H., and WOLIN, L. 1963. Eating behavior and dietary intake of girls 12 to 14 years old. J. Am. Diet. Assoc. 43:223.

HIRSCH, J. S. 1989. Diet mixes indulgence, health. Wall Street J. Dec. 6.

———. 1990. Fast-food vendors get serious with kids. Wall Street J. Jan. 19, p. B1.

HIRSHMAN, A. 1978. Exit, Voice and Loyalty. Harvard University Press, Cambridge, Mass.

HOFFMAN, G. D. 1987. New trends in food retailing. Cereal Foods World 32(6):422-424.

HOLUSHA, J. 1990. McDonald's announces end to foam packaging. Minneapolis Star Tribune, Nov. 2, p. 1A.

HORNSBY, M. 1990a. Mad cow disease hits sales of cattle. London Times, May 23, p. 1.

———. 1990b. EC pressures Gummer over beef controls. London Times, June 7, p. 1.

HOUCK, J. P. 1990. Stabilization in agriculture: An uncertain quest. Pages 173-200 in: Agricultural Policies in a New Decade. K. Allen, ed. Natl. Center for Food and Agric. Policy, Resources for the Future, Washington D.C.

HOUSE SELECT COMMITTEE ON HUNGER, U.S. HOUSE OF REPRESENTATIVES. 1989. Food Security in the United States: The Measurement of Hunger, Issue Brief. Hearing before the Select Committee on Hunger, Mar. 23. Serial 101-2.

HUANG, K. S. 1985. U.S. Demand for Food: A Complete System of Price and Income Effects. U.S. Dep. Agric., Econ. Res. Serv. Tech. Bull. 1714.

HUGHS, K. A. 1989. Diehards say the experience feels good. Wall Street J. Oct. 13.

HULL, D. B., CAPPS, O., JR., and HAVLICEK, J., JR. 1983. Demand for convenience foods in the United States. Pages 44-50 in: Proc. 29th Annu. Conf. American Council on Consumer Interest, Mar. 16-19. K. P. Goebel, ed. Kansas City, Mo.

HUME, S. 1990. Fast food faces wary public. Advertising Age, July 2, p. 1.

HUNT, I. F., JACOB, P. H., OSTERGARD, N. J., MASRI, G., CLARK, V. A., and COULSON, A. H. 1976. Effect of nutrition education on the nutritional status of low-income pregnant women of Mexican descent. Am. J. Clin. Nutr. 29:675.

HURD, M. D. 1989. The economic status of the elderly. Science 244:659-664.

———. 1990. Research on the elderly: Economic status, retirement, and consumption and saving. J. Econ. Lit. 28:565-637.

IGGERS, J. 1987. Food marketers are told of emerging consumer trends. Minneapolis Star Tribune, May 9.

INGERSOLL, B. 1988a. Eaters beware: Fish-poisoning cases lead to calls for U.S. to inspect seafood. Wall Street J. Apr. 8, p. 1.

_____ . 1988b. Bad catch: Digging for fast profit, fishermen harvest much tainted shellfish. Wall Street J. June 8, p. A1.

_____ . 1989a. Slicing it thin: Meat inspection cuts proposed by Reagan are hot issues for Bush. Wall Street J. Feb. 2, p. A1.

_____ . 1989b. Cyanide mystery: In Chilean grape case, new data raises doubt as to what happened. Wall Street J. Nov. 16, p. A1.

_____ . 1990a. Environmentalists blast chemical firms on developing herbicide-resistant crops. Wall Street J. Mar. 21, p. B5.

_____ . 1990b. FDA to propose new standards for food labels. Wall Street J. June 27, p. B1.

_____ . 1990c. FDA concludes growth hormone in cattle is safe. Wall Street J. Aug. 24, p. C16.

INGRASSIA, P., and PATTERSON, G. A. 1989. Is buying a car a choice or a chore? Wall Street J. Oct. 24.

INGWERSEN, L. W., and HAMA, M. Y. 1985. Value of food used in households with elderly members. Fam. Econ. Rev. 4:11-19.

INSTITUTE OF FOOD TECHNOLOGISTS, EXPERT PANEL ON FOOD SAFETY AND NUTRITION. 1988. The risk/benefit concept as applied to food. Food Technol. 42(3):119-126.

INTERNATIONAL FOOD INFORMATION COUNCIL. 1990. NAS releases nutrition labeling study. Food Insight Nov.-Dec., p. 7.

INTERNATIONAL HERALD TRIBUNE. 1990. American topics: Farmers cutting back on use of chemicals. May 28, p. 3.

ISI PRESS DIGEST. 1989. Farming and the changing American diet. ISI Press Dig. 31:7-9.

JAVNA, J. 1990. Fast-food containers threaten ozone layer. Minneapolis Star Tribune, Sept. 30, p. 3E.

JONES, J. 1990. Rensi says more burgers will be sold outside U.S. Minneapolis Star Tribune, Oct. 8, p. 8D.

JONES, J. Y., and RICHARDSON, J. 1988. Domestic food assistance: Overview of programs, issues and legislation. Congress. Res. Serv. Library of Congress, CRS issue brief. Nov. 15.

JONES-LEE, M. W., HAMMERTON, M., and PHILIPS, P. R. 1985. The value of safety: Results of a national sample survey. Econ. J. 95(Mar.):49-72.

KALBACHER, J. Z., and BROOKS, N. L. 1990. Farmers are part of American mainstream. Choices. 5(1):22-23.

KANTROWITZ, B. 1990. A heavyweight fuss over the new 'fake fat.' Newsweek, Mar. 5, p. 41.

KENDALL, D. 1989. USDA says salmonella taints at least 1 in 3 chickens. Minneapolis Star Tribune, July 9, p. 2T.

KENNEDY, D. 1988. Humans in the chemical decision chain. Pages 9-19 in: Chemicals in the Human Food Chain: Sources, Options and Public Policy. H. Carter and C. Nuckton, eds. Agric. Issues Center, University of California, Davis.

KERBER, S. 1990. Ice cream remains a frozen favorite. Minneapolis Star Tribune, Mar. 14.

KERR, K. 1989. Consumers sound off on supermarket shopping. Supermarket Business, Sept., p. 55.

KINDER, F., GREEN, N. R., and HARRIS, N. 1984. Meal Management, 6th ed. Macmillan Publishing Co., New York.

KINSEY, J. 1983. Working wives and the marginal propensity to consume food away from home. Am. J. Agric. Econ. 65:10-19.

_____. 1986a. Demographic and lifestyle trends that impact food consumption patterns. Pages 32-43 in: Consumer Demand and Welfare: Implications for Food and Agricultural Policy. J. Kinsey, ed. Univ. of Minnesota Agric. Exp. Stn. Item AD-SB-2718. North Central Regional Res. Publ. 311. March.

_____. 1986b. Consumer's stake in food and agricultural policies. Pages 99-104 in: The American Council on Consumer Interest's 32nd Annu. Conf. Proc.

_____. 1987. Changing food market demographics: Implications for food processors. Cereal Foods World 32(6):425-428.

_____. 1990. Food quality and prices. Pages 143-165 in: Agricultural and Food Policy Issues for the 1990s. R. G. F. Spitze, ed. Dep. Agric. Econ., University of Illinois, Urbana.

KINSEY, J., and COLLINS, M. 1991. The consumer sentiment index: National expectations and behavior. Pages 205-218 in: Enhancing Consumer Choice. R. Mayer, ed. Am. Council on Consumer Interests, Columbia, Mo.

KINSEY, J., and HOUCK, J. 1991. The growing demand for food quality: Implications for international trade. In: Public Goods in International Trade, Food Quality and Environmental Regulation. M. Shane and H. von Witzke, eds. U.S. Dep. Agric. Econ. Res. Serv., Washington, D.C. (In press.)

KIPLINGER AGRICULTURE LETTER. 1987a. Jan. 30.

_____. 1987b. July 2.

_____. 1987c. Sept. 25.

_____. 1987d. Dec. 30.

_____. 1988a. Mar. 11.

_____. 1988b. Mar. 25.

_____. 1988c. Sept. 9.

_____. 1988d. Oct. 7.

_____. 1988e. Dec. 2.

_____. 1989a. Jan. 27.

_____. 1989b. Feb. 3.

_____. 1989c. June 2.

_____. 1989d. Aug. 25.

_____. 1989e. Sept. 9.

_____. 1989f. Oct. 20.

_____. 1989g. Nov. 3.

_____. 1989h. Nov. 30.

_____. 1990a. Feb. 9.

_____. 1990b. Feb. 23.

_____. 1990c. May 4.

_____. 1990d. May 11.

_____. 1990e. June 1.

KLEINMAN, D. 1990. Faster! Faster! Faster! St. Paul Pioneer Press, Jan. 3, p. 10.

KOHLS, R. L., and UHL, J. N. 1985. Marketing of Agricultural Products, 6th ed. Macmillan Publishing Co., New York.

_____. 1990. Marketing of Agricultural Products, 7th ed. Macmillan Publishing Co., New York.

KOHRS, M. B., DZAJKA-NARINS, D. C., and NORDSTROM, J. W. 1989. Factors affecting nutritional status of the elderly. Pages 305-333 in: Nutrition, Aging, and the Elderly. H. N. Munro and D. E. Danford, eds. Plenum Press, New York.

KORB, P. 1987. Comparing international food expenditures. U.S. Dep. Agric., Econ. Res. Serv., Natl. Food Rev. NFR-38, Fall, pp. 18-21.

KORB, P., and COCHRANE, N. 1989. World food expenditures. U.S. Dep. Agric., Econ. Res. Serv., Natl. Food Rev. 12(4):26-29.

KOTEN, J. 1984. Fast-food firms: New items undergo exhaustive testing. Wall Street J. Jan. 5, p. 21.

_____. 1987. Upheaval in middle-class market forces changes in selling strategies. Wall Street J. Mar. 13, p. 21.

KRAMER, C. S. 1988. Food safety: Consumer preferences, policy options, research needs. Pages 143-170 in: Consumer Demands in the Marketplace: Public Policies Related to Food Safety, Quality and Human Health. K. Clancy, ed. Natl. Center for Food and Agric. Policy, Resources for the Future, Washington, D.C.

KRAMER, C. S., and ELLIOTT, B. J. 1989. The consumer's stake in food policy: the United States and the European Community. Disc. Pap. Ser. FAP89-04. Natl. Center for Food and Agric. Policy, Resources for the Future, Washington, D.C. June.

KRAMER, C. S., and PENNER, K.P. 1986. Food safety: Consumers report their concerns. U.S. Dep. Agric., Econ. Res. Serv. Natl. Food Rev. 33(Spring):21-24.

KRIER, B. A. 1989. Overchoice. Los Angeles Times, Feb. 12, Part VI, p. 1.

KRISSOFF, B. 1989. The European ban on livestock hormones and the implications for international trade. U.S. Dep. Agric., Econ. Res. Serv., Natl. Food Rev. 12(3):34-36.

KUTTNER, R. 1989. Economists really should get out more often. Business Week, Apr. 24, p. 16.

LABELL, F. 1990. Microwave oven, flavor systems, packages, enhance eating experience. Food Process. 51(8):128-131.

LABUZA, T. P. 1977. Food and Your Well-being. West Publishing Co., St. Paul, Minn.

LADD, G. W., and SUVANNUNT, V. 1976. A model of consumer goods characteristics. Am. J. Agric. Econ. 58(3):504-510.

LAMBERT, C. 1990. Global spin. Harvard Magazine, Jan.-Feb. pp. 17-30.

LANCASTER, K. J. 1966a. A new approach to consumer theory. J. Political Econ. 74:132-157.

LANCASTER, K. J. 1966b. Change and innovation in the technology of consumption. Am. Econ. Rev. 56:14-23.

LARSON, J. 1990. Farewell to coupons? Am. Demogr. 12(2):14-18.

LAWLER, E. F. 1988. New perspectives on poverty in old age. In: The Public Policy and Aging Report. Policy Research Associates, Inc., Chicago, Ill. 2(1).

LAZER, W., and SHAW, E. H. 1987. How older Americans spend their money. Am. Demogr. 9(Sept.):36-41.

LEE, J. Y., and BROWN, M. G. 1989. Consumer demand for food diversity. South. J. Agric. Econ. 7(Dec.):47-53.

LELYVELD, J. 1985. Hunger in America: The safety net has shrunk but it's still in place. New York Times Magazine, June 16, pp. 20-24, 52-53, 59, 68-69.

LEONARD, R. E. 1982. Nutrition profiles: Diet in the '80s. Comm. Nutr. 1(5):12-17.

LIEB, M. E. 1989. Single-source turns electronic. Food Business, May 8, pp. 46-48.

LEVY, F. 1987. Dollars and Dreams: The Changing American Income Distribution. Russel Sage Foundation, New York.

_____. 1988. Incomes, families, and living standards. Pages 108-153 in: American Living Standards: Threats and Challenges. M. Baily, R. E. Litan, R. Z. Lawrence, and C. L. Schultze, eds. The Brookings Institute, Washington D.C.

LEVY, F., and MICHEL, R. C. 1986. An economic bust for the baby boom. Challenge, Mar.-Apr., pp. 33-39.

LINDER, S. B. 1970. The Harried Leisure Class. Columbia University Press, New York.

LINGLE, R. 1990a. Source reduction, when less is more. Prep. Foods 159(5):217-220.

_____. 1990b. Packaging reminiscences: The year in review. Prep. Foods New Prod.

Annu. 159(8):55-61.

LIPMAN, J. 1989. TV ads' influence found wanting. Wall Street J. Feb. 15, p. B6.

LITAN, R. E., LAWRENCE, R. Z., and SCHULTZE, C. L. 1988. Improving American living standards. Brookings Rev. 7(1):23-31.

LITWAK, D., and CEPEDA, J. T. 1989. 42nd annual consumer expenditures study. Supermarket Business, Sept., p. 56.

LOWRANCE, W. W. 1976. Of Acceptable Risk: Science and Determination of Safety. William Kaufman, Los Altos, Calif.

LUBIN, J. S. 1986. Rise in never-marrieds affects social customs and buying patterns. Wall Street J. May 28.

MAGNUSON, K. M. 1985. Uses and functionality of vital wheat gluten. Cereal Foods World 30(2):179-181.

MANCHESTER, A. 1987. Developing an Integrated Information System for the Food Sector. U.S. Dep. Agric., Econ. Res. Serv., Commodity Econ. Div. Agric. Econ. Rep. 575. Washington, D.C.

———. 1990. Data for Demand Analysis: Availability, Characteristics, Options. U.S. Dep. Agric., Econ. Res. Serv., Commodity Econ. Div. Agric. Econ. Rep. 613. Washington, D.C.

MANGES, M. 1989. Trying to lure back seafood consumers. Wall Street J. June 27, p. B1.

MARCOTTY, J. 1990. Survivor Hormel carving a new niche. Minneapolis Star Tribune, May 7, p. 1D.

MARINUCCI, C. 1990. If times get hard, firms may switch from ads to coupons. Minneapolis Star Tribune, Sept. 17, p. 3D.

MARION, B. W. 1986. The Organization and Performance of the U.S. Food System. Lexington Books, Lexington, Mass.

MARTIN, R. E. 1988. Seafood products, technology and research in the U.S. Food Technol. 42(3):58-62.

MAURICE, C. S., and SMITHSON, C. W. 1988. Managerial Economics, 3rd ed. Irwin, Homewood, IL.

MAYER, M. 1990. Scanning the future. Forbes, Oct. 15, pp. 114-117.

MCADAMS, J. 1987. How to use time use diaries. Am. Demogr. 9(Jan.):46-48.

MCCARTHY, C. 1988. Will U.S. forego pretty produce? Minneapolis Star Tribune, July 25, p. 17.

MCCARTHY, M. J. 1990. Restaurants search for winning recipes. Wall Street J. Jan. 29, p. B1.

MCCRACKEN, V. A., and BRANDT, J. A. 1987. Household consumption of food-away-from-home: Total expenditure and by type of food facility. Am. J. Agric. Econ. 69(2):274-284.

MCGLOUGHLIN, I. 1983. The scanner revolution–collection of purchasing data from consumer panel households. Proc. Am. Stat. Assoc. Annu. Mtg. pp. 719-720.

MEHEGAN, D. 1988. Baby boom gives retailers a jolt. St. Paul Pioneer Press, Sept. 24, p. 5B.

MEINERS, J., and HELTSLEY, M. E. 1985. The Rural Elderly: Shopping Patterns and Attitudes. Proc. 25th Annu. Western Regional Home Management/Family Economics Educators Conf., Scottsdale, Ariz.

MEYERHOFF, A. 1989. Poisons in the food we eat. Minneapolis Star Tribune, May 18, p. 25A.

MEYERS, M. 1989. ScanAmerica trying to peer into America's mind. Minneapolis Star Tribune, Feb. 5, pp. 1D, 3D.

MIDDLEKAUFF, R. D. 1988. Issues of food safety and quality relating to food ingredients. Pages 45-49 in: Consumer Demands in the Marketplace: Public Policies Related to

Food Safety, Quality and Human Health. K. Clancy, ed. Natl. Center for Food and Agric. Policy, Resources for the Future, Washington, D.C.

_____. 1989. Regulating the safety of food. Food Technol. 43(9):296-307.

MINNEAPOLIS STAR TRIBUNE. 1987a. May 5, p. 1T.

_____. 1987b. Experts say trash crisis will soon be upon us. Nov. 16.

_____. 1987c. Education of U.S. adults climbs steeply in 45 years. Dec. 2.

_____. 1988a. Report: U.S. policies encourage fat in foods. Apr. 6, p. 1A.

_____. 1988b. Tidbits. June 29, p. 1T.

_____. 1988c. Oct. 26, p. 1T.

_____. 1988d. Study says almost 600,000 homeless. Nov. 4, p. 17A.

_____. 1989a. What's bugging you? It may be something you ate. Apr. 21, p. 6A.

_____. 1989b. Plastic money comes to fast food. May 1, p. 4B.

_____. 1989c. 13 convicted in cooking-oil deaths trial. May 21, p. 11A.

_____. 1989d. Tidbits. June 14, p. 1T.

_____. 1989e. Hard liquor sales slide in 18-year low in 1988. Aug. 16.

_____. 1989f. Science board wants U.S. to stop promoting agricultural chemicals. Sept. 8, p. 1A.

_____. 1989g. Survey finds third of homeless dependent on drugs or alcohol. Oct. 11, p. 7A.

_____. 1989h. California ballot measure proposes broad steps to protect air, food, and water. Oct. 11.

_____. 1989i. Healthy, wealthy tend to be wise about nutrition. Oct. 24.

_____. 1989j. Bush to propose pesticide rule change. Oct. 26, p. 7A.

_____. 1989k. Report says homeless include more families, addicts. Dec. 21, p. 7A.

_____. 1990a. U.S. Diet panel urges major shift toward less fat and cholesterol. Feb. 28.

_____. 1990b. We're still overweight and not exercising enough. June 5.

_____. 1990c. Diet better but must improve. Oct. 16, p. 7A.

_____. 1990d. Hey baby boomers: Make way for organic coffee and 'gourmet ice.' Oct. 29.

_____. 1990e. Governments' revised dietary guidelines include 'waist to hip' ratio, fat intake limited. Nov. 6.

MINNESOTA FOOD EDUCATION AND RESOURCE CENTER. 1985. Homegrown Hunger: A Study of People Who Use Emergency Food Shelves in Minnesota. A project of the Urban Coalition of Minneapolis. Dec.

MITCHELL, A. 1983. The Nine American Lifestyles: Who We Are and Where We Are Going. Macmillan Publishing Co., New York.

MITCHELL, R. 1989. With a little bit of luck, farmers could clean up. Business Week, Jan. 9, p. 99.

MONSEN, E. R. 1987. The Journal adopts SI units for clinical laboratory values. J. Am. Diet. Assoc. 87:356-378.

_____. 1989. The 10th edition of the recommended dietary allowances: What's new in the 1989 RDAs? J. Am. Diet. Assoc. 89:1748-1752.

MONSON, G. 1990. Paint by the number portrait. Minneapolis Star Tribune, Jan. 11, p. 1E.

MOORE, C. 1989. Fast-food chains make play for kids with toy premiums. Minneapolis Star Tribune, Nov. 13.

MOORE, T. J. 1989. The cholesterol myth. Atlantic Monthly, Sept., pp. 37-70.

MORGAN, K. J., METZEN, E. J., and JOHNSON, S. R. 1979. An hedonic index for breakfast cereals. J. Consumer Res. 6:67-75.

MORRIS, B. 1984. Study to detect true eating habits finds junk-food fans in the health-food ranks. Wall Street J. Feb. 3, p. 19.

_____. 1988a. Are square meals headed for extinction? Wall Street J. Apr. 29, p. 16.

_____. 1988b. Coke and Pepsi step up bitter price war. Wall Street J. Oct. 10, p. B1.

MORRISON, R. M. 1990. The market for fat substitutes. U.S. Dep. Agric., Econ. Res. Serv., Natl. Food Rev. 13(2):24-30.

MUELLER, W. 1989. Are Americans eating better? Am. Demogr. 11(Feb):30-33.

MUNRO, H. N. 1980. Major gaps in nutrient allowances. J. Am. Diet. Assoc. 76:137-141.

_____. 1989. The challenges of research into nutrition and aging: Introduction to a multifaceted problem. Pages 1-21 in: Nutrition, Aging, and the Elderly. H. N. Munro and D. E. Danford, eds. Plenum Press: New York.

MYERS, D. 1987. How to ride the local demographic waves. Am. Demogr. April, pp. 48-51.

NAISBITT, J. 1982. Megatrends. Warner Books, New York.

NATIONAL ACADEMY OF SCIENCES, COMMITTEE ON THE SCIENTIFIC BASIS OF THE NATION'S MEAT AND POULTRY INSPECTION PROGRAM. 1985. Meat and Poultry Inspection: The Scientific Basis of the Nation's Program. Natl. Acad. Press, Washington, D.C.

NATIONAL ACADEMY OF SCIENCES, NATIONAL RESEARCH COUNCIL, COMMITTEE ON DIET, NUTRITION AND CANCER. 1982. Diet, Nutrition and Cancer. Natl. Acad. Press, Washington, D.C.

NATIONAL COMMISSION ON FOOD MARKETING. 1966. Food from Farmer to Consumer. U.S. Government Printing Office. June.

NATIONAL CHOLESTEROL EDUCATION PROGRAM. 1990. Report of the National Cholesterol Education Program Expert Panel on Population Strategies for Blood Cholesterol Reduction. U.S. Dep. Health and Human Services, Public Health Service, National Institutes of Health, National Heart, Lung and Blood Institute, Bethesda, Md.

NATIONAL DAIRY COUNCIL. 1981. The food group approach to good eating. Dairy Council Dig. 52(6):31-36.

_____. 1987. Nutrition advice for the healthy United States population. Dairy Council Dig. 58(6):31-36.

_____. 1989. Recommended dietary allowances. Dairy Council Dig. 60(6):31-38.

NATIONAL DECISION SYSTEMS. 1987. VISION Marketing Guide. Book 1. Natl. Decision Systems, Encinitas, CA.

_____. 1988. VISION Target Marketing Systems. Natl. Decision Systems, Encinitas, CA.

_____. 1989. Your Single Source Guide for Demographic and Marketing Information. Natl. Decision Systems, Encinitas, Calif., 1989.

NATIONAL RESEARCH COUNCIL, BOARD ON AGRICULTURE, COMMITTEE ON TECHNOLOGICAL OPTIONS TO IMPROVE THE NUTRITIONAL ATTRIBUTES OF ANIMAL PRODUCTS. 1988. Designing Foods: Animal Product Options in the Marketplace. Natl. Acad. Press, Washington, D.C.

NATIONAL RESEARCH COUNCIL, COMMITTEE ON DIET AND HEALTH. 1989a. Diet and Health. Natl. Acad. Press, Washington, D.C.

NATIONAL RESEARCH COUNCIL, COMMISSION ON LIFE SCIENCES, FOOD AND NUTRITION BOARD, SUBCOMMITTEE ON THE TENTH EDITION OF THE RDAS. 1989b. Recommended Dietary Allowances, 10th ed. Natl. Acad. Press, Washington, D.C.

NATIONAL RESEARCH COUNCIL, FOOD AND NUTRITION BOARD. 1980. Toward Healthful Diets. Natl. Acad. Press, Washington, D.C.

NATIONAL RESTAURANT ASSOCIATION. 1978. N.R.A. Rep. 21:1.

NATIONAL SAFETY COUNCIL. 1987. Accident Facts, 1987 Edition. Chicago.

NAZARIO, S. L. 1989a. Big firms get high on organic farming. Wall Street J. Mar. 21, p. B1.

_____. 1989b. EPA under fire for pesticide standards. Wall Street J. Feb. 17, p. B1.

_____ . 1990. Microwave packages that add crunch to lunch may also pose chemical risks. Wall Street J. Mar. 1, p. B1.

NELSON, P. 1970. Information and consumer behavior. J. Political Econ. 78:311-329.

NESTLE, M. 1988. The Surgeon General's report on nutrition and health: New federal dietary guidance policy. J. Nutr. Ed. 20(5):252-254.

NEW YORK TIMES. 1989. New study finds the poor getting poorer, younger and more urban. Mar. 12.

NIXON, D. W. 1990. Nutrition and cancer: American Cancer Society guidelines, programs, and initiatives. CA—A Cancer Journal for Clinicians 40(2):71-75.

NOBLE, K. B. 1986. Nearly half of U.S. married mothers work. St. Paul Pioneer Press, Mar. 17.

NUTRITION TODAY. 1988. The Surgeon General's report on nutrition and health. Nutr. Today 23(5):22-30.

NYBERG, B. 1989. Grocery chains ban milk from cows given growth drug. St. Paul Pioneer Press, Aug. 24, p. 1A.

O'BEIRNE, D. 1988. A corresponding viewpoint: Some food safety and quality issues in the European community. Pages 177-187 in: Consumer Demands in the Marketplace: Public Policies Related to Food Safety, Quality and Human Health. K. Clancy, ed. Natl. Center for Food and Agric. Policy, Resources for the Future: Washington, D.C.

O'REILLY, B. 1989. New truths about staying healthy. Fortune, Sept. 25, pp. 57-66.

ORGANIZATION FOR ECONOMIC COOPERATION AND DEVELOPMENT. 1986. Food Consumption Statistics, 1973–1982. The Organization, Paris.

OSTEEN, C. D., and SZMEDRA, P. I. 1989. Agricultural pesticide use trends and policy issues. U.S. Dep. Agric., Econ. Res. Serv., Agric. Econ. Rep. 622.

OSTENSO, G. L. 1984. National nutrition monitoring system: A historical perspective. J. Am. Diet. Assoc. 84:1181-1185.

OSTMAN, E. 1990. Onward and upward in the kitchen. St. Paul Pioneer Press, Jan. 3, p. 10.

OTTEN, A. L. 1984. Ever more Americans live into 80s and 90s, causing big problems. Wall Street J. July 30, pp. 1 and 10.

_____ . 1986. Deceptive picture: If you see families staging a comeback, it's probably a mirage. Wall Street J. Sept. 25, p. 1.

_____ . 1988. People patterns. Wall Street J. Nov. 10, p. B1.

_____ . 1989. Cohabiting didn't start with college kids. Wall Street J. April 6.

_____ . 1990a. People patterns. Wall Street J. Feb. 20.

_____ . 1990b. The 80's merger mania applies to families, too. Wall Street J. Feb. 20.

_____ . 1990c. People patterns. Wall Street J. Dec. 24.

OWEN, A. L. 1990. The impact of future foods on nutrition and health. J. Am. Diet. Assoc. 90:1217-1222.

PARIS, J. A. 1985. The group quarters. Am. Demogr. 7(Feb.):34-37.

PAARLBERG, D. 1980. Farm and Food Policy: Issues of the 1980s. University of Nebraska Press, Lincoln.

PADBERG, D. I. 1977. Non-use benefits of mandatory consumer information programs. J. Consumer Policy 1:6-13.

PARK, Y. K., and YETLEY, E. A. 1990. Trend changes in use and current intakes of tropical oils in the United States. Am. J. Clin. Nutr. 51:738-748.

PASSELL, P. 1989. For safety's sake. St. Paul Pioneer Press, May 21, p. G1.

PEAR, R. 1990. Welfare on rise, reflecting slump in economy of U.S. New York Times, Aug. 20, p. A1.

PENNER, K. 1989. The free market has triumphed, but what about the losers. Business Week, Sept. 25, p. 178.

PENNINGTON, J. A. T. 1983. Revision of the Total Diet Study food lists and diets. J. Am. Diet. Assoc. 82:166-173.

PENNINGTON, J. A. T., and GUNDERSON, E. L. 1987. History of the food and drug administration's Total Diet Study. J. Assoc. Anal. Chem. 70:772-782.

PETERKIN, B. G. 1982. Presentation at Session 25, 1983 Agricultural Outlook Conference. Consumer Nutrition Center. U.S. Dep. Agric., HNIS: Washington, D.C.

PETERKIN, B. B., and RIZEK, R. L. 1984. National nutrition monitoring system. Family Econ. Rev. 4:15-19.

PETERKIN, B. B., RIZEK, R. L., and TIPPETT, K. S. 1988. Nationwide food consumption survey, 1987. Nutr. Today 23(1):18-24.

PHELPS, D. 1987. Study questions safety of U.S. meat imports. Minneapolis Star Tribune, Nov. 14, p. 1A.

PHYSICIAN TASK FORCE ON HUNGER IN AMERICA. 1985. Hunger in America: the Growing Epidemic. Wesleyan University Press: Middletown, CT.

PIERSON, T. R., and ALLEN, J. W. 1988. Directions in Food Marketing: Responding to Consumers of Tomorrow. Annu. Agric. Outlook Conf., U.S. Dep. Agric., Washington, D.C., Nov. 29.

PILLSBURY COMPANY. 1988. What's Cookin', A Pillsbury Study of Trends in American Eating Behavior. Consumer Communications. The Pillsbury Company: Minneapolis, Minn.

PINSTRUP-ANDERSEN, P. 1986. Changing patterns of consumption underlying changes in trade and agricultural development. Paper prepared for the meeting of the Int. Agric. Trade Res. Consortium, CIMMYT, El Batan, Mexico, Dec. 1986. Int. Food Policy Res. Inst., Washington, D.C.

PITTS, J. M. 1989. Expenditures of black households—Housing, transportation, food and clothing. Fam. Econ. Rev. 2(3):8-12.

PLESSER, D. R., SIEGEL, M. A., JACOBS, N. R., eds. 1988. Growing Old in America. Information Aids, Inc., Plano, Texas.

POGREBIN, R. 1988. Among the elderly, togetherness is selling. New York Times, Aug. 28.

POLMAN, D. 1989. Fiftysomething? It's hip to be old, new ads croon. Des Moines Register, Aug. 26.

PORUBCANSKY, M. J. 1989. Yeltsin gives life in the U.S. rave reviews. St. Paul Pioneer Press, Sept. 24, p. 2A.

PREPARED FOODS. 1989. Is food shopping a state of mind? Prep. Foods 158(5):77.

PRESIDENT'S TASK FORCE ON FOOD ASSISTANCE. 1984. Report of the President's Task Force on Food Assistance. Washington, D.C., Jan.

PRICE, C. 1988. Take-out food in convenience stores. U.S. Dep. Agric., Econ. Res. Serv., Natl. Food Rev. 11(4):14-17.

PRICE, C. C., and NEWTON, D. J. 1986. Supermarket characteristics: A continual evolution. U.S. Dep. Agric., Econ. Res. Serv., Natl. Food Rev. 35(Fall):20-22.

PRICE, D. 1988. Estimating food use by age, sex and household size. Res. Bull. XB1002. Washington State University, Pullman.

PROCHASKA, F. J., and SCHRIMPER, R. A. 1973. Opportunity cost of time and other socioeconomic effects on away-from-home food consumption. Am. J. Agric. Econ. 55:595-603.

PUTNAM, J. J. 1989a. Food consumption, prices and expenditures, 1966–1987. Stat. Bull. 773. U.S. Dep. Agric., Econ. Res. Serv., Washington, D.C.

_____. 1989b. Food consumption. U.S. Dep. Agric., Econ. Res. Serv., Natl. Food Rev. 12(2):1-9.

_____. 1990a. Food consumption, prices and expenditures, 1967–88. Stat. Bull. 804. U.S. Dep. Agric., Econ. Res. Serv., Washington, D.C.

_____. 1990b. Food consumption. U.S. Dep. Agric., Econ. Res. Serv., Natl. Food Rev. 13(3):1-9.

PUZE, D. P. 1989. Ignorance blamed for most U.S. food-borne illnesses. Minneapolis Star Tribune, Jan. 11, p. 5T.

RAPER, N., and MARSTON, R. 1988. Nutrient Content of the U.S. Food Supply. HNIS Admin. Rep. 299-21. U.S. Dep. Agric., HNIS, Washington, D.C.

RAUNIKAR, R., and HUANG, C. L. 1987. Food Demand Analysis. Iowa State University Press, Ames.

REEVES, J. B., and WEIHRAUCH, J. L. 1979. Composition of Foods. Agric. Handb. 8-4. U.S. Dep. Agric., Washington, D.C.

REYNOLDS, P. D., and SPONAUGLE, G. C. 1982. A Guide to Survey Research: How to Plan a Survey, Estimate Costs, and Use a Survey Research Service. Publ. CURA 82-4. Center for Urban and Regional Affairs, Minneapolis, Minn.

RICH, S. 1986. Most mothers still stay home while children are under 18. Washington Post, Nov. 2.

_____. 1987. Hyping the family's decline. Washington Post, July 26.

_____. 1990. Data give portrait of working poor. St. Paul Pioneer Press, Jan. 7, p. 8G.

RICHARDS, B. 1989. Sour reception greets milk hormone. Wall Street J. Sept. 15, p. B1.

RICHE, M. F. 1987. Mysterious young adults. Am. Demogr. 9(Feb.):38-43.

_____. 1988a. America's new workers. Am. Demogr. 10(Feb.):34-38.

_____. 1988b. The postmarital society. Am. Demogr. 10(Nov.):23-26,60.

_____. 1989. Psychographics for the 1990s. Am. Demogr. 11(7):24-26, 30-31, 53.

_____. 1990. Look before leaping. Am. Demogr. 12(2):18-20.

RITSON, C., GOFTON, L., and MCKENZIE, J. 1986. The Food Consumer. John Wiley and Sons, New York.

RIZEK, R. L., and POSATI, L. P. 1985. Continuing survey of food intakes by individuals. Family Econ. Rev. 1:16-17.

ROBE, K. 1990. Completely automated warehouse: The low-cost solution. Food Process. 51(4):93-94,96,98,100-101.

ROBERTS, T. 1989. Human illness costs of foodborne bacteria. Am. J. Agric. Econ. 71:468-474.

ROBERTS, T., and VAN RAVENSWAAY, E. 1989. The economics of food safety. U.S. Dep. Agric., Econ. Res. Serv., Natl. Food Rev. 12(3):1-8.

ROBICHAUX, M. 1989. Boom in fancy coffee pits big marketers, little firms. Wall Street J. Nov. 6.

ROBINSON, J. P. 1976. Changes in America's use of time, 1965–1975. Rep. Communication Research Center, Cleveland State University.

_____. 1989. Time's up. Am. Demogr. 11(July):33-35.

ROGAN, A., and GLAROS, G. 1988. Food irradiation: The process and implications of dietitians. J. Am. Diet. Assoc. 88:833-838.

ROSENBERGER, A. T. 1979. Estimates of income specific price response for policy analysis. Mimeo. Dep. Nutrition, Cornell University, Ithaca.

ROSEVILLE AREA SCHOOLS, DISTRICT 623, MINNESOTA. 1989. School Newsletter. July 19.

ROSEWICZ, B. 1989. Pesticide risk from apples: Who's right? Wall Street J. Mar. 10, p. B1.

ROTHENBERG, R. 1988. Time-savers don't lure older buyers, sellers find. Minneapolis Star Tribune, June 29.

ROUNDS, T. Q. 1988. Where in the world have you been? Am. Demogr. 10(May):30-33.

RUNGE, C. F. 1989. Trade in disservices: Environmental regulation and agricultural trade competitiveness. Staff Pap. P89-23. Dep. Agric. Appl. Econ., University of Minnesota, St. Paul.

RUNYON, K. E. 1977. Consumer Behavior and the Practices of Marketing. Charles E. Merrill Publishing, Columbus, Ohio.

SACHS, S. 1989. Safe meat and poultry. U.S. Dep. Agric., Econ. Res. Serv., Natl. Food Rev. 12(3):31-33.

SALATHE, L. 1979. Demographics and food consumption. U.S. Dep. Agric., Econ. Stat. Coop. Serv., Natl. Food Rev. 8(Fall):31-33.

SANJUR, D. 1982. Social and Cultural Perspectives in Nutrition. Prentice-Hall, Inc., Englewood Cliffs, N.J.

SANSOLO, M. 1989. Rethinking the shopper. Prog. Grocer 68(5):63-66.

SCHILLER, Z. 1989. Stalking the new consumer: as markets fracture, P & G, and others sharpen micro marketing. Business Week, Aug. 28, pp. 54-62.

SCHLOSBERG, J. 1987. The demographics of dieting. Am. Demogr. 9(July):35-62.

SCHMICKLE, S. 1989a. Biotechnology gives rise to debate on food safety. Minneapolis Star Tribune, Mar. 27, p. 1A.

_____ . 1989b. Co-op won't take milk from cows treated with hormone. Minneapolis Star Tribune, Aug. 30, p. 1A.

_____ . 1989c. Huge agricultural research effort sought. Minneapolis Star Tribune, Oct. 6, 1989, p. 5B.

_____ . 1990a. Farmers forced to consider whether livestock is fat-and-happy. Minneapolis Star Tribune, Jan. 14, p. 1A.

_____ . 1990b. City dwellers have more to say on farm bill. Minneapolis Star Tribune, May 6, p. 5B.

_____ . 1990c. FDA delays approving bovine drug for a year. Minneapolis Star Tribune, Apr. 24, p. 7B.

_____ . 1990d. FDA OK's irradiation, but poultry industry balks. Minneapolis Star Tribune, May 2, p. 1A.

_____ . 1990e. Report finds irradiation inspection data lacking. Minneapolis Star Tribune, May 5, p. 6A.

SCHUBRING, R. 1989. Who are your customers? Minnesota Grocer 4(3):15-17.

SCHULTZ, D. E. 1989. Sorting out your options in electronic marketing. Presented at the Food Marketing Institute 1989 Supermarket Industry Convention, May 7-10, Chicago, Ill.

SCHULTZ, T. W. 1961. Investment in human capital. Am. Econ. Rev. 51(1):1-17.

SCHUR, S. 1989. Revolution in the kitchen. Supermarket Business, Sept., pp. 46-50.

SCHWADEL, F. 1989a. Consumer trust: An elusive quarry. Wall Street J. Sept. 20. p. B1.

SCHWADEL, F. 1989b. Dropouts cite poor service, tight schedules. Wall Street J. Oct. 13.

SCHWARTZ, J. 1988. Hispanics in the eighties. Am. Demogr. 10(Jan.):43-45.

_____ . 1989. Back to the source. Am. Demogr. 11(1):22-26.

SCHWARTZ, J., and EXTER, T. 1989. All our children. Am. Demogr. 11(May):34-37.

SCHWARTZ, J., and HOWARD, J. 1989. Move over, moo shu pork. Business Week, Feb. 20, p. 42.

SCHWENK, F. N. 1981. Two measures of inflation: The consumer price index and the personal consumption expenditure implicit price deflator. U.S. Dep. Agric., Sci. Educ. Admin., Fam. Econ. Rev. Winter, pp. 13-18.

SCHWERIN, H. S., STANTON, J. L., RILEY, A. M., and BRETT, B. E. 1981. How have the quantity and quality of the American diet changed during the past decade? Food Technol. 35(9):50-57.

SCIENCE. 1987. Industry toxicologists keen on reducing animal use. Science 236:252.

SENAUER, B. 1982. The current status of food and nutrition policy and the food programs. Am. J. Agric. Econ. 64:1009-1016.

_____ . 1986. Economics and nutrition. Pages 46-57 in: What is America Eating? National Research Council, Food and Nutrition Board. Natl. Acad. Press, Washington, D.C.

SENAUER, B., and YOUNG, N. 1986. The impact of food stamps on food expenditures: Rejection of the traditional model. Am. J. Agric. Econ. 68:37-43.

SENAUER, B., SAHN, D., and ALDERMAN, H. 1986. The effect of the value of time on food consumption patterns in developing countries: Evidence from Sri Lanka. Am. J. Agric. Econ. 68:920-927.

SEXAUER, B., and MANN, J. S. 1979. Food Expenditure Patterns of Single Person Households. U.S. Dep. Agric., Econ. Stat. Coop. Serv., Agric. Econ. Rep. 428. Washington, D.C.

SHABECOFF, P. 1989. The nation is getting ready to cut its dose of pesticides. New York Times, Apr. 16, p. E6.

SHAPIRO, E. 1990a. Con Agra moving toward head of table. Minneapolis Star Tribune, June 17, p. 1D.

———. 1990b. The people who are putting taste back on the table. New York Times, July 22, p. 5.

SHAPIRO, L. 1988. Health or hype? Newsweek, Feb. 22, pp. 67-68.

———. 1990. The zap generation. Newsweek, Feb. 26, pp. 56-57.

SHERATON, M. 1988. Taking out, eating in. Time, Apr. 11, pp. 75-76.

SHERMAN, E., and SCHIFFMAN, L. 1984. Applying age-gender theory from social gerontology to understand the consumer well-being of the elderly. Pages 569-573 in: Advances in Consumer Research, Vol. 2. T. Kinnear, ed. Association for Consumer Research, Provo, Utah.

SHIPP, S. 1988. How singles spend. Am. Demogr. 10(Apr.):22-27.

SHRIMPER, R. 1986. Effects of increasing elderly population on future food demands and consumption. Pages 163-176 in: Food Demand Analysis. O. Capps, Jr., and B. Senauer, eds. Southern Regional Research Committee and Farm Foundation: Blacksburg, Va.

SIEBER, J. N. 1988. Sources: Nonpesticides. Pages 23-36 in: Chemicals in the Human Food Chain: Sources, Options and Public Policy. H. O. Carter and C. F. Nuckson, eds. Agric. Issues Center, University of California, Davis.

SILLS-LEVY, E. 1989. U.S. food trends leading to the year 2000. Food Technol. 42(4):128-132.

SIMON, J. L. 1989. The Economic Consequences of Immigration. Basil Blackwell, New York.

SIMS, L. S. 1988a. Contributions of the U.S. Department of Agriculture. Am. J. Clin. Nutr. 47:329-332.

SIMS, L. S. 1988b. Nutrition Policy Through the Reagan Era: Feast or Famine. PEW/Cornell Lecture Ser. Food and Nutrition Policy, Cornell University, Ithaca. Nov. 1.

SINCLAIR, U. 1906. The Jungle. Doubleday/Page, New York.

SLOVIC, P. 1987. Perception of risk. Science 236:280-285.

SLOVUT, G. 1989. Wisconsin cheesemaker is source of salmonella, says Minnesota official. Minneapolis Star Tribune, Sept. 2, p. 1A.

SMALLWOOD, D., and BLAYLOCK, J. 1981. Impact of household size and income on food spending patterns. U.S. Dep. Agric., Econ. Res. Serv. Tech. Bull. 1650. Washington, D.C.

SMEEDING, T. 1984. Non-money income and the elderly: The case of the 'tweeners.' Institute for Research on Poverty, University of Wisconsin, Madison.

SMITH, B. J., and YONKERS, R. D. 1990. The importance of cereal to fluid milk consumption. Marketing Res. Rep. 8, AE&RS 211. Pennsylvania State University, University Park.

SMITH, B. J., HERRMANN, R. O., and WARLAND, R. H. 1990. Milk consumption and consumer concerns about fat, cholesterol, and calories. Marketing Res. Rep. 7, AE&RS 210. Pennsylvania State University, University Park.

SOLOMON, J. 1989. Firms address workers cultural variety. Wall Street J. Feb. 10.

SPENCER, G. 1986. Projections of the Hispanic population: 1983 to 2080. Current

Population Rep., Ser. P-25, no. 995. U.S. Dep. Commerce, Bureau of the Census. U.S. Government Printing Office, Washington, D.C.

SPRINGER, K., SCHWARTZ, J., and MILLER, A. 1990. How low can they go? Newsweek, Aug. 20, pp. 66-67.

SRI INTERNATIONAL. 1989. Descriptive materials for the VALS 2 segmentation system. SRI International, Menlo Park, CA.

ST. PAUL PIONEER PRESS. 1988a. Aug. 12, p. 3A.

_____. 1988b. Men do more at home, but not whole lot. Nov. 30.

_____. 1990. First genetic food enzyme wins government OK. Mar. 25, p. 18A.

STEINBURG, B. 1983. The mass market is splitting apart. Fortune, Nov. 28, pp. 76-82.

STIGLER, G. J. 1961. The economics of information. J. Political Econ. 64(3):213-225.

_____. 1966. The Theory of Price, 3rd ed. Macmillan Publishing Co., New York.

STIGLER, G., and BECKER, G. S. 1977. De gustibus non est disputandum. Am. Econ. Rev. 67(2):76-90.

STIMMANN, M. 1988. Sources: Pesticides. In: Chemicals in the Human Food Chain: Sources, Options and Public Policy. H. Carter and C. Nuckson, eds. Agric. Issues Center, University of California, Davis.

STIPP, H. H. 1988. What is a working woman? Am. Demogr. 10(July):24-27,59.

STIPP, D. 1989. Apple of our eye could soon have made in Japan tag. Wall Street J. Oct. 25, p. A16.

_____. 1990. Science is pushing heart disease's toll farther into old age. Wall Street J. Jan. 24.

STOVER, J. 1989. The latest figures on world population growth. Challenge, July-Aug., p. 56.

STUCKER, T. A., FALLERT, R. F., and LIPTON, K. L. 1986. Bovine growth hormone brings progress to dairy farms. U.S. Dep. Agric., Econ. Res. Serv., Natl. Food Rev. 35(Fall):12-15.

SUPERMARKET BUSINESS. 1989. Helping elderly shoppers. Sept., p. 53.

SWASY, A. 1989. Despite skepticism, a once-lowly bran now aspires to the level of oat cuisine. Wall Street J. Mar. 28, p. B1.

_____. 1990. You can slice it, dice it, or ice it, but to some it'll still be the pits. Wall Street J. April 5.

SWASY, A., and STRICHARCHUK, G. 1988. Grocery chains pressure supplier for uniform prices. Wall Street J. Oct. 21, p. B1.

TANNAHILL, R. 1988. Food in History. Penguin Books, London.

THAYER, A. M. 1990. Dependable plastics generate controversy in solid waste issues. Chem. Eng. News 68(26):7-14.

THE ECONOMIST. 1988. The year of the brand. Dec. 24, pp. 95-100.

_____. 1989a. Mar. 4, p. 68.

_____. 1989b. Farming: Green land. Nov. 4, pp. 36-37.

_____. 1990a. Good times are back on the farm, for a bit. Mar. 10, pp. 25-26.

_____. 1990b. Mad cows and ministry men. May 19, p. 24.

THERRIEN, L. 1989. Want shelf space at the supermarket? Ante up. Business Week, Aug. 7, p. 60-61.

TOMEK, W. G., and ROBINSON, K. L. 1972. Agricultural Product Prices. Cornell University Press, Ithaca.

TOMLINSON, R. 1984. Where population control cuts a different way. Wall Street J. June 20.

TONGREN, H. N. 1988. Determinant behavior characteristics of older consumers. J. Consumer Affairs 22:136-157.

TOWNSEND, B., and RICHE, M. F. 1987. Two paychecks and seven lifestyles. Am. Demogr. 9(Aug.):24-29.

TRAVIS, C. 1987. Old age is not what it used to be. Good Health Magazine, Sept. 27, p. 25.

UNITED FRESH FRUIT AND VEGETABLE ASSOCIATION. 1988. The Produce Industry Fact Book. The Association, Alexandria, VA.

_____. 1989. Produce, Pesticides, and Perceptions. The Association, Alexandria, VA.

USDA. *See* U.S. Department of Agriculture.

U.S. DEPARTMENT OF AGRICULTURE. 1988. Agricultural Statistics 1988. U.S. Government Printing Office, Washington, D.C.

_____. 1989. Agricultural Statistics 1989. U.S. Government Printing Office, Washington, D.C.

U.S. DEPARTMENT OF AGRICULTURE AND U.S. DEPARTMENT OF HEALTH AND HUMAN SERVICES. 1990. Nutrition and Your Health: Dietary Guidelines for Americans, 3rd ed. Home Gard. Bull. 232. Washington, D.C.

U.S. DEPARTMENT OF AGRICULTURE, AGRICULTURAL MARKETING SERVICE. 1981. A Review of Federal Marketing Orders for Fruits, Vegetables and Specialty Crops: Economic Efficiency and Welfare Implications. Agric. Econ. Rep. 477. Washington, D.C.

U.S. DEPARTMENT OF AGRICULTURE, AGRICULTURAL RESEARCH SERVICE. 1958. Food for Fitness, a Daily Food Guide. Leafl. 424. Washington, D.C.

_____. 1963. Composition of Foods—Raw, Processed, Prepared. Agric. Handb. 8. Washington, D.C.

_____. 1976–1989. Composition of Foods—Raw, Processed, Prepared. Rev. Agric. Handb. 8-1 to 8-17, 8-20, 8-21. U.S. Government Printing Office, Washington, D.C.

_____. 1989. Cost of food at home. Fam. Econ. Rev. 2(2):26.

U.S. DEPARTMENT OF AGRICULTURE, BUREAU OF AGRICULTURAL ECONOMICS. 1949. Consumption of Food in the United States, 1909–48. Misc. Publ. 691. Washington, D.C.

U.S. DEPARTMENT OF AGRICULTURE, ECONOMIC RESEARCH SERVICE. 1981. Food Consumption, Prices and Expenditures, 1960–80. Stat. Bull. 672. Washington, D.C.

_____. 1984. Oil Crops, Situation and Outlook Rep. U.S. Dep. Agric., Econ. Res. Serv. OCS-8. Washington, D.C.

_____. 1985. Food Consumption, Prices, and Expenditures, 1964–84. Stat. Bull. 736. Washington, D.C.

_____. 1988. Food Marketing Review, 1987. Agric. Econ. Rep. 590. Washington, D.C.

_____. 1989a. Economic indicators of the farm sector. Farm Sector Rev., 1987, ECIFS 7-4.

_____. 1989b. Food Marketing Review, 1988. Agric. Econ. Rep. 614. Washington, D.C.

_____. 1989c. Economic Indicators of the Farm Sector: National Financial Summary, 1988. ECIFS 8-1.

_____. 1990a. The government's role in agriculture. U.S. Dep. Agric., Econ. Res. Serv., Natl. Food Rev. 13(1):1.

_____. 1990b. Oil Crops, Situation and Outlook Report. OCS-25.

U.S. DEPARTMENT OF AGRICULTURE, FOOD AND NUTRITION SERVICE. 1986. Evaluation of the Special Supplemental Food Program for Women, Infants, and Children (WIC): Volume I—Summary. Prepared by Research Triangle Institute. U.S. Government Printing Office, Washington, D.C.

_____. 1988. Midwest Region, FNS Food Assistance Programs. Chicago, June.

_____. 1989. Annual Historical Review of FNS Programs—Fiscal Year 1988. U.S. Government Printing Office, Washington, D.C.

U.S. DEPARTMENT OF AGRICULTURE, HUMAN NUTRITION INFORMATION SERVICE. 1987. Research on Survey Methodology. Admin. Rep. 382. Washington, D.C.

_____ . 1989. Preparing Foods and Planning Menus Using the Dietary Guidelines. Home Gard. Bull. 232-8, p. 11. Washington, D.C.

U.S. DEPARTMENT OF AGRICULTURE, HUMAN NUTRITION INFORMATION SERVICE, DIETARY GUIDELINES ADVISORY COMMITTEE. 1990. Report of the Dietary Guidelines Advisory Committee on the Dietary Guidelines for Americans, 1990. U.S. Government Printing Office, Washington, D.C.

U.S. DEPARTMENT OF AGRICULTURE, HUMAN NUTRITION INFORMATION SERVICE, NUTRITION MONITORING DIVISION. 1985. Nationwide Food Consumption Survey, Continuing Survey of Food Intakes by Individuals. Women 19–50 Years and Their Children 1–5 Years, 1 Day, 1985. CSFII Rep. 85-1. Washington, D.C.

_____ . 1986a. Nationwide Food Consumption Survey, Continuing Survey of Food Intakes by Individuals. Low-income Women 19–50 Years and Their Children 1–5 Years, 1 Day, 1985. CSFII Rep. 85-2. Washington, D.C.

_____ . 1986b. Nationwide Food Consumption Survey, Continuing Survey of Food Intakes by Individuals. Men 19–50 Years, 1 Day, 1985. CSFII Rep. 85-3. Washington, D.C.

_____ . 1987a. Nationwide Food Consumption Survey, Continuing Survey of Food Intakes by Individuals. Women 19–50 Years and Their Children 1–5 Years, 1 Day, 1986. CSFII Rep. 86-1. Washington, D.C.

_____ . 1987b. Nationwide Food Consumption Survey, Continuing Survey of Food Intakes by Individuals. Low-income Women 19–50 Years and Their Children 1–5 Years, 1 Day, 1986. CSFII Rep. 86-2. Washington, D.C.

_____ . 1987c. Nationwide Food Consumption Survey, Continuing Survey of Food Intakes by Individuals. Women 19–50 Years and Their Children 1–5 Years, 4 days, 1985. CSFII Rep. 85-4. Washington, D.C.

_____ . 1988a. Nationwide Food Consumption Survey, Continuing Survey of Food Intakes by Individuals. Low-income Women 19–50 Years and Their Children 1–5 Years, 4 Days, 1985. CSFII Rep. 85-5. Washington, D.C.

_____ . 1988b. Nationwide Food Consumption Survey, Continuing Survey of Food Intakes by Individuals. Women 19–50 Years and Their Children 1–5 Years, 4 Days, 1986. CSFII Rep. 86-3. Washington, D.C.

_____ . 1989. Nationwide Food Consumption Survey, Continuing Survey of Food Intakes by Individuals. Low-income Women 19–50 Years and Their Children 1–5 Years, 4 Days, 1986. CSFII Rep. 86-4. Washington, D.C.

U.S. DEPARTMENT OF AGRICULTURE, SCIENCE AND EDUCATION ADMINISTRA-TION. 1979a. Money Value of Food Used by Households in the United States, Spring 1977. Prelim. Rep. 1, Nationwide Food Consumption Survey 1977–78. U.S. Government Printing Office, Washington, D.C.

_____ . 1979b. Food. Home Gard. Bull. 228. Washington, D.C.

U.S. DEPARTMENT OF COMMERCE, BUREAU OF THE CENSUS. 1965. Population Estimates: Estimates of the Population of the U.S. by Single Years of Age, Color and Sex: 1900 to 1959. Curr. Pop. Rep. Ser. P-25, no. 311.

_____ . 1970. Statistical Abstract of the United States, 1970. U.S. Government Printing Office, Washington, D.C.

_____ . 1981. Household and Family Characteristics: March 1980. Curr. Pop. Rep. Ser. P-20, no. 366. Washington, D.C.

_____ . 1984a. Estimates of the Population of the United States to April 1, 1984. Curr. Pop. Rep. Ser. P-25, no. 953. Washington, D.C.

_____ . 1984b. School Enrollment—Social and Economic Characteristics of Students: October 1983. Curr. Pop. Rep. Ser. P-20, no. 394. Washington, D.C.

_____ . 1984c. Projections of the Population of the U.S. by age, sex, and race: 1983 to 2020. Curr. Pop. Rep. Ser. P-25, no. 952. Washington, D.C.

_____ . 1984d. News, CB84-02, Jan. 9. Washington, D.C.

_____ . 1984e. News, CB84-84, April 27. Washington, D.C.

_____ . 1984f. News, CB84-184, Oct. 16. Washington, D.C.

_____ . 1985a. Households, Families, Marital Status and Living Arrangements: March 1985. (adv. rep.) Curr. Pop. Rep. Ser. P-20, no. 402. Washington, D.C.

_____ . 1985b. Population Profile of the United States: 1983–84. Curr. Pop. Rep. Ser. P-23, no. 145. Washington, D.C.

_____ . 1986a. Household and Family Characteristics: March 1985. Curr. Pop. Rep. Ser. P-20, no. 411. Washington, D.C.

_____ . 1986b. News, CB86-71, May 7. Washington, D.C.

_____ . 1986c. News, CB86-100, June 26. Washington, D.C.

_____ . 1986d. News, CB86-195, Dec. 5. Washington, D.C.

_____ . 1987a. Statistical Abstract of the United States, 1988. U.S. Government Printing Office, Washington D.C.

_____ . 1987b. What's it Worth. Curr. Pop. Rep. Ser. P-20, no. 11, pp. 7-8. Washington, D.C.

_____ . 1987c. Households, Families, Marital Status and Living Arrangements: March 1987. (adv. rep.) Curr. Pop. Rep. Ser. P-20, no. 417. Washington, D.C.

_____ . 1987d. Household and Family Characteristics: March 1986. Curr. Pop. Rep. Ser. P-20, no. 419. Washington, D.C.

_____ . 1987e. Population Profile of the United States 1984/85. Curr. Pop. Rep. Spec. Stud., Ser. P-23, no. 150. Washington, D.C. April.

_____ . 1987f. News. CB87-114, Sept. 7. Washington, D.C.

_____ . 1987g. News, CB87-188, Dec. 2. Washington, D.C.

_____ . 1988a. Statistical Abstract of the United States, 1989, 109th ed. U.S. Government Printing Office, Washington D.C.

_____ . 1988b. Families, Marital Status and Living Arrangements: March 1987. Curr. Pop. Rep. Ser. P-20, no. 423. Washington, D.C.

_____ . 1988c. News, CB88-04, Jan. 6. Washington, D.C.

_____ . 1988d. News, CB88-48, April 1. Washington, D.C.

_____ . 1988e. News, CB88-59, April 8. Washington, D.C.

_____ . 1988f. News, CB88-102, June 16. Washington, D.C.

_____ . 1988g. News, CB88-119, July 20. Washington, D.C.

_____ . 1988h. News, CB88-142, Sept. 7. Washington, D.C.

_____ . 1988i. News, CB88-151, Sept. 22. Washington, D.C.

_____ . 1988j. News, CB88-157, Sept. 30. Washington, D.C.

_____ . 1988k. News, CB88-176, Nov. 16. Washington, D.C.

_____ . 1988l. News, CB88-205, Dec. 30. Washington, D.C.

_____ . 1989a. Statistical Abstract of the United States, 1989. U.S. Government Printing Office, Washington, D.C.

_____ . 1989b. Projections of the Population of the U.S. by Age, Sex, and Race: 1988 to 2080. Curr. Pop. Rep. Ser. P-25, no. 1018. Washington, D.C.

_____ . 1989c. News, CB89-73, May 5. Washington, D.C.

_____ . 1989d. News, CB89-77, May 11. Washington, D.C.

_____ . 1989e. News, CB89-95, June 7. Washington, D.C.

_____ . 1989f. News, CB89-118, July 26. Washington, D.C.

_____ . 1989g. News, CB89-158, Oct. 12. Washington, D.C.

_____ . 1990a. Statistical Abstract of the United States, 1990. 110th ed. U.S. Government Printing Office, Washington D.C.

_____ . 1990b. News, CB90-07, Jan. 10. Washington, D.C.

_____ . 1990c. News, CB90-171, Sept. 26. Washington, D.C.

_____ . 1990d. News, CB90-204, Nov. 9. Washington, D.C.

_____ . 1991. News, CB91-07, Jan. 7. Washington, D.C.

U.S. DEPARTMENT OF HEALTH AND HUMAN SERVICES AND U.S DEPARTMENT OF AGRICULTURE. 1986. Nutrition Monitoring in the United States: A Progress Report from the Joint Nutrition Monitoring Committee. DHHS (PHS) Publ. 86-1255. National Center for Health Statistics, Hyattsville, Md.

U.S. DEPARTMENT OF HEALTH AND HUMAN SERVICES, NATIONAL CENTER FOR HEALTH STATISTICS. 1988a. Vital Statistics of the United States, 1986. Life Tables Vol. 2, Sect. 6. Publ. 88-1147. Hyattsville, Md. p. 13.

———. 1988b. Vital Statistics of the United States, 1986. Vol. 1. Natality. DHHS (PHS) Publ. 88-1123. Public Health Service, Washington D.C. pp. 1,4, and 5.

———. 1988c. Vital Statistics of the United States, 1986. Vol. 2. Mortality. Part A, DHHS (PHS) Publ. 88-1122. Public Health Service, Washington, D.C.

———. 1989. Health United States, 1988. DHHS (PHS) Publ. 89-1232. Public Health Service, Washington, D.C.

U.S. DEPARTMENT OF HEALTH AND HUMAN SERVICES, PUBLIC HEALTH SERVICE. 1988. The Surgeon General's Report on Nutrition and Health. DHHS (PHS) Publ. 88-50210. Washington, D.C.

U.S. DEPARTMENT OF HEALTH AND HUMAN SERVICES, PUBLIC HEALTH SERVICE AND U.S. DEPARTMENT OF AGRICULTURE, FOOD AND CONSUMER SERVICES. 1989. Nutrition monitoring in the United States. DHHS (PHS) Publ. 89-1255. Hyattsville, Md.

U.S. DEPARTMENT OF HEALTH, EDUCATION AND WELFARE. 1976. The Measure of Poverty: A Report to Congress as Mandated by the Education Amendments of 1974. U.S. Government Printing Office, Washington, D.C.

U.S. DEPARTMENT OF HEALTH, EDUCATION AND WELFARE, PUBLIC HEALTH SERVICE. 1979. Healthy People: The Surgeon General's Report on Health Promotion and Disease Prevention. DHEW (PHS) Publ. no. 79-55071. Washington, D.C.

U.S. DEPARTMENT OF LABOR, BUREAU OF LABOR STATISTICS. 1987. Consumer Expenditure Survey Results for 1985. News, USDL 87-399, Sept. 24. Washington, D.C.

———. 1989a. News Rep. 790,795,797. Washington, D.C.

———. 1989b. Consumer Expenditure Survey: Integrated Survey Data, 1984–86. Bull. 2333. Washington, D.C.

U.S. SENATE SELECT COMMITTEE ON NUTRITION AND HUMAN NEEDS. 1977a. Dietary Goals for the United States, 1st ed. Feb. U.S. Government Printing Office, Washington, D.C. 79 pp.

———. 1977b. Dietary Goals for the United States, 2nd ed. Dec. U.S. Government Printing Office, Washington, D.C. 83 pp.

VAN DUYNE, C. 1982. Food prices, expectations and inflation. Am. J. Agric. Econ. 64:420-430.

VAN RAVENSWAAY, E. 1988. How much food safety do consumers want? An analysis of current studies and strategies for future research. Pages 89-114 in: Consumer Demands in the Marketplace: Public Policies Related to Food Safety, Quality and Human Health. K. Clancy, ed. Natl. Center for Food and Agric. Policy, Resources for the Future, Washington, D.C.

VAN RAVENSWAAY, E., and SMITH, M. 1986. Food contamination: Consumer reactions and producer losses. U.S. Dep. Agric., Econ. Res. Serv., Natl. Food Rev. 33(Spring):14-16.

VENTO, B. F. 1989. Food for thought: What are we really eating. Congressional Newsl. U.S. Congress: Washington, D.C., July.

VER MEULEN, M., RYAN, M., CLEMENTS, M., and UBELL, E. 1987. What America eats. Parade. Oct. 25, pp. 4-16.

WALDHOLZ, M. 1990. Weight is cardiac risk in women. Wall Street J. Mar. 29.

WALDMAN, S. 1989. Do warning labels work? Newsweek, July 18, pp. 40-41.

WALDROP, J. 1989a. Inside America's households. Am. Demogr. 11(Mar.):20-27.

_____. 1989b. A lesson in home economics. Am. Demogr. 11(Aug.):26-61.

WALL STREET JOURNAL. 1988a. People patterns. Feb. 4.

_____. 1988b. July 28, p. 25.

_____. 1988c. Consumers find fault with food advertising. Aug. 18, p. 23.

_____. 1988d. People patterns. Nov. 17, p. B1.

_____. 1989a. People patterns. Feb. 7, p. B1.

_____. 1989b. People patterns. July 5.

_____. 1989c. People patterns. Aug. 21.

_____. 1989d. People patterns. Sept. 20.

_____. 1989e. People patterns. Nov. 17.

_____. 1990. Sept. 25.

WALLACE, L. T. 1987. Agriculture's Futures: America's Food System. Springer-Verlag, New York.

WALLACE, W. H., and CULLISON, W. E. 1979. Measuring Price Changes: a Study of the Price Indexes, 4th ed. Federal Reserve Bank of Richmond, Richmond, VA.

WALSH, R. 1990. The drive to buy. Int. Org. Consumers Unions Newsl. 4:180.

WASCOE, D., JR. 1989. Survey studies elderly in all shades of gray. Minneapolis Star Tribune, Dec. 6.

_____. 1990. Days of double coupons are increasingly numbered. Minneapolis Star Tribune, Sept. 17, p. 3D.

WAUGH, F. F. 1929. Quality as a Determinant of Vegetable Prices. Columbia University Press, New York.

WESSEL, D. 1989a. Sure ways to annoy consumers. Wall Street J. Nov. 11.

_____. 1989b. After the beep: The message is convenience matters most. Wall Street J. Sept. 19.

WEST, D., and PRICE, D. 1976. The effects of income, assets, food programs, and household size on food consumption. Am. J. Agric. Econ. 58:725-730.

WHOLE FOODS. 1989. 12(4):28, 30, 32, 35.

WILKERSON, I. 1987. Growth of the very poor is focus of new studies. New York Times. Dec. 20.

WILLIAMSON, T. H. 1987. Superwarehouse markets: What they are, how they operate, why they succeed. Cereal Foods World 32(6):431-432.

WOLF, D. 1987. The ageless market. Am. Demogr. 9(July):26-29, 55-56.

WOLF, I. D., and LECHOWICH, R. V. 1989. Current issues in microbiological food safety. Cereal Foods World 34(6)468-472.

WOTEKI, C. E., BRIEFEL, R. R., and KUCZMARSKI, R. 1988a. Contributions of the National Center for Health Statistics. Am. J. Clin. Nutr. 47:320-328.

WOTEKI, C. E., HITCHCOCK, D. C., BRIEFEL, R. R., and WINN, D. M. 1988b. National health and nutrition examination survey—NHANES. Nutr. Today 23(1):25-27.

YAUKEY, D. 1985. Demography. St. Martin's Press, New York.

YOUNG, C. M. 1981. Dietary methodology. In: Assessing Changing Food Consumption Patterns. Committee on Food Consumption Patterns, Food and Nutrition Board, National Research Council. Natl. Acad. Press: Washington, D.C.

YOUNG, D. R. 1986. America in Perspective: Major Trends in the United States Through the 1990s. (Oxford Analytical) Houghton Mifflin Co., Boston, Mass.

ZELINSKY, W. 1987. You are where you eat. Am. Demogr. 9(July):30-58.

ZELLNER, J. A. 1986. Information remedies: Can they be effective? (mimeo) U.S. Dep. Agric., Econ. Res. Serv. May 27.

_____. 1988. Market responses to public policies affecting the quality and safety of food and diets. Pages 54-74 in: Consumer Demands in the Marketplace: Public Policies

Related to Food Safety, Quality, and Human Health. K. Clancy, ed. Natl. Center for Food and Agric. Policy, Resources for the Future: Washington, D.C.

ZELLNER, W. 1989. Why the Pizza King may abdicate the throne. Business Week, Sept. 25, p. 46.

Index